50% OFF
Online Praxis Core Prep Course!

By Mometrix

Dear Customer,

We consider it an honor and a privilege that you chose our Praxis Core Study Guide. As a way of showing our appreciation and to help us better serve you, we are offering **50% off our online Praxis Core Online Course.** Many Praxis courses are needlessly expensive and don't deliver enough value. With our course, you get access to the best Praxis Core prep material, and **you only pay half price.**

We have structured our online course to perfectly complement your printed study guide. The Praxis Core Online Course contains **in-depth lessons** that cover all the most important topics, **230+ video reviews** that explain difficult concepts, over **700 practice questions** to ensure you feel prepared, and more than **550 digital flashcards,** so you can study while you're on the go.

Online Praxis Core Prep Course

Topics Covered:

- Reading
  - Literary Analysis
  - Theme and Plot
  - Elements of a Text

- Writing
  - Foundations of Grammar
  - Parts of an Essay
  - Style and Form

- Mathematics
  - Numbers and Operations
  - Proportions and Ratios
  - Systems of Equations

Course Features:

- Praxis Core Study Guide
  - Get content that complements our best-selling study guide.
- Full-Length Practice Tests
  - With over 700 practice questions, you can test yourself again and again.
- Mobile Friendly
  - If you need to study on the go, the course is easily accessible from your mobile device.
- Praxis Core Flashcards
  - Our course includes a flashcards mode with over 550 content cards for you to study.

To receive this discount, visit our website at mometrix.com/university/praxis-core or simply scan this QR code with your smartphone. At the checkout page, enter the discount code: **core50off**

If you have any questions or concerns, please contact us at support@mometrix.com.

TEST PREPARATION

SCAN HERE

FREE Study Skills Videos/DVD Offer

Dear Customer,

Thank you for your purchase from Mometrix! We consider it an honor and a privilege that you have purchased our product and we want to ensure your satisfaction.

As part of our ongoing effort to meet the needs of test takers, we have developed a set of Study Skills Videos that we would like to give you for FREE. These videos cover our *best practices* for getting ready for your exam, from how to use our study materials to how to best prepare for the day of the test.

All that we ask is that you email us with feedback that would describe your experience so far with our product. Good, bad, or indifferent, we want to know what you think!

To get your FREE Study Skills Videos, you can use the **QR code** below, or send us an **email** at studyvideos@mometrix.com with *FREE VIDEOS* in the subject line and the following information in the body of the email:

- The name of the product you purchased.
- Your product rating on a scale of 1-5, with 5 being the highest rating.
- Your feedback. It can be long, short, or anything in between. We just want to know your impressions and experience so far with our product. (Good feedback might include how our study material met your needs and ways we might be able to make it even better. You could highlight features that you found helpful or features that you think we should add.)

If you have any questions or concerns, please don't hesitate to contact me directly.

Thanks again!

Sincerely,

Jay Willis
Vice President
jay.willis@mometrix.com
1-800-673-8175

Praxis Core

Study Guide
2024-2025

5 **Full-Length**
Practice Tests

**Academic Skills for Educators
Secrets for Reading 5713,
Writing 5723, and Math 5733
with Step-by-Step
Video Tutorials**

5th Edition

Written and edited by the Mometrix Teacher Certification Test Team

Printed in the United States of America

This paper meets the requirements of ANSI/NISO Z39.48-1992 (Permanence of Paper).

Mometrix offers volume discount pricing to institutions. For more information or a price quote, please contact our sales department at sales@mometrix.com or 888-248-1219.

Mometrix Media LLC is not affiliated with or endorsed by any official testing organization. All organizational and test names are trademarks of their respective owners.

Paperback
ISBN 13: 978-1-5167-2421-5

DEAR FUTURE EXAM SUCCESS STORY

First of all, **THANK YOU** for purchasing Mometrix study materials!

Second, congratulations! You are one of the few determined test-takers who are committed to doing whatever it takes to excel on your exam. **You have come to the right place.** We developed these study materials with one goal in mind: to deliver you the information you need in a format that's concise and easy to use.

In addition to optimizing your guide for the content of the test, we've outlined our recommended steps for breaking down the preparation process into small, attainable goals so you can make sure you stay on track.

We've also analyzed the entire test-taking process, identifying the most common pitfalls and showing how you can overcome them and be ready for any curveball the test throws you.

Standardized testing is one of the biggest obstacles on your road to success, which only increases the importance of doing well in the high-pressure, high-stakes environment of test day. Your results on this test could have a significant impact on your future, and this guide provides the information and practical advice to help you achieve your full potential on test day.

Your success is our success

We would love to hear from you! If you would like to share the story of your exam success or if you have any questions or comments in regard to our products, please contact us at **800-673-8175** or **support@mometrix.com**.

Thanks again for your business and we wish you continued success!

Sincerely,
The Mometrix Test Preparation Team

Need more help? Check out our flashcards at:
http://MometrixFlashcards.com/Praxis

TABLE OF CONTENTS

Introduction

Thank you for purchasing this resource! You have made the choice to prepare yourself for a test that could have a huge impact on your future, and this guide is designed to help you be fully ready for test day. Obviously, it's important to have a solid understanding of the test material, but you also need to be prepared for the unique environment and stressors of the test, so that you can perform to the best of your abilities.

For this purpose, the first section that appears in this guide is the **Secret Keys**. We've devoted countless hours to meticulously researching what works and what doesn't, and we've boiled down our findings to the five most impactful steps you can take to improve your performance on the test. We start at the beginning with study planning and move through the preparation process, all the way to the testing strategies that will help you get the most out of what you know when you're finally sitting in front of the test.

We recommend that you start preparing for your test as far in advance as possible. However, if you've bought this guide as a last-minute study resource and only have a few days before your test, we recommend that you skip over the first two Secret Keys since they address a long-term study plan.

If you struggle with **test anxiety**, we strongly encourage you to check out our recommendations for how you can overcome it. Test anxiety is a formidable foe, but it can be beaten, and we want to make sure you have the tools you need to defeat it.

Review Video Directory

As you work your way through this guide, you will see numerous review video links interspersed with the written content. If you would like to access all of these review videos in one place, click on the video directory link found on the bonus page: **mometrix.com/bonus948/praxcore**

1

Secret Key #1 – Plan Big, Study Small

There's a lot riding on your performance. If you want to ace this test, you're going to need to keep your skills sharp and the material fresh in your mind. You need a plan that lets you review everything you need to know while still fitting in your schedule. We'll break this strategy down into three categories.

Information Organization

Start with the information you already have: the official test outline. From this, you can make a complete list of all the concepts you need to cover before the test. Organize these concepts into groups that can be studied together, and create a list of any related vocabulary you need to learn so you can brush up on any difficult terms. You'll want to keep this vocabulary list handy once you actually start studying since you may need to add to it along the way.

Time Management

Once you have your set of study concepts, decide how to spread them out over the time you have left before the test. Break your study plan into small, clear goals so you have a manageable task for each day and know exactly what you're doing. Then just focus on one small step at a time. When you manage your time this way, you don't need to spend hours at a time studying. Studying a small block of content for a short period each day helps you retain information better and avoid stressing over how much you have left to do. You can relax knowing that you have a plan to cover everything in time. In order for this strategy to be effective though, you have to start studying early and stick to your schedule. Avoid the exhaustion and futility that comes from last-minute cramming!

Study Environment

The environment you study in has a big impact on your learning. Studying in a coffee shop, while probably more enjoyable, is not likely to be as fruitful as studying in a quiet room. It's important to keep distractions to a minimum. You're only planning to study for a short block of time, so make the most of it. Don't pause to check your phone or get up to find a snack. It's also important to **avoid multitasking**. Research has consistently shown that multitasking will make your studying dramatically less effective. Your study area should also be comfortable and well-lit so you don't have the distraction of straining your eyes or sitting on an uncomfortable chair.

 The time of day you study is also important. You want to be rested and alert. Don't wait until just before bedtime. Study when you'll be most likely to comprehend and remember. Even better, if you know what time of day your test will be, set that time aside for study. That way your brain will be used to working on that subject at that specific time and you'll have a better chance of recalling information.

Finally, it can be helpful to team up with others who are studying for the same test. Your actual studying should be done in as isolated an environment as possible, but the work of organizing the information and setting up the study plan can be divided up. In between study sessions, you can discuss with your teammates the concepts that you're all studying and quiz each other on the details. Just be sure that your teammates are as serious about the test as you are. If you find that your study time is being replaced with social time, you might need to find a new team.

Secret Key #2 – Make Your Studying Count

You're devoting a lot of time and effort to preparing for this test, so you want to be absolutely certain it will pay off. This means doing more than just reading the content and hoping you can remember it on test day. It's important to make every minute of study count. There are two main areas you can focus on to make your studying count.

Retention

It doesn't matter how much time you study if you can't remember the material. You need to make sure you are retaining the concepts. To check your retention of the information you're learning, try recalling it at later times with minimal prompting. Try carrying around flashcards and glance at one or two from time to time or ask a friend who's also studying for the test to quiz you.

To enhance your retention, look for ways to put the information into practice so that you can apply it rather than simply recalling it. If you're using the information in practical ways, it will be much easier to remember. Similarly, it helps to solidify a concept in your mind if you're not only reading it to yourself but also explaining it to someone else. Ask a friend to let you teach them about a concept you're a little shaky on (or speak aloud to an imaginary audience if necessary). As you try to summarize, define, give examples, and answer your friend's questions, you'll understand the concepts better and they will stay with you longer. Finally, step back for a big picture view and ask yourself how each piece of information fits with the whole subject. When you link the different concepts together and see them working together as a whole, it's easier to remember the individual components.

Finally, practice showing your work on any multi-step problems, even if you're just studying. Writing out each step you take to solve a problem will help solidify the process in your mind, and you'll be more likely to remember it during the test.

Modality

Modality simply refers to the means or method by which you study. Choosing a study modality that fits your own individual learning style is crucial. No two people learn best in exactly the same way, so it's important to know your strengths and use them to your advantage.

For example, if you learn best by visualization, focus on visualizing a concept in your mind and draw an image or a diagram. Try color-coding your notes, illustrating them, or creating symbols that will trigger your mind to recall a learned concept. If you learn best by hearing or discussing information, find a study partner who learns the same way or read aloud to yourself. Think about how to put the information in your own words. Imagine that you are giving a lecture on the topic and record yourself so you can listen to it later.

For any learning style, flashcards can be helpful. Organize the information so you can take advantage of spare moments to review. Underline key words or phrases. Use different colors for different categories. Mnemonic devices (such as creating a short list in which every item starts with the same letter) can also help with retention. Find what works best for you and use it to store the information in your mind most effectively and easily.

3

Secret Key #3 – Practice the Right Way

Your success on test day depends not only on how many hours you put into preparing, but also on whether you prepared the right way. It's good to check along the way to see if your studying is paying off. One of the most effective ways to do this is by taking practice tests to evaluate your progress. Practice tests are useful because they show exactly where you need to improve. Every time you take a practice test, pay special attention to these three groups of questions:

- The questions you got wrong
- The questions you had to guess on, even if you guessed right
- The questions you found difficult or slow to work through

This will show you exactly what your weak areas are, and where you need to devote more study time. Ask yourself why each of these questions gave you trouble. Was it because you didn't understand the material? Was it because you didn't remember the vocabulary? Do you need more repetitions on this type of question to build speed and confidence? Dig into those questions and figure out how you can strengthen your weak areas as you go back to review the material.

 Additionally, many practice tests have a section explaining the answer choices. It can be tempting to read the explanation and think that you now have a good understanding of the concept. However, an explanation likely only covers part of the question's broader context. Even if the explanation makes perfect sense, **go back and investigate** every concept related to the question until you're positive you have a thorough understanding.

As you go along, keep in mind that the practice test is just that: practice. Memorizing these questions and answers will not be very helpful on the actual test because it is unlikely to have any of the same exact questions. If you only know the right answers to the sample questions, you won't be prepared for the real thing. **Study the concepts** until you understand them fully, and then you'll be able to answer any question that shows up on the test.

It's important to wait on the practice tests until you're ready. If you take a test on your first day of study, you may be overwhelmed by the amount of material covered and how much you need to learn. Work up to it gradually.

On test day, you'll need to be prepared for answering questions, managing your time, and using the test-taking strategies you've learned. It's a lot to balance, like a mental marathon that will have a big impact on your future. Like training for a marathon, you'll need to start slowly and work your way up. When test day arrives, you'll be ready.

Start with the strategies you've read in the first two Secret Keys—plan your course and study in the way that works best for you. If you have time, consider using multiple study resources to get different approaches to the same concepts. It can be helpful to see difficult concepts from more than one angle. Then find a good source for practice tests. Many times, the test website will suggest potential study resources or provide sample tests.

Practice Test Strategy

If you're able to find at least three practice tests, we recommend this strategy:

UNTIMED AND OPEN-BOOK PRACTICE

Take the first test with no time constraints and with your notes and study guide handy. Take your time and focus on applying the strategies you've learned.

TIMED AND OPEN-BOOK PRACTICE

Take the second practice test open-book as well, but set a timer and practice pacing yourself to finish in time.

TIMED AND CLOSED-BOOK PRACTICE

Take any other practice tests as if it were test day. Set a timer and put away your study materials. Sit at a table or desk in a quiet room, imagine yourself at the testing center, and answer questions as quickly and accurately as possible.

Keep repeating timed and closed-book tests on a regular basis until you run out of practice tests or it's time for the actual test. Your mind will be ready for the schedule and stress of test day, and you'll be able to focus on recalling the material you've learned.

Secret Key #4 – Pace Yourself

Once you're fully prepared for the material on the test, your biggest challenge on test day will be managing your time. Just knowing that the clock is ticking can make you panic even if you have plenty of time left. Work on pacing yourself so you can build confidence against the time constraints of the exam. Pacing is a difficult skill to master, especially in a high-pressure environment, so **practice is vital**.

Set time expectations for your pace based on how much time is available. For example, if a section has 60 questions and the time limit is 30 minutes, you know you have to average 30 seconds or less per question in order to answer them all. Although 30 seconds is the hard limit, set 25 seconds per question as your goal, so you reserve extra time to spend on harder questions. When you budget extra time for the harder questions, you no longer have any reason to stress when those questions take longer to answer.

Don't let this time expectation distract you from working through the test at a calm, steady pace, but keep it in mind so you don't spend too much time on any one question. Recognize that taking extra time on one question you don't understand may keep you from answering two that you do understand later in the test. If your time limit for a question is up and you're still not sure of the answer, mark it and move on, and come back to it later if the time and the test format allow. If the testing format doesn't allow you to return to earlier questions, just make an educated guess; then put it out of your mind and move on.

On the easier questions, be careful not to rush. It may seem wise to hurry through them so you have more time for the challenging ones, but it's not worth missing one if you know the concept and just didn't take the time to read the question fully. Work efficiently but make sure you understand the question and have looked at all of the answer choices, since more than one may seem right at first.

Even if you're paying attention to the time, you may find yourself a little behind at some point. You should speed up to get back on track, but do so wisely. Don't panic; just take a few seconds less on each question until you're caught up. Don't guess without thinking, but do look through the answer choices and eliminate any you know are wrong. If you can get down to two choices, it is often worthwhile to guess from those. Once you've chosen an answer, move on and don't dwell on any that you skipped or had to hurry through. If a question was taking too long, chances are it was one of the harder ones, so you weren't as likely to get it right anyway.

On the other hand, if you find yourself getting ahead of schedule, it may be beneficial to slow down a little. The more quickly you work, the more likely you are to make a careless mistake that will affect your score. You've budgeted time for each question, so don't be afraid to spend that time. Practice an efficient but careful pace to get the most out of the time you have.

Secret Key #5 – Have a Plan for Guessing

When you're taking the test, you may find yourself stuck on a question. Some of the answer choices seem better than others, but you don't see the one answer choice that is obviously correct. What do you do?

The scenario described above is very common, yet most test takers have not effectively prepared for it. Developing and practicing a plan for guessing may be one of the single most effective uses of your time as you get ready for the exam.

In developing your plan for guessing, there are three questions to address:

- When should you start the guessing process?
- How should you narrow down the choices?
- Which answer should you choose?

When to Start the Guessing Process

Unless your plan for guessing is to select C every time (which, despite its merits, is not what we recommend), you need to leave yourself enough time to apply your answer elimination strategies. Since you have a limited amount of time for each question, that means that if you're going to give yourself the best shot at guessing correctly, you have to decide quickly whether or not you will guess.

Of course, the best-case scenario is that you don't have to guess at all, so first, see if you can answer the question based on your knowledge of the subject and basic reasoning skills. Focus on the key words in the question and try to jog your memory of related topics. Give yourself a chance to bring the knowledge to mind, but once you realize that you don't have (or you can't access) the knowledge you need to answer the question, it's time to start the guessing process.

It's almost always better to start the guessing process too early than too late. It only takes a few seconds to remember something and answer the question from knowledge. Carefully eliminating wrong answer choices takes longer. Plus, going through the process of eliminating answer choices can actually help jog your memory.

Summary: Start the guessing process as soon as you decide that you can't answer the question based on your knowledge.

7

How to Narrow Down the Choices

The next chapter in this book (**Test-Taking Strategies**) includes a wide range of strategies for how to approach questions and how to look for answer choices to eliminate. You will definitely want to read those carefully, practice them, and figure out which ones work best for you. Here though, we're going to address a mindset rather than a particular strategy.

Your odds of guessing an answer correctly depend on how many options you are choosing from.

Number of options left	5	4	3	2	1
Odds of guessing correctly	20%	25%	33%	50%	100%

You can see from this chart just how valuable it is to be able to eliminate incorrect answers and make an educated guess, but there are two things that many test takers do that cause them to miss out on the benefits of guessing:

- Accidentally eliminating the correct answer
- Selecting an answer based on an impression

We'll look at the first one here, and the second one in the next section.

To avoid accidentally eliminating the correct answer, we recommend a thought exercise called **the $5 challenge**. In this challenge, you only eliminate an answer choice from contention if you are willing to bet $5 on it being wrong. Why $5? Five dollars is a small but not insignificant amount of money. It's an amount you could afford to lose but wouldn't want to throw away. And while losing $5 once might not hurt too much, doing

it twenty times will set you back $100. In the same way, each small decision you make—eliminating a choice here, guessing on a question there—won't by itself impact your score very much, but when you put them all together, they can make a big difference. By holding each answer choice elimination decision to a higher standard, you can reduce the risk of accidentally eliminating the correct answer.

The $5 challenge can also be applied in a positive sense: If you are willing to bet $5 that an answer choice *is* correct, go ahead and mark it as correct.

Summary: Only eliminate an answer choice if you are willing to bet $5 that it is wrong.

8

Which Answer to Choose

You're taking the test. You've run into a hard question and decided you'll have to guess. You've eliminated all the answer choices you're willing to bet $5 on. Now you have to pick an answer. Why do we even need to talk about this? Why can't you just pick whichever one you feel like when the time comes?

The answer to these questions is that if you don't come into the test with a plan, you'll rely on your impression to select an answer choice, and if you do that, you risk falling into a trap. The test writers know that everyone who takes their test will be guessing on some of the questions, so they intentionally write wrong answer choices to seem plausible. You still have to pick an answer though, and if the wrong answer choices are designed to look right, how can you ever be sure that you're not falling for their trap? The best solution we've found to this dilemma is to take the decision out of your hands entirely. Here is the process we recommend:

Once you've eliminated any choices that you are confident (willing to bet $5) are wrong, select the first remaining choice as your answer.

Whether you choose to select the first remaining choice, the second, or the last, the important thing is that you use some preselected standard. Using this approach guarantees that you will not be enticed into selecting an answer choice that looks right, because you are not basing your decision on how the answer choices look.

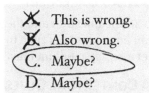

This is not meant to make you question your knowledge. Instead, it is to help you recognize the difference between your knowledge and your impressions. There's a huge difference between thinking an answer is right because of what you know, and thinking an answer is right because it looks or sounds like it should be right.

Summary: To ensure that your selection is appropriately random, make a predetermined selection from among all answer choices you have not eliminated.

Test-Taking Strategies

This section contains a list of test-taking strategies that you may find helpful as you work through the test. By taking what you know and applying logical thought, you can maximize your chances of answering any question correctly!

It is very important to realize that every question is different and every person is different: no single strategy will work on every question, and no single strategy will work for every person. That's why we've included all of them here, so you can try them out and determine which ones work best for different types of questions and which ones work best for you.

Question Strategies

☑ READ CAREFULLY

Read the question and the answer choices carefully. Don't miss the question because you misread the terms. You have plenty of time to read each question thoroughly and make sure you understand what is being asked. Yet a happy medium must be attained, so don't waste too much time. You must read carefully and efficiently.

☑ CONTEXTUAL CLUES

Look for contextual clues. If the question includes a word you are not familiar with, look at the immediate context for some indication of what the word might mean. Contextual clues can often give you all the information you need to decipher the meaning of an unfamiliar word. Even if you can't determine the meaning, you may be able to narrow down the possibilities enough to make a solid guess at the answer to the question.

☑ PREFIXES

If you're having trouble with a word in the question or answer choices, try dissecting it. Take advantage of every clue that the word might include. Prefixes can be a huge help. Usually, they allow you to determine a basic meaning. *Pre-* means before, *post-* means after, *pro-* is positive, *de-* is negative. From prefixes, you can get an idea of the general meaning of the word and try to put it into context.

☑ HEDGE WORDS

Watch out for critical hedge words, such as *likely, may, can, sometimes, often, almost, mostly, usually, generally, rarely,* and *sometimes*. Question writers insert these hedge phrases to cover every possibility. Often an answer choice will be wrong simply because it leaves no room for exception. Be on guard for answer choices that have definitive words such as *exactly* and *always*.

☑ SWITCHBACK WORDS

Stay alert for *switchbacks*. These are the words and phrases frequently used to alert you to shifts in thought. The most common switchback words are *but, although,* and *however*. Others include *nevertheless, on the other hand, even though, while, in spite of, despite,* and *regardless of*. Switchback words are important to catch because they can change the direction of the question or an answer choice.

☑ FACE VALUE

When in doubt, use common sense. Accept the situation in the problem at face value. Don't read too much into it. These problems will not require you to make wild assumptions. If you have to go beyond creativity and warp time or space in order to have an answer choice fit the question, then you should move on and consider the other answer choices. These are normal problems rooted in reality. The applicable relationship or explanation may not be readily apparent, but it is there for you to figure out. Use your common sense to interpret anything that isn't clear.

Answer Choice Strategies

⊘ ANSWER SELECTION

The most thorough way to pick an answer choice is to identify and eliminate wrong answers until only one is left, then confirm it is the correct answer. Sometimes an answer choice may immediately seem right, but be careful. The test writers will usually put more than one reasonable answer choice on each question, so take a second to read all of them and make sure that the other choices are not equally obvious. As long as you have time left, it is better to read every answer choice than to pick the first one that looks right without checking the others.

⊘ ANSWER CHOICE FAMILIES

An answer choice family consists of two (in rare cases, three) answer choices that are very similar in construction and cannot all be true at the same time. If you see two answer choices that are direct opposites or parallels, one of them is usually the correct answer. For instance, if one answer choice says that quantity x increases and another either says that quantity x decreases (opposite) or says that quantity y increases (parallel), then those answer choices would fall into the same family. An answer choice that doesn't match the construction of the answer choice family is more likely to be incorrect. Most questions will not have answer choice families, but when they do appear, you should be prepared to recognize them.

⊘ ELIMINATE ANSWERS

Eliminate answer choices as soon as you realize they are wrong, but make sure you consider all possibilities. If you are eliminating answer choices and realize that the last one you are left with is also wrong, don't panic. Start over and consider each choice again. There may be something you missed the first time that you will realize on the second pass.

⊘ AVOID FACT TRAPS

Don't be distracted by an answer choice that is factually true but doesn't answer the question. You are looking for the choice that answers the question. Stay focused on what the question is asking for so you don't accidentally pick an answer that is true but incorrect. Always go back to the question and make sure the answer choice you've selected actually answers the question and is not merely a true statement.

⊘ EXTREME STATEMENTS

In general, you should avoid answers that put forth extreme actions as standard practice or proclaim controversial ideas as established fact. An answer choice that states the "process should be used in certain situations, if..." is much more likely to be correct than one that states the "process should be discontinued completely." The first is a calm rational statement and doesn't even make a definitive, uncompromising stance, using a hedge word *if* to provide wiggle room, whereas the second choice is far more extreme.

⊘ BENCHMARK

As you read through the answer choices and you come across one that seems to answer the question well, mentally select that answer choice. This is not your final answer, but it's the one that will help you evaluate the other answer choices. The one that you selected is your benchmark or standard for judging each of the other answer choices. Every other answer choice must be compared to your benchmark. That choice is correct until proven otherwise by another answer choice beating it. If you find a better answer, then that one becomes your new benchmark. Once you've decided that no other choice answers the question as well as your benchmark, you have your final answer.

11

⊘ PREDICT THE ANSWER

Before you even start looking at the answer choices, it is often best to try to predict the answer. When you come up with the answer on your own, it is easier to avoid distractions and traps because you will know exactly what to look for. The right answer choice is unlikely to be word-for-word what you came up with, but it should be a close match. Even if you are confident that you have the right answer, you should still take the time to read each option before moving on.

General Strategies

⊘ TOUGH QUESTIONS

If you are stumped on a problem or it appears too hard or too difficult, don't waste time. Move on! Remember though, if you can quickly check for obviously incorrect answer choices, your chances of guessing correctly are greatly improved. Before you completely give up, at least try to knock out a couple of possible answers. Eliminate what you can and then guess at the remaining answer choices before moving on.

⊘ CHECK YOUR WORK

Since you will probably not know every term listed and the answer to every question, it is important that you get credit for the ones that you do know. Don't miss any questions through careless mistakes. If at all possible, try to take a second to look back over your answer selection and make sure you've selected the correct answer choice and haven't made a costly careless mistake (such as marking an answer choice that you didn't mean to mark). This quick double check should more than pay for itself in caught mistakes for the time it costs.

⊘ PACE YOURSELF

It's easy to be overwhelmed when you're looking at a page full of questions; your mind is confused and full of random thoughts, and the clock is ticking down faster than you would like. Calm down and maintain the pace that you have set for yourself. Especially as you get down to the last few minutes of the test, don't let the small numbers on the clock make you panic. As long as you are on track by monitoring your pace, you are guaranteed to have time for each question.

⊘ DON'T RUSH

It is very easy to make errors when you are in a hurry. Maintaining a fast pace in answering questions is pointless if it makes you miss questions that you would have gotten right otherwise. Test writers like to include distracting information and wrong answers that seem right. Taking a little extra time to avoid careless mistakes can make all the difference in your test score. Find a pace that allows you to be confident in the answers that you select.

⊘ KEEP MOVING

Panicking will not help you pass the test, so do your best to stay calm and keep moving. Taking deep breaths and going through the answer elimination steps you practiced can help to break through a stress barrier and keep your pace.

Final Notes

The combination of a solid foundation of content knowledge and the confidence that comes from practicing your plan for applying that knowledge is the key to maximizing your performance on test day. As your foundation of content knowledge is built up and strengthened, you'll find that the strategies included in this chapter become more and more effective in helping you quickly sift through the distractions and traps of the test to isolate the correct answer.

Now that you're preparing to move forward into the test content chapters of this book, be sure to keep your goal in mind. As you read, think about how you will be able to apply this information on the test. If you've already seen sample questions for the test and you have an idea of the question format and style, try to come up with questions of your own that you can answer based on what you're reading. This will give you valuable practice applying your knowledge in the same ways you can expect to on test day.

Good luck and good studying!

Reading

Transform passive reading into active learning! After immersing yourself in this chapter, put your comprehension to the test by taking a quiz. The insights you gained will stay with you longer this way. Scan the QR code to go directly to the chapter quiz interface for this study guide. If you're using a computer, simply visit the bonus page at **mometrix.com/bonus948/praxcore** and click the Chapter Quizzes link.

Key Ideas and Details

READING INFORMATIONAL TEXTS

TEXT FEATURES IN INFORMATIONAL TEXTS

The **title of a text** gives readers some idea of its content. The **table of contents** is a list near the beginning of a text, showing the book's sections and chapters and their coinciding page numbers. This gives readers an overview of the whole text and helps them find specific chapters easily. An **appendix**, at the back of the book or document, includes important information that is not present in the main text. Also at the back, an **index** lists the book's important topics alphabetically with their page numbers to help readers find them easily. **Glossaries**, usually found at the backs of books, list technical terms alphabetically with their definitions to aid vocabulary learning and comprehension. Boldface print is used to emphasize certain words, often identifying words included in the text's glossary where readers can look up their definitions. **Headings** separate sections of text and show the topic of each. **Subheadings** divide subject headings into smaller, more specific categories to help readers organize information. **Footnotes**, at the bottom of the page, give readers more information, such as citations or links. **Bullet points** list items separately, making facts and ideas easier to see and understand. A **sidebar** is a box of information to one side of the main text giving additional information, often on a more focused or in-depth example of a topic.

Illustrations and **photographs** are pictures that visually emphasize important points in text. The captions below the illustrations explain what those images show. Charts and tables are visual forms of information that make something easier to understand quickly. Diagrams are drawings that show relationships or explain a process. Graphs visually show the relationships among multiple sets of information plotted along vertical and horizontal axes. Maps show geographical information visually to help readers understand the relative locations of places covered in the text. Timelines are visual graphics that show historical events in chronological order to help readers see their sequence.

> **Review Video: Informative Text**
> Visit mometrix.com/academy and enter code: 924964

LANGUAGE USE

LITERAL AND FIGURATIVE LANGUAGE

As in fictional literature, informational text also uses both **literal language**, which means just what it says, and **figurative language**, which imparts more than literal meaning. For example, an informational text author might use a simile or direct comparison, such as writing that a racehorse "ran like the wind." Informational text authors also use metaphors or implied comparisons, such as "the cloud of the Great Depression." Imagery may also appear in informational texts to increase the reader's understanding of ideas and concepts discussed in the text.

15

EXPLICIT AND IMPLICIT INFORMATION

When informational text states something explicitly, the reader is told by the author exactly what is meant, which can include the author's interpretation or perspective of events. For example, a professor writes, "I have seen students go into an absolute panic just because they weren't able to complete the exam in the time they were allotted." This explicitly tells the reader that the students were afraid, and by using the words "just because," the writer indicates their fear was exaggerated out of proportion relative to what happened. However, another professor writes, "I have had students come to me, their faces drained of all color, saying 'We weren't able to finish the exam.'" This is an example of implicit meaning: the second writer did not state explicitly that the students were panicked. Instead, he wrote a description of their faces being "drained of all color." From this description, the reader can infer that the students were so frightened that their faces paled.

> **Review Video: Explicit and Implicit Information**
> Visit mometrix.com/academy and enter code: 735771

TECHNICAL LANGUAGE

Technical language is more impersonal than literary and vernacular language. Passive voice makes the tone impersonal. For example, instead of writing, "We found this a central component of protein metabolism," scientists write, "This was found a central component of protein metabolism." While science professors have traditionally instructed students to avoid active voice because it leads to first-person ("I" and "we") usage, science editors today find passive voice dull and weak. Many journal articles combine both. Tone in technical science writing should be detached, concise, and professional. While one may normally write, "This chemical has to be available for proteins to be digested," professionals write technically, "The presence of this chemical is required for the enzyme to break the covalent bonds of proteins." The use of technical language appeals to both technical and non-technical audiences by displaying the author or speaker's understanding of the subject and suggesting their credibility regarding the message they are communicating.

TECHNICAL MATERIAL FOR NON-TECHNICAL READERS

Writing about **technical subjects** for **non-technical readers** differs from writing for colleagues because authors place more importance on delivering a critical message than on imparting the maximum technical content possible. Technical authors also must assume that non-technical audiences do not have the expertise to comprehend extremely scientific or technical messages, concepts, and terminology. They must resist the temptation to impress audiences with their scientific knowledge and expertise and remember that their primary purpose is to communicate a message that non-technical readers will understand, feel, and respond to. Non-technical and technical styles include similarities. Both should formally cite any references or other authors' work utilized in the text. Both must follow intellectual property and copyright regulations. This includes the author's protecting his or her own rights, or a public domain statement, as he or she chooses.

> **Review Video: Technical Passages**
> Visit mometrix.com/academy and enter code: 478923

NON-TECHNICAL AUDIENCES

Writers of technical or scientific material may need to write for many non-technical audiences. Some readers have no technical or scientific background, and those who do may not be in the same field as the authors. Government and corporate policymakers and budget managers need technical information they can understand for decision-making. Citizens affected by technology or science are a different audience. Non-governmental organizations can encompass many of the preceding groups. Elementary and secondary school programs also need non-technical language for presenting technical subject matter. Additionally, technical authors will need to use non-technical language when collecting consumer responses to surveys, presenting scientific or para-scientific material to the public, writing about the history of science, and writing about science and technology in developing countries.

USE OF EVERYDAY LANGUAGE

Authors of technical information sometimes must write using non-technical language that readers outside their disciplinary fields can comprehend. They should use not only non-technical terms, but also normal, everyday language to accommodate readers whose native language is different than the language the text is written in. For example, instead of writing that "eustatic changes like thermal expansion are causing hazardous conditions in the littoral zone," an author would do better to write that "a rising sea level is threatening the coast." When technical terms cannot be avoided, authors should also define or explain them using non-technical language. Although authors must cite references and acknowledge their use of others' work, they should avoid the kinds of references or citations that they would use in scientific journals—unless they reinforce author messages. They should not use endnotes, footnotes, or any other complicated referential techniques because non-technical journal publishers usually do not accept them. Including high-resolution illustrations, photos, maps, or satellite images and incorporating multimedia into digital publications will enhance non-technical writing about technical subjects. Technical authors may publish using non-technical language in e-journals, trade journals, specialty newsletters, and daily newspapers.

MAKING INFERENCES ABOUT INFORMATIONAL TEXT

With informational text, reader comprehension depends not only on recalling important statements and details, but also on reader inferences based on examples and details. Readers add information from the text to what they already know to draw inferences about the text. These inferences help the readers to fill in the information that the text does not explicitly state, enabling them to understand the text better. When reading a nonfictional autobiography or biography, for example, the most appropriate inferences might concern the events in the book, the actions of the subject of the autobiography or biography, and the message the author means to convey. When reading a nonfictional expository (informational) text, the reader would best draw inferences about problems and their solutions, and causes and their effects. When reading a nonfictional persuasive text, the reader will want to infer ideas supporting the author's message and intent.

STRUCTURES OR ORGANIZATIONAL PATTERNS IN INFORMATIONAL TEXTS

Informational text can be **descriptive**, appealing to the five senses and answering the questions what, who, when, where, and why. Another method of structuring informational text is sequence and order. **Chronological** texts relate events in the sequence that they occurred, from start to finish, while how-to texts organize information into a series of instructions in the sequence in which the steps should be followed. **Comparison-contrast** structures of informational text describe various ideas to their readers by pointing out how things or ideas are similar and how they are different. **Cause and effect** structures of informational text describe events that occurred and identify the causes or reasons that those events occurred. **Problem and solution** structures of informational texts introduce and describe problems and offer one or more solutions for each problem described.

DETERMINING AN INFORMATIONAL AUTHOR'S PURPOSE

Informational authors' purposes are why they write texts. Readers must determine authors' motivations and goals. Readers gain greater insight into a text by considering the author's motivation. This develops critical reading skills. Readers perceive writing as a person's voice, not simply printed words. Uncovering author motivations and purposes empowers readers to know what to expect from the text, read for relevant details, evaluate authors and their work critically, and respond effectively to the motivations and persuasions of the text. The main idea of a text is what the reader is supposed to understand from reading it; the purpose of the text is why the author has written it and what the author wants readers to do with its information. Authors state some purposes clearly, while other purposes may be unstated but equally significant. When stated purposes contradict other parts of a text, the author may have a hidden agenda. Readers can better evaluate a text's effectiveness, whether they agree or disagree with it, and why they agree or disagree through identifying unstated author purposes.

IDENTIFYING AUTHOR'S POINT OF VIEW OR PURPOSE

In some informational texts, readers find it easy to identify the author's point of view and purpose, such as when the author explicitly states his or her position and reason for writing. But other texts are more difficult, either because of the content or because the authors give neutral or balanced viewpoints. This is particularly true in scientific texts, in which authors may state the purpose of their research in the report, but never state their point of view except by interpreting evidence or data.

To analyze text and identify point of view or purpose, readers should ask themselves the following four questions:

1. With what main point or idea does this author want to persuade readers to agree?
2. How does this author's word choice affect the way that readers consider this subject?
3. How do this author's choices of examples and facts affect the way that readers consider this subject?
4. What is it that this author wants to accomplish by writing this text?

> **Review Video: Understanding the Author's Intent**
> Visit mometrix.com/academy and enter code: 511819
>
> **Review Video: Author's Position**
> Visit mometrix.com/academy and enter code: 827954

EVALUATING ARGUMENTS MADE BY INFORMATIONAL TEXT WRITERS

When evaluating an informational text, the first step is to identify the argument's conclusion. Then identify the author's premises that support the conclusion. Try to paraphrase premises for clarification and make the conclusion and premises fit. List all premises first, sequentially numbered, then finish with the conclusion. Identify any premises or assumptions not stated by the author but required for the stated premises to support the conclusion. Read word assumptions sympathetically, as the author might. Evaluate whether premises reasonably support the conclusion. For inductive reasoning, the reader should ask if the premises are true, if they support the conclusion, and if so, how strongly. For deductive reasoning, the reader should ask if the argument is valid or invalid. If all premises are true, then the argument is valid unless the conclusion can be false. If it can, then the argument is invalid. An invalid argument can be made valid through alterations such as the addition of needed premises.

USE OF RHETORIC IN INFORMATIONAL TEXTS

There are many ways authors can support their claims, arguments, beliefs, ideas, and reasons for writing in informational texts. For example, authors can appeal to readers' sense of **logic** by communicating their reasoning through a carefully sequenced series of logical steps to help "prove" the points made. Authors can appeal to readers' **emotions** by using descriptions and words that evoke feelings of sympathy, sadness, anger, righteous indignation, hope, happiness, or any other emotion to reinforce what they express and share with their audience. Authors may appeal to the **moral** or **ethical values** of readers by using words and descriptions that can convince readers that something is right or wrong. By relating personal anecdotes, authors can supply readers with more accessible, realistic examples of points they make, as well as appealing to their emotions. They can provide supporting evidence by reporting case studies. They can also illustrate their points by making analogies to which readers can better relate.

CHARTS, GRAPHS, AND VISUALS
PIE CHART

A pie chart, also known as a circle graph, is useful for depicting how a single unit or category is divided. The standard pie chart is a circle with designated wedges. Each wedge is **proportional** in size to a part of the whole. For instance, consider Shawna, a student at City College, who uses a pie chart to represent her budget. If she spends half of her money on rent, then the pie chart will represent that amount with a line through the center of the pie. If she spends a quarter of her money on food, there will be a line extending from the edge of the circle to the center at a right angle to the line depicting rent. This illustration would make it clear that the student spends twice the amount of money on rent as she does on food.

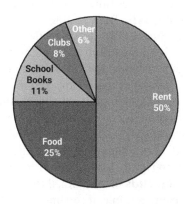

A pie chart is effective at showing how a single entity is divided into parts. They are not effective at demonstrating the relationships between parts of different wholes. For example, an unhelpful use of a pie chart would be to compare the respective amounts of state and federal spending devoted to infrastructure since these values are only meaningful in the context of the entire budget.

BAR GRAPH

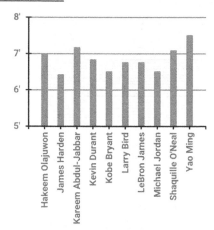

The bar graph is one of the most common visual representations of information. **Bar graphs** are used to illustrate sets of numerical **data**. The graph has a vertical axis (along which numbers are listed) and a horizontal axis (along which categories, words, or some other indicators are placed). One example of a bar graph is a depiction of the respective heights of famous basketball players: the vertical axis would contain numbers ranging from five to eight feet, and the horizontal axis would contain the names of the players. The length of the bar above the player's name would illustrate his height, and the top of the bar would stop perpendicular to the height listed along the left side. In this representation, one would see that Yao Ming is taller than Michael Jordan because Yao's bar would be higher.

LINE GRAPH

A line graph is a type of graph that is typically used for measuring trends over time. The graph is set up along a vertical and a horizontal **axis**. The variables being measured are listed along the left side and the bottom side of the axes. Points are then plotted along the graph as they correspond with their values for each variable. For instance, consider a line graph measuring a person's income for each month of the year. If the person earned $1500 in January, there should be a point directly above January (perpendicular to the horizontal axis) and directly to the right of $1500 (perpendicular to the vertical axis). Once all of the lines are plotted, they are connected with a line from left to right. This line provides a nice visual illustration of the general **trends** of the data, if they exist. For instance, using the earlier example, if the line sloped up, then one would see that the person's income had increased over the course of the year.

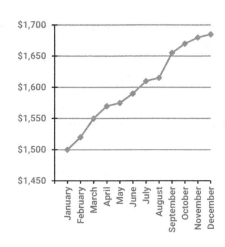

PICTOGRAPHS

A **pictograph** is a graph, generally in the horizontal orientation, that uses pictures or symbols to represent the data. Each pictograph must have a key that defines the picture or symbol and gives the quantity each picture or symbol represents. Pictures or symbols on a pictograph are not always shown as whole elements. In this case, the fraction of the picture or symbol shown represents the same fraction of the quantity a whole picture or symbol stands for.

> **Review Video: Pictographs**
> Visit mometrix.com/academy and enter code: 147860

TYPES OF PRINTED COMMUNICATION
MEMO

A memo (short for *memorandum*) is a common form of written communication. There is a standard format for these documents. It is typical for there to be a **heading** at the top indicating the author, date, and recipient. In some cases, this heading will also include the author's title and the name of his or her institution. Below this information will be the **body** of the memo. These documents are typically written by and for members of the same organization. They usually contain a plan of action, a request for information on a specific topic, or a response to such a request. Memos are considered to be official documents, so they are usually written in a **formal** style. Many memos are organized with numbers or bullet points, which make it easier for the reader to identify key ideas.

POSTED ANNOUNCEMENT

People post **announcements** for all sorts of occasions. Many people are familiar with notices for lost pets, yard sales, and landscaping services. In order to be effective, these announcements need to *contain all of the information* the reader requires to act on the message. For instance, a lost pet announcement needs to include a good description of the animal and a contact number for the owner. A yard sale notice should include the address, date, and hours of the sale, as well as a brief description of the products that will be available there. When composing an announcement, it is important to consider the perspective of the **audience**—what will they need to know in order to respond to the message? Although a posted announcement can have color and decoration to attract the eye of the passerby, it must also convey the necessary information clearly.

CLASSIFIED ADVERTISEMENT

Classified advertisements, or **ads**, are used to sell or buy goods, to attract business, to make romantic connections, and to do countless other things. They are an inexpensive, and sometimes free, way to make a

brief **pitch**. Classified ads used to be found only in newspapers or special advertising circulars, but there are now online listings as well. The style of these ads has remained basically the same. An ad usually begins with a word or phrase indicating what is being **sold** or **sought**. Then, the listing will give a brief **description** of the product or service. Because space is limited and costly in newspapers, classified ads there will often contain abbreviations for common attributes. For instance, two common abbreviations are *bk* for *black*, and *obo* for *or best offer*. Classified ads will then usually conclude by listing the **price** (or the amount the seeker is willing to pay), followed by **contact information** like a telephone number or email address.

SCALE READINGS OF STANDARD MEASUREMENT INSTRUMENTS

The scales used on **standard measurement instruments** are fairly easy to read with a little practice. Take the **ruler** as an example. A typical ruler has different units along each long edge. One side measures inches, and the other measures centimeters. The units are specified close to the zero reading for the ruler. Note that the ruler does not begin measuring from its outermost edge. The zero reading is a black line a tiny distance inside of the edge. On the inches side, each inch is indicated with a long black line and a number. Each half-inch is noted with a slightly shorter line. Quarter-inches are noted with still shorter lines, eighth-inches are noted with even shorter lines, and sixteenth-inches are noted with the shortest lines of all. On the centimeter side, the second-largest black lines indicate half-centimeters, and the smaller lines indicate tenths of centimeters, otherwise known as millimeters.

COMMON ORGANIZATIONS OF TEXTS

ORGANIZATION OF THE TEXT

The way a text is organized can help readers understand the author's intent and his or her conclusions. There are various ways to organize a text, and each one has a purpose and use. Usually, authors will organize information logically in a passage so the reader can follow and locate the information within the text. However, since not all passages are written with the same logical structure, you need to be familiar with several different types of passage structure.

> **Review Video: Organizational Methods to Structure Text**
> Visit mometrix.com/academy and enter code: 606263
>
> **Review Video: Sequence of Events in a Story**
> Visit mometrix.com/academy and enter code: 807512

CHRONOLOGICAL

When using **chronological** order, the author presents information in the order that it happened. For example, biographies are typically written in chronological order. The subject's birth and childhood are presented first, followed by their adult life, and lastly the events leading up to the person's death.

CAUSE AND EFFECT

One of the most common text structures is **cause and effect**. A **cause** is an act or event that makes something happen, and an **effect** is the thing that happens as a result of the cause. A cause-and-effect relationship is not always explicit, but there are some terms in English that signal causes, such as *since*, *because*, and *due to*. Furthermore, terms that signal effects include *consequently, therefore, this leads to*. As an example, consider the sentence *Because the sky was clear, Ron did not bring an umbrella*. The cause is the clear sky, and the effect is that Ron did not bring an umbrella. However, readers may find that sometimes the cause-and-effect relationship will not be clearly noted. For instance, the sentence *He was late and missed the meeting* does not contain any signaling words, but the sentence still contains a cause (he was late) and an effect (he missed the meeting).

> **Review Video: Cause and Effect**
> Visit mometrix.com/academy and enter code: 868099

MULTIPLE EFFECTS

Be aware of the possibility for a single cause to have **multiple effects.** (e.g., *Single cause*: Because you left your homework on the table, your dog engulfed the assignment. *Multiple effects*: As a result, you receive a failing grade, your parents do not allow you to go out with your friends, you miss out on the new movie, and one of your classmates spoils it for you before you have another chance to watch it).

MULTIPLE CAUSES

Also, there is the possibility for a single effect to have **multiple causes.** (e.g., *Single effect*: Alan has a fever. *Multiple causes*: An unexpected cold front came through the area, and Alan forgot to take his multi-vitamin to avoid getting sick.) Additionally, an effect can in turn be the cause of another effect, in what is known as a cause-and-effect chain. (e.g., As a result of her disdain for procrastination, Lynn prepared for her exam. This led to her passing her test with high marks. Hence, her resume was accepted and her application was approved.)

CAUSE AND EFFECT IN PERSUASIVE ESSAYS

Persuasive essays, in which an author tries to make a convincing argument and change the minds of readers, usually include cause-and-effect relationships. However, these relationships should not always be taken at face value. Frequently, an author will assume a cause or take an effect for granted. To read a persuasive essay effectively, readers need to judge the cause-and-effect relationships that the author is presenting. For instance, imagine an author wrote the following: *The parking deck has been unprofitable because people would prefer to ride their bikes.* The relationship is clear: the cause is that people prefer to ride their bikes, and the effect is that the parking deck has been unprofitable. However, readers should consider whether this argument is conclusive. Perhaps there are other reasons for the failure of the parking deck: a down economy, excessive fees, etc. Too often, authors present causal relationships as if they are fact rather than opinion. Readers should be on the alert for these dubious claims.

PROBLEM-SOLUTION

Some nonfiction texts are organized to **present a problem** followed by a solution. For this type of text, the problem is often explained before the solution is offered. In some cases, as when the problem is well known, the solution may be introduced briefly at the beginning. Other passages may focus on the solution, and the problem will be referenced only occasionally. Some texts will outline multiple solutions to a problem, leaving readers to choose among them. If the author has an interest or an allegiance to one solution, he or she may fail to mention or describe accurately some of the other solutions. Readers should be careful of the author's agenda when reading a problem-solution text. Only by understanding the author's perspective and interests can one develop a proper judgment of the proposed solution.

COMPARE AND CONTRAST

Many texts follow the **compare-and-contrast** model in which the similarities and differences between two ideas or things are explored. Analysis of the similarities between ideas is called **comparison**. In an ideal comparison, the author places ideas or things in an equivalent structure, i.e., the author presents the ideas in the same way. If an author wants to show the similarities between cricket and baseball, then he or she may do so by summarizing the equipment and rules for each game. Be mindful of the similarities as they appear in the passage and take note of any differences that are mentioned. Often, these small differences will only reinforce the more general similarity.

Thinking critically about ideas and conclusions can seem like a daunting task. One way to ease this task is to understand the basic elements of ideas and writing techniques. Looking at the ways different ideas relate to each other can be a good way for readers to begin their analysis. For instance, sometimes authors will write about two ideas that are in opposition to each other. Or, one author will provide his or her ideas on a topic, and another author may respond in opposition. The analysis of these opposing ideas is known as **contrast**. Contrast is often marred by the author's obvious partiality to one of the ideas. A discerning reader will be put off by an author who does not engage in a fair fight. In an analysis of opposing ideas, both ideas should be presented in clear and reasonable terms. If the author does prefer a side, you need to read carefully to determine the areas where the author shows or avoids this preference. In an analysis of opposing ideas, you should proceed through the passage by marking the major differences point by point with an eye that is looking for an explanation of each side's view. For instance, in an analysis of capitalism and communism, there is an importance in outlining each side's view on labor, markets, prices, personal responsibility, etc. Additionally, as you read through the passages, you should note whether the opposing views present each side in a similar manner.

SEQUENCE

Readers must be able to identify a text's **sequence**, or the order in which things happen. Often, when the sequence is very important to the author, the text is indicated with signal words like *first*, *then*, *next*, and *last*. However, a sequence can be merely implied and must be noted by the reader. Consider the sentence *He walked through the garden and gave water and fertilizer to the plants*. Clearly, the man did not walk through the garden before he collected water and fertilizer for the plants. So, the implied sequence is that he first collected water, then he collected fertilizer, next he walked through the garden, and last he gave water or fertilizer as necessary to the plants. Texts do not always proceed in an orderly sequence from first to last. Sometimes they begin at the end and start over at the beginning. As a reader, you can enhance your understanding of the passage by taking brief notes to clarify the sequence.

> **Review Video: Sequence**
> Visit mometrix.com/academy and enter code: 489027

MAIN IDEAS AND SUPPORTING DETAILS
IDENTIFYING TOPICS AND MAIN IDEAS

One of the most important skills in reading comprehension is the identification of **topics** and **main ideas**. There is a subtle difference between these two features. The topic is the subject of a text (i.e., what the text is all about). The main idea, on the other hand, is the most important point being made by the author. The topic is usually expressed in a few words at the most while the main idea often needs a full sentence to be completely defined. As an example, a short passage might be written on the topic of penguins, and the main idea could be written as *Penguins are different from other birds in many ways*. In most nonfiction writing, the topic and the main idea will be **stated directly** and often appear in a sentence at the very beginning or end of the text. When being tested on an understanding of the author's topic, you may be able to skim the passage for the general idea by reading only the first sentence of each paragraph. A body paragraph's first sentence is often—but not always—the main **topic sentence** which gives you a summary of the content in the paragraph.

However, there are cases in which the reader must figure out an **unstated** topic or main idea. In these instances, you must read every sentence of the text and try to come up with an overarching idea that is supported by each of those sentences.

Note: The main idea should not be confused with the thesis statement. While the main idea gives a brief, general summary of a text, the thesis statement provides a **specific perspective** on an issue that the author supports with evidence.

> **Review Video: Topics and Main Ideas**
> Visit mometrix.com/academy and enter code: 407801

SUPPORTING DETAILS

Supporting details are smaller pieces of evidence that provide backing for the main point. In order to show that a main idea is correct or valid, an author must add details that prove their point. All texts contain details, but they are only classified as supporting details when they serve to reinforce some larger point. Supporting details are most commonly found in informative and persuasive texts. In some cases, they will be clearly indicated with terms like *for example* or *for instance*, or they will be enumerated with terms like *first*, *second*, and *last*. However, you need to be prepared for texts that do not contain those indicators. As a reader, you should consider whether the author's supporting details really back up his or her main point. Details can be factual and correct, yet they may not be **relevant** to the author's point. Conversely, details can be relevant, but be ineffective because they are based on opinion or assertions that cannot be proven.

> **Review Video: <u>Supporting Details</u>**
> Visit mometrix.com/academy and enter code: 396297

An example of a main idea is: *Giraffes live in the Serengeti of Africa.* A supporting detail about giraffes could be: *A giraffe in this region benefits from a long neck by reaching twigs and leaves on tall trees.* The main idea gives the general idea that the text is about giraffes. The supporting detail gives a specific fact about how the giraffes eat.

MAKING PREDICTIONS AND INFERENCES

MAKING PREDICTIONS

When we read literature, **making predictions** about what will happen in the writing reinforces our purpose for reading and prepares us mentally. A **prediction** is a guess about what will happen next. Readers constantly make predictions based on what they have read and what they already know. We can make predictions before we begin reading and during our reading. Consider the following sentence: *Staring at the computer screen in shock, Kim blindly reached over for the brimming glass of water on the shelf to her side.* The sentence suggests that Kim is distracted, and that she is not looking at the glass that she is going to pick up. So, a reader might predict that Kim is going to knock over the glass. Of course, not every prediction will be accurate: perhaps Kim will pick the glass up cleanly. Nevertheless, the author has certainly created the expectation that the water might be spilled.

As we read on, we can test the accuracy of our predictions, revise them in light of additional reading, and confirm or refute our predictions. Predictions are always subject to revision as the reader acquires more information. A reader can make predictions by observing the title and illustrations; noting the structure, characters, and subject; drawing on existing knowledge relative to the subject; and asking "why" and "who" questions. Connecting reading to what we already know enables us to learn new information and construct meaning. For example, before third-graders read a book about Johnny Appleseed, they may start a KWL chart—a list of what they *Know*, what they *Want* to know or learn, and what they have *Learned* after reading. Activating existing background knowledge and thinking about the text before reading improves comprehension.

> **Review Video: <u>Predictive Reading</u>**
> Visit mometrix.com/academy and enter code: 437248

Test-taking tip: To respond to questions requiring future predictions, your answers should be based on evidence of past or present behavior and events.

EVALUATING PREDICTIONS

When making predictions, readers should be able to explain how they developed their prediction. One way readers can defend their thought process is by citing textual evidence. Textual evidence to evaluate reader predictions about literature includes specific synopses of the work, paraphrases of the work or parts of it, and direct quotations from the work. These references to the text must support the prediction by indicating, clearly

24

or unclearly, what will happen later in the story. A text may provide these indications through literary devices such as foreshadowing. Foreshadowing is anything in a text that gives the reader a hint about what is to come by emphasizing the likelihood of an event or development. Foreshadowing can occur through descriptions, exposition, and dialogue. Foreshadowing in dialogue usually occurs when a character gives a warning or expresses a strong feeling that a certain event will occur. Foreshadowing can also occur through irony. However, unlike other forms of foreshadowing, the events that seem the most likely are the opposite of what actually happens. Instances of foreshadowing and irony can be summarized, paraphrased, or quoted to defend a reader's prediction.

> **Review Video: Textual Evidence for Predictions**
> Visit mometrix.com/academy and enter code: 261070

DRAWING CONCLUSIONS FROM INFERENCES

Inferences about literary text are logical conclusions that readers make based on their observations and previous knowledge. An inference is based on both what is found in a passage or a story and what is known from personal experience. For instance, a story may say that a character is frightened and can hear howling in the distance. Based on both what is in the text and personal knowledge, it is a logical conclusion that the character is frightened because he hears the sound of wolves. A good inference is supported by the information in a passage.

IMPLICIT AND EXPLICIT INFORMATION

By inferring, readers construct meanings from text that are personally relevant. By combining their own schemas or concepts and their background information pertinent to the text with what they read, readers interpret it according to both what the author has conveyed and their own unique perspectives. Inferences are different from **explicit information**, which is clearly stated in a passage. Authors do not always explicitly spell out every meaning in what they write; many meanings are implicit. Through inference, readers can comprehend implied meanings in the text, and also derive personal significance from it, making the text meaningful and memorable to them. Inference is a natural process in everyday life. When readers infer, they can draw conclusions about what the author is saying, predict what may reasonably follow, amend these predictions as they continue to read, interpret the import of themes, and analyze the characters' feelings and motivations through their actions.

EXAMPLE OF DRAWING CONCLUSIONS FROM INFERENCES

Read the excerpt and decide why Jana finally relaxed.

> Jana loved her job, but the work was very demanding. She had trouble relaxing. She called a friend, but she still thought about work. She ordered a pizza, but eating it did not help. Then, her kitten jumped on her lap and began to purr. Jana leaned back and began to hum a little tune. She felt better.

You can draw the conclusion that Jana relaxed because her kitten jumped on her lap. The kitten purred, and Jana leaned back and hummed a tune. Then she felt better. The excerpt does not explicitly say that this is the reason why she was able to relax. The text leaves the matter unclear, but the reader can infer or make a "best guess" that this is the reason she is relaxing. This is a logical conclusion based on the information in the passage. It is the best conclusion a reader can make based on the information he or she has read. Inferences are based on the information in a passage, but they are not directly stated in the passage.

Test-taking tip: While being tested on your ability to make correct inferences, you must look for **contextual clues**. An answer can be true, but not the best or most correct answer. The contextual clues will help you find the answer that is the **best answer** out of the given choices. Be careful in your reading to understand the context in which a phrase is stated. When asked for the implied meaning of a statement made in the passage,

you should immediately locate the statement and read the **context** in which the statement was made. Also, look for an answer choice that has a similar phrase to the statement in question.

Review Video: <u>Inference</u>
Visit mometrix.com/academy and enter code: 379203

Review Video: <u>How to Support a Conclusion</u>
Visit mometrix.com/academy and enter code: 281653

RECOGNIZING AN AUTHOR'S PURPOSE
AUTHOR'S POSITION AND PURPOSE

In order to be an effective reader, one must pay attention to the author's **position** and **purpose**. Even those texts that seem objective and impartial, like textbooks, have a position and bias. Readers need to take these positions into account when considering the author's message. When an author uses emotional language or clearly favors one side of an argument, his or her position is clear. However, the author's position may be evident not only in what he or she writes, but also in what he or she doesn't write. In a normal setting, a reader would want to review some other texts on the same topic in order to develop a view of the author's position. If this was not possible, then you would want to at least acquire some background about the author. However, since you are in the middle of an exam and the only source of information is the text, you should look for language and argumentation that seems to indicate a particular stance on the subject.

Review Video: <u>Author's Position</u>
Visit mometrix.com/academy and enter code: 827954

AUTHOR'S PURPOSE

Usually, identifying the author's **purpose** is easier than identifying his or her position. In most cases, the author has no interest in hiding his or her purpose. A text that is meant to entertain, for instance, should be written to please the reader. Most narratives, or stories, are written to entertain, though they may also inform or persuade. Informative texts are easy to identify, while the most difficult purpose of a text to identify is persuasion because the author has an interest in making this purpose hard to detect. When a reader discovers that the author is trying to persuade, he or she should be skeptical of the argument. For this reason, persuasive texts often try to establish an entertaining tone and hope to amuse the reader into agreement. On the other hand, an informative tone may be implemented to create an appearance of authority and objectivity.

An author's purpose is evident often in the organization of the text (e.g., section headings in bold font points to an informative text). However, you may not have such organization available to you in your exam. Instead, if the author makes his or her main idea clear from the beginning, then the likely purpose of the text is to inform. If the author begins by making a claim and provides various arguments to support that claim, then the purpose is probably to persuade. If the author tells a story or wants to gain the reader's attention more than to push a particular point or deliver information, then his or her purpose is most likely to entertain. As a reader, you must judge authors on how well they accomplish their purpose. In other words, you need to consider the type of passage (e.g., technical, persuasive, etc.) that the author has written and if the author has followed the requirements of the passage type.

READING COMPREHENSION AND CONNECTING WITH TEXTS
COMPARING TWO STORIES

When presented with two different stories, there will be **similarities** and **differences** between the two. A reader needs to make a list, or other graphic organizer, of the points presented in each story. Once the reader has written down the main point and supporting points for each story, the two sets of ideas can be compared. The reader can then present each idea and show how it is the same or different in the other story. This is called **comparing and contrasting ideas**.

The reader can compare ideas by stating, for example: "In Story 1, the author believes that humankind will one day land on Mars, whereas in Story 2, the author believes that Mars is too far away for humans to ever step foot on." Note that the two viewpoints are different in each story that the reader is comparing. A reader may state that: "Both stories discussed the likelihood of humankind landing on Mars." This statement shows how the viewpoint presented in both stories is based on the same topic, rather than how each viewpoint is different. The reader will complete a comparison of two stories with a conclusion.

> **Review Video: How to Compare and Contrast**
> Visit mometrix.com/academy and enter code: 833765

OUTLINING A PASSAGE

As an aid to drawing conclusions, **outlining** the information contained in the passage should be a familiar skill to readers. An effective outline will reveal the structure of the passage and will lead to solid conclusions. An effective outline will have a title that refers to the basic subject of the text, though the title does not need to restate the main idea. In most outlines, the main idea will be the first major section. Each major idea in the passage will be established as the head of a category. For instance, the most common outline format calls for the main ideas of the passage to be indicated with Roman numerals. In an effective outline of this kind, each of the main ideas will be represented by a Roman numeral and none of the Roman numerals will designate minor details or secondary ideas. Moreover, all supporting ideas and details should be placed in the appropriate place on the outline. An outline does not need to include every detail listed in the text, but it should feature all of those that are central to the argument or message. Each of these details should be listed under the corresponding main idea.

> **Review Video: Outlining as an Aid to Drawing Conclusions**
> Visit mometrix.com/academy and enter code: 584445

USING GRAPHIC ORGANIZERS

Ideas from a text can also be organized using **graphic organizers**. A graphic organizer is a way to simplify information and take key points from the text. A graphic organizer such as a timeline may have an event listed for a corresponding date on the timeline, while an outline may have an event listed under a key point that occurs in the text. Each reader needs to create the type of graphic organizer that works the best for him or her in terms of being able to recall information from a story. Examples include a spider-map, which takes a main idea from the story and places it in a bubble with supporting points branching off the main idea. An outline is useful for diagramming the main and supporting points of the entire story, and a Venn diagram compares and contrasts characteristics of two or more ideas.

> **Review Video: Graphic Organizers**
> Visit mometrix.com/academy and enter code: 665513

MAKING LOGICAL CONCLUSIONS ABOUT A PASSAGE

A reader should always be drawing conclusions from the text. Sometimes conclusions are **implied** from written information, and other times the information is **stated directly** within the passage. One should always aim to draw conclusions from information stated within a passage, rather than to draw them from mere

27

implications. At times an author may provide some information and then describe a counterargument. Readers should be alert for direct statements that are subsequently rejected or weakened by the author. Furthermore, you should always read through the entire passage before drawing conclusions. Many readers are trained to expect the author's conclusions at either the beginning or the end of the passage, but many texts do not adhere to this format.

Drawing conclusions from information implied within a passage requires confidence on the part of the reader. **Implications** are things that the author does not state directly, but readers can assume based on what the author does say. Consider the following passage: *I stepped outside and opened my umbrella. By the time I got to work, the cuffs of my pants were soaked.* The author never states that it is raining, but this fact is clearly implied. Conclusions based on implication must be well supported by the text. In order to draw a solid conclusion, readers should have **multiple pieces of evidence**. If readers have only one piece, they must be assured that there is no other possible explanation than their conclusion. A good reader will be able to draw many conclusions from information implied by the text, which will be a great help on the exam.

DRAWING CONCLUSIONS

A common type of inference that a reader has to make is **drawing a conclusion**. The reader makes this conclusion based on the information provided within a text. Certain facts are included to help a reader come to a specific conclusion. For example, a story may open with a man trudging through the snow on a cold winter day, dragging a sled behind him. The reader can logically **infer** from the setting of the story that the man is wearing heavy winter clothes in order to stay warm. Information is implied based on the setting of a story, which is why **setting** is an important element of the text. If the same man in the example was trudging down a beach on a hot summer day, dragging a surf board behind him, the reader would assume that the man is not wearing heavy clothes. The reader makes inferences based on their own experiences and the information presented to them in the story.

Test-taking tip: When asked to identify a conclusion that may be drawn, look for critical "hedge" phrases, such as *likely*, *may*, *can*, and *will often*, among many others. When you are being tested on this knowledge, remember the question that writers insert into these hedge phrases to cover every possibility. Often an answer will be wrong simply because there is no room for exception. Extreme positive or negative answers (such as *always* or *never*) are usually not correct. When answering these questions, the reader **should not** use any outside knowledge that is not gathered directly or reasonably inferred from the passage. Correct answers can be derived straight from the passage.

EXAMPLE

Read the following sentence from *Little Women* by Louisa May Alcott and draw a conclusion based upon the information presented:

> *You know the reason Mother proposed not having any presents this Christmas was because it is going to be a hard winter for everyone; and she thinks we ought not to spend money for pleasure, when our men are suffering so in the army.*

Based on the information in the sentence, the reader can conclude, or **infer**, that the men are away at war while the women are still at home. The pronoun *our* gives a clue to the reader that the character is speaking about men she knows. In addition, the reader can assume that the character is speaking to a brother or sister, since the term "Mother" is used by the character while speaking to another person. The reader can also come to the conclusion that the characters celebrate Christmas, since it is mentioned in the **context** of the sentence. In the sentence, the mother is presented as an unselfish character who is opinionated and thinks about the wellbeing of other people.

SUMMARIZING

A helpful tool is the ability to **summarize** the information that you have read in a paragraph or passage format. This process is similar to creating an effective outline. First, a summary should accurately define the main idea of the passage, though the summary does not need to explain this main idea in exhaustive detail. The summary should continue by laying out the most important supporting details or arguments from the passage. All of the significant supporting details should be included, and none of the details included should be irrelevant or insignificant. Also, the summary should accurately report all of these details. Too often, the desire for brevity in a summary leads to the sacrifice of clarity or accuracy. Summaries are often difficult to read because they omit all of the graceful language, digressions, and asides that distinguish great writing. However, an effective summary should communicate the same overall message as the original text.

Review Video: <u>Summarizing Text</u>
Visit mometrix.com/academy and enter code: 172903

PARAPHRASING

Paraphrasing is another method that the reader can use to aid in comprehension. When paraphrasing, one puts what they have read into their own words by rephrasing what the author has written, or one "translates" all of what the author shared into their own words by including as many details as they can.

EVALUATING A PASSAGE

It is important to understand the logical conclusion of the ideas presented in an informational text. **Identifying a logical conclusion** can help you determine whether you agree with the writer or not. Coming to this conclusion is much like making an inference: the approach requires you to combine the information given by the text with what you already know and make a logical conclusion. If the author intended for the reader to draw a certain conclusion, then you can expect the author's argumentation and detail to be leading in that direction.

One way to approach the task of drawing conclusions is to make brief **notes** of all the points made by the author. When the notes are arranged on paper, they may clarify the logical conclusion. Another way to approach conclusions is to consider whether the reasoning of the author raises any pertinent questions. Sometimes you will be able to draw several conclusions from a passage. On occasion these will be conclusions that were never imagined by the author. Therefore, be aware that these conclusions must be **supported directly by the text**.

EVALUATION OF SUMMARIES

A summary of a literary passage is a condensation in the reader's own words of the passage's main points. Several guidelines can be used in evaluating a summary. The summary should be complete yet concise. It should be accurate, balanced, fair, neutral, and objective, excluding the reader's own opinions or reactions. It should reflect in similar proportion how much each point summarized was covered in the original passage. Summary writers should include tags of attribution, like "Macaulay argues that" to reference the original author whose ideas are represented in the summary. Summary writers should not overuse quotations; they should only quote central concepts or phrases they cannot precisely convey in words other than those of the original author. Another aspect of evaluating a summary is considering whether it can stand alone as a coherent, unified composition. In addition, evaluation of a summary should include whether its writer has cited the original source of the passage they have summarized so that readers can find it.

MAKING CONNECTIONS TO ENHANCE COMPREHENSION

Reading involves thinking. For good comprehension, readers make **text-to-self**, **text-to-text**, and **text-to-world connections**. Making connections helps readers understand text better and predict what might occur next based on what they already know, such as how characters in the story feel or what happened in another text. Text-to-self connections with the reader's life and experiences make literature more personally relevant and meaningful to readers. Readers can make connections before, during, and after reading—including whenever the text reminds them of something similar they have encountered in life or other texts. The genre, setting, characters, plot elements, literary structure and devices, and themes an author uses allow a reader to make connections to other works of literature or to people and events in their own lives. Venn diagrams and

29

other graphic organizers help visualize connections. Readers can also make double-entry notes: key content, ideas, events, words, and quotations on one side, and the connections with these on the other.

Craft, Structure, and Language Skills

WORD ROOTS AND PREFIXES AND SUFFIXES

AFFIXES

Affixes in the English language are morphemes that are added to words to create related but different words. Derivational affixes form new words based on and related to the original words. For example, the affix *–ness* added to the end of the adjective *happy* forms the noun *happiness.* Inflectional affixes form different grammatical versions of words. For example, the plural affix *–s* changes the singular noun *book* to the plural noun *books,* and the past tense affix *–ed* changes the present tense verb *look* to the past tense *looked.* Prefixes are affixes placed in front of words. For example, *heat* means to make hot; *preheat* means to heat in advance. Suffixes are affixes placed at the ends of words. The *happiness* example above contains the suffix *–ness.* Circumfixes add parts both before and after words, such as how *light* becomes *enlighten* with the prefix *en-* and the suffix *–en.* Interfixes create compound words via central affixes: *speed* and *meter* become *speedometer* via the interfix *–o–.*

> **Review Video: Affixes**
> Visit mometrix.com/academy and enter code: 782422

WORD ROOTS, PREFIXES, AND SUFFIXES TO HELP DETERMINE MEANINGS OF WORDS

Many English words were formed from combining multiple sources. For example, the Latin *habēre* means "to have," and the prefixes *in-* and *im-* mean a lack or prevention of something, as in *insufficient* and *imperfect.* Latin combined *in-* with *habēre* to form *inhibēre,* whose past participle was *inhibitus.* This is the origin of the English word *inhibit,* meaning to prevent from having. Hence by knowing the meanings of both the prefix and the root, one can decipher the word meaning. In Greek, the root *enkephalo-* refers to the brain. Many medical terms are based on this root, such as encephalitis and hydrocephalus. Understanding the prefix and suffix meanings (*-itis* means inflammation; *hydro-* means water) allows a person to deduce that encephalitis refers to brain inflammation and hydrocephalus refers to water (or other fluid) in the brain.

> **Review Video: Determining Word Meanings**
> Visit mometrix.com/academy and enter code: 894894

PREFIXES

While knowing prefix meanings helps ESL and beginning readers learn new words, other readers take for granted the meanings of known words. However, prefix knowledge will also benefit them for determining meanings or definitions of unfamiliar words. For example, native English speakers and readers familiar with recipes know what *preheat* means. Knowing that *pre-* means in advance can also inform them that *presume* means to assume in advance, that *prejudice* means advance judgment, and that this understanding can be applied to many other words beginning with *pre-*. Knowing that the prefix *dis-* indicates opposition informs the meanings of words like *disbar, disagree, disestablish,* and many more. Knowing *dys-* means bad, impaired, abnormal, or difficult informs *dyslogistic, dysfunctional, dysphagia,* and *dysplasia.*

SUFFIXES

In English, certain suffixes generally indicate both that a word is a noun, and that the noun represents a state of being or quality. For example, *-ness* is commonly used to change an adjective into its noun form, as with *happy* and *happiness, nice* and *niceness,* and so on. The suffix *–tion* is commonly used to transform a verb into its noun

form, as with *converse* and *conversation or move* and *motion*. Thus, if readers are unfamiliar with the second form of a word, knowing the meaning of the transforming suffix can help them determine meaning.

PREFIXES FOR NUMBERS

Prefix	Definition	Examples
bi-	two	bisect, biennial
mono-	one, single	monogamy, monologue
poly-	many	polymorphous, polygamous
semi-	half, partly	semicircle, semicolon
uni-	one	uniform, unity

PREFIXES FOR TIME, DIRECTION, AND SPACE

Prefix	Definition	Examples
a-	in, on, of, up, to	abed, afoot
ab-	from, away, off	abdicate, abjure
ad-	to, toward	advance, adventure
ante-	before, previous	antecedent, antedate
anti-	against, opposing	antipathy, antidote
cata-	down, away, thoroughly	catastrophe, cataclysm
circum-	around	circumspect, circumference
com-	with, together, very	commotion, complicate
contra-	against, opposing	contradict, contravene
de-	from	depart
dia-	through, across, apart	diameter, diagnose
dis-	away, off, down, not	dissent, disappear
epi-	upon	epilogue
ex-	out	extract, excerpt
hypo-	under, beneath	hypodermic, hypothesis
inter-	among, between	intercede, interrupt
intra-	within	intramural, intrastate
ob-	against, opposing	objection
per-	through	perceive, permit
peri-	around	periscope, perimeter
post-	after, following	postpone, postscript
pre-	before, previous	prevent, preclude
pro-	forward, in place of	propel, pronoun
retro-	back, backward	retrospect, retrograde
sub-	under, beneath	subjugate, substitute
super-	above, extra	supersede, supernumerary
trans-	across, beyond, over	transact, transport
ultra-	beyond, excessively	ultramodern, ultrasonic

NEGATIVE PREFIXES

Prefix	Definition	Examples
a-	without, lacking	atheist, agnostic
in-	not, opposing	incapable, ineligible
non-	not	nonentity, nonsense
un-	not, reverse of	unhappy, unlock

EXTRA PREFIXES

Prefix	Definition	Examples
for-	away, off, from	forget, forswear
fore-	previous	foretell, forefathers
homo-	same, equal	homogenized, homonym
hyper-	excessive, over	hypercritical, hypertension
in-	in, into	intrude, invade
mal-	bad, poorly, not	malfunction, malpractice
mis-	bad, poorly, not	misspell, misfire
neo-	new	Neolithic, neoconservative
omni-	all, everywhere	omniscient, omnivore
ortho-	right, straight	orthogonal, orthodox
over-	above	overbearing, oversight
pan-	all, entire	panorama, pandemonium
para-	beside, beyond	parallel, paradox
re-	backward, again	revoke, recur
sym-	with, together	sympathy, symphony

Below is a list of common suffixes and their meanings:

ADJECTIVE SUFFIXES

Suffix	Definition	Examples
-able (-ible)	capable of being	toler*able*, ed*ible*
-esque	in the style of, like	picturesque, grotesque
-ful	filled with, marked by	thankful, zestful
-ific	make, cause	terrific, beatific
-ish	suggesting, like	churlish, childish
-less	lacking, without	hopeless, countless
-ous	marked by, given to	religious, riotous

NOUN SUFFIXES

Suffix	Definition	Examples
-acy	state, condition	accuracy, privacy
-ance	act, condition, fact	acceptance, vigilance
-ard	one that does excessively	drunkard, sluggard
-ation	action, state, result	occupation, starvation
-dom	state, rank, condition	serfdom, wisdom
-er (-or)	office, action	teach*er*, elevat*or*, hon*or*
-ess	feminine	waitress, duchess
-hood	state, condition	manhood, statehood
-ion	action, result, state	union, fusion
-ism	act, manner, doctrine	barbarism, socialism
-ist	worker, follower	monopolist, socialist
-ity (-ty)	state, quality, condition	acid*ity*, civil*ity*, twen*ty*
-ment	result, action	Refreshment
-ness	quality, state	greatness, tallness
-ship	position	internship, statesmanship
-sion (-tion)	state, result	revi*sion*, expedi*tion*
-th	act, state, quality	warmth, width
-tude	quality, state, result	magnitude, fortitude

VERB SUFFIXES

Suffix	Definition	Examples
-ate	having, showing	separate, desolate
-en	cause to be, become	deepen, strengthen
-fy	make, cause to have	glorify, fortify
-ize	cause to be, treat with	sterilize, mechanize

DETERMINING WORD MEANINGS

SYNONYMS AND ANTONYMS

When you understand how words relate to each other, you will discover more in a passage. This is explained by understanding **synonyms** (e.g., words that mean the same thing) and **antonyms** (e.g., words that mean the opposite of one another). As an example, *dry* and *arid* are synonyms, and *dry* and *wet* are antonyms.

There are many pairs of words in English that can be considered synonyms, despite having slightly different definitions. For instance, the words *friendly* and *collegial* can both be used to describe a warm interpersonal relationship, and one would be correct to call them synonyms. However, *collegial* (kin to *colleague*) is often used in reference to professional or academic relationships, and *friendly* has no such connotation.

If the difference between the two words is too great, then they should not be called synonyms. *Hot* and *warm* are not synonyms because their meanings are too distinct. A good way to determine whether two words are synonyms is to substitute one word for the other word and verify that the meaning of the sentence has not changed. Substituting *warm* for *hot* in a sentence would convey a different meaning. Although warm and hot may seem close in meaning, warm generally means that the temperature is moderate, and hot generally means that the temperature is excessively high.

Antonyms are words with opposite meanings. *Light* and *dark*, *up* and *down*, *right* and *left*, *good* and *bad*: these are all sets of antonyms. Be careful to distinguish between antonyms and pairs of words that are simply different. *Black* and *gray*, for instance, are not antonyms because gray is not the opposite of black. *Black* and *white*, on the other hand, are antonyms.

Not every word has an antonym. For instance, many nouns do not. What would be the antonym of *chair*? During your exam, the questions related to antonyms are more likely to concern adjectives. You will recall that adjectives are words that describe a noun. Some common adjectives include *purple*, *fast*, *skinny*, and *sweet*. From those four adjectives, *purple* is the item that lacks a group of obvious antonyms.

> **Review Video: What Are Synonyms and Antonyms?**
> Visit mometrix.com/academy and enter code: 105612

DENOTATIVE VS. CONNOTATIVE MEANING

The **denotative** meaning of a word is the literal meaning. The **connotative** meaning goes beyond the denotative meaning to include the emotional reaction that a word may invoke. The connotative meaning often takes the denotative meaning a step further due to associations the reader makes with the denotative meaning. Readers can differentiate between the denotative and connotative meanings by first recognizing how authors use each meaning. Most non-fiction, for example, is fact-based and authors do not use flowery, figurative language. The reader can assume that the writer is using the denotative meaning of words. In fiction, the author may use the connotative meaning. Readers can determine whether the author is using the denotative or connotative meaning of a word by implementing context clues.

> **Review Video: Connotation and Denotation**
> Visit mometrix.com/academy and enter code: 310092

NUANCES OF WORD MEANING RELATIVE TO CONNOTATION, DENOTATION, DICTION, AND USAGE

A word's denotation is simply its objective dictionary definition. However, its connotation refers to the subjective associations, often emotional, that specific words evoke in listeners and readers. Two or more words can have the same dictionary meaning, but very different connotations. Writers use diction (word choice) to convey various nuances of thought and emotion by selecting synonyms for other words that best communicate the associations they want to trigger for readers. For example, a car engine is naturally greasy; in this sense, "greasy" is a neutral term. But when a person's smile, appearance, or clothing is described as "greasy," it has a negative connotation. Some words have even gained additional or different meanings over time. For example, *awful* used to be used to describe things that evoked a sense of awe. When *awful* is separated into its root word, awe, and suffix, -ful, it can be understood to mean "full of awe." However, the word is now commonly used to describe things that evoke repulsion, terror, or another intense, negative reaction.

> **Review Video: Word Usage in Sentences**
> Visit mometrix.com/academy and enter code: 197863

CONTEXT CLUES

Readers of all levels will encounter words that they have either never seen or have encountered only on a limited basis. The best way to define a word in **context** is to look for nearby words that can assist in revealing the meaning of the word. For instance, unfamiliar nouns are often accompanied by examples that provide a definition. Consider the following sentence: *Dave arrived at the party in hilarious garb: a leopard-print shirt, buckskin trousers, and bright green sneakers.* If a reader was unfamiliar with the meaning of garb, he or she could read the examples (i.e., a leopard-print shirt, buckskin trousers, and high heels) and quickly determine that the word means *clothing*. Examples will not always be this obvious. Consider this sentence: *Parsley, lemon, and flowers were just a few of the items he used as garnishes.* Here, the word *garnishes* is exemplified by parsley, lemon, and flowers. Readers who have eaten in a variety of restaurants will probably be able to identify a garnish as something used to decorate a plate.

> **Review Video: Reading Comprehension: Using Context Clues**
> Visit mometrix.com/academy and enter code: 613660

USING CONTRAST IN CONTEXT CLUES

In addition to looking at the context of a passage, readers can use contrast to define an unfamiliar word in context. In many sentences, the author will not describe the unfamiliar word directly; instead, he or she will describe the opposite of the unfamiliar word. Thus, you are provided with some information that will bring you closer to defining the word. Consider the following example: *Despite his intelligence, Hector's low brow and bad posture made him look obtuse.* The author writes that Hector's appearance does not convey intelligence. Therefore, *obtuse* must mean unintelligent. Here is another example: *Despite the horrible weather, we were beatific about our trip to Alaska.* The word *despite* indicates that the speaker's feelings were at odds with the weather. Since the weather is described as *horrible*, then *beatific* must mean something positive.

SUBSTITUTION TO FIND MEANING

In some cases, there will be very few contextual clues to help a reader define the meaning of an unfamiliar word. When this happens, one strategy that readers may employ is **substitution**. A good reader will brainstorm some possible synonyms for the given word, and he or she will substitute these words into the sentence. If the sentence and the surrounding passage continue to make sense, then the substitution has revealed at least some information about the unfamiliar word. Consider the sentence: *Frank's admonition rang in her ears as she climbed the mountain.* A reader unfamiliar with *admonition* might come up with some substitutions like *vow, promise, advice, complaint,* or *compliment.* All of these words make general sense of the sentence, though their meanings are diverse. However, this process has suggested that an admonition is some sort of message. The substitution strategy is rarely able to pinpoint a precise definition, but this process can be effective as a last resort.

Occasionally, you will be able to define an unfamiliar word by looking at the descriptive words in the context. Consider the following sentence: *Fred dragged the recalcitrant boy kicking and screaming up the stairs.* The words *dragged*, *kicking*, and *screaming* all suggest that the boy does not want to go up the stairs. The reader may assume that *recalcitrant* means something like unwilling or protesting. In this example, an unfamiliar adjective was identified.

Additionally, using description to define an unfamiliar noun is a common practice compared to unfamiliar adjectives, as in this sentence: *Don's wrinkled frown and constantly shaking fist identified him as a curmudgeon of the first order.* Don is described as having a *wrinkled frown and constantly shaking fist,* suggesting that a *curmudgeon* must be a grumpy person. Contrasts do not always provide detailed information about the unfamiliar word, but they at least give the reader some clues.

WORDS WITH MULTIPLE MEANINGS

When a word has more than one meaning, readers can have difficulty determining how the word is being used in a given sentence. For instance, the verb *cleave*, can mean either *join* or *separate*. When readers come upon this word, they will have to select the definition that makes the most sense. Consider the following sentence: *Hermione's knife cleaved the bread cleanly.* Since a knife cannot join bread together, the word must indicate separation. A slightly more difficult example would be the sentence: *The birds cleaved to one another as they flew from the oak tree.* Immediately, the presence of the words *to one another* should suggest that in this sentence *cleave* is being used to mean *join*. Discovering the intent of a word with multiple meanings requires the same tricks as defining an unknown word: look for contextual clues and evaluate the substituted words.

CONTEXT CLUES TO HELP DETERMINE MEANINGS OF WORDS

If readers simply bypass unknown words, they can reach unclear conclusions about what they read. However, looking for the definition of every unfamiliar word in the dictionary can slow their reading progress. Moreover, the dictionary may list multiple definitions for a word, so readers must search the word's context for meaning. Hence context is important to new vocabulary regardless of reader methods. Four types of context clues are examples, definitions, descriptive words, and opposites. Authors may use a certain word, and then follow it with several different examples of what it describes. Sometimes authors actually supply a definition of a word they use, which is especially true in informational and technical texts. Authors may use descriptive words that elaborate upon a vocabulary word they just used. Authors may also use opposites with negation that help define meaning.

EXAMPLES AND DEFINITIONS

An author may use a word and then give examples that illustrate its meaning. Consider this text: "Teachers who do not know how to use sign language can help students who are deaf or hard of hearing understand certain instructions by using gestures instead, like pointing their fingers to indicate which direction to look or go; holding up a hand, palm outward, to indicate stopping; holding the hands flat, palms up, curling a finger toward oneself in a beckoning motion to indicate 'come here'; or curling all fingers toward oneself repeatedly to indicate 'come on', 'more', or 'continue.'" The author of this text has used the word "gestures" and then followed it with examples, so a reader unfamiliar with the word could deduce from the examples that "gestures" means "hand motions." Readers can find examples by looking for signal words "for example," "for instance," "like," "such as," and "e.g."

While readers sometimes have to look for definitions of unfamiliar words in a dictionary or do some work to determine a word's meaning from its surrounding context, at other times an author may make it easier for readers by defining certain words. For example, an author may write, "The company did not have sufficient capital, that is, available money, to continue operations." The author defined "capital" as "available money," and heralded the definition with the phrase "that is." Another way that authors supply word definitions is with appositives. Rather than being introduced by a signal phrase like "that is," "namely," or "meaning," an appositive comes after the vocabulary word it defines and is enclosed within two commas. For example, an author may write, "The Indians introduced the Pilgrims to pemmican, cakes they made of lean meat dried and

mixed with fat, which proved greatly beneficial to keep settlers from starving while trapping." In this example, the appositive phrase following "pemmican" and preceding "which" defines the word "pemmican."

DESCRIPTIONS

When readers encounter a word they do not recognize in a text, the author may expand on that word to illustrate it better. While the author may do this to make the prose more picturesque and vivid, the reader can also take advantage of this description to provide context clues to the meaning of the unfamiliar word. For example, an author may write, "The man sitting next to me on the airplane was obese. His shirt stretched across his vast expanse of flesh, strained almost to bursting." The descriptive second sentence elaborates on and helps to define the previous sentence's word "obese" to mean extremely fat. A reader unfamiliar with the word "repugnant" can decipher its meaning through an author's accompanying description: "The way the child grimaced and shuddered as he swallowed the medicine showed that its taste was particularly repugnant."

OPPOSITES

Text authors sometimes introduce a contrasting or opposing idea before or after a concept they present. They may do this to emphasize or heighten the idea they present by contrasting it with something that is the reverse. However, readers can also use these context clues to understand familiar words. For example, an author may write, "Our conversation was not cheery. We sat and talked very solemnly about his experience and a number of similar events." The reader who is not familiar with the word "solemnly" can deduce by the author's preceding use of "not cheery" that "solemn" means the opposite of cheery or happy, so it must mean serious or sad. Or if someone writes, "Don't condemn his entire project because you couldn't find anything good to say about it," readers unfamiliar with "condemn" can understand from the sentence structure that it means the opposite of saying anything good, so it must mean reject, dismiss, or disapprove. "Entire" adds another context clue, meaning total or complete rejection.

SYNTAX TO DETERMINE PART OF SPEECH AND MEANINGS OF WORDS

Syntax refers to sentence structure and word order. Suppose that a reader encounters an unfamiliar word when reading a text. To illustrate, consider an invented word like "splunch." If this word is used in a sentence like "Please splunch that ball to me," the reader can assume from syntactic context that "splunch" is a verb. We would not use a noun, adjective, adverb, or preposition with the object "that ball," and the prepositional phrase "to me" further indicates "splunch" represents an action. However, in the sentence, "Please hand that splunch to me," the reader can assume that "splunch" is a noun. Demonstrative adjectives like "that" modify nouns. Also, we hand someone some*thing*—a thing being a noun; we do not hand someone a verb, adjective, or adverb. Some sentences contain further clues. For example, from the sentence, "The princess wore the glittering splunch on her head," the reader can deduce that it is a crown, tiara, or something similar from the syntactic context, without knowing the word.

SYNTAX TO INDICATE DIFFERENT MEANINGS OF SIMILAR SENTENCES

The syntax, or structure, of a sentence affords grammatical cues that aid readers in comprehending the meanings of words, phrases, and sentences in the texts that they read. Seemingly minor differences in how the words or phrases in a sentence are ordered can make major differences in meaning. For example, two sentences can use exactly the same words but have different meanings based on the word order:

- "The man with a broken arm sat in a chair."
- "The man sat in a chair with a broken arm."

While both sentences indicate that a man sat in a chair, differing syntax indicates whether the man's or chair's arm was broken.

DETERMINING MEANING OF PHRASES AND PARAGRAPHS

Like unknown words, the meanings of phrases, paragraphs, and entire works can also be difficult to discern. Each of these can be better understood with added context. However, for larger groups of words, more context

36

is needed. Unclear phrases are similar to unclear words, and the same methods can be used to understand their meaning. However, it is also important to consider how the individual words in the phrase work together. Paragraphs are a bit more complicated. Just as words must be compared to other words in a sentence, paragraphs must be compared to other paragraphs in a composition or a section.

DETERMINING MEANING IN VARIOUS TYPES OF COMPOSITIONS

To understand the meaning of an entire composition, the type of composition must be considered. **Expository writing** is generally organized so that each paragraph focuses on explaining one idea, or part of an idea, and its relevance. **Persuasive writing** uses paragraphs for different purposes to organize the parts of the argument. **Unclear paragraphs** must be read in the context of the paragraphs around them for their meaning to be fully understood. The meaning of full texts can also be unclear at times. The purpose of composition is also important for understanding the meaning of a text. To quickly understand the broad meaning of a text, look to the introductory and concluding paragraphs. Fictional texts are different. Some fictional works have implicit meanings, but some do not. The target audience must be considered for understanding texts that do have an implicit meaning, as most children's fiction will clearly state any lessons or morals. For other fiction, the application of literary theories and criticism may be helpful for understanding the text.

ADDITIONAL RESOURCES FOR DETERMINING WORD MEANING AND USAGE

While these strategies are useful for determining the meaning of unknown words and phrases, sometimes additional resources are needed to properly use the terms in different contexts. Some words have multiple definitions, and some words are inappropriate in particular contexts or modes of writing. The following tools are helpful for understanding all meanings and proper uses for words and phrases.

- **Dictionaries** provide the meaning of a multitude of words in a language. Many dictionaries include additional information about each word, such as its etymology, its synonyms, or variations of the word.
- **Glossaries** are similar to dictionaries, as they provide the meanings of a variety of terms. However, while dictionaries typically feature an extensive list of words and comprise an entire publication, glossaries are often included at the end of a text and only include terms and definitions that are relevant to the text they follow.
- **Spell Checkers** are used to detect spelling errors in typed text. Some spell checkers may also detect the misuse of plural or singular nouns, verb tenses, or capitalization. While spell checkers are a helpful tool, they are not always reliable or attuned to the author's intent, so it is important to review the spell checker's suggestions before accepting them.
- **Style Manuals** are guidelines on the preferred punctuation, format, and grammar usage according to different fields or organizations. For example, the Associated Press Stylebook is a style guide often used for media writing. The guidelines within a style guide are not always applicable across different contexts and usages, as the guidelines often cover grammatical or formatting situations that are not objectively correct or incorrect.

Integration of Knowledge and Ideas

PERSUASION AND RHETORIC

PERSUASIVE TECHNIQUES

To **appeal using reason**, writers present logical arguments, such as using "If... then... because" statements. To **appeal to emotions**, authors may ask readers how they would feel about something or to put themselves in another's place, present their argument as one that will make the audience feel good, or tell readers how they should feel. To **appeal to character**, **morality**, or **ethics**, authors present their points to readers as the right or most moral choices. Authors cite expert opinions to show readers that someone very knowledgeable about the subject or viewpoint agrees with the author's claims. **Testimonials**, usually via anecdotes or quotations regarding the author's subject, help build the audience's trust in an author's message through positive support from ordinary people. **Bandwagon appeals** claim that everybody else agrees with the author's argument and persuade readers to conform and agree, also. Authors **appeal to greed** by presenting their choice as cheaper, free, or more valuable for less cost. They **appeal to laziness** by presenting their views as more convenient, easy, or relaxing. Authors also anticipate potential objections and argue against them before audiences think of them, thereby depicting those objections as weak.

Authors can use **comparisons** like analogies, similes, and metaphors to persuade audiences. For example, a writer might represent excessive expenses as "hemorrhaging" money, which the author's recommended solution will stop. Authors can use negative word connotations to make some choices unappealing to readers, and positive word connotations to make others more appealing. Using **humor** can relax readers and garner their agreement. However, writers must take care: ridiculing opponents can be a successful strategy for appealing to readers who already agree with the author, but can backfire by angering other readers. **Rhetorical questions** need no answer, but create effect that can force agreement, such as asking the question, "Wouldn't you rather be paid more than less?" **Generalizations** persuade readers by being impossible to disagree with. Writers can easily make generalizations that appear to support their viewpoints, like saying, "We all want peace, not war" regarding more specific political arguments. **Transfer** and **association** persuade by example: if advertisements show attractive actors enjoying their products, audiences imagine they will experience the same. **Repetition** can also sometimes effectively persuade audiences.

> **Review Video: Using Rhetorical Strategies for Persuasion**
> Visit mometrix.com/academy and enter code: 302658

CLASSICAL AUTHOR APPEALS

In his *On Rhetoric,* ancient Greek philosopher Aristotle defined three basic types of appeal used in writing, which he called *pathos*, *ethos*, and *logos*. **Pathos** means suffering or experience and refers to appeals to the emotions (the English word *pathetic* comes from this root). Writing that is meant to entertain audiences, by making them either happy, as with comedy, or sad, as with tragedy, uses *pathos*. Aristotle's *Poetics* states that evoking the emotions of terror and pity is one of the criteria for writing tragedy. **Ethos** means character and connotes ideology (the English word *ethics* comes from this root). Writing that appeals to credibility, based on academic, professional, or personal merit, uses *ethos*. **Logos** means "I say" and refers to a plea, opinion, expectation, word or speech, account, opinion, or reason (the English word *logic* comes from this root.) Aristotle used it to mean persuasion that appeals to the audience through reasoning and logic to influence their opinions.

CRITICAL EVALUATION OF EFFECTIVENESS OF PERSUASIVE METHODS

First, readers should identify the author's **thesis**—what he or she argues for or against. They should consider the argument's content and the author's reason for presenting it. Does the author offer **solutions** to problems raised? If so, are they realistic? Note all central ideas and evidence supporting the author's thesis. Research any unfamiliar subjects or vocabulary. Readers should then outline or summarize the work in their own words. Identify which types of appeals the author uses. Readers should evaluate how well the author communicated meaning from the reader's perspective: Did they respond to emotional appeals with anger, concern, happiness, etc.? If so, why? Decide if the author's reasoning sufficed for changing the reader's mind. Determine whether the content and presentation were accurate, cohesive, and clear. Readers should also ask themselves whether they found the author believable or not, and why or why not.

EVALUATING AN ARGUMENT

Argumentative and persuasive passages take a stand on a debatable issue, seek to explore all sides of the issue, and find the best possible solution. Argumentative and persuasive passages should not be combative or abusive. The word *argument* may remind you of two or more people shouting at each other and walking away in anger. However, an argumentative or persuasive passage should be a calm and reasonable presentation of an author's ideas for others to consider. When an author writes reasonable arguments, his or her goal is not to win or have the last word. Instead, authors want to reveal current understanding of the question at hand and

suggest a solution to a problem. The purpose of argument and persuasion in a free society is to reach the best solution.

EVIDENCE

The term **text evidence** refers to information that supports a main point or minor points and can help lead the reader to a conclusion about the text's credibility. Information used as text evidence is precise, descriptive, and factual. A main point is often followed by supporting details that provide evidence to back up a claim. For example, a passage may include the claim that winter occurs during opposite months in the Northern and Southern hemispheres. Text evidence for this claim may include examples of countries where winter occurs in opposite months. Stating that the tilt of the Earth as it rotates around the sun causes winter to occur at different times in separate hemispheres is another example of text evidence. Text evidence can come from common knowledge, but it is also valuable to include text evidence from credible, relevant outside sources.

> **Review Video: Textual Evidence**
> Visit mometrix.com/academy and enter code: 486236

Evidence that supports the thesis and additional arguments needs to be provided. Most arguments must be supported by facts or statistics. A fact is something that is known with certainty, has been verified by several independent individuals, and can be proven to be true. In addition to facts, examples and illustrations can support an argument by adding an emotional component. With this component, you persuade readers in ways that facts and statistics cannot. The emotional component is effective when used alongside objective information that can be confirmed.

CREDIBILITY

The text used to support an argument can be the argument's downfall if the text is not credible. A text is **credible**, or believable, when its author is knowledgeable and objective, or unbiased. The author's motivations for writing the text play a critical role in determining the credibility of the text and must be evaluated when assessing that credibility. Reports written about the ozone layer by an environmental scientist and a hairdresser will have a different level of credibility.

> **Review Video: Author Credibility**
> Visit mometrix.com/academy and enter code: 827257

APPEAL TO EMOTION

Sometimes, authors will appeal to the reader's emotion in an attempt to persuade or to distract the reader from the weakness of the argument. For instance, the author may try to inspire the pity of the reader by delivering a heart-rending story. An author also might use the bandwagon approach, in which he suggests that his opinion is correct because it is held by the majority. Some authors resort to name-calling, in which insults and harsh words are delivered to the opponent in an attempt to distract. In advertising, a common appeal is the celebrity testimonial, in which a famous person endorses a product. Of course, the fact that a famous person likes something should not really mean anything to the reader. These and other emotional appeals are usually evidence of poor reasoning and a weak argument.

> **Review Video: Emotional Language in Literature**
> Visit mometrix.com/academy and enter code: 759390

COUNTER ARGUMENTS

When authors give both sides to the argument, they build trust with their readers. As a reader, you should start with an undecided or neutral position. If an author presents only his or her side to the argument, then they are not exhibiting credibility and are weakening their argument.

Building common ground with readers can be effective for persuading neutral, skeptical, or opposed readers. Sharing values with undecided readers can allow people to switch positions without giving up what they feel is important. People who may oppose a position need to feel that they can change their minds without betraying who they are as a person. This appeal to having an open mind can be a powerful tool in arguing a position without antagonizing other views. Objections can be countered on a point-by-point basis or in a summary paragraph. Be mindful of how an author points out flaws in counter arguments. If they are unfair to the other side of the argument, then you should lose trust with the author.

RHETORICAL DEVICES

- An **anecdote** is a brief story authors may relate to their argument, which can illustrate their points in a more real and relatable way.
- **Aphorisms** concisely state common beliefs and may rhyme. For example, Benjamin Franklin's "Early to bed and early to rise / Makes a man healthy, wealthy, and wise" is an aphorism.
- **Allusions** refer to literary or historical figures to impart symbolism to a thing or person and to create reader resonance. In John Steinbeck's *Of Mice and Men,* protagonist George's last name is Milton. This alludes to John Milton, who wrote *Paradise Lost*, and symbolizes George's eventual loss of his dream.
- **Satire** exaggerates, ridicules, or pokes fun at human flaws or ideas, as in the works of Jonathan Swift and Mark Twain.
- A **parody** is a form of satire that imitates another work to ridicule its topic or style.
- A **paradox** is a statement that is true despite appearing contradictory.
- **Hyperbole** is overstatement using exaggerated language.
- An **oxymoron** combines seeming contradictions, such as "deafening silence."
- **Analogies** compare two things that share common elements.
- **Similes** (stated comparisons using the words *like* or *as*) and **metaphors** (stated comparisons that do not use *like* or *as*) are considered forms of analogy.
- When using logic to reason with audiences, **syllogism** refers either to deductive reasoning or a deceptive, very sophisticated, or subtle argument.
- **Deductive reasoning** moves from general to specific, **inductive reasoning** from specific to general.
- **Diction** is author word choice that establishes tone and effect.
- **Understatement** achieves effects like contrast or irony by downplaying or describing something more subtly than warranted.
- **Chiasmus** uses parallel clauses, the second reversing the order of the first. Examples include T. S. Eliot's "Has the Church failed mankind, or has mankind failed the Church?" and John F. Kennedy's "Ask not what your country can do for you; ask what you can do for your country."
- **Anaphora** regularly repeats a word or phrase at the beginnings of consecutive clauses or phrases to add emphasis to an idea. A classic example of anaphora was Winston Churchill's emphasis of determination: "[W]e shall fight on the beaches, we shall fight on the landing grounds, we shall fight in the fields and in the streets, we shall fight in the hills; we shall never surrender..."

READING ARGUMENTATIVE WRITING
AUTHOR'S ARGUMENT IN ARGUMENTATIVE WRITING

In argumentative writing, the argument is a belief, position, or opinion that the author wants to convince readers to believe as well. For the first step, readers should identify the **issue**. Some issues are controversial, meaning people disagree about them. Gun control, foreign policy, and the death penalty are all controversial issues. The next step is to determine the **author's position** on the issue. That position or viewpoint constitutes the author's argument. Readers should then identify the **author's assumptions**: things he or she accepts, believes, or takes for granted without needing proof. Inaccurate or illogical assumptions produce flawed arguments and can mislead readers. Readers should identify what kinds of **supporting evidence** the author

offers, such as research results, personal observations or experiences, case studies, facts, examples, expert testimony and opinions, and comparisons. Readers should decide how relevant this support is to the argument.

Review Video: <u>Argumentative Writing</u>
Visit mometrix.com/academy and enter code: 561544

EVALUATING AN AUTHOR'S ARGUMENT

The first three reader steps to **evaluate an author's argument** are to identify the **author's assumptions**, identify the **supporting evidence**, and decide **whether the evidence is relevant**. For example, if an author is not an expert on a particular topic, then that author's personal experience or opinion might not be relevant. The fourth step is to assess the **author's objectivity**. For example, consider whether the author introduces clear, understandable supporting evidence and facts to support the argument. The fifth step is evaluating whether the author's **argument is complete**. When authors give sufficient support for their arguments and also anticipate and respond effectively to opposing arguments or objections to their points, their arguments are complete. However, some authors omit information that could detract from their arguments. If instead they stated this information and refuted it, it would strengthen their arguments. The sixth step in evaluating an author's argumentative writing is to assess whether the **argument is valid**. Providing clear, logical reasoning makes an author's argument valid. Readers should ask themselves whether the author's points follow a sequence that makes sense, and whether each point leads to the next. The seventh step is to determine whether the author's **argument is credible**, meaning that it is convincing and believable. Arguments that are not valid are not credible, so step seven depends on step six. Readers should be mindful of their own biases as they evaluate and should not expect authors to conclusively prove their arguments, but rather to provide effective support and reason.

EVALUATING AN AUTHOR'S METHOD OF APPEAL

To evaluate the effectiveness of an appeal, it is important to consider the author's purpose for writing. Any appeals an author uses in their argument must be relevant to the argument's goal. For example, a writer that argues for the reclassification of Pluto, but primarily uses appeals to emotion, will not have an effective argument. This writer should focus on using appeals to logic and support their argument with provable facts. While most arguments should include appeals to logic, emotion, and credibility, some arguments only call for one or two of these types of appeal. Evidence can support an appeal, but the evidence must be relevant to truly strengthen the appeal's effectiveness. If the writer arguing for Pluto's reclassification uses the reasons for Jupiter's classification as evidence, their argument would be weak. This information may seem relevant because it is related to the classification of planets. However, this classification is highly dependent on the size of the celestial object, and Jupiter is significantly bigger than Pluto. This use of evidence is illogical and does not support the appeal. Even when appropriate evidence and appeals are used, appeals and arguments lose their effectiveness when they create logical fallacies.

OPINIONS, FACTS, AND FALLACIES

Critical thinking skills are mastered through understanding various types of writing and the different purposes of authors can have for writing different passages. Every author writes for a purpose. When you understand their purpose and how they accomplish their goal, you will be able to analyze their writing and determine whether or not you agree with their conclusions.

Readers must always be aware of the difference between fact and opinion. A **fact** can be subjected to analysis and proven to be true. An **opinion**, on the other hand, is the author's personal thoughts or feelings and may not be altered by research or evidence. If the author writes that the distance from New York City to Boston is about two hundred miles, then he or she is stating a fact. If the author writes that New York City is too crowded, then he or she is giving an opinion because there is no objective standard for overpopulation. Opinions are often supported by facts. For instance, an author might use a comparison between the population density of New York City and that of other major American cities as evidence of an overcrowded population. An opinion supported by facts tends to be more convincing. On the other hand, when authors support their opinions with other opinions, readers should employ critical thinking and approach the argument with skepticism.

> **Review Video: Distinguishing Fact and Opinion**
> Visit mometrix.com/academy and enter code: 870899

RELIABLE SOURCES

When you have an argumentative passage, you need to be sure that facts are presented to the reader from **reliable sources**. An opinion is what the author thinks about a given topic. An opinion is not common knowledge or proven by expert sources, instead the information is the personal beliefs and thoughts of the author. To distinguish between fact and opinion, a reader needs to consider the type of source that is presenting information, the information that backs-up a claim, and the author's motivation to have a certain point-of-view on a given topic. For example, if a panel of scientists has conducted multiple studies on the effectiveness of taking a certain vitamin, then the results are more likely to be factual than those of a company that is selling a vitamin and simply claims that taking the vitamin can produce positive effects. The company is motivated to sell their product, and the scientists are using the scientific method to prove a theory. Remember, if you find sentences that contain phrases such as "I think...", then the statement is an opinion.

BIASES

In their attempts to persuade, writers often make mistakes in their thought processes and writing choices. These processes and choices are important to understand so you can make an informed decision about the author's credibility. Every author has a point of view, but authors demonstrate a **bias** when they ignore reasonable counterarguments or distort opposing viewpoints. A bias is evident whenever the author's claims are presented in a way that is unfair or inaccurate. Bias can be intentional or unintentional, but readers should be skeptical of the author's argument in either case. Remember that a biased author may still be correct. However, the author will be correct in spite of, not because of, his or her bias.

A **stereotype** is a bias applied specifically to a group of people or a place. Stereotyping is considered to be particularly abhorrent because it promotes negative, misleading generalizations about people. Readers should be very cautious of authors who use stereotypes in their writing. These faulty assumptions typically reveal the author's ignorance and lack of curiosity.

> **Review Video: Bias and Stereotype**
> Visit mometrix.com/academy and enter code: 644829

SETTING, MOOD, TONE, AND PERSPECTIVE IN LITERARY TEXTS
SETTING AND TIME FRAME

A literary text has both a setting and time frame. A **setting** is the place in which the story as a whole is set. The **time frame** is the period in which the story is set. This may refer to the historical period the story takes place in or if the story takes place over a single day. Both setting and time frame are relevant to a text's meaning because they help the reader place the story in time and space. An author uses setting and time frame to anchor a text, create a mood, and enhance its meaning. This helps a reader understand why a character acts the way he does, or why certain events in the story are important. The setting impacts the **plot** and character **motivations**, while the time frame helps place the story in **chronological context**.

EXAMPLE

Read the following excerpt from The Adventures of Huckleberry Finn by Mark Twain and analyze the relevance of setting to the text's meaning:

> We said there warn't no home like a raft, after all. Other places do seem so cramped up and smothery, but a raft don't. You feel mighty free and easy and comfortable on a raft.

This excerpt from *The Adventures of Huckleberry Finn* by Mark Twain reveals information about the **setting** of the book. By understanding that the main character, Huckleberry Finn, lives on a raft, the reader can place the story on a river, in this case, the Mississippi River in the South before the Civil War. The information about the setting also gives the reader clues about the **character** of Huck Finn: he clearly values independence and freedom, and he likes the outdoors. The information about the setting in the quote helps the reader to better understand the rest of the text.

SYNTAX AND WORD CHOICE

Authors use words and **syntax**, or sentence structure, to make their texts unique, convey their own writing style, and sometimes to make a point or emphasis. They know that word choice and syntax contribute to the reader's understanding of the text as well as to the tone and mood of a text.

> **Review Video: What is Syntax?**
> Visit mometrix.com/academy and enter code: 242280

MOOD AND TONE

Mood is a story's atmosphere, or the feelings the reader gets from reading it. The way authors set the mood in writing is comparable to the way filmmakers use music to set the mood in movies. Instead of music, though, writers judiciously select descriptive words to evoke certain **moods**. The mood of a work may convey joy, anger, bitterness, hope, gloom, fear, apprehension, or any other emotion the author wants the reader to feel. In addition to vocabulary choices, authors also use figurative expressions, particular sentence structures, and choices of diction that project and reinforce the moods they want to create. Whereas mood is the reader's emotions evoked by reading what is written, **tone** is the emotions and attitudes of the writer that she or he expresses in the writing. Authors use the same literary techniques to establish tone as they do to establish mood. An author may use a humorous tone, an angry or sad tone, a sentimental or unsentimental tone, or something else entirely.

MOOD AND TONE IN THE GREAT GATSBY

To understand the difference between mood and tone, look at this excerpt from F. Scott Fitzgerald's *The Great Gatsby*. In this passage, Nick Caraway, the novel's narrator, is describing his affordable house, which sits in a neighborhood full of expensive mansions.

> "I lived at West Egg, the—well the less fashionable of the two, though this is a most superficial tag to express the bizarre and not a little sinister contrast between them. My house was at the very tip of the egg, only fifty yard from the Sound, and squeezed between two huge places that rented for twelve or fifteen thousand a season … My own house was an eyesore, but it was a small eyesore, and it had been overlooked, so I had a view of the water, a partial view of my neighbor's lawn, and the consoling proximity of millionaires—all for eighty dollars a month."

In this description, the mood created for the reader does not match the tone created through the narrator. The mood in this passage is one of dissatisfaction and inferiority. Nick compares his home to his neighbors', saying he lives in the "less fashionable" neighborhood and that his house is "overlooked," an "eyesore," and "squeezed between two huge" mansions. He also adds that his placement allows him the "consoling proximity of millionaires." A literal reading of these details leads the reader to have negative feelings toward Nick's house and his economic inferiority to his neighbors, creating the mood.

However, Fitzgerald also conveys an opposing attitude, or tone, through Nick's description. Nick calls the distinction between the neighborhoods "superficial," showing a suspicion of the value suggested by the neighborhoods' titles, properties, and residents. Nick also undermines his critique of his own home by calling it "a small eyesore" and claiming it has "been overlooked." However, he follows these statements with a description of his surroundings, claiming that he has "a view of the water" and can see some of his wealthy neighbor's property from his home, and a comparison between the properties' rent. While the mental image created for the reader depicts a small house shoved between looming mansions, the tone suggests that Nick

enjoys these qualities about his home, or at least finds it charming. He acknowledges its shortcomings, but includes the benefits of his home's unassuming appearance.

> **Review Video: <u>Style, Tone, and Mood</u>**
> Visit mometrix.com/academy and enter code: 416961

POINT OF VIEW

Another element that impacts a text is the author's point of view. The **point of view** of a text is the perspective from which a passage is told. An author will always have a point of view about a story before he or she draws up a plot line. The author will know what events they want to take place, how they want the characters to interact, and how they want the story to resolve. An author will also have an opinion on the topic or series of events which is presented in the story that is based on their prior experience and beliefs.

The two main points of view that authors use, especially in a work of fiction, are first person and third person. If the narrator of the story is also the main character, or *protagonist*, the text is written in first-person point of view. In first person, the author writes from the perspective of *I*. Third-person point of view is probably the most common that authors use in their passages. Using third person, authors refer to each character by using *he* or *she*. In third-person omniscient, the narrator is not a character in the story and tells the story of all of the characters at the same time.

> **Review Video: <u>Point of View</u>**
> Visit mometrix.com/academy and enter code: 383336

FIRST-PERSON NARRATION

First-person narratives let narrators express inner feelings and thoughts, especially when the narrator is the protagonist as Lemuel Gulliver is in Jonathan Swift's *Gulliver's Travels*. The narrator may be a close friend of the protagonist, like Dr. Watson in Sir Arthur Conan Doyle's *Sherlock Holmes*. Or, the narrator can be less involved with the main characters and plot, like Nick Carraway in F. Scott Fitzgerald's *The Great Gatsby*. When a narrator reports others' narratives, she or he is a "**frame narrator**," like the nameless narrator of Joseph Conrad's *Heart of Darkness* or Mr. Lockwood in Emily Brontë's *Wuthering Heights*. **First-person plural** is unusual but can be effective. Isaac Asimov's *I, Robot*, William Faulkner's *A Rose for Emily*, Maxim Gorky's *Twenty-Six Men and a Girl*, and Jeffrey Eugenides' *The Virgin Suicides* all use first-person plural narration. Author Kurt Vonnegut is the first-person narrator in his semi-autobiographical novel *Timequake*. Also unusual, but effective, is a **first-person omniscient** (rather than the more common third-person omniscient) narrator, like Death in Markus Zusak's *The Book Thief* and the ghost in Alice Sebold's *The Lovely Bones*.

SECOND-PERSON NARRATION

While **second-person** address is very commonplace in popular song lyrics, it is the least used form of narrative voice in literary works. Popular serial books of the 1980s like *Fighting Fantasy* or *Choose Your Own Adventure* employed second-person narratives. In some cases, a narrative combines both second-person and first-person voices, using the pronouns *you* and *I*. This can draw readers into the story, and it can also enable the authors to compare directly "your" and "my" feelings, thoughts, and actions. When the narrator is also a character in the story, as in Edgar Allan Poe's short story "The Tell-Tale Heart" or Jay McInerney's novel *Bright Lights, Big City*, the narrative is better defined as first-person despite it also addressing "you."

THIRD-PERSON NARRATION

Narration in the third person is the most prevalent type, as it allows authors the most flexibility. It is so common that readers simply assume without needing to be informed that the narrator is not a character in the story, or involved in its events. **Third-person singular** is used more frequently than **third-person plural**, though some authors have also effectively used plural. However, both singular and plural are most often included in stories according to which characters are being described. The third-person narrator may be either objective or subjective, and either omniscient or limited. **Objective third-person** narration does not include

44

what the characters described are thinking or feeling, while **subjective third-person** narration does. The **third-person omniscient** narrator knows everything about all characters, including their thoughts and emotions, and all related places, times, and events. However, the **third-person limited** narrator may know everything about a particular character, but is limited to that character. In other words, the narrator cannot speak about anything that character does not know.

ALTERNATING-PERSON NARRATION

Although authors more commonly write stories from one point of view, there are also instances wherein they alternate the narrative voice within the same book. For example, they may sometimes use an omniscient third-person narrator and a more intimate first-person narrator at other times. In J. K. Rowling's series of *Harry Potter* novels, she often writes in a third-person limited narrative, but sometimes changes to narration by characters other than the protagonist. George R. R. Martin's series *A Song of Ice and Fire* changes the point of view to coincide with divisions between chapters. The same technique is used by Erin Hunter (a pseudonym for several authors of the *Warriors, Seekers,* and *Survivors* book series). Authors using first-person narrative sometimes switch to third-person to describe significant action scenes, especially those where the narrator was absent or uninvolved, as Barbara Kingsolver does in her novel *The Poisonwood Bible.*

HISTORICAL AND SOCIAL CONTEXT

Fiction that is heavily influenced by a historical or social context cannot be comprehended as the author intended if the reader does not keep this context in mind. Many important elements of the text will be influenced by any context, including symbols, allusions, settings, and plot events. These contexts, as well as the identity of the work's author, can help to inform the reader about the author's concerns and intended meanings. For example, George Orwell published his novel *1984* in the year 1949, soon after the end of World War II. At that time, following the defeat of the Nazis, the Cold War began between the Western Allied nations and the Eastern Soviet Communists. People were therefore concerned about the conflict between the freedoms afforded by Western democracies versus the oppression represented by Communism. Orwell had also previously fought in the Spanish Civil War against a Spanish regime that he and his fellows viewed as oppressive. From this information, readers can infer that Orwell was concerned about oppression by totalitarian governments. This informs *1984*'s story of Winston Smith's rebellion against the oppressive "Big Brother" government, of the fictional dictatorial state of Oceania, and his capture, torture, and ultimate conversion by that government. Some literary theories also seek to use historical and social contexts to reveal deeper meanings and implications in a text.

PLOT AND STORY STRUCTURE

THEME

The **theme** of a passage is what the reader learns from the text or the passage. It is the lesson or **moral** contained in the passage. It also is a unifying idea that is used throughout the text; it can take the form of a common setting, idea, symbol, design, or recurring event. A passage can have two or more themes that convey its overall idea. The theme or themes of a passage are often based on **universal themes**. They can frequently be expressed using well-known sayings about life, society, or human nature, such as "Hard work pays off" or "Good triumphs over evil." Themes are not usually stated **explicitly**. The reader must figure them out by carefully reading the passage. Themes are often the reason why passages are written; they give a passage unity and meaning. Themes are created through **plot development**. The events of a story help shape the themes of a passage.

EXAMPLE

Explain why "Take care of what you care about" accurately describes the theme of the following excerpt.

> Luca collected baseball cards, but he wasn't very careful with them. He left them around the house. His dog liked to chew. One day, Luca and his friend Bart were looking at his collection. Then they went outside. When Luca got home, he saw his dog chewing on his cards. They were ruined.

This excerpt tells the story of a boy who is careless with his baseball cards and leaves them lying around. His dog ends up chewing them and ruining them. The lesson is that if you care about something, you need to take care of it. This is the theme, or point, of the story. Some stories have more than one theme, but this is not really true of this excerpt. The reader needs to figure out the theme based on what happens in the story. Sometimes, as in the case of fables, the theme is stated directly in the text. However, this is not usually the case.

> **Review Video: Themes in Literature**
> Visit mometrix.com/academy and enter code: 732074

PLOT AND STORY STRUCTURE

The **plot** includes the events that happen in a story and the order in which they are told to the reader. There are several types of plot structures, as stories can be told in many ways. The most common plot structure is the chronological plot, which presents the events to the reader in the same order they occur for the characters in the story. Chronological plots usually have five main parts, the **exposition**, **rising action**, the **climax**, **falling action**, and the **resolution**. This type of plot structure guides the reader through the story's events as the characters experience them and is the easiest structure to understand and identify. While this is the most common plot structure, many stories are nonlinear, which means the plot does not sequence events in the same order the characters experience them. Such stories might include elements like flashbacks that cause the story to be nonlinear.

> **Review Video: How to Make a Story Map**
> Visit mometrix.com/academy and enter code: 261719

EXPOSITION

The **exposition** is at the beginning of the story and generally takes place before the rising action begins. The purpose of the exposition is to give the reader context for the story, which the author may do by introducing one or more characters, describing the setting or world, or explaining the events leading up to the point where the story begins. The exposition may still include events that contribute to the plot, but the **rising action** and main conflict of the story are not part of the exposition. Some narratives skip the exposition and begin the story with the beginning of the rising action, which causes the reader to learn the context as the story intensifies.

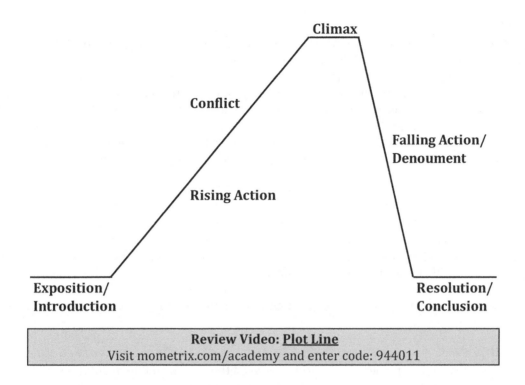

CONFLICT

A **conflict** is a problem to be solved. Literary plots typically include one conflict or more. Characters' attempts to resolve conflicts drive the narrative's forward movement. **Conflict resolution** is often the protagonist's primary occupation. Physical conflicts like exploring, wars, and escapes tend to make plots most suspenseful and exciting. Emotional, mental, or moral conflicts tend to make stories more personally gratifying or rewarding for many audiences. Conflicts can be external or internal. A major type of internal conflict is some inner personal battle, or **man versus self**. Major types of external conflicts include **man versus nature**, **man versus man**, and **man versus society**. Readers can identify conflicts in literary plots by identifying the protagonist and antagonist and asking why they conflict, what events develop the conflict, where the climax occurs, and how they identify with the characters.

Read the following paragraph and discuss the type of conflict present:

> Timothy was shocked out of sleep by the appearance of a bear just outside his tent. After panicking for a moment, he remembered some advice he had read in preparation for this trip: he should make noise so the bear would not be startled. As Timothy started to hum and sing, the bear wandered away.

There are three main types of conflict in literature: **man versus man**, **man versus nature**, and **man versus self**. This paragraph is an example of man versus nature. Timothy is in conflict with the bear. Even though no physical conflict like an attack exists, Timothy is pitted against the bear. Timothy uses his knowledge to "defeat" the bear and keep himself safe. The solution to the conflict is that Timothy makes noise, the bear wanders away, and Timothy is safe.

RISING ACTION

The **rising action** is the part of the story where conflict **intensifies**. The rising action begins with an event that prompts the main conflict of the story. This may also be called the **inciting incident**. The main conflict generally occurs between the protagonist and an antagonist, but this is not the only type of conflict that may occur in a narrative. After this event, the protagonist works to resolve the main conflict by preparing for an altercation, pursuing a goal, fleeing an antagonist, or doing some other action that will end the conflict. The rising action is composed of several additional events that increase the story's tension. Most often, other developments will occur alongside the growth of the main conflict, such as character development or the development of minor conflicts. The rising action ends with the **climax**, which is the point of highest tension in the story.

CLIMAX

The **climax** is the event in the narrative that marks the height of the story's conflict or tension. The event that takes place at the story's climax will end the rising action and bring about the results of the main conflict. If the conflict was between a good protagonist and an evil antagonist, the climax may be a final battle between the two characters. If the conflict is an adventurer looking for heavily guarded treasure, the climax may be the adventurer's encounter with the final obstacle that protects the treasure. The climax may be made of multiple scenes, but can usually be summarized as one event. Once the conflict and climax are complete, the **falling action** begins.

FALLING ACTION

The **falling action** shows what happens in the story between the climax and the resolution. The falling action often composes a much smaller portion of the story than the rising action does. While the climax includes the end of the main conflict, the falling action may show the results of any minor conflicts in the story. For example, if the protagonist encountered a troll on the way to find some treasure, and the troll demanded the protagonist share the treasure after retrieving it, the falling action would include the protagonist returning to share the treasure with the troll. Similarly, any unexplained major events are usually made clear during the falling action. Once all significant elements of the story are resolved or addressed, the story's resolution will occur. The **resolution** is the end of the story, which shows the final result of the plot's events and shows what life is like for the main characters once they are no longer experiencing the story's conflicts.

RESOLUTION

The way the conflict is **resolved** depends on the type of conflict. The plot of any book starts with the lead up to the conflict, then the conflict itself, and finally the solution, or **resolution**, to the conflict. In **man versus man** conflicts, the conflict is often resolved by two parties coming to some sort of agreement or by one party triumphing over the other party. In **man versus nature** conflicts, the conflict is often resolved by man coming to some realization about some aspect of nature. In **man versus self** conflicts, the conflict is often resolved by the character growing or coming to an understanding about part of himself.

CHARACTER DEVELOPMENT

When depicting characters or figures in a written text, authors generally use actions, dialogue, and descriptions as characterization techniques. Characterization can occur in both fiction and nonfiction and is used to show a character or figure's personality, demeanor, and thoughts. This helps create a more engaging experience for the reader by providing a more concrete picture of a character or figure's tendencies and features. Characterizations also gives authors the opportunity to integrate elements such as dialects, activities, attire, and attitudes into their writing.

To understand the meaning of a story, it is vital to understand the characters as the author describes them. We can look for contradictions in what a character thinks, says, and does. We can notice whether the author's observations about a character differ from what other characters in the story say about that character. A character may be dynamic, meaning they change significantly during the story, or static, meaning they remain the same from beginning to end. Characters may be two-dimensional, not fully developed, or may be well

48

developed with characteristics that stand out vividly. Characters may also symbolize universal properties. Additionally, readers can compare and contrast characters to analyze how each one developed.

A well-known example of character development can be found in Charles Dickens's *Great Expectations*. The novel's main character, Pip, is introduced as a young boy, and he is depicted as innocent, kind, and humble. However, as Pip grows up and is confronted with the social hierarchy of Victorian England, he becomes arrogant and rejects his loved ones in pursuit of his own social advancement. Once he achieves his social goals, he realizes the merits of his former lifestyle, and lives with the wisdom he gained in both environments and life stages. Dickens shows Pip's ever-changing character through his interactions with others and his inner thoughts, which evolve as his personal values and personality shift.

Review Video: <u>Character Changes</u>
Visit mometrix.com/academy and enter code: 408719

DIALOGUE

Effectively written dialogue serves at least one, but usually several, purposes. It advances the story and moves the plot, develops the characters, sheds light on the work's theme or meaning, and can, often subtly, account for the passage of time not otherwise indicated. It can alter the direction that the plot is taking, typically by introducing some new conflict or changing existing ones. **Dialogue** can establish a work's narrative voice and the characters' voices and set the tone of the story or of particular characters. When fictional characters display enlightenment or realization, dialogue can give readers an understanding of what those characters have discovered and how. Dialogue can illuminate the motivations and wishes of the story's characters. By using consistent thoughts and syntax, dialogue can support character development. Skillfully created, it can also represent real-life speech rhythms in written form. Via conflicts and ensuing action, dialogue also provides drama.

DIALOGUE IN FICTION

In fictional works, effectively written dialogue does more than just break up or interrupt sections of narrative. While **dialogue** may supply exposition for readers, it must nonetheless be believable. Dialogue should be dynamic, not static, and it should not resemble regular prose. Authors should not use dialogue to write clever similes or metaphors, or to inject their own opinions. Nor should they use dialogue at all when narrative would be better. Most importantly, dialogue should not slow the plot movement. Dialogue must seem natural, which means careful construction of phrases rather than actually duplicating natural speech, which does not necessarily translate well to the written word. Finally, all dialogue must be pertinent to the story, rather than just added conversation.

FIGURATIVE LANGUAGE AND LITERARY DEVICES

LITERARY ANALYSIS

The best literary analysis shows special insight into at least one important aspect of a text. When analyzing literary texts, it can be difficult to find a starting place. Many texts can be analyzed several different ways, often leaving an overwhelming number of options for writers to consider. However, narrowing the focus to a particular element of literature can be helpful when preparing to analyze a text. Symbolism, themes, and motifs are common starting points for literary analysis. These three methods of analysis can lead to a holistic analysis of a text, since they involve elements that are often distributed throughout the text. However, not all texts feature these elements in a way that facilitates a strong analysis, if they are present at all. It is also common to focus on character or plot development for analysis. These elements are compatible with theme, symbolism, and allusion. Setting and imagery, figurative language, and any external contexts can also contribute to analysis or complement one of these other elements. The application of a critical, or literary, theory to a text can also provide a thorough and strong analysis.

LITERAL AND FIGURATIVE MEANING

When language is used **literally**, the words mean exactly what they say and nothing more. When language is used **figuratively**, the words mean something beyond their literal meaning. For example, "The weeping willow tree has long, trailing branches and leaves" is a literal description. But "The weeping willow tree looks as if it is bending over and crying" is a figurative description—specifically, a **simile** or stated comparison. Another figurative language form is **metaphor**, or an implied comparison. A good example is the metaphor of a city, state, or city-state as a ship, and its governance as sailing that ship. Ancient Greek lyrical poet Alcaeus is credited with first using this metaphor, and ancient Greek tragedian Aeschylus then used it in *Seven Against Thebes,* and then Plato used it in the *Republic.*

FIGURES OF SPEECH

A **figure of speech** is a verbal expression whose meaning is figurative rather than literal. For example, the phrase "butterflies in the stomach" does not refer to actual butterflies in a person's stomach. It is a metaphor representing the fluttery feelings experienced when a person is nervous or excited—or when one "falls in love," which does not mean physically falling. "Hitting a sales target" does not mean physically hitting a target with arrows as in archery; it is a metaphor for meeting a sales quota. "Climbing the ladder of success" metaphorically likens advancing in one's career to ascending ladder rungs. Similes, such as "light as a feather" (meaning very light, not a feather's actual weight), and hyperbole, like "I'm starving/freezing/roasting," are also figures of speech. Figures of speech are often used and crafted for emphasis, freshness of expression, or clarity.

> **Review Video: Figures of Speech**
> Visit mometrix.com/academy and enter code: 111295

FIGURATIVE LANGUAGE

Figurative language extends past the literal meanings of words. It offers readers new insight into the people, things, events, and subjects covered in a work of literature. Figurative language also enables readers to feel they are sharing the authors' experiences. It can stimulate the reader's senses, make comparisons that readers find intriguing or even startling, and enable readers to view the world in different ways. When looking for figurative language, it is important to consider the context of the sentence or situation. Phrases that appear out of place or make little sense when read literally are likely instances of figurative language. Once figurative language has been recognized, context is also important to determining the type of figurative language being used and its function. For example, when a comparison is being made, a metaphor or simile is likely being used. This means the comparison may emphasize or create irony through the things being compared. Seven specific types of figurative language include: alliteration, onomatopoeia, personification, imagery, similes, metaphors, and hyperbole.

> **Review Video: Figurative Language**
> Visit mometrix.com/academy and enter code: 584902

ALLITERATION AND ONOMATOPOEIA

Alliteration describes a series of words beginning with the same sounds. **Onomatopoeia** uses words imitating the sounds of things they name or describe. For example, in his poem "Come Down, O Maid," Alfred Tennyson writes of "The moan of doves in immemorial elms, / And murmuring of innumerable bees." The word "moan" sounds like some sounds doves make, "murmuring" represents the sounds of bees buzzing. Onomatopoeia also includes words that are simply meant to represent sounds, such as "meow," "kaboom," and "whoosh."

> **Review Video: Alliteration in Everyday Expressions**
> Visit mometrix.com/academy and enter code: 462837

PERSONIFICATION

Another type of figurative language is **personification**. This is describing a non-human thing, like an animal or an object, as if it were human. The general intent of personification is to describe things in a manner that will be comprehensible to readers. When an author states that a tree *groans* in the wind, he or she does not mean that the tree is emitting a low, pained sound from a mouth. Instead, the author means that the tree is making a noise similar to a human groan. Of course, this personification establishes a tone of sadness or suffering. A different tone would be established if the author said that the tree was *swaying* or *dancing*. Alfred Tennyson's poem "The Eagle" uses all of these types of figurative language: "He clasps the crag with crooked hands." Tennyson used alliteration, repeating /k/ and /kr/ sounds. These hard-sounding consonants reinforce the imagery, giving visual and tactile impressions of the eagle.

> **Review Video: Personification**
> Visit mometrix.com/academy and enter code: 260066

SIMILES AND METAPHORS

Similes are stated comparisons using "like" or "as." Similes can be used to stimulate readers' imaginations and appeal to their senses. Because a simile includes *like* or *as*, the device creates more space between the description and the thing being described than a metaphor does. If an author says that *a house was like a shoebox*, then the tone is different than the author saying that the house *was* a shoebox. Authors will choose between a metaphor and a simile depending on their intended tone.

Similes also help compare fictional characters to well-known objects or experiences, so the reader can better relate to them. William Wordsworth's poem about "Daffodils" begins, "I wandered lonely as a cloud." This simile compares his loneliness to that of a cloud. It is also personification, giving a cloud the human quality loneliness. In his novel *Lord Jim* (1900), Joseph Conrad writes in Chapter 33, "I would have given anything for the power to soothe her frail soul, tormenting itself in its invincible ignorance like a small bird beating about the cruel wires of a cage." Conrad uses the word "like" to compare the girl's soul to a small bird. His description of the bird beating at the cage shows the similar helplessness of the girl's soul to gain freedom.

> **Review Video: Similes**
> Visit mometrix.com/academy and enter code: 642949

A **metaphor** is a type of figurative language in which the writer equates something with another thing that is not particularly similar, instead of using *like* or *as*. For instance, *the bird was an arrow arcing through the sky*. In this sentence, the arrow is serving as a metaphor for the bird. The point of a metaphor is to encourage the reader to consider the item being described in a *different way*. Let's continue with this metaphor for a flying bird. You are asked to envision the bird's flight as being similar to the arc of an arrow. So, you imagine the flight to be swift and bending. Metaphors are a way for the author to describe an item *without being direct and obvious*. This literary device is a lyrical and suggestive way of providing information. Note that the reference for a metaphor will not always be mentioned explicitly by the author. Consider the following description of a forest in winter: *Swaying skeletons reached for the sky and groaned as the wind blew through them.* In this example, the author is using *skeletons* as a metaphor for leafless trees. This metaphor creates a spooky tone while inspiring the reader's imagination.

LITERARY EXAMPLES OF METAPHOR

A **metaphor** is an implied comparison, i.e., it compares something to something else without using "like", "as", or other comparative words. For example, in "The Tyger" (1794), William Blake writes, "Tyger Tyger, burning bright, / In the forests of the night." Blake compares the tiger to a flame not by saying it is like a fire, but by simply describing it as "burning." Henry Wadsworth Longfellow's poem "O Ship of State" (1850) uses an extended metaphor by referring consistently throughout the entire poem to the state, union, or republic as a seagoing vessel, referring to its keel, mast, sail, rope, anchors, and to its braving waves, rocks, gale, tempest,

and "false lights on the shore." Within the extended metaphor, Wordsworth uses a specific metaphor: "the anchors of thy hope!"

TED HUGHES' ANIMAL METAPHORS

Ted Hughes frequently used animal metaphors in his poetry. In "The Thought Fox," a model of concise, structured beauty, Hughes characterizes the poet's creative process with succinct, striking imagery of an idea entering his head like a wild fox. Repeating "loneliness" in the first two stanzas emphasizes the poet's lonely work: "Something else is alive / Beside the clock's loneliness." He treats an idea's arrival as separate from himself. Three stanzas detail in vivid images a fox's approach from the outside winter forest at starless midnight—its nose, "Cold, delicately" touching twigs and leaves; "neat" paw prints in snow; "bold" body; brilliant green eyes; and self-contained, focused progress—"Till, with a sudden sharp hot stink of fox," he metaphorically depicts poetic inspiration as the fox's physical entry into "the dark hole of the head." Hughes ends by summarizing his vision of a poet as an interior, passive idea recipient, with the outside world unchanged: "The window is starless still; the clock ticks, / The page is printed."

> **Review Video: Metaphors in Writing**
> Visit mometrix.com/academy and enter code: 133295

METONYMY

Metonymy is naming one thing with words or phrases of a closely related thing. This is similar to metaphor. However, the comparison has a close connection, unlike metaphor. An example of metonymy is to call the news media *the press*. Of course, *the press* is the machine that prints newspapers. Metonymy is a way of naming something without using the same name constantly.

SYNECDOCHE

Synecdoche points to the whole by naming one of the parts. An example of synecdoche would be calling a construction worker a *hard hat*. Like metonymy, synecdoche is an easy way of naming something without having to overuse a name. The device allows writers to highlight pieces of the thing being described. For example, referring to businessmen as *suits* suggests professionalism and unity.

HYPERBOLE

Hyperbole is excessive exaggeration used for humor or emphasis rather than for literal meaning. For example, in *To Kill a Mockingbird*, Harper Lee wrote, "People moved slowly then. There was no hurry, for there was nowhere to go, nothing to buy and no money to buy it with, nothing to see outside the boundaries of Maycomb County." This was not literally true; Lee exaggerates the scarcity of these things for emphasis. In "Old Times on the Mississippi," Mark Twain wrote, "I... could have hung my hat on my eyes, they stuck out so far." This is not literal, but makes his description vivid and funny. In his poem "As I Walked Out One Evening", W. H. Auden wrote, "I'll love you, dear, I'll love you / Till China and Africa meet, / And the river jumps over the mountain / And the salmon sing in the street." He used things not literally possible to emphasize the duration of his love.

UNDERSTATEMENT

Understatement is the opposite of hyperbole. This device discounts or downplays something. Think about someone who climbs Mount Everest. Then, they say that the journey was *a little stroll*. As with other types of figurative language, understatement has a range of uses. The device may show self-defeat or modesty as in the Mount Everest example. However, some may think of understatement as false modesty (i.e., an attempt to bring attention to you or a situation). For example, a woman is praised on her diamond engagement ring. The woman says, *Oh, this little thing?* Her understatement might be heard as stuck-up or unfeeling.

> **Review Video: Hyperbole and Understatement**
> Visit mometrix.com/academy and enter code: 308470

LITERARY IRONY

In literature, irony demonstrates the opposite of what is said or done. The three types of irony are **verbal irony**, **situational irony**, and **dramatic irony**. Verbal irony uses words opposite to the meaning. Sarcasm may use verbal irony. One common example is describing something that is confusing as "clear as mud." For example, in his 1986 movie *Hannah and Her Sisters,* author, director, and actor Woody Allen says to his character's date, "I had a great evening; it was like the Nuremburg Trials." Notice these employ similes. In situational irony, what happens contrasts with what was expected. O. Henry's short story *The Gift of the Magi* uses situational irony: a husband and wife each sacrifice their most prized possession to buy each other a Christmas present. The irony is that she sells her long hair to buy him a watch fob, while he sells his heirloom pocket-watch to buy her the jeweled combs for her hair she had long wanted; in the end, neither of them can use their gifts. In dramatic irony, narrative informs audiences of more than its characters know. For example, in *Romeo and Juliet,* the audience is made aware that Juliet is only asleep, while Romeo believes her to be dead, which then leads to Romeo's death.

> **Review Video: What is Irony?**
> Visit mometrix.com/academy and enter code: 374204

IDIOMS

Idioms create comparisons, and often take the form of similes or metaphors. Idioms are always phrases and are understood to have a meaning that is different from its individual words' literal meaning. For example, "break a leg" is a common idiom that is used to wish someone luck or tell them to perform well. Literally, the phrase "break a leg" means to injure a person's leg, but the phrase takes on a different meaning when used as an idiom. Another example is "call it a day," which means to temporarily stop working on a task, or find a stopping point, rather than literally referring to something as "a day." Many idioms are associated with a region or group. For example, an idiom commonly used in the American South is "'til the cows come home." This phrase is often used to indicate that something will take or may last for a very long time, but not that it will literally last until the cows return to where they reside.

ALLUSION

An allusion is an uncited but recognizable reference to something else. Authors use language to make allusions to places, events, artwork, and other books in order to make their own text richer. For example, an author may allude to a very important text in order to make his own text seem more important. Martin Luther King, Jr. started his "I Have a Dream" speech by saying "Five score years ago..." This is a clear allusion to President Abraham Lincoln's "Gettysburg Address" and served to remind people of the significance of the event. An author may allude to a place to ground his text or make a cultural reference to make readers feel included. There are many reasons that authors make allusions.

> **Review Video: Allusions**
> Visit mometrix.com/academy and enter code: 294065

COMIC RELIEF

Comic relief is the use of comedy by an author to break up a dramatic or tragic scene and infuse it with a bit of **lightheartedness**. In William Shakespeare's *Hamlet*, two gravediggers digging the grave for Ophelia share a joke while they work. The death and burial of Ophelia are tragic moments that directly follow each other. Shakespeare uses an instance of comedy to break up the tragedy and give his audience a bit of a break from the tragic drama. Authors sometimes use comic relief so that their work will be less depressing; other times they use it to create irony or contrast between the darkness of the situation and the lightness of the joke. Often, authors will use comedy to parallel what is happening in the tragic scenes.

> **Review Video: Comic Relief**
> Visit mometrix.com/academy and enter code: 779604

FORESHADOWING

Foreshadowing is a device authors use to give readers **hints** about events that will take place later in a story. Foreshadowing most often takes place through a character's dialogue or actions. Sometimes the character will know what is going to happen and will purposefully allude to future events. For example, consider a protagonist who is about to embark on a journey through the woods. Just before the protagonist begins the trip, another character says, "Be careful, you never know what could be out in those woods!" This alerts the reader that the woods may be dangerous and prompts the reader to expect something to attack the protagonist in the woods. This is an example of foreshadowing through warning. Alternatively, a character may unknowingly foreshadow later events. For example, consider a story where a brother and sister run through their house and knock over a vase and break it. The brother says, "Don't worry, we'll clean it up! Mom will never know!" However, the reader knows that their mother will most likely find out what they have done, so the reader expects the siblings to later get in trouble for running, breaking the vase, and hiding it from their mother.

SYMBOLISM

Symbolism describes an author's use of a **symbol**, an element of the story that **represents** something else. Symbols can impact stories in many ways, including deepening the meaning of a story or its elements, comparing a story to another work, or foreshadowing later events in a story. Symbols can be objects, characters, colors, numbers, or anything else the author establishes as a symbol. Symbols can be clearly established through direct comparison or repetition, but they can also be established subtly or gradually over a large portion of the story. Another form of symbolism is **allusion**, which is when something in a story is used to prompt the reader to think about another work. Many well-known works use **Biblical allusions**, which are allusions to events or details in the Bible that inform a work or an element within it.

EXAMPLES OF THEMES AND PLOTS IN LITERATURE

THEMES IN LITERATURE

When we read parables, their themes are the lessons they aim to teach. When we read fables, the moral of each story is its theme. When we read fictional works, the authors' perspectives regarding life and human behavior are their themes. Unlike in parables and fables, themes in literary fiction are usually not meant to preach or teach the readers a lesson. Hence, themes in fiction are not as explicit as they are in parables or fables. Instead, they are implicit, and the reader only infers them. By analyzing the fictional characters through thinking about their actions and behavior, understanding the setting of the story, and reflecting on how its plot develops, the reader comes to infer the main theme of the work. When writers succeed, they communicate with their readers such that common ground is established between author and audience. While a reader's individual experience may differ in its details from the author's written story, both may share universal underlying truths which allow author and audience to connect.

DETERMINING THEME

In well-crafted literature, theme, structure, and plot are interdependent and inextricable: each element informs and reflects the others. The structure of a work is how it is organized. The theme is the central idea or meaning found in it. The plot is what happens in the story. Titles can also inform us of a work's theme. For instance, the title of Edgar Allan Poe's "The Tell-Tale Heart" informs readers of the story's theme of guilt before they even read about the repeated heartbeat the protagonist hears immediately before and constantly after committing and hiding a murder. Repetitive patterns of events or behaviors also give clues to themes. The same is true of symbols. For example, in F. Scott Fitzgerald's *The Great Gatsby,* for Jay Gatsby the green light at the end of the dock symbolizes Daisy Buchanan and his own dreams for the future. More generally, it is also understood as a symbol of the American Dream, and narrator Nick Carraway explicitly compares it to early settlers' sight of America rising from the ocean.

THEMATIC DEVELOPMENT
THEME IN THE GREAT GATSBY

In *The Great Gatsby*, F. Scott Fitzgerald portrayed 1920s America as greedy, cynical, and rife with moral decay. Jay Gatsby's lavish weekly parties symbolize the reckless excesses of the Jazz Age. The growth of bootlegging and organized crime in reaction to Prohibition is symbolized by the character of Meyer Wolfsheim and by Gatsby's own ill-gotten wealth. Fitzgerald symbolized social divisions using geography. The "old money" aristocrats like the Buchanans lived on East Egg, while the "new money" bourgeois like Gatsby lived on West Egg. Fitzgerald also used weather, as many authors have, to reinforce narrative and emotional tones in the novel. Just as in *Romeo and Juliet*, where William Shakespeare set the confrontation of Tybalt and Mercutio and its deadly consequences on the hottest summer day under a burning sun, in *The Great Gatsby*, Fitzgerald did the same with Tom Wilson's deadly confrontation with Gatsby. Both works are ostensible love stories carrying socially critical themes about the destructiveness of pointless and misguided behaviors—family feuds in the former, pursuit of money in the latter.

> **Review Video: Thematic Development**
> Visit mometrix.com/academy and enter code: 576507

THEME IN LES MISÉRABLES

In Victor Hugo's novel *Les Misérables*, the overall metamorphosis of protagonist Jean Valjean from a cynical ex-convict into a noble benefactor demonstrates Hugo's theme of the importance of love and compassion for others. Hugo also reflects this in more specific plot events. For example, Valjean's love for Cosette sustains him through many difficult periods and trying events. Hugo illustrates how love and compassion for others beget the same in them: Bishop Myriel's kindness to Valjean eventually inspires him to become honest. Years later, Valjean, as M. Madeleine, has rescued Fauchelevent from under a fallen carriage, Fauchelevent returns the compassionate act by giving Valjean sanctuary in the convent. M. Myriel's kindness also ultimately enables Valjean to rescue Cosette from the Thénardiers. Receiving Valjean's father-like love enables Cosette to fall in love with and marry Marius, and the love between Cosette and Marius enables the couple to forgive Valjean for his past crimes when they are revealed.

THEME IN "THE TELL-TALE HEART"

In one of his shortest stories, "The Tell-Tale Heart," Poe used economy of language to emphasize the murderer-narrator's obsessive focus on bare details like the victim's cataract-milky eye, the sound of a heartbeat, and insistence he is sane. The narrator begins by denying he is crazy, even citing his extreme agitation as proof of sanity. Contradiction is then extended: the narrator loves the old man, yet kills him. His motives are irrational—not greed or revenge, but to relieve the victim of his "evil eye." Because "eye" and "I" are homonyms, readers may infer that eye/I symbolizes the old man's identity, contradicting the killer's delusion that he can separate them. The narrator distances himself from the old man by perceiving his eye as separate, and dismembering his dead body. This backfires when he imagines the victim's heartbeat, which is really his own, just before he kills him and frequently afterward. Guilty and paranoid, he gives himself away. Poe predated Freud in exploring the paradox of killing those we love and the concept of projecting our own processes onto others.

THEME IN THE WORKS OF WILLIAM FAULKNER AND CHARLES DICKENS

William Faulkner contrasts the traditions of the antebellum South with the rapid changes of post-Civil War industrialization in his short story "A Rose for Emily." Living inside the isolated world of her house, Emily Grierson denies the reality of modern progress. Contradictorily, she is both a testament to time-honored history and a mysterious, eccentric, unfathomable burden. Faulkner portrays her with deathlike imagery even in life, comparing her to a drowned woman and referring to her skeleton. Emily symbolizes the Old South; as her social status is degraded, so is the antebellum social order. Like Miss Havisham in Charles Dickens' *Great Expectations*, Emily preserves her bridal bedroom, denying change and time's passage. Emily tries to control death through denial, shown in her necrophilia with her father's corpse and her killing of Homer Barron to stop him from leaving her, then also denying his death. Faulkner uses the motif of dust throughout to represent

not only the decay of Emily, her house, and Old Southern traditions, but also how her secrets are obscured from others.

THEME IN MOBY-DICK

The great White Whale in *Moby-Dick* plays various roles to different characters. In Captain Ahab's obsessive, monomaniacal quest to kill it, the whale represents all evil, and Ahab believes it his duty and destiny to rid the world of it. Ishmael attempts through multiple scientific disciplines to understand the whale objectively, but fails—it is hidden underwater and mysterious to humans—reinforcing Melville's theme that humans can never know everything; here the whale represents the unknowable. Melville reverses white's usual connotation of purity in Ishmael's dread of white, associated with crashing waves, polar animals, albinos—all frightening and unnatural. White is often viewed as an absence of color, yet white light is the sum total of all colors in the spectrum. In the same way, white can signify both absence of meaning, and totality of meaning incomprehensible to humans. As a creature of nature, the whale also symbolizes how 19th-century white men's exploitative expansionistic actions were destroying the natural environment.

THEME IN THE OLD MAN AND THE SEA

Because of the old fisherman Santiago's struggle to capture a giant marlin, some people characterize Ernest Hemingway's *The Old Man and the Sea* as telling of man against nature. However, it can more properly be interpreted as telling of man's role as part of nature. Both man and fish are portrayed as brave, proud, and honorable. In Hemingway's world, all creatures, including humans, must either kill or be killed. Santiago reflects, "man can be destroyed but not defeated," following this principle in his life. As heroes are often created through their own deaths, Hemingway seems to believe that while being destroyed is inevitable, destruction enables living beings to transcend it by fighting bravely with honor and dignity. Hemingway echoes Romantic poet John Keats' contention that only immediately before death can we understand beauty as it is about to be destroyed. He also echoes ancient Greek and Roman myths and the Old Testament with the tragic flaw of overweening pride or overreaching. Like Icarus, Prometheus, and Adam and Eve, the old man "went out too far."

UNIVERSAL THEMES

The Old Testament book of Genesis, the Quran, and the Epic of Gilgamesh all contain flood stories. Versions differ somewhat, yet marketed similarities also exist. Genesis describes a worldwide flood, attributing it to God's decision that mankind, his creation, had become incontrovertibly wicked in spirit and must be destroyed for the world to start anew. The Quran describes the flood as regional, caused by Allah after sending Nuh (notice the similarity in name to Noah) as a messenger to his people to cease their evil. The Quran stipulates that Allah only destroys those who deny or ignore messages from his messengers. In the Gilgamesh poems Utnapishtim, like Noah, is instructed to build a ship to survive the flood. Both men also send out birds afterward as tests, using doves and a raven, though with different outcomes. Many historians and archeologists believe a Middle Eastern tidal wave was a real basis for these stories. However, their universal themes remain the same: the flood was seen as God's way of wiping out humans whose behavior had become ungodly.

THEME OF OVERREACHING

A popular theme throughout literature is the human trait of **reaching too far** or **presuming too much**. In Greek mythology, Daedalus constructed wings of feathers and wax that men might fly like birds. He permitted his son Icarus to try them, but cautioned the boy not to fly too close to the sun. The impetuous youth (in what psychologist David Elkind later named adolescence's myth of invincibility) ignored this, flying too close to the sun. The wax melted, the wings disintegrated, and Icarus fell into the sea and perished. In the Old Testament, God warned Adam and Eve not to eat fruit from the tree of knowledge of good and evil. Because they ignored this command, they were banished from Eden's eternal perfection, condemning them to mortality and suffering. The Romans were themselves examples of overreaching in their conquest and assimilation of most of the then-known world and their ultimate demise. In Christopher Marlowe's *Dr. Faustus* and Johann Wolfgang von Goethe's *Faust,* the protagonist sells his soul to the Devil for unlimited knowledge and success, ultimately leading to his own tragic end.

STORY VS. DISCOURSE

In terms of plot, "story" is the characters, places, and events originating in the author's mind, while "discourse" is how the author arranges and sequences events—which may be chronological or not. Story is imaginary; discourse is words on the page. Discourse allows a story to be told in different ways. One element of plot structure is relating events differently from the order in which they occurred. This is easily done with cause-and-effect; for example, in the sentence, "He died following a long illness," we know the illness preceded the death, but the death precedes the illness in words. In Kate Chopin's short story "The Story of an Hour" (1894), she tells some of the events out of chronological order, which has the effect of amplifying the surprise of the ending for the reader. Another element of plot structure is selection. Chopin omits some details, such as Mr. Mallard's trip home; this allows readers to be as surprised at his arrival as Mrs. Mallard is.

PLOT AND MEANING

Novelist E. M. Forster has made the distinction between story as relating a series of events, such as a king dying and then his queen dying, versus plot as establishing motivations for actions and causes for events, such as a king dying and then his queen dying from grief over his death. Thus, plot fulfills the function of helping readers understand cause-and-effect in events and underlying motivations in characters' actions, which in turn helps them understand life. This affects a work's meaning by supporting its ability to explain why things happen, why people do things, and ultimately the meaning of life. Some authors find that while story events convey meaning, they do not tell readers there is any one meaning in life or way of living, but rather are mental experiments with various meanings, enabling readers to explore. Hence stories may not necessarily be constructed to impose one definitive meaning, but rather to find some shape, direction, and meaning within otherwise random events.

CLASSIC ANALYSIS OF PLOT STRUCTURE

In *Poetics,* Aristotle defined plot as "the arrangement of the incidents." He meant not the story, but how it is structured for presentation. In tragedies, Aristotle found results driven by chains of cause and effect preferable to those driven by the protagonist's personality or character. He identified "unity of action" as necessary for a plot's wholeness, meaning its events must be internally connected, not episodic or relying on *deus ex machina* or other external intervention. A plot must have a beginning, middle, and end. Gustav Freytag adapted Aristotle's ideas into his Pyramid (1863). The beginning, today called the exposition, incentive, or inciting moment, emphasizes causes and de-emphasizes effects. Aristotle called the ensuing cause and effect *desis*, or tying up, today called complications which occur during the rising action. These culminate in a crisis or climax, Aristotle's *peripateia*. This occurs at the plot's middle, where cause and effect are both emphasized. The falling action, which Aristotle called the *lusis* or unraveling, is today called the dénouement. The resolution comes at the catastrophe, outcome, or end, when causes are emphasized and effects de-emphasized.

> **Review Video: Plot Line**
> Visit mometrix.com/academy and enter code: 944011

ANALYSIS OF PLOT STRUCTURES THROUGH RECURRING PATTERNS

Authors of fiction select characters, places, and events from their imaginations and arrange them to create a story that will affect their readers. One way to analyze plot structure is to compare and contrast different events in a story. For example, in Kate Chopin's "The Story of an Hour," a very simple but key pattern of repetition is the husband's leaving and then returning. Such patterns fulfill the symmetrical aspect that Aristotle said was required of sound plot structure. In James Baldwin's short story, "Sonny's Blues," the narrator is Sonny's brother. In an encounter with one of Sonny's old friends early in the story, the brother initially disregards his communication. In a subsequent flashback, Baldwin informs us that this was the same way he had treated Sonny. In Nathaniel Hawthorne's "Young Goodman Brown," a pattern is created by the protagonist's recurrent efforts not to go farther into the wood. In Herman Melville's "Bartleby the Scrivener" and in William Faulkner's "Barn Burning," patterns are also created by repetition such as Bartleby's repeated refusals and the history of barn-burning episodes, respectively.

LITERARY THEORIES AND CRITICISM AND INTERPRETATION

Literary theory includes ideas that guide readers through the process of interpreting literature. Literary theory, as a subject, encompasses several specific, focused theories that lead readers to interpret or analyze literature through the context of the theory using the subjects and elements it involves. Some commonly used and discussed literary theories include **postcolonial theory**, **gender and feminist theory**, **structuralism**, **new historicism**, **reader-response theory**, and **sociological criticism**.

- **Postcolonial theory** involves the historical and geographical context of a work and leads readers to consider how colonization informs the plot, characters, setting, and other elements in the work.
- **Gender and feminist theory** invites readers to interpret a text by looking at its treatment of and suggestions about women and a culture's treatment of women. As with most literary theories, this information can be clearly stated or strongly implied in a work, but it may also be gleaned through looking closely at symbols, characters, and plot elements in a work.
- **Structuralism** uses the structure and organization of a work and the foundations of language to examine how and what a text conveys about the human experience and how those findings connect to common human experiences.
- **New historicism** heavily relies on the cultural and historical context of a work, including when it was written, where the author lives or lived, the culture and history of that location, and other works from the same culture. New historical readings seek to examine these details to expose the ideologies of the location and culture that influenced the work.
- **Reader-response theory** uses the individual reader's response to the text and experience while reading the text to examine the meaning of the reader's relationship with the text and what that relationship suggests about the reader or the factors impacting their experience.
- **Sociological criticism** considers the societies that are relevant to a text. The author's society and any reader's society are important to the text, as sociological criticism seeks to uncover what the text implies or reveals about those societies. This method of criticism can also involve studying the presentation of a society within the text and applying it to the author's society or their other writings.

MEDIA TYPES

MEDIA AND FORMAT CHOICES

Effective communication depends on choosing the correct method. Media and format choices are influenced by the target audience, the budget, and the needs of the audience.

INSTRUCTIONAL VIDEOS

Instructional videos have potential for excellent two-way communication because questions and feedback can be built in. Videos can be targeted to particular audiences, and they can be paused for discussion or replayed to reinforce concepts. Viewers can see processes, including "before," "during," and "after" phases. Videos are accessible because most communities have at least one DVD player or computer. Moreover, video players and computers are continually becoming less expensive to buy and use. Disadvantages include the necessity of editing software and equipment in some cases, as well as the need for support from other print materials. There is also danger of overuse, if other media or methods are more appropriate, and higher up-front costs. Producers of instructional videos must account for the costs of script development and hiring local performers as needed.

DVDS AND CDS

Interactive DVDs and CDs, such as games, give viewers the opportunity to actively participate as they learn information. Additionally, videos are considered to be a professional method of sharing information. Compared to many other media formats, discs are comparatively inexpensive to make and are easy to transport due to their small size and weight. They are more resistant to damage and aging than older videotape technology, making them more durable. Some disadvantages include needing access to technology to play what is stored on the disc and access to certain software programs to add new content to a disc, especially if the producer wants to include video animation or audio commentary. Producers must also consider expenses concerning

58

paid staff and production and labeling expenses. Content that would appear on DVDs and CDs can alternatively be shared through streaming services or digital files stored on a computer or other compatible device.

TELEVISION AND RADIO

Both television and radio are forms of mass media that reach many people. TV has the broadest reach and can market to the general public or be customized for target audiences, while radio only tends to reach specific target audiences. TV has the advantage of video plus audio, while radio broadcasts only feature audio. However, access to television programs is more expensive than access to radio broadcasts. A shared disadvantage is that TV and radio audiences can only interact directly during call-in programs. Additionally, programming times may be inconvenient, but tape, digital sound, and digital video recording (DVR) can remedy this. Many streaming services also provide access to these programs. Both television and radio are useful for communicating simple slogans and messages, and both can generate awareness, interest, and excitement.

NEWSPAPERS

Except for the occasional community columns, news releases, and letters to the editor, newspaper pages and features afford little opportunity for audience input or participation. However, they do reach and appeal to the general public. Cost is an advantage: hiring a PR writer and paying for a news advertisement costs much less than a radio or TV spot. Additionally, newspaper features are high-status, and audiences can reread and review them as often as they like. However, newspaper ads may have difficulty affecting the reader as deeply without audio or video, and they require a literate audience. Their publication is also subject to editors' whims and biases. Newspaper pieces combining advertising and editorial content—"advertorials"—provide inclusion of paid material, but are viewed as medium-status and cost more.

WEBSITES, BLOGS, MOBILE PHONES, AND TEXT MESSAGING

Computer literacy is required for online material, but participation potential is high via websites, e-networking, and blogging. Mobile phones and text messaging are used for enormous direct, public, two-way and one-on-one communication, with timely information and reminders. Web media need a literate public and can be tailored for specific audiences. They afford global information, are accessible by increasingly technology-literate populations, and are high-status. Web media disadvantages include the necessity of computers and people to design, manage, and supply content, as well as to provide technical support. Mobile and text media are globally popular, but appeal especially to certain demographics like teens and young adults. They are increasingly available, especially in rural regions, and are decreasing in cost. Mobile and text media disadvantages include required brevity in texts and provider messaging charges. Links to related websites and pages within existing sites are also advantages of digital media.

PUBLIC PRESENTATIONS AND SLIDESHOWS

Public presentations have great potential for audience participation and can directly target various audiences. They can encourage the establishment of partnerships and groups, stimulate local ownership of issues and projects, and make information public. A drawback to public presentations is that they are limited to nights, weekends, or whenever audiences are available and do not always attract the intended audience.

Another method of presentation is to use **slideshows**. These presentations are best for sophisticated audiences like professionals, civil servants, and service organizations. Well-designed slideshows are good for stimulating audience interest, selling ideas, and marketing products. Also, they are accessible online as well as in-person so they can reach a broader audience. Slideshow disadvantages include the necessity of projectors and other equipment. They are also limited to communicating more general points, outlines, and summaries rather than conveying a multitude of information in more detail.

POSTERS AND BROCHURES

Both **posters** and **brochures** can target audiences of the general public and more specific public sectors. Posters are better for communicating simple slogans and messages, while brochures can include more detail and are better for printing instructional information. Both can be inexpensive to produce, especially if printed only as needed and in-house. Posters can often be printed in-house without using outside printing companies. However, it is difficult to get feedback on both posters and brochures—unless they have been broadly tested, or if their publication is accompanied by workshops and other participatory events. A disadvantage of using posters is that they are designed to draw attention and communicate quickly, as they are mostly viewed in passing. This means that their messages must be simple and communicate efficiently. A disadvantage of using brochures is that they can only be distributed to a specific, limited group or area. Posters and brochures are also only understood when audiences are literate in both written language and visual elements.

FLYERS AND FACT SHEETS

Flyers and fact sheets have one-way communication potential because readers cannot give feedback. Their target audiences are general. Some advantages of using this form of media include flexibility: people can distribute them at meetings or events, put them on car windshields in parking lots, leave them in stores or on bulletin boards at community agencies and schools, hand them out from booths and other displays, or mail them. When printed in black and white, they can be very inexpensive. They afford recipients the convenience of being able to review them at their leisure. Organizations and individuals can produce flyers and fact sheets in-house, or even at home with desktop publishing software. Disadvantages include their limitation to single facts or tips and specific information on specified topics.

EVALUATING MEDIA INFORMATION SOURCES

With the wealth of media in different formats available today, users are more likely to take media at face value. However, to understand the content of media, consumers must **critically evaluate each source**.

Users should ask themselves the following questions about media sources:

- Who is delivering this message and why?
- What methods do a media source's publishers employ to gain and maintain users' attention?
- Which points of view is the media source representing?
- What are the various ways this message could be interpreted?
- What information is missing from the message?
- Is the source scholarly, i.e., peer-reviewed?
- Does it include author names and their credentials as they relate to the topic?
- Who publishes it and why?
- Who is the target audience?
- Is the language technically specific or non-technical?
- Are sources cited, research claims documented, conclusions based on furnished evidence, and references provided?
- Is the publication current?

OTHER CONSIDERATIONS FOR THE VALIDITY OF SOURCES

For books, consider whether information is **up-to-date** and whether **historical perspectives** apply. Content is more likely to be **scholarly** if publishers are universities, government, or professional organizations. Book reviews can also provide useful information. For articles, identify the author, publisher, frequency of the periodical's publication, and what kind of advertising, if any, is included. Looking for book reviews also informs users. For articles, look for biographical author information, publisher name, frequency of the periodical's publication, and whether advertising is included and, if so, whether it is for certain occupations or disciplines. For web pages, check their domain names, identify publishers or sponsors, look for the author or publisher's contact information, check dates of most recent page updates, be alert to biases, and verify the validity of the information on the webpage. The quality and accuracy of web pages located through search engines rather than library databases varies widely and requires careful user inspection. Web page recommendations from reliable sources like university faculties can help indicate quality and accuracy. Citations of websites by credible or scholarly sources also show reliability. Authors' names, relevant credentials, affiliations, and

contact information support their authority. Site functionality, such as ease of navigation, ability to search, site maps, and indexes, is also a criterion to consider.

PERSUASIVE MEDIA

Advertising, public relations, and advocacy media all use **persuasion**. Advertisers use persuasion to sell goods and services. The public relations field uses persuasion to give good impressions of companies, governments, or organizations. Advocacy groups use persuasion to garner support or votes. Persuasion can come through commercials, public service announcements, speeches, websites, and newsletters, among other channels. Activists, lobbyists, government officials, and politicians use political rhetoric involving persuasive techniques. Basic techniques include using celebrity spokespersons, whom consumers admire or aspire to resemble, or conversely, "everyday people" (albeit often portrayed by actors) with whom consumers identify. Using expert testimonials lends credibility. Explicit claims of content, effectiveness, quality, and reliability—which often cannot be proven or disproven—are used to persuade. While news and advocacy messages mostly eschew humor for credibility's sake (except in political satire), advertising often persuades via humor, which gets consumer attention and associates its pleasure with advertised products and services. Qualifiers and other misleading terms, sometimes called "Weasel words," are often combined with exaggerated claims. Intensifiers, such as hyperboles, superlatives, repetitions, and sentimental appeals are also persuasive.

INTERMEDIATE TECHNIQUES

Dangerous propagandist Adolf Hitler said people suspect little lies more than big ones; hence the "Big Lie" is a persuasion method that cannot be identified without consumers' keen critical thinking. A related method is **charisma**, which can induce people to believe messages they would otherwise reject. **Euphemisms** substitute abstract, vague, or bland terms in place of more graphic, clear, and unpleasant ones. For example, the terms "layoffs" and "firing" are replaced by "downsizing," and "torture" is replaced with "intensive interrogation techniques." **Extrapolation** bases sweeping conclusions on small amounts of minor information to appeal to what consumers wish or hope. Flattery appeals to consumer self-esteem needs, such as L'Oréal's "You're worth it." Flattery is sometimes accomplished through contrast, like ads showing others' mistakes to make consumers feel superior and smarter. "Glittering generalities" refer to claims based on concepts such as beauty, love, health, democracy, freedom, and science. Persuaders use this tactic to gain consumer acceptance without consumers questioning what they mean. The opposite is name-calling to persuade consumers to reject someone or something.

American citizens love new ideas and technology. Persuaders exploit this by emphasizing the **newness** of products, services, and candidates. Conversely, they also use **nostalgia** to evoke consumers' happy memories, which they often remember more than unhappy ones. Citing "scientific evidence" is an intermediate version of the basic technique of expert testimonials. Consumers may accept this as proof, but some advertisers, politicians, and other persuaders may present inaccurate or misleading "evidence." Another intermediate technique is the "simple solution." Although the natures of people and life are complex, when consumers feel overwhelmed by complexity, persuaders exploit this by offering policies, products, or services they claim will solve complicated problems by simple means. Persuaders also use symbols, images, words, and names we associate with more general, emotional concepts like lifestyle, country, family, religion, and gender. While symbols have power, their significance also varies across individuals. For example, some consumers regard the Hummer SUV as a prestigious status symbol, while others regard it as environmentally harmful and irresponsible.

ADVANCED TECHNIQUES

Ad hominem, Latin for "against the man" attacks the person behind an idea rather than criticizing the idea itself. It operates by association: if a person is considered immoral or uneducated, then his or her ideas must be bad as well. **"Stacking the deck"** misleads by presenting only selected information that supports one position. **Apophasis**, or a false denial, allows the speaker or writer to indirectly bring attention to a flaw in an opponent's credibility. For example, a politician saying, "I won't mention my opponent's tax evasion issues" manages to mention them while seeming less accusatory. Persuaders may also use **majority belief**, making

statements such as "Four out of five dentists recommend this brand" or "[insert number] people can't be wrong." In an intensified version, persuaders exploit group dynamics at rallies, speeches, and other live-audience events where people are vulnerable to surrounding crowd influences. **Scapegoating**, blaming one person or group for complex problems, is a form of the intermediate "simple solution" technique, a practice common in politics. **Timing** also persuades, like advertising flowers and candy in the weeks preceding Valentine's Day, ad campaigns preceding new technology rollouts, and politician speeches following big news events.

VISUAL MEDIA

Some images have the power to communicate more information than an entire paragraph. Images can contain several elements and be interpreted different ways, making them an effective vessel for abstract and emotionally appealing ideas. Humans are also able to understand images before they fully acquire language, meaning that images can reach more people than language can at any time. Images are also more quickly comprehended than text, making them a highly efficient method of communication. People can remember or memorize images more easily than text, also. Historically, images have been used for propaganda and subliminal messaging. Images are also used by different companies as an effective technique to entice customers to buy their products. Though images do not always contain text, they can still convey explicit and implicit meanings. An image's explicit meaning would be the most recognizable shape or concept in the image. The implicit meaning may be obscured within the image through the use of negative space, background images, or out-of-focus shapes.

INTERPRETING AND EVALUATING PERSUASIVE MEDIA

Most messages can be interpreted in different ways. They can be interpreted explicitly, where the literal meaning of the words in the message creates the meaning of the message, and no context is considered. Alternatively, other contexts can be considered alongside the explicit meaning of the message. These create alternative, not clearly stated meanings called **implicit meanings**. Politics, current events, regional norms, and even emotions are examples of contexts that can add implicit meanings to a message. These implicit meanings can change the effect a message has on its recipient. Many products have slogans with both implicit and explicit meanings. These implicit meanings must be considered to fully interpret a message.

Messages come in different forms, and each form has a unique way of communicating both explicit and implicit meanings. Images can come with captions that communicate a message, but some images carry subliminal messages. This means that their implicit meaning is received by the viewer, but the viewer is not aware of it. The term **propaganda** describes messages that advocate for a specific opinion or way of thinking. Most propaganda is politically driven and has been used during historical periods, most notably World War II. Unlike messages with hidden or veiled implicit meanings, most propaganda aggressively communicates its entire meaning and is difficult to misinterpret. Documentaries are another prominent form of communication. Documentaries are informational videos that focus on a specific figure, subject, phenomenon, or time period. While documentaries are primarily fact based and contain excerpts from interviews and testimonials, documentaries feature a limited view of their subject and sometimes attempt to persuade viewers to take action or embrace their central message. While some documentaries communicate this clearly, some hide an implicit meaning through the way they present each piece of information.

Chapter Quiz

Ready to see how well you retained what you just read? Scan the QR code to go directly to the chapter quiz interface for this study guide. If you're using a computer, simply visit the bonus page at **mometrix.com/bonus948/praxcore** and click the Chapter Quizzes link.

Writing

Transform passive reading into active learning! After immersing yourself in this chapter, put your comprehension to the test by taking a quiz. The insights you gained will stay with you longer this way. Scan the QR code to go directly to the chapter quiz interface for this study guide. If you're using a computer, simply visit the bonus page at **mometrix.com/bonus948/praxcore** and click the Chapter Quizzes link.

Language Skills

PARTS OF SPEECH

NOUNS

A noun is a person, place, thing, or idea. The two main types of nouns are **common** and **proper** nouns. Nouns can also be categorized as abstract (i.e., general) or concrete (i.e., specific).

COMMON NOUNS

Common nouns are generic names for people, places, and things. Common nouns are not usually capitalized.

Examples of common nouns:

People: boy, girl, worker, manager

Places: school, bank, library, home

Things: dog, cat, truck, car

> **Review Video: What is a Noun?**
> Visit mometrix.com/academy and enter code: 344028

PROPER NOUNS

Proper nouns name specific people, places, or things. All proper nouns are capitalized.

Examples of proper nouns:

People: Abraham Lincoln, George Washington, Martin Luther King, Jr.

Places: Los Angeles, California; New York; Asia

Things: Statue of Liberty, Earth, Lincoln Memorial

Note: Some nouns can be either common or proper depending on their use. For example, when referring to the planet that we live on, *Earth* is a proper noun and is capitalized. When referring to the dirt, rocks, or land on our planet, *earth* is a common noun and is not capitalized.

GENERAL AND SPECIFIC NOUNS

General nouns are the names of conditions or ideas. **Specific nouns** name people, places, and things that are understood by using your senses.

63

General nouns:

Condition: beauty, strength

Idea: truth, peace

Specific nouns:

People: baby, friend, father

Places: town, park, city hall

Things: rainbow, cough, apple, silk, gasoline

COLLECTIVE NOUNS

Collective nouns are the names for a group of people, places, or things that may act as a whole. The following are examples of collective nouns: *class, company, dozen, group, herd, team,* and *public*. Collective nouns usually require an article, which denotes the noun as being a single unit. For instance, a choir is a group of singers. Even though there are many singers in a choir, the word choir is grammatically treated as a single unit. If we refer to the members of the group, and not the group itself, it is no longer a collective noun.

Incorrect: The *choir are* going to compete nationally this year.

Correct: The *choir is* going to compete nationally this year.

Incorrect: The *members* of the choir *is* competing nationally this year.

Correct: The *members* of the choir *are* competing nationally this year.

PRONOUNS

Pronouns are words that are used to stand in for nouns. A pronoun may be classified as personal, intensive, relative, interrogative, demonstrative, indefinite, and reciprocal.

Personal: *Nominative* is the case for nouns and pronouns that are the subject of a sentence. *Objective* is the case for nouns and pronouns that are an object in a sentence. *Possessive* is the case for nouns and pronouns that show possession or ownership.

Singular

	Nominative	Objective	Possessive
First Person	I	me	my, mine
Second Person	you	you	your, yours
Third Person	he, she, it	him, her, it	his, her, hers, its

Plural

	Nominative	Objective	Possessive
First Person	we	us	our, ours
Second Person	you	you	your, yours
Third Person	they	them	their, theirs

Intensive: I myself, you yourself, he himself, she herself, the (thing) itself, we ourselves, you yourselves, they themselves

Relative: which, who, whom, whose

Interrogative: what, which, who, whom, whose

Demonstrative: this, that, these, those

Indefinite: all, any, each, everyone, either/neither, one, some, several

Reciprocal: each other, one another

> **Review Video: Nouns and Pronouns**
> Visit mometrix.com/academy and enter code: 312073

VERBS

A verb is a word or group of words that indicates action or being. In other words, the verb shows something's action or state of being or the action that has been done to something. If you want to write a sentence, then you need a verb. Without a verb, you have no sentence.

TRANSITIVE AND INTRANSITIVE VERBS

A **transitive verb** is a verb whose action indicates a receiver. **Intransitive verbs** do not indicate a receiver of an action. In other words, the action of the verb does not point to an object.

Transitive: He drives a car. | She feeds the dog.

Intransitive: He runs every day. | She voted in the last election.

A dictionary will tell you whether a verb is transitive or intransitive. Some verbs can be transitive or intransitive.

ACTION VERBS AND LINKING VERBS

Action verbs show what the subject is doing. In other words, an action verb shows action. Unlike most types of words, a single action verb, in the right context, can be an entire sentence. **Linking verbs** link the subject of a sentence to a noun or pronoun, or they link a subject with an adjective. You always need a verb if you want a complete sentence. However, linking verbs on their own cannot be a complete sentence.

Common linking verbs include *appear, be, become, feel, grow, look, seem, smell, sound,* and *taste.* However, any verb that shows a condition and connects to a noun, pronoun, or adjective that describes the subject of a sentence is a linking verb.

Action: He sings. | Run! | Go! | I talk with him every day. | She reads.

Linking:

Incorrect: I am.

Correct: I am John. | The roses smell lovely. | I feel tired.

Note: Some verbs are followed by words that look like prepositions, but they are a part of the verb and a part of the verb's meaning. These are known as phrasal verbs, and examples include *call off, look up,* and *drop off.*

> **Review Video: Action Verbs and Linking Verbs**
> Visit mometrix.com/academy and enter code: 743142

VOICE

Transitive verbs may be in active voice or passive voice. The difference between active voice and passive voice is whether the subject is acting or being acted upon. When the subject of the sentence is doing the action, the verb is in **active voice**. When the subject is being acted upon, the verb is in **passive voice**.

> **Active**: Jon drew the picture. (The subject *Jon* is doing the action of *drawing a picture.*)

> **Passive**: The picture is drawn by Jon. (The subject *picture* is receiving the action from Jon.)

VERB TENSES

Verb **tense** is a property of a verb that indicates when the action being described takes place (past, present, or future) and whether or not the action is completed (simple or perfect). Describing an action taking place in the present (*I talk*) requires a different verb tense than describing an action that took place in the past (*I talked*). Some verb tenses require an auxiliary (helping) verb. These helping verbs include *am, are, is | have, has, had | was, were, will* (or *shall*).

Present: I talk	Present perfect: I have talked
Past: I talked	Past perfect: I had talked
Future: I will talk	Future perfect: I will have talked

Present: The action is happening at the current time.

> Example: He *walks* to the store every morning.

To show that something is happening right now, use the progressive present tense: I *am walking*.

Past: The action happened in the past.

> Example: She *walked* to the store an hour ago.

Future: The action will happen later.

> Example: I *will walk* to the store tomorrow.

Present perfect: The action started in the past and continues into the present or took place previously at an unspecified time.

> Example: I *have walked* to the store three times today.

Past perfect: The action was completed at some point in the past. This tense is usually used to describe an action that was completed before some other reference time or event.

> Example: I *had eaten* already before they arrived.

Future perfect: The action will be completed before some point in the future. This tense may be used to describe an action that has already begun or has yet to begin.

> Example: The project *will have been completed* by the deadline.

Review Video: <u>Present Perfect, Past Perfect, and Future Perfect Verb Tenses</u>
Visit mometrix.com/academy and enter code: 269472

66

CONJUGATING VERBS

When you need to change the form of a verb, you are **conjugating** a verb. The key forms of a verb are present tense (sing/sings), past tense (sang), present participle (singing), and past participle (sung). By combining these forms with helping verbs, you can make almost any verb tense. The following table demonstrate some of the different ways to conjugate a verb:

Tense	First Person	Second Person	Third Person Singular	Third Person Plural
Simple Present	I sing	You sing	He, she, it sings	They sing
Simple Past	I sang	You sang	He, she, it sang	They sang
Simple Future	I will sing	You will sing	He, she, it will sing	They will sing
Present Progressive	I am singing	You are singing	He, she, it is singing	They are singing
Past Progressive	I was singing	You were singing	He, she, it was singing	They were singing
Present Perfect	I have sung	You have sung	He, she, it has sung	They have sung
Past Perfect	I had sung	You had sung	He, she, it had sung	They had sung

MOOD

There are three **moods** in English: the indicative, the imperative, and the subjunctive.

The **indicative mood** is used for facts, opinions, and questions.

Fact: You can do this.

Opinion: I think that you can do this.

Question: Do you know that you can do this?

The **imperative** is used for orders or requests.

Order: You are going to do this!

Request: Will you do this for me?

The **subjunctive mood** is for wishes and statements that go against fact.

Wish: I wish that I were famous.

Statement against fact: If I were you, I would do this. (This goes against fact because I am not you. You have the chance to do this, and I do not have the chance.)

ADJECTIVES

An **adjective** is a word that is used to modify a noun or pronoun. An adjective answers a question: *Which one? What kind?* or *How many?* Usually, adjectives come before the words that they modify, but they may also come after a linking verb.

Which one? The *third* suit is my favorite.

What kind? This suit is *navy blue*.

How many? I am going to buy *four* pairs of socks to match the suit.

> **Review Video: Descriptive Text**
> Visit mometrix.com/academy and enter code: 174903

ARTICLES

Articles are adjectives that are used to distinguish nouns as definite or indefinite. *A*, *an*, and *the* are the only articles. **Definite** nouns are preceded by *the* and indicate a specific person, place, thing, or idea. **Indefinite** nouns are preceded by *a* or *an* and do not indicate a specific person, place, thing, or idea.

Note: *An* comes before words that start with a vowel sound. For example, "Are you going to get an **u**mbrella?"

Definite: I lost *the* bottle that belongs to me.

Indefinite: Does anyone have *a* bottle to share?

> **Review Video: Function of Articles in a Sentence**
> Visit mometrix.com/academy and enter code: 449383

COMPARISON WITH ADJECTIVES

Some adjectives are relative and other adjectives are absolute. Adjectives that are **relative** can show the comparison between things. **Absolute** adjectives can also show comparison, but they do so in a different way. Let's say that you are reading two books. You think that one book is perfect, and the other book is not exactly perfect. It is not possible for one book to be more perfect than the other. Either you think that the book is perfect, or you think that the book is imperfect. In this case, perfect and imperfect are absolute adjectives.

Relative adjectives will show the different **degrees** of something or someone to something else or someone else. The three degrees of adjectives include positive, comparative, and superlative.

The **positive** degree is the normal form of an adjective.

Example: This work is *difficult*. | She is *smart*.

The **comparative** degree compares one person or thing to another person or thing.

Example: This work is *more difficult* than your work. | She is *smarter* than me.

The **superlative** degree compares more than two people or things.

Example: This is the *most difficult* work of my life. | She is the *smartest* lady in school.

> **Review Video: What is an Adjective?**
> Visit mometrix.com/academy and enter code: 470154

ADVERBS

An **adverb** is a word that is used to **modify** a verb, an adjective, or another adverb. Usually, adverbs answer one of these questions: *When? Where? How?* and *Why?* The negatives *not* and *never* are considered adverbs. Adverbs that modify adjectives or other adverbs **strengthen** or **weaken** the words that they modify.

Examples:

He walks *quickly* through the crowd.

The water flows *smoothly* on the rocks.

Note: Adverbs are usually indicated by the morpheme *-ly*, which has been added to the root word. For instance, *quick* can be made into an adverb by adding *-ly* to construct *quickly*. Some words that end in *-ly* do not follow this rule and can behave as other parts of speech. Examples of adjectives ending in *-ly* include: *early, friendly, holy, lonely, silly*, and *ugly*. To know if a word that ends in *-ly* is an adjective or adverb, check your dictionary. Also, while many adverbs end in *-ly*, you need to remember that not all adverbs end in *-ly*.

Examples:

He is *never* angry.

You are *too* irresponsible to travel alone.

Review Video: What is an Adverb?
Visit mometrix.com/academy and enter code: 713951

Review Video: Adverbs that Modify Adjectives
Visit mometrix.com/academy and enter code: 122570

COMPARISON WITH ADVERBS

The rules for comparing adverbs are the same as the rules for adjectives.

The **positive** degree is the standard form of an adverb.

Example: He arrives *soon*. | She speaks *softly* to her friends.

The **comparative** degree compares one person or thing to another person or thing.

Example: He arrives *sooner* than Sarah. | She speaks *more softly* than him.

The **superlative** degree compares more than two people or things.

Example: He arrives *soonest* of the group. | She speaks the *most softly* of any of her friends.

PREPOSITIONS

A **preposition** is a word placed before a noun or pronoun that shows the relationship between that noun or pronoun and another word in the sentence.

Common prepositions:

about	before	during	on	under
after	beneath	for	over	until
against	between	from	past	up
among	beyond	in	through	with
around	by	of	to	within
at	down	off	toward	without

Examples:

> The napkin is *in* the drawer.

> The Earth rotates *around* the Sun.

> The needle is *beneath* the haystack.

> Can you find "me" *among* the words?

> **Review Video: Prepositions**
> Visit mometrix.com/academy and enter code: 946763

CONJUNCTIONS

Conjunctions join words, phrases, or clauses and they show the connection between the joined pieces. **Coordinating conjunctions** connect equal parts of sentences. **Correlative conjunctions** show the connection between pairs. **Subordinating conjunctions** join subordinate (i.e., dependent) clauses with independent clauses.

COORDINATING CONJUNCTIONS

The **coordinating conjunctions** include: *and, but, yet, or, nor, for,* and *so*

Examples:

> The rock was small, *but* it was heavy.

> She drove in the night, *and* he drove in the day.

CORRELATIVE CONJUNCTIONS

The **correlative conjunctions** are: *either...or | neither...nor | not only...but also*

Examples:

Either you are coming *or* you are staying.

He *not only* ran three miles *but also* swam 200 yards.

> **Review Video: Coordinating and Correlative Conjunctions**
> Visit mometrix.com/academy and enter code: 390329
>
> **Review Video: Adverb Equal Comparisons**
> Visit mometrix.com/academy and enter code: 231291

SUBORDINATING CONJUNCTIONS

Common **subordinating conjunctions** include:

after	since	whenever
although	so that	where
because	unless	wherever
before	until	whether
in order that	when	while

Examples:

I am hungry *because* I did not eat breakfast.

He went home *when* everyone left.

> **Review Video: Subordinating Conjunctions**
> Visit mometrix.com/academy and enter code: 958913

INTERJECTIONS

Interjections are words of exclamation (i.e., audible expression of great feeling) that are used alone or as a part of a sentence. Often, they are used at the beginning of a sentence for an introduction. Sometimes, they can be used in the middle of a sentence to show a change in thought or attitude.

Common Interjections: Hey! | Oh, | Ouch! | Please! | Wow!

AGREEMENT AND SENTENCE STRUCTURE
SUBJECTS AND PREDICATES
SUBJECTS

The **subject** of a sentence names who or what the sentence is about. The subject may be directly stated in a sentence, or the subject may be the implied *you*. The **complete subject** includes the simple subject and all of its modifiers. To find the complete subject, ask *Who* or *What* and insert the verb to complete the question. The answer, including any modifiers (adjectives, prepositional phrases, etc.), is the complete subject. To find the **simple subject**, remove all of the modifiers in the complete subject. Being able to locate the subject of a sentence helps with many problems, such as those involving sentence fragments and subject-verb agreement.

Examples:

simple
subject
The small, red car is the one that he wants for Christmas.
complete
subject

simple
subject
The young artist is coming over for dinner.
complete
subject

> **Review Video: Subjects in English**
> Visit mometrix.com/academy and enter code: 444771

In **imperative** sentences, the verb's subject is understood (e.g., [You] Run to the store), but is not actually present in the sentence. Normally, the subject comes before the verb. However, the subject comes after the verb in sentences that begin with *There are* or *There was*.

Direct:

John knows the way to the park.	Who knows the way to the park?	John
The cookies need ten more minutes.	What needs ten minutes?	The cookies
By five o'clock, Bill will need to leave.	Who needs to leave?	Bill
There are five letters on the table for him.	What is on the table?	Five letters
There were coffee and doughnuts in the house.	What was in the house?	Coffee and doughnuts

Implied:

Go to the post office for me.	Who is going to the post office?	You
Come and sit with me, please?	Who needs to come and sit?	You

PREDICATES

In a sentence, you always have a predicate and a subject. The subject tells who or what the sentence is about, and the **predicate** explains or describes the subject. The predicate includes the verb or verb phrase and any direct or indirect objects of the verb, as well as any words or phrases modifying these.

Think about the sentence *He sings*. In this sentence, we have a subject (He) and a predicate (sings). This is all that is needed for a sentence to be complete. Most sentences contain more information, but if this is all the information that you are given, then you have a complete sentence.

Now, let's look at another sentence: *John and Jane sing on Tuesday nights at the dance hall.*

subject   predicate
John and Jane sing on Tuesday nights at the dance hall.

SUBJECT-VERB AGREEMENT

Verbs must **agree** with their subjects in number and in person. To agree in number, singular subjects need singular verbs and plural subjects need plural verbs. A **singular** noun refers to **one** person, place, or thing. A **plural** noun refers to **more than one** person, place, or thing. To agree in person, the correct verb form must be

72

chosen to match the first, second, or third person subject. The present tense ending *-s* or *-es* is used on a verb if its subject is third person singular; otherwise, the verb's ending is not modified.

> **Review Video: Subject-Verb Agreement**
> Visit mometrix.com/academy and enter code: 479190

NUMBER AGREEMENT EXAMPLES:

singular singular
subject verb

Single Subject and Verb: Dan calls home.

Dan is one person. So, the singular verb *calls* is needed.

plural plural
subject verb

Plural Subject and Verb: Dan and Bob call home.

More than one person needs the plural verb *call*.

PERSON AGREEMENT EXAMPLES:

First Person: I *am* walking.

Second Person: You *are* walking.

Third Person: He *is* walking.

COMPLICATIONS WITH SUBJECT-VERB AGREEMENT
WORDS BETWEEN SUBJECT AND VERB

Words that come between the simple subject and the verb have no bearing on subject-verb agreement.

Examples:

singular singular
subject verb

The joy of my life returns home tonight.

The phrase *of my life* does not influence the verb *returns*.

singular singular
subject verb

The question that still remains unanswered is "Who are you?"

Don't let the phrase "*that still remains…*" trouble you. The subject *question* goes with *is*.

COMPOUND SUBJECTS

A compound subject is formed when two or more nouns joined by *and*, *or*, or *nor* jointly act as the subject of the sentence.

JOINED BY AND

When a compound subject is joined by *and*, it is treated as a plural subject and requires a plural verb.

Examples:

plural subject — plural verb
You and Jon are invited to come to my house.

plural subject — plural verb
The pencil and paper belong to me.

JOINED BY OR/NOR

For a compound subject joined by *or* or *nor*, the verb must agree in number with the part of the subject that is closest to the verb (italicized in the examples below).

Examples:

subject — verb
Today or tomorrow is the day.

subject — verb
Stan or Phil wants to read the book.

subject — verb
Neither the pen nor the book is on the desk.

subject — verb
Either the blanket or pillows arrive this afternoon.

INDEFINITE PRONOUNS AS SUBJECT

An indefinite pronoun is a pronoun that does not refer to a specific noun. Some indefinite pronouns function as only singular, some function as only plural, and some can function as either singular or plural depending on how they are used.

ALWAYS SINGULAR

Pronouns such as *each*, *either*, *everybody*, *anybody*, *somebody*, and *nobody* are always singular.

Examples:

singular subject — singular verb
Each of the runners has a different bib number.

singular verb — singular subject
Is either of you ready for the game?

Note: The words *each* and *either* can also be used as adjectives (e.g., *each* person is unique). When one of these adjectives modifies the subject of a sentence, it is always a singular subject.

singular
subject   singular
          verb
Everybody grows a day older every day.

singular   singular
subject   verb
Anybody   is   welcome to bring a tent.

ALWAYS PLURAL

Pronouns such as *both*, *several*, and *many* are always plural.

Examples:

plural
subject   plural
               verb
Both of the siblings were too tired to argue.

plural   plural
subject verb
Many have tried, but none have succeeded.

DEPEND ON CONTEXT

Pronouns such as *some*, *any*, *all*, *none*, *more*, and *most* can be either singular or plural depending on what they are representing in the context of the sentence.

Examples:

singular
subject   singular
                verb
All of my dog's food was still there in his bowl.

plural
subject   plural
                  verb
By the end of the night, all of my guests were already excited about coming to my next party.

OTHER CASES INVOLVING PLURAL OR IRREGULAR FORM

Some nouns are **singular in meaning but plural in form**: news, mathematics, physics, and economics.

The *news is* coming on now.

Mathematics is my favorite class.

Some nouns are plural in form and meaning, and have **no singular equivalent**: scissors and pants.

Do these *pants come* with a shirt?

The *scissors are* for my project.

Mathematical operations are **irregular** in their construction, but are normally considered to be **singular in meaning**.

One plus one is two.

Three times three is nine.

Note: Look to your **dictionary** for help when you aren't sure whether a noun with a plural form has a singular or plural meaning.

COMPLEMENTS

A complement is a noun, pronoun, or adjective that is used to give more information about the subject or object in the sentence.

DIRECT OBJECTS

A direct object is a noun or pronoun that tells who or what **receives** the action of the verb. A sentence will only include a direct object if the verb is a transitive verb. If the verb is an intransitive verb or a linking verb, there will be no direct object. When you are looking for a direct object, find the verb and ask *who* or *what*.

Examples:

I took *the blanket*.

Jane read *books*.

INDIRECT OBJECTS

An indirect object is a noun or pronoun that indicates what or whom the action had an **influence** on. If there is an indirect object in a sentence, then there will also be a direct object. When you are looking for the indirect object, find the verb and ask *to/for whom or what*.

Examples:

indirect   direct
object   object
We taught the old dog a new trick.

indirect   direct
object   object
I gave them a math lesson.

> **Review Video: Direct and Indirect Objects**
> Visit mometrix.com/academy and enter code: 817385

PREDICATE NOMINATIVES AND PREDICATE ADJECTIVES

As we looked at previously, verbs may be classified as either action verbs or linking verbs. A linking verb is so named because it links the subject to words in the predicate that describe or define the subject. These words are called predicate nominatives (if nouns or pronouns) or predicate adjectives (if adjectives).

Examples:

           predicate
subject   nominative
My father is a lawyer.

           predicate
subject   adjective
Your mother is patient.

PRONOUN USAGE

The **antecedent** is the noun that has been replaced by a pronoun. A pronoun and its antecedent **agree** when they have the same number (singular or plural) and gender (male, female, or neutral).

Examples:

Singular agreement: John came into town, and he played for us.

(antecedent) (pronoun)

Plural agreement: John and Rick came into town, and they played for us.

(antecedent) (pronoun)

To determine which is the correct pronoun to use in a compound subject or object, try each pronoun **alone** in place of the compound in the sentence. Your knowledge of pronouns will tell you which one is correct.

Example:

Bob and (I, me) will be going.

Test: (1) *I will be going* or (2) *Me will be going*. The second choice cannot be correct because *me* cannot be used as the subject of a sentence. Instead, *me* is used as an object.

Answer: Bob and I will be going.

When a pronoun is used with a noun immediately following (as in "we boys"), try the sentence **without the added noun**.

Example:

(We/Us) boys played football last year.

Test: (1) *We played football last year* or (2) *Us played football last year*. Again, the second choice cannot be correct because *us* cannot be used as a subject of a sentence. Instead, *us* is used as an object.

Answer: We boys played football last year.

> **Review Video: <u>Pronoun Usage</u>**
> Visit mometrix.com/academy and enter code: 666500
>
> **Review Video: <u>What is Pronoun-Antecedent Agreement?</u>**
> Visit mometrix.com/academy and enter code: 919704

A pronoun should point clearly to the **antecedent**. Here is how a pronoun reference can be unhelpful if it is puzzling or not directly stated.

Unhelpful: Ron and Jim went to the store, and he bought soda.

(antecedent) (pronoun)

Who bought soda? Ron or Jim?

Helpful: Jim went to the store, and he bought soda.

(antecedent) (pronoun)

The sentence is clear. Jim bought the soda.

Some pronouns change their form by their placement in a sentence. A pronoun that is a **subject** in a sentence comes in the **subjective case**. Pronouns that serve as **objects** appear in the **objective case**. Finally, the pronouns that are used as **possessives** appear in the **possessive case**.

Examples:

> **Subjective case**: *He* is coming to the show.

> The pronoun *He* is the subject of the sentence.

> **Objective case**: Josh drove *him* to the airport.

> The pronoun *him* is the object of the sentence.

> **Possessive case**: The flowers are *mine*.

> The pronoun *mine* shows ownership of the flowers.

The word *who* is a subjective-case pronoun that can be used as a **subject**. The word *whom* is an objective-case pronoun that can be used as an **object**. The words *who* and *whom* are common in subordinate clauses or in questions.

Examples:

> $\overbrace{subject}$ $\overbrace{verb}$
> He knows who wants to come.

> $\overbrace{object}$ $\overbrace{verb}$
> He knows the man whom we want at the party.

CLAUSES

A clause is a group of words that contains both a subject and a predicate (verb). There are two types of clauses: independent and dependent. An **independent clause** contains a complete thought, while a **dependent (or subordinate) clause** does not. A dependent clause includes a subject and a verb, and may also contain objects or complements, but it cannot stand as a complete thought without being joined to an independent clause. Dependent clauses function within sentences as adjectives, adverbs, or nouns.

Example:

> independent   dependent
> clause   clause
> I am running because I want to stay in shape.

The clause *I am running* is an independent clause: it has a subject and a verb, and it gives a complete thought. The clause *because I want to stay in shape* is a dependent clause: it has a subject and a verb, but it does not express a complete thought. It adds detail to the independent clause to which it is attached.

> **Review Video: What is a Clause?**
> Visit mometrix.com/academy and enter code: 940170
>
> **Review Video: Independent and Dependent Clauses**
> Visit mometrix.com/academy and enter code: 556903

TYPES OF DEPENDENT CLAUSES
ADJECTIVE CLAUSES

An **adjective clause** is a dependent clause that modifies a noun or a pronoun. Adjective clauses begin with a relative pronoun (*who, whose, whom, which,* and *that*) or a relative adverb (*where, when,* and *why*).

Also, adjective clauses usually come immediately after the noun that the clause needs to explain or rename. This is done to ensure that it is clear which noun or pronoun the clause is modifying.

Examples:

```
        independent                  adjective
          clause                      clause
```
I learned the reason why I won the award.

```
        independent                  adjective
          clause                      clause
```
This is the place where I started my first job.

An adjective clause can be an essential or nonessential clause. An essential clause is very important to the sentence. **Essential clauses** explain or define a person or thing. **Nonessential clauses** give more information about a person or thing but are not necessary to define them. Nonessential clauses are set off with commas while essential clauses are not.

Examples:

```
                essential
                 clause
```
A person who works hard at first can often rest later in life.

```
                nonessential
                  clause
```
Neil Armstrong, who walked on the moon, is my hero.

> **Review Video: Adjective Clauses and Phrases**
> Visit mometrix.com/academy and enter code: 520888

ADVERB CLAUSES

An **adverb clause** is a dependent clause that modifies a verb, adjective, or adverb. In sentences with multiple dependent clauses, adverb clauses are usually placed immediately before or after the independent clause. An adverb clause is introduced with words such as *after, although, as, before, because, if, since, so, unless, when, where*, and *while*.

Examples:

```
            adverb
            clause
```
When you walked outside, I called the manager.

```
                    adverb
                    clause
```
I will go with you unless you want to stay.

NOUN CLAUSES

A **noun clause** is a dependent clause that can be used as a subject, object, or complement. Noun clauses begin with words such as *how, that, what, whether, which, who,* and *why*. These words can also come with an adjective clause. Unless the noun clause is being used as the subject of the sentence, it should come after the verb of the independent clause.

Examples:

noun
clause

The real mystery is how you avoided serious injury.

noun
clause

What you learn from each other depends on your honesty with others.

SUBORDINATION

When two related ideas are not of equal importance, the ideal way to combine them is to make the more important idea an independent clause and the less important idea a dependent or subordinate clause. This is called **subordination**.

Example:

> **Separate ideas**: The team had a perfect regular season. The team lost the championship.

> **Subordinated**: Despite having a perfect regular season, *the team lost the championship.*

PHRASES

A phrase is a group of words that functions as a single part of speech, usually a noun, adjective, or adverb. A **phrase** is not a complete thought and does not contain a subject and predicate, but it adds detail or explanation to a sentence, or renames something within the sentence.

PREPOSITIONAL PHRASES

One of the most common types of phrases is the prepositional phrase. A **prepositional phrase** begins with a preposition and ends with a noun or pronoun that is the object of the preposition. Normally, the prepositional phrase functions as an **adjective** or an **adverb** within the sentence.

Examples:

prepositional
phrase

The picnic is on the blanket.

prepositional
phrase

I am sick with a fever today.

prepositional
phrase

Among the many flowers, John found a four-leaf clover.

VERBAL PHRASES

A **verbal** is a word or phrase that is formed from a verb but does not function as a verb. Depending on its particular form, it may be used as a noun, adjective, or adverb. A verbal does **not** replace a verb in a sentence.

Examples:

verb

Correct: Walk a mile daily.

This is a complete sentence with the implied subject *you.*

verbal

Incorrect: To walk a mile.

This is not a sentence since there is no functional verb.

There are three types of verbal: **participles**, **gerunds**, and **infinitives**. Each type of verbal has a corresponding **phrase** that consists of the verbal itself along with any complements or modifiers.

PARTICIPLES

A **participle** is a type of verbal that always functions as an adjective. The present participle always ends with -*ing*. Past participles end with -*d*, -*ed*, -*n*, or -*t*. Participles are combined with helping verbs to form certain verb tenses, but a participle by itself cannot function as a verb.

Examples: dance (verb) | dancing (present participle) | danced (past participle)

Participial phrases most often come right before or right after the noun or pronoun that they modify.

Examples:

participial phrase
Shipwrecked on an island, the boys started to fish for food.

participial phrase
Having been seated for five hours, we got out of the car to stretch our legs.

participial phrase
Praised for their work, the group accepted the first-place trophy.

GERUNDS

A **gerund** is a type of verbal that always functions as a **noun**. Like present participles, gerunds always end with -*ing*, but they can be easily distinguished from participles by the part of speech they represent (participles always function as adjectives). Since a gerund or gerund phrase always functions as a noun, it can be used as the subject of a sentence, the predicate nominative, or the object of a verb or preposition.

Examples:

gerund
We want to be known for teaching the poor.
object of preposition

gerund
Coaching this team is the best job of my life.
subject

gerund
We like practicing our songs in the basement.
object of verb

INFINITIVES

An **infinitive** is a type of verbal that can function as a noun, an adjective, or an adverb. An infinitive is made of the word *to* and the basic form of the verb. As with all other types of verbal phrases, an infinitive phrase includes the verbal itself and all of its complements or modifiers.

81

Examples:

infinitive
To join the team is my goal in life.
noun

infinitive
The animals have enough food to eat for the night.
adjective

infinitive
People lift weights to exercise their muscles.
adverb

> **Review Video: Verbals**
> Visit mometrix.com/academy and enter code: 915480

APPOSITIVE PHRASES

An **appositive** is a word or phrase that is used to explain or rename nouns or pronouns. Noun phrases, gerund phrases, and infinitive phrases can all be used as appositives.

Examples:

appositive
Terriers, hunters at heart, have been dressed up to look like lap dogs.

The noun phrase *hunters at heart* renames the noun *terriers*.

appositive
His plan, to save and invest his money, was proven as a safe approach.

The infinitive phrase explains what the plan is.

Appositive phrases can be **essential** or **nonessential**. An appositive phrase is essential if the person, place, or thing being described or renamed is too general for its meaning to be understood without the appositive.

Examples:

essential
Two of America's Founding Fathers, George Washington and Thomas Jefferson, served as presidents.

nonessential
George Washington and Thomas Jefferson, two Founding Fathers, served as presidents.

ABSOLUTE PHRASES

An absolute phrase is a phrase that consists of **a noun followed by a participle**. An absolute phrase provides **context** to what is being described in the sentence, but it does not modify or explain any particular word; it is essentially independent.

Examples:

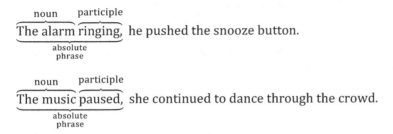

The alarm ringing, he pushed the snooze button.

The music paused, she continued to dance through the crowd.

PARALLELISM

When multiple items or ideas are presented in a sentence in series, such as in a list, the items or ideas must be stated in grammatically equivalent ways. For example, if two ideas are listed in parallel and the first is stated in gerund form, the second cannot be stated in infinitive form. (e.g., *I enjoy reading and to study.* [incorrect]) An infinitive and a gerund are not grammatically equivalent. Instead, you should write *I enjoy reading and studying* OR *I like to read and to study.* In lists of more than two, all items must be parallel.

Example:

Incorrect: He stopped at the office, grocery store, and the pharmacy before heading home.

The first and third items in the list of places include the article *the*, so the second item needs it as well.

Correct: He stopped at the office, *the* grocery store, and the pharmacy before heading home.

Example:

Incorrect: While vacationing in Europe, she went biking, skiing, and climbed mountains.

The first and second items in the list are gerunds, so the third item must be as well.

Correct: While vacationing in Europe, she went biking, skiing, and *mountain climbing*.

> **Review Video: Parallel Sentence Construction**
> Visit mometrix.com/academy and enter code: 831988

SENTENCE PURPOSE

There are four types of sentences: declarative, imperative, interrogative, and exclamatory.

A **declarative** sentence states a fact and ends with a period.

The football game starts at seven o'clock.

An **imperative** sentence tells someone to do something and generally ends with a period. An urgent command might end with an exclamation point instead.

Don't forget to buy your ticket.

An **interrogative** sentence asks a question and ends with a question mark.

Are you going to the game on Friday?

An **exclamatory** sentence shows strong emotion and ends with an exclamation point.

I can't believe we won the game!

SENTENCE STRUCTURE

Sentences are classified by structure based on the type and number of clauses present. The four classifications of sentence structure are the following:

Simple: A simple sentence has one independent clause with no dependent clauses. A simple sentence may have **compound elements** (i.e., compound subject or verb).

Examples:

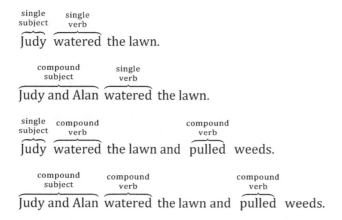

Compound: A compound sentence has two or more independent clauses with no dependent clauses. Usually, the independent clauses are joined with a comma and a coordinating conjunction or with a semicolon.

Examples:

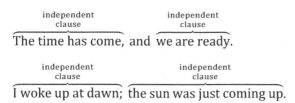

Complex: A complex sentence has one independent clause and at least one dependent clause.

Examples:

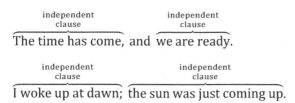

Compound-Complex: A compound-complex sentence has at least two independent clauses and at least one dependent clause.

Examples:

independent   dependent   independent
clause   clause   clause

John is my friend who went to India, and he brought back souvenirs.

independent   independent   dependent
clause   clause   clause

You may not realize this, but we heard the music that you played last night.

> **Review Video: Sentence Structure**
> Visit mometrix.com/academy and enter code: 700478

Sentence variety is important to consider when writing an essay or speech. A variety of sentence lengths and types creates rhythm, makes a passage more engaging, and gives writers an opportunity to demonstrate their writing style. Writing that uses the same length or type of sentence without variation can be boring or difficult to read. To evaluate a passage for effective sentence variety, it is helpful to note whether the passage contains diverse sentence structures and lengths. It is also important to pay attention to the way each sentence starts and avoid beginning with the same words or phrases.

SENTENCE FRAGMENTS

Recall that a group of words must contain at least one **independent clause** in order to be considered a sentence. If it doesn't contain even one independent clause, it is called a **sentence fragment**.

The appropriate process for **repairing** a sentence fragment depends on what type of fragment it is. If the fragment is a dependent clause, it can sometimes be as simple as removing a subordinating word (e.g., when, because, if) from the beginning of the fragment. Alternatively, a dependent clause can be incorporated into a closely related neighboring sentence. If the fragment is missing some required part, like a subject or a verb, the fix might be as simple as adding the missing part.

Examples:

Fragment: Because he wanted to sail the Mediterranean.

Removed subordinating word: He wanted to sail the Mediterranean.

Combined with another sentence: Because he wanted to sail the Mediterranean, he booked a Greek island cruise.

RUN-ON SENTENCES

Run-on sentences consist of multiple independent clauses that have not been joined together properly. Run-on sentences can be corrected in several different ways:

Join clauses properly: This can be done with a comma and coordinating conjunction, with a semicolon, or with a colon or dash if the second clause is explaining something in the first.

Example:

Incorrect: I went on the trip, we visited lots of castles.

Corrected: I went on the trip, and we visited lots of castles.

85

Split into separate sentences: This correction is most effective when the independent clauses are very long or when they are not closely related.

Example:

> **Incorrect**: The drive to New York takes ten hours, my uncle lives in Boston.

> **Corrected**: The drive to New York takes ten hours. My uncle lives in Boston.

Make one clause dependent: This is the easiest way to make the sentence correct and more interesting at the same time. It's often as simple as adding a subordinating word between the two clauses or before the first clause.

Example:

> **Incorrect**: I finally made it to the store and I bought some eggs.

> **Corrected**: When I finally made it to the store, I bought some eggs.

Reduce to one clause with a compound verb: If both clauses have the same subject, remove the subject from the second clause, and you now have just one clause with a compound verb.

Example:

> **Incorrect**: The drive to New York takes ten hours, it makes me very tired.

> **Corrected**: The drive to New York takes ten hours and makes me very tired.

Note: While these are the simplest ways to correct a run-on sentence, often the best way is to completely reorganize the thoughts in the sentence and rewrite it.

> **Review Video: <u>Fragments and Run-on Sentences</u>**
> Visit mometrix.com/academy and enter code: 541989

DANGLING AND MISPLACED MODIFIERS
DANGLING MODIFIERS
A dangling modifier is a dependent clause or verbal phrase that does not have a clear logical connection to a word in the sentence.

Example:

> dangling
> modifier
> **Incorrect**: Reading each magazine article, the stories caught my attention.

The word *stories* cannot be modified by *Reading each magazine article*. People can read, but stories cannot read. Therefore, the subject of the sentence must be a person.

> gerund
> phrase
> **Corrected**: Reading each magazine article, I was entertained by the stories.

86

Example:

Incorrect: Ever since childhood, my grandparents have visited me for Christmas.

dangling modifier — Ever since childhood

The speaker in this sentence can't have been visited by her grandparents when *they* were children, since she wouldn't have been born yet. Either the modifier should be clarified or the sentence should be rearranged to specify whose childhood is being referenced.

Clarified: Ever since I was a child, my grandparents have visited for Christmas.

dependent clause — Ever since I was a child

Rearranged: Ever since childhood, I have enjoyed my grandparents visiting for Christmas.

adverb phrase — Ever since childhood

MISPLACED MODIFIERS

Because modifiers are grammatically versatile, they can be put in many different places within the structure of a sentence. The danger of this versatility is that a modifier can accidentally be placed where it is modifying the wrong word or where it is not clear which word it is modifying.

Example:

Incorrect: She read the book to a crowd that was filled with beautiful pictures.

modifier — that was filled with beautiful pictures

The book was filled with beautiful pictures, not the crowd.

Corrected: She read the book that was filled with beautiful pictures to a crowd.

modifier — that was filled with beautiful pictures

Example:

Ambiguous: Derek saw a bus nearly hit a man on his way to work.

modifier — on his way to work

Was Derek on his way to work or was the other man?

Derek: On his way to work, Derek saw a bus nearly hit a man.

modifier — On his way to work

The other man: Derek saw a bus nearly hit a man who was on his way to work.

modifier — who was on his way to work

SPLIT INFINITIVES

A split infinitive occurs when a modifying word comes between the word *to* and the verb that pairs with *to*.

Example: To *clearly* explain vs. *To explain* clearly | To *softly* sing vs. *To sing* softly

Though considered improper by some, split infinitives may provide better clarity and simplicity in some cases than the alternatives. As such, avoiding them should not be considered a universal rule.

DOUBLE NEGATIVES

Standard English allows **two negatives** only when a **positive** meaning is intended. (e.g., The team was *not displeased* with their performance.) Double negatives to emphasize negation are not used in standard English.

Negative modifiers (e.g., never, no, and not) should not be paired with other negative modifiers or negative words (e.g., none, nobody, nothing, or neither). The modifiers *hardly, barely*, and *scarcely* are also considered negatives in standard English, so they should not be used with other negatives.

PUNCTUATION
END PUNCTUATION
PERIODS

Use a period to end all sentences except direct questions and exclamations. Periods are also used for abbreviations.

Examples: 3 p.m. | 2 a.m. | Mr. Jones | Mrs. Stevens | Dr. Smith | Bill, Jr. | Pennsylvania Ave.

Note: An abbreviation is a shortened form of a word or phrase.

QUESTION MARKS

Question marks should be used following a **direct question**. A polite request can be followed by a period instead of a question mark.

Direct Question: What is for lunch today? | How are you? | Why is that the answer?

Polite Requests: Can you please send me the item tomorrow. | Will you please walk with me on the track.

> **Review Video: Question Marks**
> Visit mometrix.com/academy and enter code: 118471

EXCLAMATION MARKS

Exclamation marks are used after a word group or sentence that shows much feeling or has special importance. Exclamation marks should not be overused. They are saved for proper **exclamatory interjections**.

Example: We're going to the finals! | You have a beautiful car! | "That's crazy!" she yelled.

> **Review Video: Exclamation Points**
> Visit mometrix.com/academy and enter code: 199367

COMMAS

The comma is a punctuation mark that can help you understand connections in a sentence. Not every sentence needs a comma. However, if a sentence needs a comma, you need to put it in the right place. A comma in the wrong place (or an absent comma) will make a sentence's meaning unclear.

These are some of the rules for commas:

Use Case	Example
Before a **coordinating conjunction** joining independent clauses	Bob caught three fish, and I caught two fish.
After an **introductory phrase**	After the final out, we went to a restaurant to celebrate.
After an **adverbial clause**	Studying the stars, I was awed by the beauty of the sky.
Between **items in a series**	I will bring the turkey, the pie, and the coffee.
For **interjections**	Wow, you know how to play this game.
After *yes* and *no* responses	No, I cannot come tomorrow.
Separate **nonessential modifiers**	John Frank, who coaches the team, was promoted today.
Separate **nonessential appositives**	Thomas Edison, an American inventor, was born in Ohio.
Separate **nouns of direct address**	You, John, are my only hope in this moment.
Separate **interrogative tags**	This is the last time, correct?
Separate **contrasts**	You are my friend, not my enemy.
Writing **dates**	July 4, 1776, is an important date to remember.
Writing **addresses**	He is meeting me at 456 Delaware Avenue, Washington, D.C., tomorrow morning.
Writing **geographical names**	Paris, France, is my favorite city.
Writing **titles**	John Smith, PhD, will be visiting your class today.
Separate **expressions like** *he said*	"You can start," she said, "with an apology."

A comma is also used **between coordinate adjectives** not joined with *and*. However, not all adjectives are coordinate (i.e., equal or parallel). To determine if your adjectives are coordinate, try connecting them with *and* or reversing their order. If it still sounds right, they are coordinate.

Incorrect: The kind, brown dog followed me home.

Correct: The kind, loyal dog followed me home.

> **Review Video: When to Use a Comma**
> Visit mometrix.com/academy and enter code: 786797

SEMICOLONS

The semicolon is used to join closely related independent clauses without the need for a coordinating conjunction. Semicolons are also used in place of commas to separate list elements that have internal commas. Some rules for semicolons include:

Use Case	Example
Between closely connected independent clauses **not connected with a coordinating conjunction**	You are right; we should go with your plan.
Between independent clauses **linked with a transitional word**	I think that we can agree on this; however, I am not sure about my friends.
Between items in a **series that has internal punctuation**	I have visited New York, New York; Augusta, Maine; and Baltimore, Maryland.

> **Review Video: How to Use Semicolons**
> Visit mometrix.com/academy and enter code: 370605

COLONS

The colon is used to call attention to the words that follow it. When used in a sentence, a colon should only come at the **end** of a **complete sentence**. The rules for colons are as follows:

Use Case	Example
After an independent clause to **make a list**	I want to learn many languages: Spanish, German, and Italian.
For **explanations**	There is one thing that stands out on your resume: responsibility.
To give a **quote**	He started with an idea: "We are able to do more than we imagine."
After the **greeting in a formal letter**	To Whom It May Concern:
Show **hours and minutes**	It is 3:14 p.m.
Separate a **title and subtitle**	The essay is titled "America: A Short Introduction to a Modern Country."

> **Review Video: Using Colons**
> Visit mometrix.com/academy and enter code: 868673

PARENTHESES

Parentheses are used for additional information. Also, they can be used to put labels for letters or numbers in a series. Parentheses should be not be used very often. If they are overused, parentheses can be a distraction instead of a help.

Examples:

Extra Information: The rattlesnake (see Image 2) is a dangerous snake of North and South America.

Series: Include in the email (1) your name, (2) your address, and (3) your question for the author.

> **Review Video: Parentheses**
> Visit mometrix.com/academy and enter code: 947743

QUOTATION MARKS

Use quotation marks to close off **direct quotations** of a person's spoken or written words. Do not use quotation marks around indirect quotations. An indirect quotation gives someone's message without using the person's exact words. Use **single quotation marks** to close off a quotation inside a quotation.

Direct Quote: Nancy said, "I am waiting for Henry to arrive."

Indirect Quote: Henry said that he is going to be late to the meeting.

Quote inside a Quote: The teacher asked, "Has everyone read 'The Gift of the Magi'?"

Quotation marks should be used around the titles of **short works**: newspaper and magazine articles, poems, short stories, songs, television episodes, radio programs, and subdivisions of books or websites.

Examples:

"Rip Van Winkle" (short story by Washington Irving)

"O Captain! My Captain!" (poem by Walt Whitman)

Although it is not standard usage, quotation marks are sometimes used to highlight **irony** or the use of words to mean something other than their dictionary definition. This type of usage should be employed sparingly, if at all.

Examples:

| The boss warned Frank that he was walking on "thin ice." | Frank is not walking on real ice. Instead, he is being warned to avoid mistakes. |
| The teacher thanked the young man for his "honesty." | The quotation marks around *honesty* show that the teacher does not believe the young man's explanation. |

> **Review Video: Quotation Marks**
> Visit mometrix.com/academy and enter code: 884918

Periods and commas are put **inside** quotation marks. Colons and semicolons are put **outside** the quotation marks. Question marks and exclamation points are placed inside quotation marks when they are part of a quote. When the question or exclamation mark goes with the whole sentence, the mark is left outside of the quotation marks.

Examples:

Period and comma	We read "The Gift of the Magi," "The Skylight Room," and "The Cactus."
Semicolon	They watched "The Nutcracker"; then, they went home.
Exclamation mark that is a part of a quote	The crowd cheered, "Victory!"
Question mark that goes with the whole sentence	Is your favorite short story "The Tell-Tale Heart"?

APOSTROPHES

An apostrophe is used to show **possession** or the **deletion of letters in contractions**. An apostrophe is not needed with the possessive pronouns *his, hers, its, ours, theirs, whose,* and *yours.*

Singular Nouns: David's car | a book's theme | my brother's board game

Plural Nouns that end with -s: the scissors' handle | boys' basketball

Plural Nouns that end without -s: Men's department | the people's adventure

> **Review Video: When to Use an Apostrophe**
> Visit mometrix.com/academy and enter code: 213068
>
> **Review Video: Punctuation Errors in Possessive Pronouns**
> Visit mometrix.com/academy and enter code: 221438

HYPHENS

Hyphens are used to **separate compound words**. Use hyphens in the following cases:

Use Case	Example
Compound numbers from 21 to 99 when written out in words	This team needs twenty-five points to win the game.
Written-out fractions that are used as adjectives	The recipe says that we need a three-fourths cup of butter.
Compound adjectives that come before a noun	The well-fed dog took a nap.
Unusual compound words that would be hard to read or easily confused with other words	This is the best anti-itch cream on the market.

Note: This is not a complete set of the rules for hyphens. A dictionary is the best tool for knowing if a compound word needs a hyphen.

> **Review Video: Hyphens**
> Visit mometrix.com/academy and enter code: 981632

DASHES

Dashes are used to show a **break** or a **change in thought** in a sentence or to act as parentheses in a sentence. When typing, use two hyphens to make a dash. Do not put a space before or after the dash. The following are the functions of dashes:

Use Case	Example
Set off parenthetical statements or an **appositive with internal punctuation**	The three trees—oak, pine, and magnolia—are coming on a truck tomorrow.
Show a **break or change in tone or thought**	The first question—how silly of me—does not have a correct answer.

ELLIPSIS MARKS

The ellipsis mark has **three** periods (...) to show when **words have been removed** from a quotation. If a **full sentence or more** is removed from a quoted passage, you need to use **four** periods to show the removed text and the end punctuation mark. The ellipsis mark should not be used at the beginning of a quotation. The ellipsis mark should also not be used at the end of a quotation unless some words have been deleted from the end of the final quoted sentence.

Example:

"Then he picked up the groceries...paid for them...later he went home."

BRACKETS

There are two main reasons to use brackets:

Use Case	Example
Placing **parentheses inside of parentheses**	The hero of this story, Paul Revere (a silversmith and industrialist [see Ch. 4]), rode through towns of Massachusetts to warn of advancing British troops.
Adding **clarification or detail to a quotation** that is not part of the quotation	The father explained, "My children are planning to attend my alma mater [State University]."

> **Review Video: Brackets**
> Visit mometrix.com/academy and enter code: 727546

COMMON USAGE MISTAKES
WORD CONFUSION
WHICH, THAT, AND WHO

The words *which*, *that*, and *who* can act as **relative pronouns** to help clarify or describe a noun.

Which is used for things only.

> Example: Andrew's car, *which is old and rusty,* broke down last week.

That is used for people or things. *That* is usually informal when used to describe people.

> Example: Is this the only book *that Louis L'Amour wrote?*

> Example: Is Louis L'Amour the author *that wrote Western novels?*

Who is used for people or for animals that have an identity or personality.

> Example: Mozart was the composer *who wrote those operas.*

> Example: John's dog, *who is called Max,* is large and fierce.

HOMOPHONES

Homophones are words that sound alike (or similar) but have different **spellings** and **definitions**. A homophone is a type of **homonym**, which is a pair or group of words that are pronounced or spelled the same, but do not mean the same thing.

TO, TOO, AND TWO

To can be an adverb or a preposition for showing direction, purpose, and relationship. See your dictionary for the many other ways to use *to* in a sentence.

> Examples: I went to the store. | I want to go with you.

Too is an adverb that means *also, as well, very,* or *in excess.*

> Examples: I can walk a mile too. | You have eaten too much.

Two is a number.

> Example: You have two minutes left.

THERE, THEIR, AND THEY'RE

There can be an adjective, adverb, or pronoun. Often, *there* is used to show a place or to start a sentence.

> Examples: I went there yesterday. | There is something in his pocket.

Their is a pronoun that is used to show ownership.

> Examples: He is their father. | This is their fourth apology this week.

They're is a contraction of *they are.*

> Example: Did you know that they're in town?

KNEW AND NEW

Knew is the past tense of *know*.

> Example: I knew the answer.

New is an adjective that means something is current, has not been used, or is modern.

> Example: This is my new phone.

THEN AND THAN

Then is an adverb that indicates sequence or order:

> Example: I'm going to run to the library and then come home.

Than is special-purpose word used only for comparisons:

> Example: Susie likes chips more than candy.

ITS AND IT'S

Its is a pronoun that shows ownership.

> Example: The guitar is in its case.

It's is a contraction of *it is*.

> Example: It's an honor and a privilege to meet you.

Note: The *h* in honor is silent, so *honor* starts with the vowel sound *o*, which must have the article *an*.

YOUR AND YOU'RE

Your is a pronoun that shows ownership.

> Example: This is your moment to shine.

You're is a contraction of *you are*.

> Example: Yes, you're correct.

SAW AND SEEN

Saw is the past-tense form of *see*.

> Example: I saw a turtle on my walk this morning.

Seen is the past participle of *see*.

> Example: I have seen this movie before.

AFFECT AND EFFECT

There are two main reasons that *affect* and *effect* are so often confused: 1) both words can be used as either a noun or a verb, and 2) unlike most homophones, their usage and meanings are closely related to each other. Here is a quick rundown of the four usage options:

Affect (n): feeling, emotion, or mood that is displayed

> Example: The patient had a flat *affect*. (i.e., his face showed little or no emotion)

Affect (v): to alter, to change, to influence

> Example: The sunshine *affects* the plant's growth.

Effect (n): a result, a consequence

> Example: What *effect* will this weather have on our schedule?

Effect (v): to bring about, to cause to be

> Example: These new rules will *effect* order in the office.

The noun form of *affect* is rarely used outside of technical medical descriptions, so if a noun form is needed on the test, you can safely select *effect*. The verb form of *effect* is not as rare as the noun form of *affect*, but it's still not all that likely to show up on your test. If you need a verb and you can't decide which to use based on the definitions, choosing *affect* is your best bet.

HOMOGRAPHS

Homographs are words that share the same spelling, but have different meanings and sometimes different pronunciations. To figure out which meaning is being used, you should be looking for context clues. The context clues give hints to the meaning of the word. For example, the word *spot* has many meanings. It can mean "a place" or "a stain or blot." In the sentence "After my lunch, I saw a spot on my shirt," the word *spot* means "a stain or blot." The context clues of "After my lunch" and "on my shirt" guide you to this decision. A homograph is another type of homonym.

BANK

> (noun): an establishment where money is held for savings or lending

> (verb): to collect or pile up

CONTENT

> (noun): the topics that will be addressed within a book

> (adjective): pleased or satisfied

> (verb): to make someone pleased or satisfied

FINE

> (noun): an amount of money that acts a penalty for an offense

> (adjective): very small or thin

> (adverb): in an acceptable way

> (verb): to make someone pay money as a punishment

INCENSE

> (noun): a material that is burned in religious settings and makes a pleasant aroma

> (verb): to frustrate or anger

LEAD

> (noun): the first or highest position

> (noun): a heavy metallic element

(verb): to direct a person or group of followers

(adjective): containing lead

OBJECT

(noun): a lifeless item that can be held and observed

(verb): to disagree

PRODUCE

(noun): fruits and vegetables

(verb): to make or create something

REFUSE

(noun): garbage or debris that has been thrown away

(verb): to not allow

SUBJECT

(noun): an area of study

(verb): to force or subdue

TEAR

(noun): a fluid secreted by the eyes

(verb): to separate or pull apart

COMMONLY MISUSED WORDS AND PHRASES

A LOT

The phrase *a lot* should always be written as two words; never as *alot*.

Correct: That's a lot of chocolate!

Incorrect: He does that alot.

CAN

The word *can* is used to describe things that are possible occurrences; the word *may* is used to described things that are allowed to happen.

Correct: May I have another piece of pie?

Correct: I can lift three of these bags of mulch at a time.

Incorrect: Mom said we can stay up thirty minutes later tonight.

COULD HAVE

The phrase *could of* is often incorrectly substituted for the phrase *could have*. Similarly, *could of, may of*, and *might of* are sometimes used in place of the correct phrases *could have, may have*, and *might have*.

Correct: If I had known, I would have helped out.

Incorrect: Well, that could of gone much worse than it did.

MYSELF

The word *myself* is a reflexive pronoun, often incorrectly used in place of *I* or *me*.

> **Correct**: He let me do it myself.

> **Incorrect**: The job was given to Dave and myself.

OFF

The phrase *off of* is a redundant expression that should be avoided. In most cases, it can be corrected simply by removing *of*.

> **Correct**: My dog chased the squirrel off its perch on the fence.

> **Incorrect**: He finally moved his plate off of the table.

SUPPOSED TO

The phrase *suppose to* is sometimes used incorrectly in place of the phrase *supposed to*.

> **Correct**: I was supposed to go to the store this afternoon.

> **Incorrect**: When are we suppose to get our grades?

TRY TO

The phrase *try and* is often used in informal writing and conversation to replace the correct phrase *try to*.

> **Correct**: It's a good policy to try to satisfy every customer who walks in the door.

> **Incorrect**: Don't try and do too much.

Text Types, Purposes, and Production

THE WRITING PROCESS

BRAINSTORMING

Brainstorming is a technique that is used to find a creative approach to a subject. This can be accomplished by simple **free-association** with a topic. For example, with paper and pen, write every thought that you have about the topic in a word or phrase. This is done without critical thinking. You should put everything that comes to your mind about the topic on your scratch paper. Then, you need to read the list over a few times. Next, look for patterns, repetitions, and clusters of ideas. This allows a variety of fresh ideas to come as you think about the topic.

FREE WRITING

Free writing is a more structured form of brainstorming. The method involves taking a limited amount of time (e.g., 2 to 3 minutes) to write everything that comes to mind about the topic in complete sentences. When time expires, review everything that has been written down. Many of your sentences may make little or no sense, but the insights and observations that can come from free writing make this method a valuable approach. Usually, free writing results in a fuller expression of ideas than brainstorming because thoughts and associations are written in complete sentences. However, both techniques can be used to complement each other.

PLANNING

Planning is the process of organizing a piece of writing before composing a draft. Planning can include creating an outline or a graphic organizer, such as a Venn diagram, a spider-map, or a flowchart. These methods should help the writer identify their topic, main ideas, and the general organization of the composition. Preliminary research can also take place during this stage. Planning helps writers organize all of their ideas and decide if they have enough material to begin their first draft. However, writers should remember that the decisions they make during this step will likely change later in the process, so their plan does not have to be perfect.

DRAFTING

Writers may then use their plan, outline, or graphic organizer to compose their first draft. They may write subsequent drafts to improve their writing. Writing multiple drafts can help writers consider different ways to communicate their ideas and address errors that may be difficult to correct without rewriting a section or the whole composition. Most writers will vary in how many drafts they choose to write, as there is no "right" number of drafts. Writing drafts also takes away the pressure to write perfectly on the first try, as writers can improve with each draft they write.

REVISING, EDITING, AND PROOFREADING

Once a writer completes a draft, they can move on to the revising, editing, and proofreading steps to improve their draft. These steps begin with making broad changes that may apply to large sections of a composition and then making small, specific corrections. **Revising** is the first and broadest of these steps. Revising involves ensuring that the composition addresses an appropriate audience, includes all necessary material, maintains focus throughout, and is organized logically. Revising may occur after the first draft to ensure that the following drafts improve upon errors from the first draft. Some revision should occur between each draft to avoid repeating these errors. The **editing** phase of writing is narrower than the revising phase. Editing a composition should include steps such as improving transitions between paragraphs, ensuring each paragraph is on topic, and improving the flow of the text. The editing phase may also include correcting grammatical errors that cannot be fixed without significantly altering the text. **Proofreading** involves fixing misspelled words, typos, other grammatical errors, and any remaining surface-level flaws in the composition.

RECURSIVE WRITING PROCESS

However you approach writing, you may find comfort in knowing that the revision process can occur in any order. The **recursive writing process** is not as difficult as the phrase may make it seem. Simply put, the recursive writing process means that you may need to revisit steps after completing other steps. It also implies that the steps are not required to take place in any certain order. Indeed, you may find that planning, drafting, and revising can all take place at about the same time. The writing process involves moving back and forth between planning, drafting, and revising, followed by more planning, more drafting, and more revising until the writing is satisfactory.

> **Review Video: Recursive Writing Process**
> Visit mometrix.com/academy and enter code: 951611

TECHNOLOGY IN THE WRITING PROCESS

Modern technology has yielded several tools that can be used to make the writing process more convenient and organized. Word processors and online tools, such as databases and plagiarism detectors, allow much of the writing process to be completed in one place, using one device.

TECHNOLOGY FOR PLANNING AND DRAFTING

For the planning and drafting stages of the writing process, word processors are a helpful tool. These programs also feature formatting tools, allowing users to create their own planning tools or create digital outlines that can be easily converted into sentences, paragraphs, or an entire essay draft. Online databases and references also complement the planning process by providing convenient access to information and sources for research. Word processors also allow users to keep up with their work and update it more easily than if they wrote their work by hand. Online word processors often allow users to collaborate, making group assignments more convenient. These programs also allow users to include illustrations or other supplemental media in their compositions.

TECHNOLOGY FOR REVISING, EDITING, AND PROOFREADING

Word processors also benefit the revising, editing, and proofreading stages of the writing process. Most of these programs indicate errors in spelling and grammar, allowing users to catch minor errors and correct them quickly. There are also websites designed to help writers by analyzing text for deeper errors, such as poor sentence structure, inappropriate complexity, lack of sentence variety, and style issues. These websites can help users fix errors they may not know to look for or may have simply missed. As writers finish these steps, they may benefit from checking their work for any plagiarism. There are several websites and programs that compare text to other documents and publications across the internet and detect any similarities within the text. These websites show the source of the similar information, so users know whether or not they referenced the source and unintentionally plagiarized its contents.

TECHNOLOGY FOR PUBLISHING

Technology also makes managing written work more convenient. Digitally storing documents keeps everything in one place and is easy to reference. Digital storage also makes sharing work easier, as documents can be attached to an email or stored online. This also allows writers to publish their work easily, as they can electronically submit it to other publications or freely post it to a personal blog, profile, or website.

OUTLINING AND ORGANIZING IDEAS
MAIN IDEAS, SUPPORTING DETAILS, AND OUTLINING A TOPIC

A writer often begins the first paragraph of a paper by stating the **main idea** or point, also known as the **topic sentence**. The rest of the paragraph supplies particular details that develop and support the main point. One way to visualize the relationship between the main point and supporting information is by considering a table: the tabletop is the main point, and each of the table's legs is a supporting detail or group of details. Both professional authors and students can benefit from planning their writing by first making an outline of the topic. Outlines facilitate quick identification of the main point and supporting details without having to wade through the additional language that will exist in the fully developed essay, article, or paper. Outlining can also help readers to analyze a piece of existing writing for the same reason. The outline first summarizes the main idea in one sentence. Then, below that, it summarizes the supporting details in a numbered list. Writing the paper then consists of filling in the outline with detail, writing a paragraph for each supporting point, and adding an introduction and conclusion.

INTRODUCTION

The purpose of the introduction is to capture the reader's attention and announce the essay's main idea. Normally, the introduction contains 50-80 words, or 3-5 sentences. An introduction can begin with an interesting quote, a question, or a strong opinion—something that will **engage** the reader's interest and prompt them to keep reading. If you are writing your essay to a specific prompt, your introduction should include a **restatement or summarization** of the prompt so that the reader will have some context for your essay. Finally, your introduction should briefly state your **thesis or main idea**: the primary thing you hope to communicate to the reader through your essay. Don't try to include all of the details and nuances of your thesis, or all of your reasons for it, in the introduction. That's what the rest of the essay is for!

> **Review Video: Introduction**
> Visit mometrix.com/academy and enter code: 961328

THESIS STATEMENT

The thesis is the main idea of the essay. A temporary thesis, or working thesis, should be established early in the writing process because it will serve to keep the writer focused as ideas develop. This temporary thesis is subject to change as you continue to write.

The temporary thesis has two parts: a **topic** (i.e., the focus of your essay based on the prompt) and a **comment**. The comment makes an important point about the topic. A temporary thesis should be interesting and specific.

99

Also, you need to limit the topic to a manageable scope. These three questions are useful tools to measure the effectiveness of any temporary thesis:

- Does the focus of my essay have enough interest to hold an audience?
- Is the focus of my essay specific enough to generate interest?
- Is the focus of my essay manageable for the time limit? Too broad? Too narrow?

The thesis should be a generalization rather than a fact because the thesis prepares readers for facts and details that support the thesis. The process of bringing the thesis into sharp focus may help in outlining major sections of the work. Once the thesis and introduction are complete, you can address the body of the work.

> **Review Video: Thesis Statements**
> Visit mometrix.com/academy and enter code: 691033

SUPPORTING THE THESIS

Throughout your essay, the thesis should be **explained clearly and supported** adequately by additional arguments. The thesis sentence needs to contain a clear statement of the purpose of your essay and a comment about the thesis. With the thesis statement, you have an opportunity to state what is noteworthy of this particular treatment of the prompt. Each sentence and paragraph should build on and support the thesis.

When you respond to the prompt, use parts of the passage to support your argument or defend your position. Using supporting evidence from the passage strengths your argument because readers can see your attention to the entire passage and your response to the details and facts within the passage. You can use facts, details, statistics, and direct quotations from the passage to uphold your position. Be sure to point out which information comes from the original passage and base your argument around that evidence.

BODY

In an essay's introduction, the writer establishes the thesis and may indicate how the rest of the piece will be structured. In the body of the piece, the writer **elaborates** upon, **illustrates**, and **explains** the **thesis statement**. How writers arrange supporting details and their choices of paragraph types are development techniques. Writers may give examples of the concept introduced in the thesis statement. If the subject includes a cause-and-effect relationship, the author may explain its causality. A writer will explain or analyze the main idea of the piece throughout the body, often by presenting arguments for the veracity or credibility of the thesis statement. Writers may use development to define or clarify ambiguous terms. Paragraphs within the body may be organized using natural sequences, like space and time. Writers may employ **inductive reasoning**, using multiple details to establish a generalization or causal relationship, or **deductive reasoning**, proving a generalized hypothesis or proposition through a specific example or case.

> **Review Video: Drafting Body Paragraphs**
> Visit mometrix.com/academy and enter code: 724590

PARAGRAPHS

After the introduction of a passage, a series of body paragraphs will carry a message through to the conclusion. Each paragraph should be **unified around a main point**. Normally, a good topic sentence summarizes the paragraph's main point. A topic sentence is a general sentence that gives an introduction to the paragraph.

The sentences that follow support the topic sentence. However, though it is usually the first sentence, the topic sentence can come as the final sentence to the paragraph if the earlier sentences give a clear explanation of the paragraph's topic. This allows the topic sentence to function as a concluding sentence. Overall, the paragraphs need to stay true to the main point. This means that any unnecessary sentences that do not advance the main point should be removed.

The main point of a paragraph requires adequate development (i.e., a substantial paragraph that covers the main point). A paragraph of two or three sentences does not cover a main point. This is especially true when the main point of the paragraph gives strong support to the argument of the thesis. An occasional short paragraph is fine as a transitional device. However, a well-developed argument will have paragraphs with more than a few sentences.

METHODS OF DEVELOPING PARAGRAPHS

Common methods of adding substance to paragraphs include examples, illustrations, analogies, and cause and effect.

- **Examples** are supporting details to the main idea of a paragraph or a passage. When authors write about something that their audience may not understand, they can provide an example to show their point. When authors write about something that is not easily accepted, they can give examples to prove their point.
- **Illustrations** are extended examples that require several sentences. Well-selected illustrations can be a great way for authors to develop a point that may not be familiar to their audience.
- **Analogies** make comparisons between items that appear to have nothing in common. Analogies are employed by writers to provoke fresh thoughts about a subject. These comparisons may be used to explain the unfamiliar, to clarify an abstract point, or to argue a point. Although analogies are effective literary devices, they should be used carefully in arguments. Two things may be alike in some respects but completely different in others.
- **Cause and effect** is an excellent device to explain the connection between an action or situation and a particular result. One way that authors can use cause and effect is to state the effect in the topic sentence of a paragraph and add the causes in the body of the paragraph. This method can give an author's paragraphs structure, which always strengthens writing.

TYPES OF PARAGRAPHS

A **paragraph of narration** tells a story or a part of a story. Normally, the sentences are arranged in chronological order (i.e., the order that the events happened). However, flashbacks (i.e., an anecdote from an earlier time) can be included.

A **descriptive paragraph** makes a verbal portrait of a person, place, or thing. When specific details are used that appeal to one or more of the senses (i.e., sight, sound, smell, taste, and touch), authors give readers a sense of being present in the moment.

A **process paragraph** is related to time order (i.e., First, you open the bottle. Second, you pour the liquid, etc.). Usually, this describes a process or teaches readers how to perform a process.

Comparing two things draws attention to their similarities and indicates a number of differences. When authors contrast, they focus only on differences. Both comparing and contrasting may be done point-by-point, noting both the similarities and differences of each point, or in sequential paragraphs, where you discuss all the similarities and then all the differences, or vice versa.

BREAKING TEXT INTO PARAGRAPHS

For most forms of writing, you will need to use multiple paragraphs. As such, determining when to start a new paragraph is very important. Reasons for starting a new paragraph include:

- To mark off the introduction and concluding paragraphs
- To signal a shift to a new idea or topic
- To indicate an important shift in time or place
- To explain a point in additional detail
- To highlight a comparison, contrast, or cause and effect relationship

PARAGRAPH LENGTH

Most readers find that their comfort level for a paragraph is between 100 and 200 words. Shorter paragraphs cause too much starting and stopping and give a choppy effect. Paragraphs that are too long often test the attention span of readers. Two notable exceptions to this rule exist. In scientific or scholarly papers, longer paragraphs suggest seriousness and depth. In journalistic writing, constraints are placed on paragraph size by the narrow columns in a newspaper format.

The first and last paragraphs of a text will usually be the introduction and conclusion. These special-purpose paragraphs are likely to be shorter than paragraphs in the body of the work. Paragraphs in the body of the essay follow the subject's outline (e.g., one paragraph per point in short essays and a group of paragraphs per point in longer works). Some ideas require more development than others, so it is good for a writer to remain flexible. A paragraph of excessive length may be divided, and shorter ones may be combined.

COHERENT PARAGRAPHS

A smooth flow of sentences and paragraphs without gaps, shifts, or bumps will lead to paragraph **coherence**. Ties between old and new information can be smoothed using several methods:

- **Linking ideas clearly**, from the topic sentence to the body of the paragraph, is essential for a smooth transition. The topic sentence states the main point, and this should be followed by specific details, examples, and illustrations that support the topic sentence. The support may be direct or indirect. In **indirect support**, the illustrations and examples may support a sentence that in turn supports the topic directly.
- The **repetition of key words** adds coherence to a paragraph. To avoid dull language, variations of the key words may be used.
- **Parallel structures** are often used within sentences to emphasize the similarity of ideas and connect sentences giving similar information.
- Maintaining a **consistent verb tense** throughout the paragraph helps. Shifting tenses affects the smooth flow of words and can disrupt the coherence of the paragraph.

> **Review Video: How to Write a Good Paragraph**
> Visit mometrix.com/academy and enter code: 682127

SEQUENCE WORDS AND PHRASES

When a paragraph opens with the topic sentence, the second sentence may begin with a phrase like *first of all*, introducing the first supporting detail or example. The writer may introduce the second supporting item with words or phrases like *also*, *in addition*, and *besides*. The writer might introduce succeeding pieces of support with wording like, *another thing*, *moreover*, *furthermore*, or *not only that, but*. The writer may introduce the last piece of support with *lastly*, *finally*, or *last but not least*. Writers get off the point by presenting off-target items not supporting the main point. For example, a main point *my dog is not smart* is supported by the statement, *he's six years old and still doesn't answer to his name*. But *he cries when I leave for school* is not supportive, as it does not indicate lack of intelligence. Writers stay on point by presenting only supportive statements that are directly relevant to and illustrative of their main point.

> **Review Video: Sequence**
> Visit mometrix.com/academy and enter code: 489027

TRANSITIONS

Transitions between sentences and paragraphs guide readers from idea to idea and indicate relationships between sentences and paragraphs. Writers should be judicious in their use of transitions, inserting them sparingly. They should also be selected to fit the author's purpose—transitions can indicate time, comparison, and conclusion, among other purposes. Tone is also important to consider when using transitional phrases,

varying the tone for different audiences. For example, in a scholarly essay, *in summary* would be preferable to the more informal *in short*.

When working with transitional words and phrases, writers usually find a natural flow that indicates when a transition is needed. In reading a draft of the text, it should become apparent where the flow is disrupted. At this point, the writer can add transitional elements during the revision process. Revising can also afford an opportunity to delete transitional devices that seem heavy handed or unnecessary.

> **Review Video: Transitions in Writing**
> Visit mometrix.com/academy and enter code: 233246

TYPES OF TRANSITIONAL WORDS

Time	afterward, immediately, earlier, meanwhile, recently, lately, now, since, soon, when, then, until, before, etc.
Sequence	too, first, second, further, moreover, also, again, and, next, still, besides, finally
Comparison	similarly, in the same way, likewise, also, again, once more
Contrasting	but, although, despite, however, instead, nevertheless, on the one hand... on the other hand, regardless, yet, in contrast
Cause and Effect	because, consequently, thus, therefore, then, to this end, since, so, as a result, if... then, accordingly
Examples	for example, for instance, such as, to illustrate, indeed, in fact, specifically
Place	near, far, here, there, to the left/right, next to, above, below, beyond, opposite, beside
Concession	granted that, naturally, of course, it may appear, although it is true that
Repetition, Summary, or Conclusion	as mentioned earlier, as noted, in other words, in short, on the whole, to summarize, therefore, as a result, to conclude, in conclusion
Addition	and, also, furthermore, moreover
Generalization	in broad terms, broadly speaking, in general

> **Review Video: Transition Words**
> Visit mometrix.com/academy and enter code: 707563
>
> **Review Video: How to Effectively Connect Sentences**
> Visit mometrix.com/academy and enter code: 948325

CONCLUSION

Two important principles to consider when writing a conclusion are strength and closure. A strong conclusion gives the reader a sense that the author's main points are meaningful and important, and that the supporting facts and arguments are convincing, solid, and well developed. When a conclusion achieves closure, it gives the impression that the writer has stated all necessary information and points and completed the work, rather than simply stopping after a specified length. Some things to avoid when writing concluding paragraphs include:

- Introducing a completely new idea
- Beginning with obvious or unoriginal phrases like "In conclusion" or "To summarize"
- Apologizing for one's opinions or writing
- Repeating the thesis word for word rather than rephrasing it
- Believing that the conclusion must always summarize the piece

> **Review Video: Drafting Conclusions**
> Visit mometrix.com/academy and enter code: 209408

WRITING STYLE AND FORM

WRITING STYLE AND LINGUISTIC FORM

Linguistic form encodes the literal meanings of words and sentences. It comes from the phonological, morphological, syntactic, and semantic parts of a language. **Writing style** consists of different ways of encoding the meaning and indicating figurative and stylistic meanings. An author's writing style can also be referred to as his or her **voice**.

Writers' stylistic choices accomplish three basic effects on their audiences:

- They **communicate meanings** beyond linguistically dictated meanings,
- They communicate the **author's attitude**, such as persuasive or argumentative effects accomplished through style, and
- They communicate or **express feelings**.

Within style, component areas include:

- Narrative structure
- Viewpoint
- Focus
- Sound patterns
- Meter and rhythm
- Lexical and syntactic repetition and parallelism
- Writing genre
- Representational, realistic, and mimetic effects
- Representation of thought and speech
- Meta-representation (representing representation)
- Irony
- Metaphor and other indirect meanings
- Representation and use of historical and dialectal variations
- Gender-specific and other group-specific speech styles, both real and fictitious
- Analysis of the processes for inferring meaning from writing

LEVEL OF FORMALITY

The relationship between writer and reader is important in choosing a **level of formality** as most writing requires some degree of formality. **Formal writing** is for addressing a superior in a school or work environment. Business letters, textbooks, and newspapers use a moderate to high level of formality. **Informal writing** is appropriate for private letters, personal emails, and business correspondence between close associates.

For your exam, you will want to be aware of informal and formal writing. One way that this can be accomplished is to watch for shifts in point of view in the essay. For example, unless writers are using a personal example, they will rarely refer to themselves (e.g., "*I* think that *my* point is very clear.") to avoid being informal when they need to be formal.

Also, be mindful of an author who addresses his or her audience **directly** in their writing (e.g., "Readers, *like you*, will understand this argument.") as this can be a sign of informal writing. Good writers understand the need to be consistent with their level of formality. Shifts in levels of formality or point of view can confuse readers and cause them to discount the message.

CLICHÉS

Clichés are phrases that have been **overused** to the point that the phrase has no importance or has lost the original meaning. These phrases have no originality and add very little to a passage. Therefore, most writers will avoid the use of clichés. Another option is to make changes to a cliché so that it is not predictable and empty of meaning.

Examples:

When life gives you lemons, make lemonade.

Every cloud has a silver lining.

JARGON

Jargon is **specialized vocabulary** that is used among members of a certain trade or profession. Since jargon is understood by only a small audience, writers will use jargon in passages that will only be read by a specialized audience. For example, medical jargon should be used in a medical journal but not in a New York Times article. Jargon includes exaggerated language that tries to impress rather than inform. Sentences filled with jargon are not precise and are difficult to understand.

Examples:

"He is going to *toenail* these frames for us." (Toenail is construction jargon for nailing at an angle.)

"They brought in a *kip* of material today." (Kip refers to 1000 pounds in architecture and engineering.)

SLANG

Slang is an **informal** and sometimes private language that is understood by some individuals. Slang terms have some usefulness, but they can have a small audience. So, most formal writing will not include this kind of language.

Examples:

"Yes, the event was a blast!" (In this sentence, *blast* means that the event was a great experience.)

"That attempt was an epic fail." (By *epic fail*, the speaker means that his or her attempt was not a success.)

COLLOQUIALISM

A colloquialism is a word or phrase that is found in informal writing. Unlike slang, **colloquial language** will be familiar to a greater range of people. However, colloquialisms are still considered inappropriate for formal writing. Colloquial language can include some slang, but these are limited to contractions for the most part.

Examples:

"Can *y'all* come back another time?" (Y'all is a contraction of "you all.")

"Will you stop him from building this *castle in the air*?" (A "castle in the air" is an improbable or unlikely event.)

ACADEMIC LANGUAGE

In educational settings, students are often expected to use academic language in their schoolwork. Academic language is also commonly found in dissertations and theses, texts published by academic journals, and other forms of academic research. Academic language conventions may vary between fields, but general academic language is free of slang, regional terminology, and noticeable grammatical errors. Specific terms may also be used in academic language, and it is important to understand their proper usage. A writer's command of academic language impacts their ability to communicate in an academic or professional context. While it is acceptable to use colloquialisms, slang, improper grammar, or other forms of informal speech in social settings or at home, it is inappropriate to practice non-academic language in academic contexts.

TONE

Tone may be defined as the writer's **attitude** toward the topic, and to the audience. This attitude is reflected in the language used in the writing. The tone of a work should be **appropriate to the topic** and to the intended audience. While it may be fine to use slang or jargon in some pieces, other texts should not contain such terms. Tone can range from humorous to serious and any level in between. It may be more or less formal, depending on the purpose of the writing and its intended audience. All these nuances in tone can flavor the entire writing and should be kept in mind as the work evolves.

WORD SELECTION

A writer's choice of words is a signature of their style. Careful thought about the use of words can improve a piece of writing. A passage can be an exciting piece to read when attention is given to the use of vivid or specific nouns rather than general ones.

Example:

General: His kindness will never be forgotten.

Specific: His thoughtful gifts and bear hugs will never be forgotten.

Attention should also be given to the kind of verbs that are used in sentences. Active verbs (e.g., run, swim) are about an action. Whenever possible, an **active verb should replace a linking verb** to provide clear examples for arguments and to strengthen a passage overall. When using an active verb, one should be sure that the verb is used in the active voice instead of the passive voice. Verbs are in the active voice when the subject is the one doing the action. A verb is in the passive voice when the subject is the recipient of an action.

Example:

Passive: The winners were called to the stage by the judges.

Active: The judges called the winners to the stage.

CONCISENESS

Conciseness is writing that communicates a message in the fewest words possible. Writing concisely is valuable because short, uncluttered messages allow the reader to understand the author's message more easily and efficiently. Planning is important in writing concise messages. If you have in mind what you need to write beforehand, it will be easier to make a message short and to the point. Do not state the obvious.

Revising is also important. After the message is written, make sure you have effective, pithy sentences that efficiently get your point across. When reviewing the information, imagine a conversation taking place, and concise writing will likely result.

APPROPRIATE KINDS OF WRITING FOR DIFFERENT TASKS, PURPOSES, AND AUDIENCES

When preparing to write a composition, consider the audience and purpose to choose the best type of writing. Four common types of writing are persuasive, expository, and narrative. **Persuasive**, or argumentative writing, is used to convince the audience to take action or agree with the author's claims. **Expository** writing is meant to inform the audience of the author's observations or research on a topic. **Narrative** writing is used to tell the audience a story and often allows more room for creativity. **Descriptive** writing is when a writer provides a substantial amount of detail to the reader so he or she can visualize the topic. While task, purpose, and audience inform a writer's mode of writing, these factors also impact elements such as tone, vocabulary, and formality.

For example, students who are writing to persuade their parents to grant them some additional privilege, such as permission for a more independent activity, should use more sophisticated vocabulary and diction that sounds more mature and serious to appeal to the parental audience. However, students who are writing for younger children should use simpler vocabulary and sentence structure, as well as choose words that are more vivid and entertaining. They should treat their topics more lightly, and include humor when appropriate. Students who are writing for their classmates may use language that is more informal, as well as age-appropriate.

Review Video: **Writing Purpose and Audience**
Visit mometrix.com/academy and enter code: 146627

COMMON TYPES OF WRITING
AUTOBIOGRAPHICAL NARRATIVES

Autobiographical narratives are narratives written by an author about an event or period in their life. Autobiographical narratives are written from one person's perspective, in first person, and often include the author's thoughts and feelings alongside their description of the event or period. Structure, style, or theme varies between different autobiographical narratives, since each narrative is personal and specific to its author and his or her experience.

REFLECTIVE ESSAY

A less common type of essay is the reflective essay. **Reflective essays** allow the author to reflect, or think back, on an experience and analyze what they recall. They should consider what they learned from the experience, what they could have done differently, what would have helped them during the experience, or anything else that they have realized from looking back on the experience. Reflection essays incorporate both objective reflection on one's own actions and subjective explanation of thoughts and feelings. These essays can be written for a number of experiences in a formal or informal context.

JOURNALS AND DIARIES

A **journal** is a personal account of events, experiences, feelings, and thoughts. Many people write journals to express their feelings and thoughts or to help them process experiences they have had. Since journals are **private documents** not meant to be shared with others, writers may not be concerned with grammar, spelling, or other mechanics. However, authors may write journals that they expect or hope to publish someday; in this case, they not only express their thoughts and feelings and process their experiences, but they also attend to their craft in writing them. Some authors compose journals to record a particular time period or a series of related events, such as a cancer diagnosis, treatment, surviving the disease, and how these experiences have changed or affected them. Other experiences someone might include in a journal are recovering from addiction, journeys of spiritual exploration and discovery, time spent in another country, or anything else someone wants to personally document. Journaling can also be therapeutic, as some people use journals to work through feelings of grief over loss or to wrestle with big decisions.

EXAMPLES OF DIARIES IN LITERATURE

The Diary of a Young Girl by Dutch Jew Anne Frank (1947) contains her life-affirming, nonfictional diary entries from 1942-1944 while her family hid in an attic from World War II's genocidal Nazis. *Go Ask Alice* (1971) by Beatrice Sparks is a cautionary, fictional novel in the form of diary entries by Alice, an unhappy, rebellious teen who takes LSD, runs away from home and lives with hippies, and eventually returns home. Frank's writing reveals an intelligent, sensitive, insightful girl, raised by intellectual European parents—a girl who believes in the goodness of human nature despite surrounding atrocities. Alice, influenced by early 1970s counterculture, becomes less optimistic. However, similarities can be found between them: Frank dies in a Nazi concentration camp while the fictitious Alice dies from a drug overdose. Both young women are also unable to escape their surroundings. Additionally, adolescent searches for personal identity are evident in both books.

> **Review Video: Journals, Diaries, Letters, and Blogs**
> Visit mometrix.com/academy and enter code: 432845

LETTERS

Letters are messages written to other people. In addition to letters written between individuals, some writers compose letters to the editors of newspapers, magazines, and other publications, while some write "Open Letters" to be published and read by the general public. Open letters, while intended for everyone to read, may also identify a group of people or a single person whom the letter directly addresses. In everyday use, the most-used forms are business letters and personal or friendly letters. Both kinds share common elements: business or personal letterhead stationery; the writer's return address at the top; the addressee's address next; a salutation, such as "Dear [name]" or some similar opening greeting, followed by a colon in business letters or a comma in personal letters; the body of the letter, with paragraphs as indicated; and a closing, like "Sincerely/Cordially/Best regards/etc." or "Love," in intimate personal letters.

EARLY LETTERS

The Greek word for "letter" is *epistolē*, which became the English word "epistle." The earliest letters were called epistles, including the New Testament's epistles from the apostles to the Christians. In ancient Egypt, the writing curriculum in scribal schools included the epistolary genre. Epistolary novels frame a story in the form of letters. Examples of noteworthy epistolary novels include:

- *Pamela* (1740), by 18th-century English novelist Samuel Richardson
- *Shamela* (1741), Henry Fielding's satire of *Pamela* that mocked epistolary writing.
- *Lettres persanes* (1721) by French author Montesquieu
- *The Sorrows of Young Werther* (1774) by German author Johann Wolfgang von Goethe
- *The History of Emily Montague* (1769), the first Canadian novel, by Frances Brooke
- *Dracula* (1897) by Bram Stoker
- *Frankenstein* (1818) by Mary Shelley
- *The Color Purple* (1982) by Alice Walker

BLOGS

The word "blog" is derived from "weblog" and refers to writing done exclusively on the internet. Readers of reputable newspapers expect quality content and layouts that enable easy reading. These expectations also apply to blogs. For example, readers can easily move visually from line to line when columns are narrow, while overly wide columns cause readers to lose their places. Blogs must also be posted with layouts enabling online readers to follow them easily. However, because the way people read on computer, tablet, and smartphone screens differs from how they read print on paper, formatting and writing blog content is more complex than writing newspaper articles. Two major principles are the bases for blog-writing rules: The first is while readers of print articles skim to estimate their length, online they must scroll down to scan; therefore, blog layouts need more subheadings, graphics, and other indications of what information follows. The second is onscreen reading can be harder on the eyes than reading printed paper, so legibility is crucial in blogs.

RULES AND RATIONALES FOR WRITING BLOGS
1. Format all posts for smooth page layout and easy scanning.
2. Column width should not be too wide, as larger lines of text can be difficult to read
3. Headings and subheadings separate text visually, enable scanning or skimming, and encourage continued reading.
4. Bullet-pointed or numbered lists enable quick information location and scanning.
5. Punctuation is critical, so beginners should use shorter sentences until confident in their knowledge of punctuation rules.

6. Blog paragraphs should be far shorter—two to six sentences each—than paragraphs written on paper to enable "chunking" because reading onscreen is more difficult.
7. Sans-serif fonts are usually clearer than serif fonts, and larger font sizes are better.
8. Highlight important material and draw attention with **boldface**, but avoid overuse. Avoid hard-to-read *italics* and ALL CAPITALS.
9. Include enough blank spaces: overly busy blogs tire eyes and brains. Images not only break up text but also emphasize and enhance text and can attract initial reader attention.
10. Use background colors judiciously to avoid distracting the eye or making it difficult to read.
11. Be consistent throughout posts, since people read them in different orders.
12. Tell a story with a beginning, middle, and end.

SPECIALIZED TYPES OF WRITING

EDITORIALS

Editorials are articles in newspapers, magazines, and other serial publications. Editorials express an opinion or belief belonging to the majority of the publication's leadership. This opinion or belief generally refers to a specific issue, topic, or event. These articles are authored by a member, or a small number of members, of the publication's leadership and are often written to affect their readers, such as persuading them to adopt a stance or take a particular action.

RESUMES

Resumes are brief, but formal, documents that outline an individual's experience in a certain area. Resumes are most often used for job applications. Such resumes will list the applicant's work experience, certification, and achievements or qualifications related to the position. Resumes should only include the most pertinent information. They should also use strategic formatting to highlight the applicant's most impressive experiences and achievements, to ensure the document can be read quickly and easily, and to eliminate both visual clutter and excessive negative space.

REPORTS

Reports summarize the results of research, new methodology, or other developments in an academic or professional context. Reports often include details about methodology and outside influences and factors. However, a report should focus primarily on the results of the research or development. Reports are objective and deliver information efficiently, sacrificing style for clear and effective communication.

MEMORANDA

A memorandum, also called a memo, is a formal method of communication used in professional settings. Memoranda are printed documents that include a heading listing the sender and their job title, the recipient and their job title, the date, and a specific subject line. Memoranda often include an introductory section explaining the reason and context for the memorandum. Next, a memorandum includes a section with details relevant to the topic. Finally, the memorandum will conclude with a paragraph that politely and clearly defines the sender's expectations of the recipient.

PURPOSES FOR WRITING

ESSAYS

Essays usually focus on one topic, subject, or goal. There are several types of essays, including informative, persuasive, and narrative. An essay's structure and level of formality depend on the type of essay and its goal. While narrative essays typically do not include outside sources, other types of essays often require some research and the integration of primary and secondary sources.

The basic format of an essay typically has three major parts: the introduction, the body, and the conclusion. The body is further divided into the writer's main points. Short and simple essays may have three main points, while essays covering broader ranges and going into more depth can have almost any number of main points, depending on length.

An essay's introduction should answer three questions:

1. What is the **subject** of the essay?

   If a student writes an essay about a book, the answer would include the title and author of the book and any additional information needed—such as the subject or argument of the book.

2. How does the essay **address** the subject?

   To answer this, the writer identifies the essay's organization by briefly summarizing main points and the evidence supporting them.

3. What will the essay **prove**?

   This is the thesis statement, usually the opening paragraph's last sentence, clearly stating the writer's message.

The body elaborates on all the main points related to the thesis, introducing one main point at a time, and includes supporting evidence with each main point. Each body paragraph should state the point in a topic sentence, which is usually the first sentence in the paragraph. The paragraph should then explain the point's meaning, support it with quotations or other evidence, and then explain how this point and the evidence are related to the thesis. The writer should then repeat this procedure in a new paragraph for each additional main point.

The conclusion reiterates the content of the introduction, including the thesis, to remind the reader of the essay's main argument or subject. The essay writer may also summarize the highlights of the argument or description contained in the body of the essay, following the same sequence originally used in the body. For example, a conclusion might look like: Point 1 + Point 2 + Point 3 = Thesis, or Point 1 → Point 2 → Point 3 → Thesis Proof. Good organization makes essays easier for writers to compose and provides a guide for readers to follow. Well-organized essays hold attention better and are more likely to get readers to accept their theses as valid.

INFORMATIVE VS. PERSUASIVE WRITING

Informative writing, also called explanatory or expository writing, begins with the basis that something is true or factual, while **persuasive** writing strives to prove something that may or may not be true or factual. Whereas argumentative text is written to **persuade** readers to agree with the author's position, informative text merely **provides information and insight** to readers. Informative writing concentrates on **informing** readers about why or how something is as it is. This can include offering new information, explaining how a process works, and developing a concept for readers. To accomplish these objectives, the essay may name and distinguish various things within a category, provide definitions, provide details about the parts of something, explain a particular function or behavior, and give readers explanations for why a fact, object, event, or process exists or occurs.

NARRATIVE WRITING

Put simply, **narrative** writing tells a story. The most common examples of literary narratives are novels. Non-fictional biographies, autobiographies, memoirs, and histories are also narratives. Narratives should tell stories in such a way that the readers learn something or gain insight or understanding. Students can write more interesting narratives by describing events or experiences that were meaningful to them. Narratives should start with the story's actions or events, rather than long descriptions or introductions. Students should ensure that there is a point to each story by describing what they learned from the experience they narrate. To write an effective description, students should include sensory details, asking themselves what they saw, heard, felt or touched, smelled, and tasted during the experiences they describe. In narrative writing, the details should

be **concrete** rather than **abstract**. Using concrete details enables readers to imagine everything that the writer describes.

> **Review Video: <u>Narratives</u>**
> Visit mometrix.com/academy and enter code: 280100

SENSORY DETAILS

Writers need to use vivid descriptions when writing descriptive essays. Narratives should also include descriptions of characters, things, and events. Students should remember to describe not only the visual detail of what someone or something looks like, but details from other senses, as well. For example, they can contrast the feeling of a sea breeze to that of a mountain breeze, describe how they think something inedible would taste, and compare sounds they hear in the same location at different times of day and night. Readers have trouble visualizing images or imagining sensory impressions and feelings from abstract descriptions, so concrete descriptions make these more real.

CONCRETE VS. ABSTRACT DESCRIPTIONS IN NARRATIVE

Concrete language provides information that readers can grasp and may empathize with, while **abstract language**, which is more general, can leave readers feeling disconnected, empty, or even confused. "It was a lovely day" is abstract, but "The sun shone brightly, the sky was blue, the air felt warm, and a gentle breeze wafted across my skin" is concrete. "Ms. Couch was a good teacher" uses abstract language, giving only a general idea of the writer's opinion. But "Ms. Couch is excellent at helping us take our ideas and turn them into good essays and stories" uses concrete language, giving more specific examples of what makes Ms. Couch a good teacher. "I like writing poems but not essays" gives readers a general idea that the student prefers one genre over another, but not why. But when reading, "I like writing short poems with rhythm and rhyme, but I hate writing five-page essays that go on and on about the same ideas," readers understand that the student prefers the brevity, rhyme, and meter of short poetry over the length and redundancy of longer prose.

Chapter Quiz

Ready to see how well you retained what you just read? Scan the QR code to go directly to the chapter quiz interface for this study guide. If you're using a computer, simply visit the bonus page at **<u>mometrix.com/bonus948/praxcore</u>** and click the Chapter Quizzes link.

111

Mathematics

Number and Quantity

NUMBER BASICS

CLASSIFICATIONS OF NUMBERS

Numbers are the basic building blocks of mathematics. Specific features of numbers are identified by the following terms:

Integer – any positive or negative whole number, including zero. Integers do not include fractions $\left(\frac{1}{3}\right)$, decimals (0.56), or mixed numbers $\left(7\frac{3}{4}\right)$.

Prime number – any whole number greater than 1 that has only two factors, itself and 1; that is, a number that can be divided evenly only by 1 and itself.

Composite number – any whole number greater than 1 that has more than two different factors; in other words, any whole number that is not a prime number. For example: The composite number 8 has the factors of 1, 2, 4, and 8.

Even number – any integer that can be divided by 2 without leaving a remainder. For example: 2, 4, 6, 8, and so on.

Odd number – any integer that cannot be divided evenly by 2. For example: 3, 5, 7, 9, and so on.

Decimal number – any number that uses a decimal point to show the part of the number that is less than one. Example: 1.234.

Decimal point – a symbol used to separate the ones place from the tenths place in decimals or dollars from cents in currency.

Decimal place – the position of a number to the right of the decimal point. In the decimal 0.123, the 1 is in the first place to the right of the decimal point, indicating tenths; the 2 is in the second place, indicating hundredths; and the 3 is in the third place, indicating thousandths.

The **decimal**, or base 10, system is a number system that uses ten different digits (0, 1, 2, 3, 4, 5, 6, 7, 8, 9). An example of a number system that uses something other than ten digits is the **binary**, or base 2, number system, used by computers, which uses only the numbers 0 and 1. It is thought that the decimal system originated because people had only their 10 fingers for counting.

Rational numbers include all integers, decimals, and fractions. Any terminating or repeating decimal number is a rational number.

Irrational numbers cannot be written as fractions or decimals because the number of decimal places is infinite and there is no recurring pattern of digits within the number. For example, pi (π) begins with 3.141592 and continues without terminating or repeating, so pi is an irrational number.

Real numbers are the set of all rational and irrational numbers.

> **Review Video: Classification of Numbers**
> Visit mometrix.com/academy and enter code: 461071
>
> **Review Video: Prime and Composite Numbers**
> Visit mometrix.com/academy and enter code: 565581

NUMBERS IN WORD FORM AND PLACE VALUE

When writing numbers out in word form or translating word form to numbers, it is essential to understand how a place value system works. In the decimal or base-10 system, each digit of a number represents how many of the corresponding place value—a specific factor of 10—are contained in the number being represented. To make reading numbers easier, every three digits to the left of the decimal place is preceded by a comma. The following table demonstrates some of the place values:

Power of 10	10^3	10^2	10^1	10^0	10^{-1}	10^{-2}	10^{-3}
Value	1,000	100	10	1	0.1	0.01	0.001
Place	thousands	hundreds	tens	ones	tenths	hundredths	thousandths

For example, consider the number 4,546.09, which can be separated into each place value like this:

4: thousands
5: hundreds
4: tens
6: ones
0: tenths
9: hundredths

This number in word form would be *four thousand five hundred forty-six and nine hundredths.*

> **Review Video: Place Value**
> Visit mometrix.com/academy and enter code: 205433

RATIONAL NUMBERS

The term **rational** means that the number can be expressed as a ratio or fraction. That is, a number, r, is rational if and only if it can be represented by a fraction $\frac{a}{b}$ where a and b are integers and b does not equal 0. The set of rational numbers includes integers and decimals. If there is no finite way to represent a value with a fraction of integers, then the number is **irrational**. Common examples of irrational numbers include: $\sqrt{5}$, $\left(1 + \sqrt{2}\right)$, and π.

> **Review Video: Rational and Irrational Numbers**
> Visit mometrix.com/academy and enter code: 280645
>
> **Review Video: Ordering Rational Numbers**
> Visit mometrix.com/academy and enter code: 419578

NUMBER LINES

A number line is a graph to see the distance between numbers. Basically, this graph shows the relationship between numbers. So a number line may have a point for zero and may show negative numbers on the left side of the line. Any positive numbers are placed on the right side of the line. For example, consider the points labeled on the following number line:

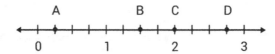

We can use the dashed lines on the number line to identify each point. Each dashed line between two whole numbers is $\frac{1}{4}$. The line halfway between two numbers is $\frac{1}{2}$.

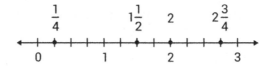

| Review Video: **The Number Line** |
| Visit mometrix.com/academy and enter code: 816439 |

ABSOLUTE VALUE

A precursor to working with negative numbers is understanding what **absolute values** are. A number's absolute value is simply the distance away from zero a number is on the number line. The absolute value of a number is always positive and is written $|x|$. For example, the absolute value of 3, written as $|3|$, is 3 because the distance between 0 and 3 on a number line is three units. Likewise, the absolute value of –3, written as $|-3|$, is 3 because the distance between 0 and –3 on a number line is three units. So $|3| = |-3|$.

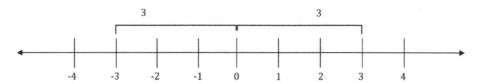

| Review Video: **Absolute Value** |
| Visit mometrix.com/academy and enter code: 314669 |

OPERATIONS

An **operation** is simply a mathematical process that takes some value(s) as input(s) and produces an output. Elementary operations are often written in the following form: *value operation value*. For instance, in the expression $1 + 2$ the values are 1 and 2 and the operation is addition. Performing the operation gives the output of 3. In this way we can say that $1 + 2$ and 3 are equal, or $1 + 2 = 3$.

ADDITION

Addition increases the value of one quantity by the value of another quantity (both called **addends**). Example: $2 + 4 = 6$ or $8 + 9 = 17$. The result is called the **sum**. With addition, the order does not matter, $4 + 2 = 2 + 4$.

When adding signed numbers, if the signs are the same simply add the absolute values of the addends and apply the original sign to the sum. For example, $(+4) + (+8) = +12$ and $(-4) + (-8) = -12$. When the original signs are different, take the absolute values of the addends and subtract the smaller value from the larger value, then apply the original sign of the larger value to the difference. Example: $(+4) + (-8) = -4$ and $(-4) + (+8) = +4$.

SUBTRACTION

Subtraction is the opposite operation to addition; it decreases the value of one quantity (the **minuend**) by the value of another quantity (the **subtrahend**). For example, $6 - 4 = 2$ or $17 - 8 = 9$. The result is called the **difference**. Note that with subtraction, the order does matter, $6 - 4 \neq 4 - 6$.

For subtracting signed numbers, change the sign of the subtrahend and then follow the same rules used for addition. Example: $(+4) - (+8) = (+4) + (-8) = -4$

MULTIPLICATION

Multiplication can be thought of as repeated addition. One number (the **multiplier**) indicates how many times to add the other number (the **multiplicand**) to itself. Example: $3 \times 2 = 2 + 2 + 2 = 6$. With multiplication, the order does not matter, $2 \times 3 = 3 \times 2$ or $3 + 3 = 2 + 2 + 2$, either way the result (the **product**) is the same.

If the signs are the same, the product is positive when multiplying signed numbers. Example: $(+4) \times (+8) = +32$ and $(-4) \times (-8) = +32$. If the signs are opposite, the product is negative. Example: $(+4) \times (-8) = -32$ and $(-4) \times (+8) = -32$. When more than two factors are multiplied together, the sign of the product is determined by how many negative factors are present. If there are an odd number of negative factors then the product is negative, whereas an even number of negative factors indicates a positive product. Example: $(+4) \times (-8) \times (-2) = +64$ and $(-4) \times (-8) \times (-2) = -64$.

DIVISION

Division is the opposite operation to multiplication; one number (the **divisor**) tells us how many parts to divide the other number (the **dividend**) into. The result of division is called the **quotient**. Example: $20 \div 4 = 5$. If 20 is split into 4 equal parts, each part is 5. With division, the order of the numbers does matter, $20 \div 4 \neq 4 \div 20$.

The rules for dividing signed numbers are similar to multiplying signed numbers. If the dividend and divisor have the same sign, the quotient is positive. If the dividend and divisor have opposite signs, the quotient is negative. Example: $(-4) \div (+8) = -0.5$.

> **Review Video: Mathematical Operations**
> Visit mometrix.com/academy and enter code: 208095

PARENTHESES

Parentheses are used to designate which operations should be done first when there are multiple operations. Example: $4 - (2 + 1) = 1$; the parentheses tell us that we must add 2 and 1, and then subtract the sum from 4, rather than subtracting 2 from 4 and then adding 1 (this would give us an answer of 3).

> **Review Video: Mathematical Parentheses**
> Visit mometrix.com/academy and enter code: 978600

EXPONENTS

An **exponent** is a superscript number placed next to another number at the top right. It indicates how many times the base number is to be multiplied by itself. Exponents provide a shorthand way to write what would be a longer mathematical expression, Example: $2^4 = 2 \times 2 \times 2 \times 2$. A number with an exponent of 2 is said to be "squared," while a number with an exponent of 3 is said to be "cubed." The value of a number raised to an exponent is called its power. So 8^4 is read as "8 to the 4th power," or "8 raised to the power of 4."

ROOTS

A **root**, such as a square root, is another way of writing a fractional exponent. Instead of using a superscript, roots use the radical symbol ($\sqrt{\ }$) to indicate the operation. A radical will have a number underneath the bar, and may sometimes have a number in the upper left: $\sqrt[n]{a}$, read as "the nth root of a." The relationship between radical notation and exponent notation can be described by this equation:

$$\sqrt[n]{a} = a^{\frac{1}{n}}$$

The two special cases of $n = 2$ and $n = 3$ are called square roots and cube roots. If there is no number to the upper left, the radical is understood to be a square root ($n = 2$). Nearly all of the roots you encounter will be square roots. A square root is the same as a number raised to the one-half power. When we say that a is the square root of b ($a = \sqrt{b}$), we mean that a multiplied by itself equals b: ($a \times a = b$).

A **perfect square** is a number that has an integer for its square root. There are 10 perfect squares from 1 to 100: 1, 4, 9, 16, 25, 36, 49, 64, 81, 100 (the squares of integers 1 through 10).

WORD PROBLEMS AND MATHEMATICAL SYMBOLS

When working on word problems, you must be able to translate verbal expressions or "math words" into math symbols. This chart contains several "math words" and their appropriate symbols:

Phrase	Symbol
equal, is, was, will be, has, costs, gets to, is the same as, becomes	=
times, of, multiplied by, product of, twice, doubles, halves, triples	×
divided by, per, ratio of/to, out of	÷
plus, added to, sum, combined, and, more than, totals of	+
subtracted from, less than, decreased by, minus, difference between	−
what, how much, original value, how many, a number, a variable	x, n, etc.

EXAMPLES OF TRANSLATED MATHEMATICAL PHRASES

- The phrase four more than twice a number can be written algebraically as $2x + 4$.
- The phrase half a number decreased by six can be written algebraically as $\frac{1}{2}x - 6$.
- The phrase the sum of a number and the product of five and that number can be written algebraically as $x + 5x$.
- You may see a test question that says, "Olivia is constructing a bookcase from seven boards. Two of them are for vertical supports and five are for shelves. The height of the bookcase is twice the width of the bookcase. If the seven boards total 36 feet in length, what will be the height of Olivia's bookcase?" You would need to make a sketch and then create the equation to determine the width of the shelves. The height can be represented as double the width. (If x represents the width of the shelves in feet, then the height of the bookcase is $2x$. Since the seven boards total 36 feet, $2x + 2x + x + x + x + x + x = 36$ or $9x = 36$; $x = 4$. The height is twice the width, or 8 feet.)

SUBTRACTION WITH REGROUPING

A great way to make use of some of the features built into the decimal system would be regrouping when attempting longform subtraction operations. When subtracting within a place value, sometimes the minuend is smaller than the subtrahend, **regrouping** enables you to 'borrow' a unit from a place value to the left in order to get a positive difference. For example, consider subtracting 189 from 525 with regrouping.

First, set up the subtraction problem in vertical form:

```
    525
  − 189
```

Notice that the numbers in the ones and tens columns of 525 are smaller than the numbers in the ones and tens columns of 189. This means you will need to use regrouping to perform subtraction:

```
     5    2    5
  −  1    8    9
```

To subtract 9 from 5 in the ones column you will need to borrow from the 2 in the tens columns:

```
     5    1   15
  −  1    8    9
                6
```

Next, to subtract 8 from 1 in the tens column you will need to borrow from the 5 in the hundreds column:

```
     4   11   15
  −  1    8    9
          3    6
```

Last, subtract the 1 from the 4 in the hundreds column:

```
     4   11   15
  −  1    8    9
     3    3    6
```

> **Review Video: Subtracting Large Numbers**
> Visit mometrix.com/academy and enter code: 603350

ORDER OF OPERATIONS

The **order of operations** is a set of rules that dictates the order in which we must perform each operation in an expression so that we will evaluate it accurately. If we have an expression that includes multiple different operations, the order of operations tells us which operations to do first. The most common mnemonic for the order of operations is **PEMDAS**, or "Please Excuse My Dear Aunt Sally." PEMDAS stands for parentheses, exponents, multiplication, division, addition, and subtraction. It is important to understand that multiplication and division have equal precedence, as do addition and subtraction, so those pairs of operations are simply worked from left to right in order.

For example, evaluating the expression $5 + 20 \div 4 \times (2 + 3)^2 - 6$ using the correct order of operations would be done like this:

- **P:** Perform the operations inside the parentheses: $(2 + 3) = 5$
- **E:** Simplify the exponents: $(5)^2 = 5 \times 5 = 25$
  - ○ The expression now looks like this: $5 + 20 \div 4 \times 25 - 6$
- **MD:** Perform multiplication and division from left to right: $20 \div 4 = 5$; then $5 \times 25 = 125$
  - ○ The expression now looks like this: $5 + 125 - 6$
- **AS:** Perform addition and subtraction from left to right: $5 + 125 = 130$; then $130 - 6 = 124$

> **Review Video: Order of Operations**
> Visit mometrix.com/academy and enter code: 259675

PROPERTIES OF EXPONENTS

The properties of exponents are as follows:

Property	Description
$a^1 = a$	Any number to the power of 1 is equal to itself
$1^n = 1$	The number 1 raised to any power is equal to 1
$a^0 = 1$	Any number raised to the power of 0 is equal to 1
$a^n \times a^m = a^{n+m}$	Add exponents to multiply powers of the same base number
$a^n \div a^m = a^{n-m}$	Subtract exponents to divide powers of the same base number
$(a^n)^m = a^{n \times m}$	When a power is raised to a power, the exponents are multiplied
$(a \times b)^n = a^n \times b^n$ $(a \div b)^n = a^n \div b^n$	Multiplication and division operations inside parentheses can be raised to a power. This is the same as each term being raised to that power.
$a^{-n} = \dfrac{1}{a^n}$	A negative exponent is the same as the reciprocal of a positive exponent

Note that exponents do not have to be integers. Fractional or decimal exponents follow all the rules above as well. Example: $5^{\frac{1}{4}} \times 5^{\frac{3}{4}} = 5^{\frac{1}{4}+\frac{3}{4}} = 5^1 = 5$.

> **Review Video: Properties of Exponents**
> Visit mometrix.com/academy and enter code: 532558

FACTORS AND MULTIPLES

FACTORS AND GREATEST COMMON FACTOR

Factors are numbers that are multiplied together to obtain a **product**. For example, in the equation $2 \times 3 = 6$, the numbers 2 and 3 are factors. A **prime number** has only two factors (1 and itself), but other numbers can have many factors.

A **common factor** is a number that divides exactly into two or more other numbers. For example, the factors of 12 are 1, 2, 3, 4, 6, and 12, while the factors of 15 are 1, 3, 5, and 15. The common factors of 12 and 15 are 1 and 3.

A **prime factor** is also a prime number. Therefore, the prime factors of 12 are 2 and 3. For 15, the prime factors are 3 and 5.

The **greatest common factor** (**GCF**) is the largest number that is a factor of two or more numbers. For example, the factors of 15 are 1, 3, 5, and 15; the factors of 35 are 1, 5, 7, and 35. Therefore, the greatest common factor of 15 and 35 is 5.

> **Review Video: Factors**
> Visit mometrix.com/academy and enter code: 920086
>
> **Review Video: Prime Numbers and Factorization**
> Visit mometrix.com/academy and enter code: 760669
>
> **Review Video: Greatest Common Factor and Least Common Multiple**
> Visit mometrix.com/academy and enter code: 838699

MULTIPLES AND LEAST COMMON MULTIPLE

Often listed out in multiplication tables, **multiples** are integer increments of a given factor. In other words, dividing a multiple by the factor will result in an integer. For example, the multiples of 7 include: $1 \times 7 = 7$, $2 \times 7 = 14$, $3 \times 7 = 21$, $4 \times 7 = 28$, $5 \times 7 = 35$. Dividing 7, 14, 21, 28, or 35 by 7 will result in the integers 1, 2, 3, 4, and 5, respectively.

The **least common multiple** (**LCM**) is the smallest number that is a multiple of two or more numbers. For example, the multiples of 3 include 3, 6, 9, 12, 15, etc.; the multiples of 5 include 5, 10, 15, 20, etc. Therefore, the least common multiple of 3 and 5 is 15.

> **Review Video: Multiples**
> Visit mometrix.com/academy and enter code: 626738

FRACTIONS, DECIMALS, AND PERCENTAGES
FRACTIONS

A **fraction** is a number that is expressed as one integer written above another integer, with a dividing line between them $\left(\frac{x}{y}\right)$. It represents the **quotient** of the two numbers "x divided by y." It can also be thought of as x out of y equal parts.

The top number of a fraction is called the **numerator**, and it represents the number of parts under consideration. The 1 in $\frac{1}{4}$ means that 1 part out of the whole is being considered in the calculation. The bottom number of a fraction is called the **denominator**, and it represents the total number of equal parts. The 4 in $\frac{1}{4}$ means that the whole consists of 4 equal parts. A fraction cannot have a denominator of zero; this is referred to as "*undefined*."

Fractions can be manipulated, without changing the value of the fraction, by multiplying or dividing (but not adding or subtracting) both the numerator and denominator by the same number. If you divide both numbers by a common factor, you are **reducing** or simplifying the fraction. Two fractions that have the same value but are expressed differently are known as **equivalent fractions**. For example, $\frac{2}{10}, \frac{3}{15}, \frac{4}{20}$, and $\frac{5}{25}$ are all equivalent fractions. They can also all be reduced or simplified to $\frac{1}{5}$.

When two fractions are manipulated so that they have the same denominator, this is known as finding a **common denominator**. The number chosen to be that common denominator should be the least common multiple of the two original denominators. Example: $\frac{3}{4}$ and $\frac{5}{6}$; the least common multiple of 4 and 6 is 12. Manipulating to achieve the common denominator: $\frac{3}{4} = \frac{9}{12}$; $\frac{5}{6} = \frac{10}{12}$.

> **Review Video: <u>Overview of Fractions</u>**
> Visit mometrix.com/academy and enter code: 262335

PROPER FRACTIONS AND MIXED NUMBERS

A fraction whose denominator is greater than its numerator is known as a **proper fraction**, while a fraction whose numerator is greater than its denominator is known as an **improper fraction**. Proper fractions have values *less than one* and improper fractions have values *greater than one*.

A **mixed number** is a number that contains both an integer and a fraction. Any improper fraction can be rewritten as a mixed number. Example: $\frac{8}{3} = \frac{6}{3} + \frac{2}{3} = 2 + \frac{2}{3} = 2\frac{2}{3}$. Similarly, any mixed number can be rewritten as an improper fraction. Example: $1\frac{3}{5} = 1 + \frac{3}{5} = \frac{5}{5} + \frac{3}{5} = \frac{8}{5}$.

> **Review Video: <u>Proper and Improper Fractions and Mixed Numbers</u>**
> Visit mometrix.com/academy and enter code: 211077

ADDING AND SUBTRACTING FRACTIONS

If two fractions have a common denominator, they can be added or subtracted simply by adding or subtracting the two numerators and retaining the same denominator. If the two fractions do not already have the same denominator, one or both of them must be manipulated to achieve a common denominator before they can be added or subtracted. Example: $\frac{1}{2} + \frac{1}{4} = \frac{2}{4} + \frac{1}{4} = \frac{3}{4}$.

> **Review Video: <u>Adding and Subtracting Fractions</u>**
> Visit mometrix.com/academy and enter code: 378080

MULTIPLYING FRACTIONS

Two fractions can be multiplied by multiplying the two numerators to find the new numerator and the two denominators to find the new denominator. Example: $\frac{1}{3} \times \frac{2}{3} = \frac{1 \times 2}{3 \times 3} = \frac{2}{9}$.

DIVIDING FRACTIONS

Two fractions can be divided by flipping the numerator and denominator of the second fraction and then proceeding as though it were a multiplication problem. Example: $\frac{2}{3} \div \frac{3}{4} = \frac{2}{3} \times \frac{4}{3} = \frac{8}{9}$.

> **Review Video: <u>Multiplying and Dividing Fractions</u>**
> Visit mometrix.com/academy and enter code: 473632

MULTIPLYING A MIXED NUMBER BY A WHOLE NUMBER OR A DECIMAL

When multiplying a mixed number by something, it is usually best to convert it to an improper fraction first. Additionally, if the multiplicand is a decimal, it is most often simplest to convert it to a fraction. For instance, to multiply $4\frac{3}{8}$ by 3.5, begin by rewriting each quantity as a whole number plus a proper fraction. Remember, a mixed number is a fraction added to a whole number and a decimal is a representation of the sum of fractions, specifically tenths, hundredths, thousandths, and so on:

$$4\frac{3}{8} \times 3.5 = \left(4 + \frac{3}{8}\right) \times \left(3 + \frac{1}{2}\right)$$

Next, the quantities being added need to be expressed with the same denominator. This is achieved by multiplying and dividing the whole number by the denominator of the fraction. Recall that a whole number is equivalent to that number divided by 1:

$$= \left(\frac{4}{1} \times \frac{8}{8} + \frac{3}{8}\right) \times \left(\frac{3}{1} \times \frac{2}{2} + \frac{1}{2}\right)$$

When multiplying fractions, remember to multiply the numerators and denominators separately:

$$= \left(\frac{4 \times 8}{1 \times 8} + \frac{3}{8}\right) \times \left(\frac{3 \times 2}{1 \times 2} + \frac{1}{2}\right)$$
$$= \left(\frac{32}{8} + \frac{3}{8}\right) \times \left(\frac{6}{2} + \frac{1}{2}\right)$$

Now that the fractions have the same denominators, they can be added:

$$= \frac{35}{8} \times \frac{7}{2}$$

Finally, perform the last multiplication and then simplify:

$$= \frac{35 \times 7}{8 \times 2} = \frac{245}{16} = \frac{240}{16} + \frac{5}{16} = 15\frac{5}{16}$$

COMPARING FRACTIONS

It is important to master the ability to compare and order fractions. This skill is relevant to many real-world scenarios. For example, carpenters often compare fractional construction nail lengths when preparing for a project, and bakers often compare fractional measurements to have the correct ratio of ingredients. There are three commonly used strategies when comparing fractions. These strategies are referred to as the common denominator approach, the decimal approach, and the cross-multiplication approach.

USING A COMMON DENOMINATOR TO COMPARE FRACTIONS

The fractions $\frac{2}{3}$ and $\frac{4}{7}$ have different denominators. $\frac{2}{3}$ has a denominator of 3, and $\frac{4}{7}$ has a denominator of 7. In order to precisely compare these two fractions, it is necessary to use a common denominator. A common denominator is a common multiple that is shared by both denominators. In this case, the denominators 3 and 7 share a multiple of 21. In general, it is most efficient to select the least common multiple for the two denominators.

Rewrite each fraction with the common denominator of 21. Then, calculate the new numerators as illustrated below.

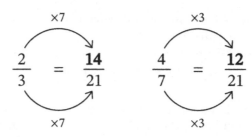

For $\frac{2}{3}$, multiply the numerator and denominator by 7. The result is $\frac{14}{21}$.

For $\frac{4}{7}$, multiply the numerator and denominator by 3. The result is $\frac{12}{21}$.

Now that both fractions have a denominator of 21, the fractions can accurately be compared by comparing the numerators. Since 14 is greater than 12, the fraction $\frac{14}{21}$ is greater than $\frac{12}{21}$. This means that $\frac{2}{3}$ is greater than $\frac{4}{7}$.

USING DECIMALS TO COMPARE FRACTIONS

Sometimes decimal values are easier to compare than fraction values. For example, $\frac{5}{8}$ is equivalent to 0.625 and $\frac{3}{5}$ is equivalent to 0.6. This means that the comparison of $\frac{5}{8}$ and $\frac{3}{5}$ can be determined by comparing the decimals 0.625 and 0.6. When both decimal values are extended to the thousandths place, they become 0.625 and 0.600, respectively. It becomes clear that 0.625 is greater than 0.600 because 625 thousandths is greater than 600 thousandths. In other words, $\frac{5}{8}$ is greater than $\frac{3}{5}$ because 0.625 is greater than 0.6.

USING CROSS-MULTIPLICATION TO COMPARE FRACTIONS

Cross-multiplication is an efficient strategy for comparing fractions. This is a shortcut for the common denominator strategy. Start by writing each fraction next to one another. Multiply the numerator of the fraction on the left by the denominator of the fraction on the right. Write down the result next to the fraction on the left. Now multiply the numerator of the fraction on the right by the denominator of the fraction on the left. Write down the result next to the fraction on the right. Compare both products. The fraction with the larger result is the larger fraction.

Consider the fractions $\frac{4}{7}$ and $\frac{5}{9}$.

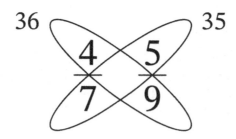

36 is greater than 35. Therefore, $\frac{4}{7}$ is greater than $\frac{5}{9}$.

DECIMALS

Decimals are one way to represent parts of a whole. Using the place value system, each digit to the right of a decimal point denotes the number of units of a corresponding *negative* power of ten. For example, consider the decimal 0.24. We can use a model to represent the decimal. Since a dime is worth one-tenth of a dollar and a penny is worth one-hundredth of a dollar, one possible model to represent this fraction is to have 2 dimes representing the 2 in the tenths place and 4 pennies representing the 4 in the hundredths place:

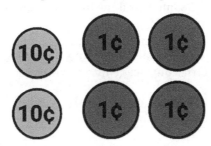

To write the decimal as a fraction, put the decimal in the numerator with 1 in the denominator. Multiply the numerator and denominator by tens until there are no more decimal places. Then simplify the fraction to lowest terms. For example, converting 0.24 to a fraction:

$$0.24 = \frac{0.24}{1} = \frac{0.24 \times 100}{1 \times 100} = \frac{24}{100} = \frac{6}{25}$$

> **Review Video: <u>Decimals</u>**
> Visit mometrix.com/academy and enter code: 837268

OPERATIONS WITH DECIMALS

ADDING AND SUBTRACTING DECIMALS

When adding and subtracting decimals, the decimal points must always be aligned. Adding decimals is just like adding regular whole numbers. Example: $4.5 + 2.0 = 6.5$.

If the problem-solver does not properly align the decimal points, an incorrect answer of 4.7 may result. An easy way to add decimals is to align all of the decimal points in a vertical column visually. This will allow you to see exactly where the decimal should be placed in the final answer. Begin adding from right to left. Add each column in turn, making sure to carry the number to the left if a column adds up to more than 9. The same rules apply to the subtraction of decimals.

> **Review Video: <u>Adding and Subtracting Decimals</u>**
> Visit mometrix.com/academy and enter code: 381101

MULTIPLYING DECIMALS

A simple multiplication problem has two components: a **multiplicand** and a **multiplier**. When multiplying decimals, work as though the numbers were whole rather than decimals. Once the final product is calculated, count the number of places to the right of the decimal in both the multiplicand and the multiplier. Then, count that number of places from the right of the product and place the decimal in that position.

For example, 12.3×2.56 has a total of three places to the right of the respective decimals. Multiply 123×256 to get 31,488. Now, beginning on the right, count three places to the left and insert the decimal. The final product will be 31.488.

> **Review Video: <u>How to Multiply Decimals</u>**
> Visit mometrix.com/academy and enter code: 731574

DIVIDING DECIMALS

Every division problem has a **divisor** and a **dividend**. The dividend is the number that is being divided. In the problem $14 \div 7$, 14 is the dividend and 7 is the divisor. In a division problem with decimals, the divisor must be converted into a whole number. Begin by moving the decimal in the divisor to the right until a whole number is created. Next, move the decimal in the dividend the same number of spaces to the right. For example, 4.9 into 24.5 would become 49 into 245. The decimal was moved one space to the right to create a whole number in the divisor, and then the same was done for the dividend. Once the whole numbers are created, the problem is carried out normally: $245 \div 49 = 5$.

PERCENTAGES

Percentages can be thought of as fractions that are based on a whole of 100; that is, one whole is equal to 100%. The word **percent** means "per hundred." Percentage problems are often presented in three main ways:

- Find what percentage of some number another number is.
  - Example: What percentage of 40 is 8?
- Find what number is some percentage of a given number.
  - Example: What number is 20% of 40?
- Find what number another number is a given percentage of.
  - Example: What number is 8 20% of?

There are three components in each of these cases: a **whole** (W), a **part** (P), and a **percentage** (%). These are related by the equation: $P = W \times \%$. This can easily be rearranged into other forms that may suit different questions better: $\% = \frac{P}{W}$ and $W = \frac{P}{\%}$. Percentage problems are often also word problems. As such, a large part of solving them is figuring out which quantities are what. For example, consider the following word problem:

In a school cafeteria, 7 students choose pizza, 9 choose hamburgers, and 4 choose tacos. What percentage of student choose tacos?

To find the whole, you must first add all of the parts: $7 + 9 + 4 = 20$. The percentage can then be found by dividing the part by the whole $\left(\% = \frac{P}{W}\right)$: $\frac{4}{20} = \frac{20}{100} = 20\%$.

CONVERTING BETWEEN PERCENTAGES, FRACTIONS, AND DECIMALS

Converting decimals to percentages and percentages to decimals is as simple as moving the decimal point. To *convert from a decimal to a percentage*, move the decimal point **two places to the right**. To *convert from a percentage to a decimal*, move it **two places to the left**. It may be helpful to remember that the percentage number will always be larger than the equivalent decimal number. Example:

$$0.23 = 23\% \quad 5.34 = 534\% \quad 0.007 = 0.7\%$$
$$700\% = 7.00 \quad 86\% = 0.86 \quad 0.15\% = 0.0015$$

To convert a fraction to a decimal, simply divide the numerator by the denominator in the fraction. To convert a decimal to a fraction, put the decimal in the numerator with 1 in the denominator. Multiply the numerator and denominator by tens until there are no more decimal places. Then simplify the fraction to lowest terms. For example, converting 0.24 to a fraction:

$$0.24 = \frac{0.24}{1} = \frac{0.24 \times 100}{1 \times 100} = \frac{24}{100} = \frac{6}{25}$$

Fractions can be converted to a percentage by finding equivalent fractions with a denominator of 100. Example:

$$\frac{7}{10} = \frac{70}{100} = 70\% \quad \frac{1}{4} = \frac{25}{100} = 25\%$$

To convert a percentage to a fraction, divide the percentage number by 100 and reduce the fraction to its simplest possible terms. Example:

$$60\% = \frac{60}{100} = \frac{3}{5} \quad 96\% = \frac{96}{100} = \frac{24}{25}$$

Review Video: Converting Fractions to Percentages and Decimals
Visit mometrix.com/academy and enter code: 306233

Review Video: Converting Percentages to Decimals and Fractions
Visit mometrix.com/academy and enter code: 287297

Review Video: Converting Decimals to Fractions and Percentages
Visit mometrix.com/academy and enter code: 986765

Review Video: Converting Decimals, Improper Fractions, and Mixed Numbers
Visit mometrix.com/academy and enter code: 696924

PROPORTIONS AND RATIOS

PROPORTIONS

A proportion is a relationship between two quantities that dictates how one changes when the other changes. A **direct proportion** describes a relationship in which a quantity increases by a set amount for every increase in the other quantity, or decreases by that same amount for every decrease in the other quantity. Example: Assuming a constant driving speed, the time required for a car trip increases as the distance of the trip increases. The distance to be traveled and the time required to travel are directly proportional.

An **inverse proportion** is a relationship in which an increase in one quantity is accompanied by a decrease in the other, or vice versa. Example: the time required for a car trip decreases as the speed increases and increases as the speed decreases, so the time required is inversely proportional to the speed of the car.

Review Video: Proportions
Visit mometrix.com/academy and enter code: 505355

RATIOS

A **ratio** is a comparison of two quantities in a particular order. Example: If there are 14 computers in a lab, and the class has 20 students, there is a student to computer ratio of 20 to 14, commonly written as 20: 14. Ratios

125

are normally reduced to their smallest whole number representation, so $20:14$ would be reduced to $10:7$ by dividing both sides by 2.

CONSTANT OF PROPORTIONALITY

When two quantities have a proportional relationship, there exists a **constant of proportionality** between the quantities. The product of this constant and one of the quantities is equal to the other quantity. For example, if one lemon costs $0.25, two lemons cost $0.50, and three lemons cost $0.75, there is a proportional relationship between the total cost of lemons and the number of lemons purchased. The constant of proportionality is the **unit price**, namely $0.25/lemon. Notice that the total price of lemons, t, can be found by multiplying the unit price of lemons, p, and the number of lemons, n: $t = pn$.

WORK/UNIT RATE

Unit rate expresses a quantity of one thing in terms of one unit of another. For example, if you travel 30 miles every two hours, a unit rate expresses this comparison in terms of one hour: in one hour you travel 15 miles, so your unit rate is 15 miles per hour. Other examples are how much one ounce of food costs (price per ounce) or figuring out how much one egg costs out of the dozen (price per 1 egg, instead of price per 12 eggs). The denominator of a unit rate is always 1. Unit rates are used to compare different situations to solve problems. For example, to make sure you get the best deal when deciding which kind of soda to buy, you can find the unit rate of each. If soda #1 costs $1.50 for a 1-liter bottle, and soda #2 costs $2.75 for a 2-liter bottle, it would be a better deal to buy soda #2, because its unit rate is only $1.375 per 1-liter, which is cheaper than soda #1. Unit rates can also help determine the length of time a given event will take. For example, if you can paint 2 rooms in 4.5 hours, you can determine how long it will take you to paint 5 rooms by solving for the unit rate per room and then multiplying that by 5.

SLOPE

On a graph with two points, (x_1, y_1) and (x_2, y_2), the **slope** is found with the formula $m = \frac{y_2 - y_1}{x_2 - x_1}$; where $x_1 \neq x_2$ and m stands for slope. If the value of the slope is **positive**, the line has an *upward direction* from left to right. If the value of the slope is **negative**, the line has a *downward direction* from left to right. Consider the following example:

A new book goes on sale in bookstores and online stores. In the first month, 5,000 copies of the book are sold. Over time, the book continues to grow in popularity. The data for the number of copies sold is in the table below.

# of Months on Sale	1	2	3	4	5
# of Copies Sold (In Thousands)	5	10	15	20	25

So, the number of copies that are sold and the time that the book is on sale is a proportional relationship. In this example, an equation can be used to show the data: $y = 5x$, where x is the number of months that the book is on sale. Also, y is the number of copies sold. So, the slope of the corresponding line is $\frac{\text{rise}}{\text{run}} = \frac{5}{1} = 5$.

CROSS MULTIPLICATION

FINDING AN UNKNOWN IN EQUIVALENT EXPRESSIONS

It is often necessary to apply information given about a rate or proportion to a new scenario. For example, if you know that Jedha can run a marathon (26.2 miles) in 3 hours, how long would it take her to run 10 miles at the same pace? Start by setting up equivalent expressions:

$$\frac{26.2 \text{ mi}}{3 \text{ hr}} = \frac{10 \text{ mi}}{x \text{ hr}}$$

Now, cross multiply and solve for x:

$$26.2x = 30$$
$$x = \frac{30}{26.2} = \frac{15}{13.1}$$
$$x \approx 1.15 \text{ hrs } or \text{ 1 hr 9 min}$$

So, at this pace, Jedha could run 10 miles in about 1.15 hours or about 1 hour and 9 minutes.

> **Review Video: Cross Multiplying Fractions**
> Visit mometrix.com/academy and enter code: 893904

Data Interpretation and Representation, Statistics, and Probability

PROBABILITY

Probability is the likelihood of a certain outcome occurring for a given event. An **event** is any situation that produces a result. It could be something as simple as flipping a coin or as complex as launching a rocket. Determining the probability of an outcome for an event can be equally simple or complex. As such, there are specific terms used in the study of probability that need to be understood:

- **Compound event**—an event that involves two or more independent events (rolling a pair of dice and taking the sum)
- **Desired outcome** (or success)—an outcome that meets a particular set of criteria (a roll of 1 or 2 if we are looking for numbers less than 3)
- **Independent events**—two or more events whose outcomes do not affect one another (two coins tossed at the same time)
- **Dependent events**—two or more events whose outcomes affect one another (two cards drawn consecutively from the same deck)
- **Certain outcome**—probability of outcome is 100% or 1
- **Impossible outcome**—probability of outcome is 0% or 0
- **Mutually exclusive outcomes**—two or more outcomes whose criteria cannot all be satisfied in a single event (a coin coming up heads and tails on the same toss)
- **Random variable**—refers to all possible outcomes of a single event which may be discrete or continuous.

> **Review Video: Intro to Probability**
> Visit mometrix.com/academy and enter code: 212374

SAMPLE SPACE

The total set of all possible results of a test or experiment is called a **sample space**, or sometimes a universal sample space. The sample space, represented by one of the variables S, Ω, or U (for universal sample space) has individual elements called outcomes. Other terms for outcome that may be used interchangeably include elementary outcome, simple event, or sample point. The number of outcomes in a given sample space could be infinite or finite, and some tests may yield multiple unique sample sets. For example, tests conducted by drawing playing cards from a standard deck would have one sample space of the card values, another sample space of the card suits, and a third sample space of suit-denomination combinations. For most tests, the sample spaces considered will be finite.

An **event**, represented by the variable E, is a portion of a sample space. It may be one outcome or a group of outcomes from the same sample space. If an event occurs, then the test or experiment will generate an outcome that satisfies the requirement of that event. For example, given a standard deck of 52 playing cards as the sample space, and defining the event as the collection of face cards, then the event will occur if the card drawn is a J, Q, or K. If any other card is drawn, the event is said to have not occurred.

For every sample space, each possible outcome has a specific likelihood, or probability, that it will occur. The probability measure, also called the **distribution**, is a function that assigns a real number probability, from zero to one, to each outcome. For a probability measure to be accurate, every outcome must have a real number probability measure that is greater than or equal to zero and less than or equal to one. Also, the probability measure of the sample space must equal one, and the probability measure of the union of multiple outcomes must equal the sum of the individual probability measures.

Probabilities of events are expressed as real numbers from zero to one. They give a numerical value to the chance that a particular event will occur. The probability of an event occurring is the sum of the probabilities of the individual elements of that event. For example, in a standard deck of 52 playing cards as the sample space and the collection of face cards as the event, the probability of drawing a specific face card is $\frac{1}{52} = 0.019$, but the probability of drawing any one of the twelve face cards is $12(0.019) = 0.228$. Note that rounding of numbers can generate different results. If you multiplied 12 by the fraction $\frac{1}{52}$ before converting to a decimal, you would get the answer $\frac{12}{52} = 0.231$.

THEORETICAL AND EXPERIMENTAL PROBABILITY

Theoretical probability can usually be determined without actually performing the event. The likelihood of an outcome occurring, or the probability of an outcome occurring, is given by the formula:

$$P(A) = \frac{\text{Number of acceptable outcomes}}{\text{Number of possible outcomes}}$$

Note that $P(A)$ is the probability of an outcome A occurring, and each outcome is just as likely to occur as any other outcome. If each outcome has the same probability of occurring as every other possible outcome, the outcomes are said to be equally likely to occur. The total number of acceptable outcomes must be less than or equal to the total number of possible outcomes. If the two are equal, then the outcome is certain to occur and the probability is 1. If the number of acceptable outcomes is zero, then the outcome is impossible and the probability is 0. For example, if there are 20 marbles in a bag and 5 are red, then the theoretical probability of randomly selecting a red marble is 5 out of 20, $\left(\frac{5}{20} = \frac{1}{4}, 0.25, \text{or } 25\%\right)$.

If the theoretical probability is unknown or too complicated to calculate, it can be estimated by an experimental probability. **Experimental probability**, also called empirical probability, is an estimate of the likelihood of a certain outcome based on repeated experiments or collected data. In other words, while theoretical probability is based on what *should* happen, experimental probability is based on what *has* happened. Experimental probability is calculated in the same way as theoretical probability, except that actual outcomes are used instead of possible outcomes. The more experiments performed or datapoints gathered, the better the estimate should be.

Theoretical and experimental probability do not always line up with one another. Theoretical probability says that out of 20 coin-tosses, 10 should be heads. However, if we were actually to toss 20 coins, we might record just 5 heads. This doesn't mean that our theoretical probability is incorrect; it just means that this particular experiment had results that were different from what was predicted. A practical application of empirical probability is the insurance industry. There are no set functions that define lifespan, health, or safety. Insurance companies look at factors from hundreds of thousands of individuals to find patterns that they then use to set the formulas for insurance premiums.

> **Review Video: Empirical Probability**
> Visit mometrix.com/academy and enter code: 513468

OBJECTIVE AND SUBJECTIVE PROBABILITY

Objective probability is based on mathematical formulas and documented evidence. Examples of objective probability include raffles or lottery drawings where there is a pre-determined number of possible outcomes and a predetermined number of outcomes that correspond to an event. Other cases of objective probability include probabilities of rolling dice, flipping coins, or drawing cards. Most gambling games are based on objective probability.

In contrast, **subjective probability** is based on personal or professional feelings and judgments. Often, there is a lot of guesswork following extensive research. Areas where subjective probability is applicable include sales trends and business expenses. Attractions set admission prices based on subjective probabilities of attendance based on varying admission rates in an effort to maximize their profit.

COMPLEMENT OF AN EVENT

Sometimes it may be easier to calculate the possibility of something not happening, or the **complement of an event**. Represented by the symbol $\bar{A}$, the complement of A is the probability that event A does not happen. When you know the probability of event A occurring, you can use the formula $P(\bar{A}) = 1 - P(A)$, where $P(\bar{A})$ is the probability of event A not occurring, and $P(A)$ is the probability of event A occurring.

ADDITION RULE

The **addition rule** for probability is used for finding the probability of a compound event. Use the formula $P(A \cup B) = P(A) + P(B) - P(A \cap B)$, where $P(A \cap B)$ is the probability of both events occurring to find the probability of a compound event. The probability of both events occurring at the same time must be subtracted to eliminate any overlap in the first two probabilities.

CONDITIONAL PROBABILITY

Given two events A and B, the **conditional probability** $P(A|B)$ is the probability that event A will occur, given that event B has occurred. The conditional probability cannot be calculated simply from $P(A)$ and $P(B)$; these probabilities alone do not give sufficient information to determine the conditional probability. It can, however, be determined if you are also given the probability of the intersection of events A and B, $P(A \cap B)$, the probability that events A and B both occur. Specifically, $P(A|B) = \frac{P(A \cap B)}{P(B)}$. For instance, suppose you have a jar containing two red marbles and two blue marbles, and you draw two marbles at random. Consider event A being the event that the first marble drawn is red, and event B being the event that the second marble drawn is blue. If we want to find the probability that B occurs given that A occurred, $P(B|A)$, then we can compute it using the fact that $P(A)$ is $\frac{1}{2}$, and $P(A \cap B)$ is $\frac{1}{3}$. (The latter may not be obvious, but may be determined by finding the product of $\frac{1}{2}$ and $\frac{2}{3}$). Therefore $P(B|A) = \frac{P(A \cap B)}{P(A)} = \frac{1/3}{1/2} = \frac{2}{3}$.

CONDITIONAL PROBABILITY IN EVERYDAY SITUATIONS

Conditional probability often arises in everyday situations in, for example, estimating the risk or benefit of certain activities. The conditional probability of having a heart attack given that you exercise daily may be smaller than the overall probability of having a heart attack. The conditional probability of having lung cancer given that you are a smoker is larger than the overall probability of having lung cancer. Note that changing the order of the conditional probability changes the meaning: the conditional probability of having lung cancer given that you are a smoker is a very different thing from the probability of being a smoker given that you have lung cancer. In an extreme case, suppose that a certain rare disease is caused only by eating a certain food, but even then, it is unlikely. Then the conditional probability of having that disease given that you eat the dangerous food is nonzero but low, but the conditional probability of having eaten that food given that you have the disease is 100%!

> **Review Video: Conditional Probability**
> Visit mometrix.com/academy and enter code: 397924

INDEPENDENCE

The conditional probability $P(A|B)$ is the probability that event A will occur given that event B occurs. If the two events are independent, we do not expect that whether or not event B occurs should have any effect on whether or not event A occurs. In other words, we expect $P(A|B) = P(A)$.

This can be proven using the usual equations for conditional probability and the joint probability of independent events. The conditional probability $P(A|B) = \frac{P(A \cap B)}{P(B)}$. If A and B are independent, then $P(A \cap B) = P(A)P(B)$. So $P(A|B) = \frac{P(A)P(B)}{P(B)} = P(A)$. By similar reasoning, if A and B are independent then $P(B|A) = P(B)$.

MULTIPLICATION RULE

The **multiplication rule** can be used to find the probability of two independent events occurring using the formula $P(A \cap B) = P(A) \times P(B)$, where $P(A \cap B)$ is the probability of two independent events occurring, $P(A)$ is the probability of the first event occurring, and $P(B)$ is the probability of the second event occurring.

The multiplication rule can also be used to find the probability of two dependent events occurring using the formula $P(A \cap B) = P(A) \times P(B|A)$, where $P(A \cap B)$ is the probability of two dependent events occurring and $P(B|A)$ is the probability of the second event occurring after the first event has already occurred.

Use a **combination of the multiplication** rule and the rule of complements to find the probability that at least one outcome of the element will occur. This is given by the general formula $P(\text{at least one event occurring}) = 1 - P(\text{no outcomes occurring})$. For example, to find the probability that at least one even number will show when a pair of dice is rolled, find the probability that two odd numbers will be rolled (no even numbers) and subtract from one. You can always use a tree diagram or make a chart to list the possible outcomes when the sample space is small, such as in the dice-rolling example, but in most cases it will be much faster to use the multiplication and complement formulas.

> **Review Video: Multiplication Rule**
> Visit mometrix.com/academy and enter code: 782598

UNION AND INTERSECTION OF TWO SETS OF OUTCOMES

If A and B are each a set of elements or outcomes from an experiment, then the **union** (symbol ∪) of the two sets is the set of elements found in set A or set B. For example, if $A = \{2, 3, 4\}$ and $B = \{3, 4, 5\}$, $A \cup B = \{2, 3, 4, 5\}$. Note that the outcomes 3 and 4 appear only once in the union. For statistical events, the union is equivalent to "or"; $P(A \cup B)$ is the same thing as $P(A \text{ or } B)$. The **intersection** (symbol ∩) of two sets is the set of outcomes common to both sets. For the above sets A and B, $A \cap B = \{3, 4\}$. For statistical events, the intersection is equivalent to "and"; $P(A \cap B)$ is the same thing as $P(A \text{ and } B)$. It is important to note that union and intersection operations commute. That is:

$$A \cup B = B \cup A \text{ and } A \cap B = B \cap A$$

PERMUTATIONS AND COMBINATIONS IN PROBABILITY

When trying to calculate the probability of an event using the $\frac{\text{desired outcomes}}{\text{total outcomes}}$ formula, you may frequently find that there are too many outcomes to individually count them. **Permutation** and **combination formulas** offer a shortcut to counting outcomes. A permutation is an arrangement of a specific number of a set of objects in a specific order. The number of **permutations** of r items given a set of n items can be calculated as $_nP_r = \frac{n!}{(n-r)!}$.

Combinations are similar to permutations, except there are no restrictions regarding the order of the elements. While ABC is considered a different permutation than BCA, ABC and BCA are considered the same combination. The number of **combinations** of r items given a set of n items can be calculated as $_nC_r = \frac{n!}{r!(n-r)!}$ or $_nC_r = \frac{_nP_r}{r!}$.

Suppose you want to calculate how many different 5-card hands can be drawn from a deck of 52 cards. This is a combination since the order of the cards in a hand does not matter. There are 52 cards available, and 5 to be selected. Thus, the number of different hands is $_{52}C_5 = \frac{52!}{5! \times 47!} = 2,598,960$.

> **Review Video: Probability - Permutation and Combination**
> Visit mometrix.com/academy and enter code: 907664

TREE DIAGRAMS

For a simple sample space, possible outcomes may be determined by using a **tree diagram** or an organized chart. In either case, you can easily draw or list out the possible outcomes. For example, to determine all the possible ways three objects can be ordered, you can draw a tree diagram:

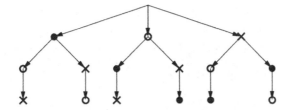

> **Review Video: Tree Diagrams**
> Visit mometrix.com/academy and enter code: 829158

You can also make a chart to list all the possibilities:

First object	Second object	Third object
●	X	O
●	O	X
O	●	X
O	X	●
X	●	O
X	O	●

Either way, you can easily see there are six possible ways the three objects can be ordered.

If two events have no outcomes in common, they are said to be **mutually exclusive**. For example, in a standard deck of 52 playing cards, the event of all card suits is mutually exclusive to the event of all card values. If two events have no bearing on each other so that one event occurring has no influence on the probability of another event occurring, the two events are said to be independent. For example, rolling a standard six-sided die multiple times does not change that probability that a particular number will be rolled from one roll to the next. If the outcome of one event does affect the probability of the second event, the two events are said to be dependent. For example, if cards are drawn from a deck, the probability of drawing an ace after an ace has been drawn is different than the probability of drawing an ace if no ace (or no other card, for that matter) has been drawn.

In probability, the **odds in favor of an event** are the number of times the event will occur compared to the number of times the event will not occur. To calculate the odds in favor of an event, use the formula $\frac{P(A)}{1-P(A)}$, where $P(A)$ is the probability that the event will occur. Many times, odds in favor is given as a ratio in the form $\frac{a}{b}$ or $a:b$, where a is the probability of the event occurring and b is the complement of the event, the probability of the event not occurring. If the odds in favor are given as 2:5, that means that you can expect the event to occur two times for every 5 times that it does not occur. In other words, the probability that the event will occur is $\frac{2}{2+5} = \frac{2}{7}$.

In probability, the **odds against an event** are the number of times the event will not occur compared to the number of times the event will occur. To calculate the odds against an event, use the formula $\frac{1-P(A)}{P(A)}$, where $P(A)$ is the probability that the event will occur. Many times, odds against is given as a ratio in the form $\frac{b}{a}$ or $b:a$, where b is the probability the event will not occur (the complement of the event) and a is the probability the event will occur. If the odds against an event are given as 3:1, that means that you can expect the event to not occur 3 times for every one time it does occur. In other words, 3 out of every 4 trials will fail.

TWO-WAY FREQUENCY TABLES

If we have a two-way frequency table, it is generally a straightforward matter to read off the probabilities of any two events A and B, as well as the joint probability of both events occurring, $P(A \cap B)$. We can then find the conditional probability $P(A|B)$ by calculating $P(A|B) = \frac{P(A \cap B)}{P(B)}$. We could also check whether or not events are independent by verifying whether $P(A)P(B) = P(A \cap B)$.

For example, a certain store's recent T-shirt sales:

	Small	Medium	Large	Total
Blue	25	40	35	100
White	27	25	22	74
Black	8	23	15	46
Total	60	88	72	220

Suppose we want to find the conditional probability that a customer buys a black shirt (event A), given that the shirt he buys is size small (event B). From the table, the probability $P(B)$ that a customer buys a small shirt is $\frac{60}{220} = \frac{3}{11}$. The probability $P(A \cap B)$ that he buys a small, black shirt is $\frac{8}{220} = \frac{2}{55}$. The conditional probability $P(A|B)$ that he buys a black shirt, given that he buys a small shirt, is therefore $P(A|B) = \frac{2/55}{3/11} = \frac{2}{15}$.

Similarly, if we want to check whether the event a customer buys a blue shirt, A, is independent of the event that a customer buys a medium shirt, B. From the table, $P(A) = \frac{100}{220} = \frac{5}{11}$ and $P(B) = \frac{88}{220} = \frac{4}{10}$. Also, $P(A \cap B) = \frac{40}{220} = \frac{2}{11}$. Since $\left(\frac{5}{11}\right)\left(\frac{4}{10}\right) = \frac{20}{110} = \frac{2}{11}$, $P(A)P(B) = P(A \cap B)$ and these two events are indeed independent.

EXPECTED VALUE

Expected value is a method of determining the expected outcome in a random situation. It is a sum of the weighted probabilities of the possible outcomes. Multiply the probability of an event occurring by the weight assigned to that probability (such as the amount of money won or lost). A practical application of the expected value is to determine whether a game of chance is really fair. If the sum of the weighted probabilities is equal to zero, the game is generally considered fair because the player has a fair chance to at least break even. If the expected value is less than zero, then players are expected to lose more than they win. For example, a lottery drawing might allow the player to choose any three-digit number, 000–999. The probability of choosing the winning number is 1:1000. If it costs \$1 to play, and a winning number receives \$500, the expected value is $\left(-\$1 \times \frac{999}{1,000}\right) + \left(\$499 \times \frac{1}{1,000}\right) = -\$0.50$. You can expect to lose on average 50 cents for every dollar you spend.

> **Review Video: Expected Value**
> Visit mometrix.com/academy and enter code: 643554

EXPECTED VALUE AND SIMULATORS

A die roll simulator will show the results of n rolls of a die. The result of each die roll may be recorded. For example, suppose a die is rolled 100 times. All results may be recorded. The numbers of 1s, 2s, 3s, 4s, 5s, and 6s, may be counted. The experimental probability of rolling each number will equal the ratio of the frequency of the rolled number to the total number of rolls. As the number of rolls increases, or approaches infinity, the experimental probability will approach the theoretical probability of $\frac{1}{6}$. Thus, the expected value for the roll of a die is shown to be $\left(1 \times \frac{1}{6}\right) + \left(2 \times \frac{1}{6}\right) + \left(3 \times \frac{1}{6}\right) + \left(4 \times \frac{1}{6}\right) + \left(5 \times \frac{1}{6}\right) + \left(6 \times \frac{1}{6}\right)$, or 3.5.

INTRODUCTION TO STATISTICS

Statistics is the branch of mathematics that deals with collecting, recording, interpreting, illustrating, and analyzing large amounts of **data**. The following terms are often used in the discussion of data and **statistics**:

- **Data** – the collective name for pieces of information (singular is datum)
- **Quantitative data** – measurements (such as length, mass, and speed) that provide information about quantities in numbers
- **Qualitative data** – information (such as colors, scents, tastes, and shapes) that cannot be measured using numbers
- **Discrete data** – information that can be expressed only by a specific value, such as whole or half numbers. (e.g., since people can be counted only in whole numbers, a population count would be discrete data.)
- **Continuous data** – information (such as time and temperature) that can be expressed by any value within a given range
- **Primary data** – information that has been collected directly from a survey, investigation, or experiment, such as a questionnaire or the recording of daily temperatures. (Primary data that has not yet been organized or analyzed is called **raw data**.)
- **Secondary data** – information that has been collected, sorted, and processed by the researcher
- **Ordinal data** – information that can be placed in numerical order, such as age or weight
- **Nominal data** – information that *cannot* be placed in numerical order, such as names or places

DATA COLLECTION
POPULATION

In statistics, the **population** is the entire collection of people, plants, etc., that data can be collected from. For example, a study to determine how well students in local schools perform on a standardized test would have a population of all the students enrolled in those schools, although a study may include just a small sample of students from each school. A **parameter** is a numerical value that gives information about the population, such as the mean, median, mode, or standard deviation. Remember that the symbol for the mean of a population is μ and the symbol for the standard deviation of a population is σ.

SAMPLE

A **sample** is a portion of the entire population. Whereas a parameter helped describe the population, a **statistic** is a numerical value that gives information about the sample, such as mean, median, mode, or standard deviation. Keep in mind that the symbols for mean and standard deviation are different when they are referring to a sample rather than the entire population. For a sample, the symbol for mean is $\bar{x}$ and the symbol for standard deviation is s. The mean and standard deviation of a sample may or may not be identical to that of the entire population due to a sample only being a subset of the population. However, if the sample is random and large enough, statistically significant values can be attained. Samples are generally used when the population is too large to justify including every element or when acquiring data for the entire population is impossible.

INFERENTIAL STATISTICS

Inferential statistics is the branch of statistics that uses samples to make predictions about an entire population. This type of statistic is often seen in political polls, where a sample of the population is questioned about a particular topic or politician to gain an understanding of the attitudes of the entire population of the country. Often, exit polls are conducted on election days using this method. Inferential statistics can have a large margin of error if you do not have a valid sample.

SAMPLING DISTRIBUTION

Statistical values calculated from various samples of the same size make up the **sampling distribution**. For example, if several samples of identical size are randomly selected from a large population and then the mean of each sample is calculated, the distribution of values of the means would be a sampling distribution.

The **sampling distribution of the mean** is the distribution of the sample mean, $\bar{x}$, derived from random samples of a given size. It has three important characteristics. First, the mean of the sampling distribution of the mean is equal to the mean of the population that was sampled. Second, assuming the standard deviation is non-zero, the standard deviation of the sampling distribution of the mean equals the standard deviation of the sampled population divided by the square root of the sample size. This is sometimes called the standard error. Finally, as the sample size gets larger, the sampling distribution of the mean gets closer to a normal distribution via the central limit theorem.

SURVEY STUDY

A **survey study** is a method of gathering information from a small group in an attempt to gain enough information to make accurate general assumptions about the population. Once a survey study is completed, the results are then put into a summary report.

Survey studies are generally in the format of surveys, interviews, or questionnaires as part of an effort to find opinions of a particular group or to find facts about a group.

It is important to note that the findings from a survey study are only as accurate as the sample chosen from the population.

CORRELATIONAL STUDIES

Correlational studies seek to determine how much one variable is affected by changes in a second variable. For example, correlational studies may look for a relationship between the amount of time a student spends studying for a test and the grade that student earned on the test or between student scores on college admissions tests and student grades in college.

It is important to note that correlational studies cannot show a cause and effect, but rather can show only that two variables are or are not potentially correlated.

EXPERIMENTAL STUDIES

Experimental studies take correlational studies one step farther, in that they attempt to prove or disprove a cause-and-effect relationship. These studies are performed by conducting a series of experiments to test the hypothesis. For a study to be scientifically accurate, it must have both an experimental group that receives the specified treatment and a control group that does not get the treatment. This is the type of study pharmaceutical companies do as part of drug trials for new medications. Experimental studies are only valid when the proper scientific method has been followed. In other words, the experiment must be well-planned and executed without bias in the testing process, all subjects must be selected at random, and the process of determining which subject is in which of the two groups must also be completely random.

OBSERVATIONAL STUDIES

Observational studies are the opposite of experimental studies. In observational studies, the tester cannot change or in any way control all of the variables in the test. For example, a study to determine which gender does better in math classes in school is strictly observational. You cannot change a person's gender, and you cannot change the subject being studied. The big downfall of observational studies is that you have no way of proving a cause-and-effect relationship because you cannot control outside influences. Events outside of school can influence a student's performance in school, and observational studies cannot take that into consideration.

RANDOM SAMPLES

For most studies, a **random sample** is necessary to produce valid results. Random samples should not have any particular influence to cause sampled subjects to behave one way or another. The goal is for the random sample to be a **representative sample**, or a sample whose characteristics give an accurate picture of the characteristics of the entire population. To accomplish this, you must make sure you have a proper **sample size**, or an appropriate number of elements in the sample.

BIASES

In statistical studies, biases must be avoided. **Bias** is an error that causes the study to favor one set of results over another. For example, if a survey to determine how the country views the president's job performance only speaks to registered voters in the president's party, the results will be skewed because a disproportionately large number of responders would tend to show approval, while a disproportionately large number of people in the opposite party would tend to express disapproval. **Extraneous variables** are, as the name implies, outside influences that can affect the outcome of a study. They are not always avoidable but could trigger bias in the result.

DATA ANALYSIS

DISPERSION

A **measure of dispersion** is a single value that helps to "interpret" the measure of central tendency by providing more information about how the data values in the set are distributed about the measure of central tendency. The measure of dispersion helps to eliminate or reduce the disadvantages of using the mean, median, or mode as a single measure of central tendency, and give a more accurate picture of the dataset as a whole. To have a measure of dispersion, you must know or calculate the range, standard deviation, or variance of the data set.

RANGE

The **range** of a set of data is the difference between the greatest and lowest values of the data in the set. To calculate the range, you must first make sure the units for all data values are the same, and then identify the greatest and lowest values. If there are multiple data values that are equal for the highest or lowest, just use one of the values in the formula. Write the answer with the same units as the data values you used to do the calculations.

> **Review Video: Statistical Range**
> Visit mometrix.com/academy and enter code: 778541

SAMPLE STANDARD DEVIATION

Standard deviation is a measure of dispersion that compares all the data values in the set to the mean of the set to give a more accurate picture. To find the **standard deviation of a sample**, use the formula

$$s = \sqrt{\frac{\sum_{i=1}^{n}(x_i - \bar{x})^2}{n - 1}}$$

Note that s is the standard deviation of a sample, x_i represents the individual values in the data set, $\bar{x}$ is the mean of the data values in the set, and n is the number of data values in the set. The higher the value of the standard deviation is, the greater the variance of the data values from the mean. The units associated with the standard deviation are the same as the units of the data values.

> **Review Video: Standard Deviation**
> Visit mometrix.com/academy and enter code: 419469

SAMPLE VARIANCE

The **variance of a sample** is the square of the sample standard deviation (denoted s^2). While the mean of a set of data gives the average of the set and gives information about where a specific data value lies in relation to the average, the variance of the sample gives information about the degree to which the data values are spread out and tells you how close an individual value is to the average compared to the other values. The units associated with variance are the same as the units of the data values squared.

PERCENTILE

Percentiles and quartiles are other methods of describing data within a set. **Percentiles** tell what percentage of the data in the set fall below a specific point. For example, achievement test scores are often given in percentiles. A score at the 80th percentile is one which is equal to or higher than 80 percent of the scores in the set. In other words, 80 percent of the scores were lower than that score.

Quartiles are percentile groups that make up quarter sections of the data set. The first quartile is the 25th percentile. The second quartile is the 50th percentile; this is also the median of the dataset. The third quartile is the 75th percentile.

SKEWNESS

Skewness is a way to describe the symmetry or asymmetry of the distribution of values in a dataset. If the distribution of values is symmetrical, there is no skew. In general the closer the mean of a data set is to the median of the data set, the less skew there is. Generally, if the mean is to the right of the median, the data set is *positively skewed*, or right-skewed, and if the mean is to the left of the median, the data set is *negatively skewed*, or left-skewed. However, this rule of thumb is not infallible. When the data values are graphed on a curve, a set with no skew will be a perfect bell curve.

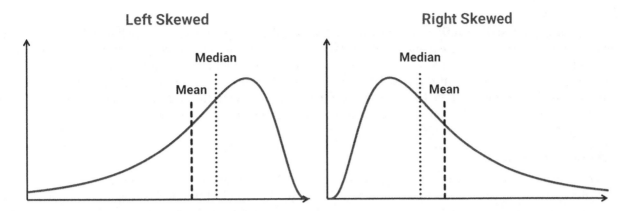

| Left Skewed | Right Skewed |

To estimate skew, use the formula:

$$\text{skew} = \frac{\sqrt{n(n-1)}}{n-2} \left(\frac{\frac{1}{n}\sum_{i=1}^{n}(x_i - \bar{x})^3}{\left(\frac{1}{n}\sum_{i=1}^{n}(x_i - \bar{x})^2\right)^{\frac{3}{2}}} \right)$$

Note that n is the datapoints in the set, x_i is the ith value in the set, and $\bar{x}$ is the mean of the set.

> **Review Video: Skew**
> Visit mometrix.com/academy and enter code: 661486

UNIMODAL VS. BIMODAL

If a distribution has a single peak, it would be considered **unimodal**. If it has two discernible peaks it would be considered **bimodal**. Bimodal distributions may be an indication that the set of data being considered is actually the combination of two sets of data with significant differences. A **uniform distribution** is a distribution in which there is *no distinct peak or variation* in the data. No values or ranges are particularly more common than any other values or ranges.

OUTLIER

An outlier is an extremely high or extremely low value in the data set. It may be the result of measurement error, in which case, the outlier is not a valid member of the data set. However, it may also be a valid member of the distribution. Unless a measurement error is identified, the experimenter cannot know for certain if an outlier is or is not a member of the distribution. There are arbitrary methods that can be employed to designate an extreme value as an outlier. One method designates an outlier (or possible outlier) to be any value less than $Q_1 - 1.5(IQR)$ or any value greater than $Q_3 + 1.5(IQR)$.

DATA ANALYSIS
SIMPLE REGRESSION

In statistics, **simple regression** is using an equation to represent a relation between independent and dependent variables. The independent variable is also referred to as the explanatory variable or the predictor and is generally represented by the variable x in the equation. The dependent variable, usually represented by the variable y, is also referred to as the response variable. The equation may be any type of function – linear, quadratic, exponential, etc. The best way to handle this task is to use the regression feature of your graphing

137

calculator. This will easily give you the curve of best fit and provide you with the coefficients and other information you need to derive an equation.

LINE OF BEST FIT

In a scatter plot, the **line of best fit** is the line that best shows the trends of the data. The line of best fit is given by the equation $\hat{y} = ax + b$, where a and b are the regression coefficients. The regression coefficient a is also the slope of the line of best fit, and b is also the y-coordinate of the point at which the line of best fit crosses the y-axis. Not every point on the scatter plot will be on the line of best fit. The differences between the y-values of the points in the scatter plot and the corresponding y-values according to the equation of the line of best fit are the residuals. The line of best fit is also called the least-squares regression line because it is also the line that has the lowest sum of the squares of the residuals.

CORRELATION COEFFICIENT

The **correlation coefficient** is the numerical value that indicates how strong the relationship is between the two variables of a linear regression equation. A correlation coefficient of -1 is a perfect negative correlation. A correlation coefficient of $+1$ is a perfect positive correlation. Correlation coefficients close to -1 or $+1$ are very strong correlations. A correlation coefficient equal to zero indicates there is no correlation between the two variables. This test is a good indicator of whether or not the equation for the line of best fit is accurate. The formula for the correlation coefficient is

$$r = \frac{\sum_{i=1}^{n}(x_i - \bar{x})(y_i - \bar{y})}{\sqrt{\sum_{i=1}^{n}(x_i - \bar{x})^2} \sqrt{\sum_{i=1}^{n}(y_i - \bar{y})^2}}$$

where r is the correlation coefficient, n is the number of data values in the set, (x_i, y_i) is a point in the set, and $\bar{x}$ and $\bar{y}$ are the means.

Z-SCORE

A **z-score** is an indication of how many standard deviations a given value falls from the sample mean. To calculate a z-score, use the formula:

$$\frac{x - \bar{x}}{\sigma}$$

In this formula x is the data value, $\bar{x}$ is the mean of the sample data, and σ is the standard deviation of the population. If the z-score is positive, the data value lies above the mean. If the z-score is negative, the data value falls below the mean. These scores are useful in interpreting data such as standardized test scores, where every piece of data in the set has been counted, rather than just a small random sample. In cases where standard deviations are calculated from a random sample of the set, the z-scores will not be as accurate.

CENTRAL LIMIT THEOREM

According to the **central limit theorem**, regardless of what the original distribution of a sample is, the distribution of the means tends to get closer and closer to a normal distribution as the sample size gets larger and larger (this is necessary because the sample is becoming more all-encompassing of the elements of the population). As the sample size gets larger, the distribution of the sample mean will approach a normal distribution with a mean of the population mean and a variance of the population variance divided by the sample size.

MEASURES OF CENTRAL TENDENCY

A **measure of central tendency** is a statistical value that gives a reasonable estimate for the center of a group of data. There are several different ways of describing the measure of central tendency. Each one has a unique way it is calculated, and each one gives a slightly different perspective on the data set. Whenever you give a measure of central tendency, always make sure the units are the same. If the data has different units, such as

138

hours, minutes, and seconds, convert all the data to the same unit, and use the same unit in the measure of central tendency. If no units are given in the data, do not give units for the measure of central tendency.

MEAN

The **statistical mean** of a group of data is the same as the arithmetic average of that group. To find the mean of a set of data, first convert each value to the same units, if necessary. Then find the sum of all the values, and count the total number of data values, making sure you take into consideration each individual value. If a value appears more than once, count it more than once. Divide the sum of the values by the total number of values and apply the units, if any. Note that the mean does not have to be one of the data values in the set, and may not divide evenly.

$$\text{mean} = \frac{\text{sum of the data values}}{\text{quantity of data values}}$$

For instance, the mean of the data set {88, 72, 61, 90, 97, 68, 88, 79, 86, 93, 97, 71, 80, 84, 89} would be the sum of the fifteen numbers divided by 15:

$$\frac{88 + 72 + 61 + 90 + 97 + 68 + 88 + 79 + 86 + 93 + 97 + 71 + 80 + 84 + 89}{15} = \frac{1242}{15}$$
$$= 82.8$$

While the mean is relatively easy to calculate and averages are understood by most people, the mean can be very misleading if it is used as the sole measure of central tendency. If the data set has outliers (data values that are unusually high or unusually low compared to the rest of the data values), the mean can be very distorted, especially if the data set has a small number of values. If unusually high values are countered with unusually low values, the mean is not affected as much. For example, if five of twenty students in a class get a 100 on a test, but the other 15 students have an average of 60 on the same test, the class average would appear as 70. Whenever the mean is skewed by outliers, it is always a good idea to include the median as an alternate measure of central tendency.

A **weighted mean**, or weighted average, is a mean that uses "weighted" values. The formula is weighted mean $= \frac{w_1 x_1 + w_2 x_2 + w_3 x_3 \ldots + w_n x_n}{w_1 + w_2 + w_3 + \cdots + w_n}$. Weighted values, such as $w_1, w_2, w_3, \ldots w_n$ are assigned to each member of the set $x_1, x_2, x_3, \ldots x_n$. When calculating the weighted mean, make sure a weight value for each member of the set is used.

> **Review Video: All About Averages**
> Visit mometrix.com/academy and enter code: 176521

MEDIAN

The **statistical median** is the value in the middle of the set of data. To find the median, list all data values in order from smallest to largest or from largest to smallest. Any value that is repeated in the set must be listed the number of times it appears. If there are an odd number of data values, the median is the value in the middle of the list. If there is an even number of data values, the median is the arithmetic mean of the two middle values.

For example, the median of the data set {88, 72, 61, 90, 97, 68, 88, 79, 86, 93, 97, 71, 80, 84, 88} is 86 since the ordered set is {61, 68, 71, 72, 79, 80, 84, **86**, 88, 88, 88, 90, 93, 97, 97}.

The big disadvantage of using the median as a measure of central tendency is that is relies solely on a value's relative size as compared to the other values in the set. When the individual values in a set of data are evenly dispersed, the median can be an accurate tool. However, if there is a group of rather large values or a group of rather small values that are not offset by a different group of values, the information that can be inferred from the median may not be accurate because the distribution of values is skewed.

MODE

The **statistical mode** is the data value that occurs the greatest number of times in the data set. It is possible to have exactly one mode, more than one mode, or no mode. To find the mode of a set of data, arrange the data like you do to find the median (all values in order, listing all multiples of data values). Count the number of times each value appears in the data set. If all values appear an equal number of times, there is no mode. If one value appears more than any other value, that value is the mode. If two or more values appear the same number of times, but there are other values that appear fewer times and no values that appear more times, all of those values are the modes.

For example, the mode of the data set {**88**, 72, 61, 90, 97, 68, **88**, 79, 86, 93, 97, 71, 80, 84, **88**} is 88.

The main disadvantage of the mode is that the values of the other data in the set have no bearing on the mode. The mode may be the largest value, the smallest value, or a value anywhere in between in the set. The mode only tells which value or values, if any, occurred the greatest number of times. It does not give any suggestions about the remaining values in the set.

> **Review Video: Mean, Median, and Mode**
> Visit mometrix.com/academy and enter code: 286207

DISPLAYING INFORMATION
FREQUENCY TABLES

Frequency tables show how frequently each unique value appears in a set. A **relative frequency table** is one that shows the proportions of each unique value compared to the entire set. Relative frequencies are given as percentages; however, the total percent for a relative frequency table will not necessarily equal 100 percent due to rounding. An example of a frequency table with relative frequencies is below.

Favorite Color	Frequency	Relative Frequency
Blue	4	13%
Red	7	22%
Green	3	9%
Purple	6	19%
Cyan	12	38%

> **Review Video: Data Interpretation of Graphs**
> Visit mometrix.com/academy and enter code: 200439

CIRCLE GRAPHS

Circle graphs, also known as *pie charts*, provide a visual depiction of the relationship of each type of data compared to the whole set of data. The circle graph is divided into sections by drawing radii to create central angles whose percentage of the circle is equal to the individual data's percentage of the whole set. Each 1% of data is equal to 3.6° in the circle graph. Therefore, data represented by a 90° section of the circle graph makes up 25% of the whole. When complete, a circle graph often looks like a pie cut into uneven wedges. The pie chart below shows the data from the frequency table referenced earlier where people were asked their favorite color.

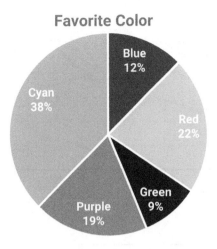

PICTOGRAPHS

A **pictograph** is a graph, generally in the horizontal orientation, that uses pictures or symbols to represent the data. Each pictograph must have a key that defines the picture or symbol and gives the quantity each picture or symbol represents. Pictures or symbols on a pictograph are not always shown as whole elements. In this case, the fraction of the picture or symbol shown represents the same fraction of the quantity a whole picture or symbol stands for. For example, a row with $3\frac{1}{2}$ ears of corn, where each ear of corn represents 100 stalks of corn in a field, would equal $3\frac{1}{2} \times 100 = 350$ stalks of corn in the field.

> **Review Video: Pictographs**
> Visit mometrix.com/academy and enter code: 147860

LINE GRAPHS

Line graphs have one or more lines of varying styles (solid or broken) to show the different values for a set of data. The individual data are represented as ordered pairs, much like on a Cartesian plane. In this case, the x- and y-axes are defined in terms of their units, such as dollars or time. The individual plotted points are joined by line segments to show whether the value of the data is increasing (line sloping upward), decreasing (line sloping downward), or staying the same (horizontal line). Multiple sets of data can be graphed on the same line graph to give an easy visual comparison. An example of this would be graphing achievement test scores for different groups of students over the same time period to see which group had the greatest increase or decrease in performance from year to year (as shown below).

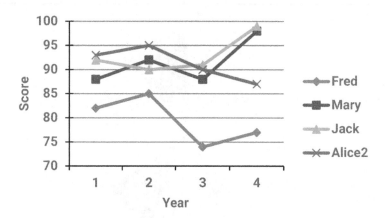

LINE PLOTS

A **line plot**, also known as a *dot plot*, has plotted points that are not connected by line segments. In this graph, the horizontal axis lists the different possible values for the data, and the vertical axis lists the number of times the individual value occurs. A single dot is graphed for each value to show the number of times it occurs. This graph is more closely related to a bar graph than a line graph. Do not connect the dots in a line plot or it will misrepresent the data.

STEM AND LEAF PLOTS

A **stem and leaf plot** is useful for depicting groups of data that fall into a range of values. Each piece of data is separated into two parts: the first, or left, part is called the stem; the second, or right, part is called the leaf. Each stem is listed in a column from smallest to largest. Each leaf that has the common stem is listed in that stem's row from smallest to largest. For example, in a set of two-digit numbers, the digit in the tens place is the stem, and the digit in the ones place is the leaf. With a stem and leaf plot, you can easily see which subset of numbers (10s, 20s, 30s, etc.) is the largest. This information is also readily available by looking at a histogram, but a stem and leaf plot also allows you to look closer and see exactly which values fall in that range. Using a sample set of test scores $(82, 88, 92, 93, 85, 90, 92, 95, 74, 88, 90, 91, 78, 87, 98, 99)$, we can assemble a stem and leaf plot like the one below.

Test Scores

7	4 8
8	2 5 7 8 8
9	0 0 1 2 2 3 5 8 9

BAR GRAPHS

A **bar graph** is one of the few graphs that can be drawn correctly in two different configurations – both horizontally and vertically. A bar graph is similar to a line plot in the way the data is organized on the graph. Both axes must have their categories defined for the graph to be useful. Rather than placing a single dot to mark the point of the data's value, a bar, or thick line, is drawn from zero to the exact value of the data, whether it is a number, percentage, or other numerical value. Longer bar lengths correspond to greater data values. To read a bar graph, read the labels for the axes to find the units being reported. Then, look where the bars end in relation to the scale given on the corresponding axis and determine the associated value.

The bar chart below represents the responses from our favorite-color survey.

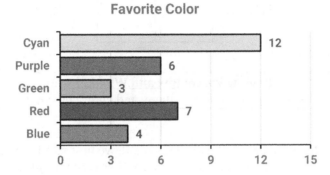

HISTOGRAMS

At first glance, a **histogram** looks like a vertical bar graph. The difference is that a bar graph has a separate bar for each piece of data and a histogram has one continuous bar for each *range* of data. For example, a histogram may have one bar for the range 0–9, one bar for 10–19, etc. While a bar graph has numerical values on one axis, a histogram has numerical values on both axes. Each range is of equal size, and they are ordered left to right from lowest to highest. The height of each column on a histogram represents the number of data values within that range. Like a stem and leaf plot, a histogram makes it easy to glance at the graph and quickly determine which range has the greatest quantity of values. A simple example of a histogram is below.

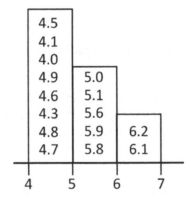

5-NUMBER SUMMARY

The **5-number summary** of a set of data gives a very informative picture of the set. The five numbers in the summary include the minimum value, maximum value, and the three quartiles. This information gives the reader the range and median of the set, as well as an indication of how the data is spread about the median.

BOX AND WHISKER PLOTS

A **box-and-whiskers plot** is a graphical representation of the 5-number summary. To draw a box-and-whiskers plot, plot the points of the 5-number summary on a number line. Draw a box whose ends are through the points for the first and third quartiles. Draw a vertical line in the box through the median to divide the box in half. Draw a line segment from the first quartile point to the minimum value, and from the third quartile point to the maximum value.

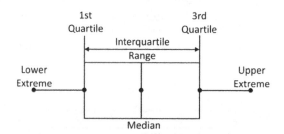

Review Video: <u>Box and Whisker Plots</u>
Visit mometrix.com/academy and enter code: 810817

EXAMPLE

Given the following data (32, 28, 29, 26, 35, 27, 30, 31, 27, 32), we first sort it into numerical order: 26, 27, 27, 28, 29, 30, 31, 32, 32, 35. We can then find the median. Since there are ten values, we take the average of the 5th and 6th values to get 29.5. We find the lower quartile by taking the median of the data smaller than the median. Since there are five values, we take the 3rd value, which is 27. We find the upper quartile by taking the median of the data larger than the overall median, which is 32. Finally, we note our minimum and maximum, which are simply the smallest and largest values in the set: 26 and 35, respectively. Now we can create our box plot:

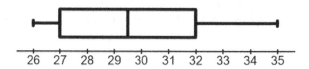

This plot is fairly "long" on the right whisker, showing one or more unusually high values (but not quite outliers). The other quartiles are similar in length, showing a fairly even distribution of data.

INTERQUARTILE RANGE

The **interquartile range, or IQR**, is the difference between the upper and lower quartiles. It measures how the data is dispersed: a high IQR means that the data is more spread out, while a low IQR means that the data is clustered more tightly around the median. To find the IQR, subtract the lower quartile value (Q_1) from the upper quartile value (Q_3).

EXAMPLE

To find the upper and lower quartiles, we first find the median and then take the median of all values above it and all values below it. In the following data set (16, 18, 13, 24, 16, 51, 32, 21, 27, 39), we first rearrange the values in numerical order: 13, 16, 16, 18, 21, 24, 27, 32, 39, 51. There are 10 values, so the median is the average of the 5th and 6th: $\frac{21+24}{2} = \frac{45}{2} = 22.5$. We do not actually need this value to find the upper and lower quartiles. We look at the set of numbers below the median: 13, 16, 16, 18, 21. There are five values, so the 3rd is the median (16), or the value of the lower quartile (Q_1). Then we look at the numbers above the median: 24, 27, 32, 39, 51. Again there are five values, so the 3rd is the median (32), or the value of the upper quartile (Q_3). We find the IQR by subtracting Q_1 from Q_3: $32 - 16 = 16$.

68-95-99.7 RULE

The **68–95–99.7 rule** describes how a normal distribution of data should appear when compared to the mean. This is also a description of a normal bell curve. According to this rule, 68 percent of the data values in a normally distributed set should fall within one standard deviation of the mean (34 percent above and 34 percent below the mean), 95 percent of the data values should fall within two standard deviations of the mean (47.5 percent above and 47.5 percent below the mean), and 99.7 percent of the data values should fall within three standard deviations of the mean, again, equally distributed on either side of the mean. This means that only 0.3 percent of all data values should fall more than three standard deviations from the mean. On the graph below, the normal curve is centered on the *y*-axis. The *x*-axis labels are how many standard deviations away from the center you are. Therefore, it is easy to see how the 68-95-99.7 rule can apply.

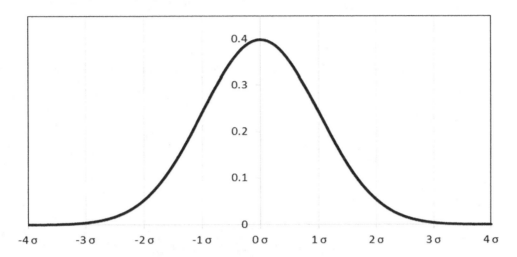

SCATTER PLOTS

BIVARIATE DATA

Bivariate data is simply data from two different variables. (The prefix *bi-* means *two*.) In a *scatter plot*, each value in the set of data is plotted on a grid similar to a Cartesian plane, where each axis represents one of the two variables. By looking at the pattern formed by the points on the grid, you can often determine whether or not there is a relationship between the two variables, and what that relationship is, if it exists. The variables may be directly proportionate, inversely proportionate, or show no proportion at all. It may also be possible to determine if the data is linear, and if so, to find an equation to relate the two variables. The following scatter plot shows the relationship between preference for brand "A" and the age of the consumers surveyed.

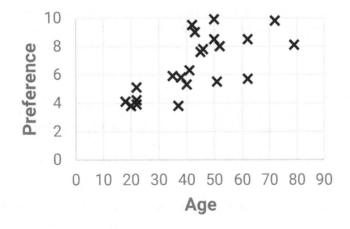

SCATTER PLOTS

Scatter plots are also useful in determining the type of function represented by the data and finding the simple regression. Linear scatter plots may be positive or negative. Nonlinear scatter plots are generally exponential or quadratic. Below are some common types of scatter plots:

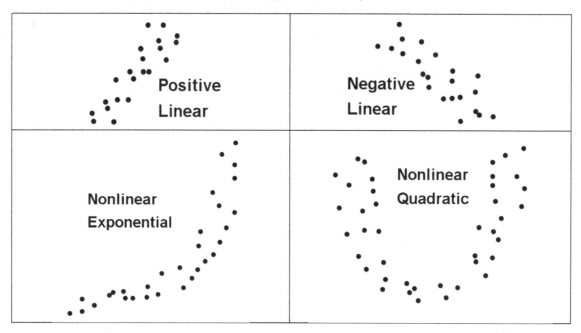

Algebra

LINEAR EXPRESSIONS

TERMS AND COEFFICIENTS

Mathematical expressions consist of a combination of one or more values arranged in terms that are added together. As such, an expression could be just a single number, including zero. A **variable term** is the product of a real number, also called a **coefficient**, and one or more variables, each of which may be raised to an exponent. Expressions may also include numbers without a variable, called **constants** or **constant terms**. The expression $6s^2$, for example, is a single term where the coefficient is the real number 6 and the variable term is s^2. Note that if a term is written as simply a variable to some exponent, like t^2, then the coefficient is 1, because $t^2 = 1t^2$.

LINEAR EXPRESSIONS

A **single variable linear expression** is the sum of a single variable term, where the variable has no exponent, and a constant, which may be zero. For instance, the expression $2w + 7$ has $2w$ as the variable term and 7 as the constant term. It is important to realize that terms are separated by addition or subtraction. Since an expression is a sum of terms, expressions such as $5x - 3$ can be written as $5x + (-3)$ to emphasize that the constant term is negative. A real-world example of a single variable linear expression is the perimeter of a square, four times the side length, often expressed: $4s$.

In general, a **linear expression** is the sum of any number of variable terms so long as none of the variables have an exponent. For example, $3m + 8n - \frac{1}{4}p + 5.5q - 1$ is a linear expression, but $3y^3$ is not. In the same way, the expression for the perimeter of a general triangle, the sum of the side lengths $(a + b + c)$ is considered to be linear, but the expression for the area of a square, the side length squared (s^2) is not.

LINEAR EQUATIONS

Equations that can be written as $ax + b = 0$, where $a \neq 0$, are referred to as **one variable linear equations**. A solution to such an equation is called a **root**. In the case where we have the equation $5x + 10 = 0$, if we solve for x we get a solution of $x = -2$. In other words, the root of the equation is –2. This is found by first subtracting 10 from both sides, which gives $5x = -10$. Next, simply divide both sides by the coefficient of the variable, in this case 5, to get $x = -2$. This can be checked by plugging –2 back into the original equation $(5)(-2) + 10 = -10 + 10 = 0$.

The **solution set** is the set of all solutions of an equation. In our example, the solution set would simply be –2. If there were more solutions (there usually are in multivariable equations) then they would also be included in the solution set. When an equation has no true solutions, it is referred to as an **empty set**. Equations with identical solution sets are **equivalent equations**. An **identity** is a term whose value or determinant is equal to 1.

Linear equations can be written many ways. Below is a list of some forms linear equations can take:

- **Standard Form**: $Ax + By = C$; the slope is $\frac{-A}{B}$ and the y-intercept is $\frac{C}{B}$
- **Slope Intercept Form**: $y = mx + b$, where m is the slope and b is the y-intercept
- **Point-Slope Form**: $y - y_1 = m(x - x_1)$, where m is the slope and (x_1, y_1) is a point on the line
- **Two-Point Form**: $\frac{y - y_1}{x - x_1} = \frac{y_2 - y_1}{x_2 - x_1}$, where (x_1, y_1) and (x_2, y_2) are two points on the given line
- **Intercept Form**: $\frac{x}{x_1} + \frac{y}{y_1} = 1$, where $(x_1, 0)$ is the point at which a line intersects the x-axis, and $(0, y_1)$
  is the point at which the same line intersects the y-axis

> **Review Video: Slope-Intercept and Point-Slope Forms**
> Visit mometrix.com/academy and enter code: 113216
>
> **Review Video: Linear Equations Basics**
> Visit mometrix.com/academy and enter code: 793005

SOLVING EQUATIONS
SOLVING ONE-VARIABLE LINEAR EQUATIONS

Multiply all terms by the lowest common denominator to eliminate any fractions. Look for addition or subtraction to undo so you can isolate the variable on one side of the equal sign. Divide both sides by the coefficient of the variable. When you have a value for the variable, substitute this value into the original equation to make sure you have a true equation. Consider the following example:

Kim's savings are represented by the table below. Represent her savings, using an equation.

X (Months)	Y (Total Savings)
2	$1,300
5	$2,050
9	$3,050
11	$3,550
16	$4,800

The table shows a function with a constant rate of change, or slope, of 250. Given the points on the table, the slopes can be calculated as $\frac{(2{,}050-1300)}{(5-2)}$, $\frac{(3{,}050-2{,}050)}{(9-5)}$, $\frac{(3{,}550-3{,}050)}{(11-9)}$, and $\frac{(4{,}800-3{,}550)}{(16-11)}$, each of which equals 250. Thus, the table shows a constant rate of change, indicating a linear function. The slope-intercept form of a linear equation is written as $y = mx + b$, where m represents the slope and b represents the y-intercept. Substituting the slope into this form gives $y = 250x + b$. Substituting corresponding x- and y-values from any point into this equation will give the y-intercept, or b. Using the point, $(2, 1{,}300)$, gives $1{,}300 = 250(2) + b$, which simplifies as $b = 800$. Thus, her savings may be represented by the equation, $y = 250x + 800$.

RULES FOR MANIPULATING EQUATIONS
LIKE TERMS

Like terms are terms in an equation that have the same variable, regardless of whether or not they also have the same coefficient. This includes terms that *lack* a variable; all constants (i.e., numbers without variables) are considered like terms. If the equation involves terms with a variable raised to different powers, the like terms are those that have the variable raised to the same power.

For example, consider the equation $x^2 + 3x + 2 = 2x^2 + x - 7 + 2x$. In this equation, 2 and –7 are like terms; they are both constants. $3x$, x, and $2x$ are like terms, they all include the variable x raised to the first power. x^2 and $2x^2$ are like terms, they both include the variable x, raised to the second power. $2x$ and $2x^2$ are not like terms; although they both involve the variable x, the variable is not raised to the same power in both terms. The fact that they have the same coefficient, 2, is not relevant.

> **Review Video: Rules for Manipulating Equations**
> Visit mometrix.com/academy and enter code: 838871

CARRYING OUT THE SAME OPERATION ON BOTH SIDES OF AN EQUATION

When solving an equation, the general procedure is to carry out a series of operations on both sides of an equation, choosing operations that will tend to simplify the equation when doing so. The reason why the same operation must be carried out on both sides of the equation is because that leaves the meaning of the equation unchanged, and yields a result that is equivalent to the original equation. This would not be the case if we carried out an operation on one side of an equation and not the other. Consider what an equation means: it is a statement that two values or expressions are equal. If we carry out the same operation on both sides of the equation—add 3 to both sides, for example—then the two sides of the equation are changed in the same way, and so remain equal. If we do that to only one side of the equation—add 3 to one side but not the other—then that wouldn't be true; if we change one side of the equation but not the other then the two sides are no longer equal.

ADVANTAGE OF COMBINING LIKE TERMS

Combining like terms refers to adding or subtracting like terms—terms with the same variable—and therefore reducing sets of like terms to a single term. The main advantage of doing this is that it simplifies the equation. Often, combining like terms can be done as the first step in solving an equation, though it can also be done later, such as after distributing terms in a product.

For example, consider the equation $2(x + 3) + 3(2 + x + 3) = -4$. The 2 and the 3 in the second set of parentheses are like terms, and we can combine them, yielding $2(x + 3) + 3(x + 5) = -4$. Now we can carry out the multiplications implied by the parentheses, distributing the outer 2 and 3 accordingly: $2x + 6 + 3x + 15 = -4$. The $2x$ and the $3x$ are like terms, and we can add them together: $5x + 6 + 15 = -4$. Now, the constants 6, 15, and –4 are also like terms, and we can combine them as well: subtracting 6 and 15 from both sides of the equation, we get $5x = -4 - 6 - 15$, or $5x = -25$, which simplifies further to $x = -5$.

> **Review Video: Solving Equations by Combining Like Terms**
> Visit mometrix.com/academy and enter code: 668506

CANCELING TERMS ON OPPOSITE SIDES OF AN EQUATION

Two terms on opposite sides of an equation can be canceled if and only if they *exactly* match each other. They must have the same variable raised to the same power and the same coefficient. For example, in the equation $3x + 2x^2 + 6 = 2x^2 - 6$, $2x^2$ appears on both sides of the equation and can be canceled, leaving $3x + 6 = -6$. The 6 on each side of the equation *cannot* be canceled, because it is added on one side of the equation and subtracted on the other. While they cannot be canceled, however, the 6 and –6 are like terms and can be combined, yielding $3x = -12$, which simplifies further to $x = -4$.

It's also important to note that the terms to be canceled must be independent terms and cannot be part of a larger term. For example, consider the equation $2(x + 6) = 3(x + 4) + 1$. We cannot cancel the x's, because even though they match each other they are part of the larger terms $2(x + 6)$ and $3(x + 4)$. We must first distribute the 2 and 3, yielding $2x + 12 = 3x + 12 + 1$. Now we see that the terms with the x's do not match, but the 12s do, and can be canceled, leaving $2x = 3x + 1$, which simplifies to $x = -1$.

PROCESS FOR MANIPULATING EQUATIONS

ISOLATING VARIABLES

To **isolate a variable** means to manipulate the equation so that the variable appears by itself on one side of the equation, and does not appear at all on the other side. Generally, an equation or inequality is considered to be solved once the variable is isolated and the other side of the equation or inequality is simplified as much as possible. In the case of a two-variable equation or inequality, only one variable needs to be isolated; it will not usually be possible to simultaneously isolate both variables.

For a linear equation—an equation in which the variable only appears raised to the first power—isolating a variable can be done by first moving all the terms with the variable to one side of the equation and all other terms to the other side. (*Moving* a term really means adding the inverse of the term to both sides; when a term is *moved* to the other side of the equation its sign is flipped.) Then combine like terms on each side. Finally, divide both sides by the coefficient of the variable, if applicable. The steps need not necessarily be done in this order, but this order will always work.

> **Review Video: Solving One-Step Equations**
> Visit mometrix.com/academy and enter code: 777004

EQUATIONS WITH MORE THAN ONE SOLUTION

Some types of non-linear equations, such as equations involving squares of variables, may have more than one solution. For example, the equation $x^2 = 4$ has two solutions: 2 and –2. Equations with absolute values can also have multiple solutions: $|x| = 1$ has the solutions $x = 1$ and $x = -1$.

It is also possible for a linear equation to have more than one solution, but only if the equation is true regardless of the value of the variable. In this case, the equation is considered to have infinitely many solutions, because any possible value of the variable is a solution. We know a linear equation has infinitely many solutions if when we combine like terms the variables cancel, leaving a true statement. For example, consider the equation $2(3x + 5) = x + 5(x + 2)$. Distributing, we get $6x + 10 = x + 5x + 10$; combining like terms gives $6x + 10 = 6x + 10$, and the $6x$-terms cancel to leave $10 = 10$. This is clearly true, so the original equation is true for any value of x. We could also have canceled the 10s leaving $0 = 0$, but again this is clearly true—in general if both sides of the equation match exactly, it has infinitely many solutions.

EQUATIONS WITH NO SOLUTION

Some types of non-linear equations, such as equations involving squares of variables, may have no solution. For example, the equation $x^2 = -2$ has no solutions in the real numbers, because the square of any real number must be positive. Similarly, $|x| = -1$ has no solution, because the absolute value of a number is always positive.

It is also possible for an equation to have no solution even if does not involve any powers greater than one, absolute values, or other special functions. For example, the equation $2(x + 3) + x = 3x$ has no solution. We can see that if we try to solve it: first we distribute, leaving $2x + 6 + x = 3x$. But now if we try to combine all the terms with the variable, we find that they cancel: we have $3x$ on the left and $3x$ on the right, canceling to leave us with $6 = 0$. This is clearly false. In general, whenever the variable terms in an equation cancel leaving different constants on both sides, it means that the equation has no solution. (If we are left with the *same* constant on both sides, the equation has infinitely many solutions instead.)

FEATURES OF EQUATIONS THAT REQUIRE SPECIAL TREATMENT
LINEAR EQUATIONS

A linear equation is an equation in which variables only appear by themselves: not multiplied together, not with exponents other than one, and not inside absolute value signs or any other functions. For example, the equation $x + 1 - 3x = 5 - x$ is a linear equation; while x appears multiple times, it never appears with an exponent other than one, or inside any function. The two-variable equation $2x - 3y = 5 + 2x$ is also a linear equation. In contrast, the equation $x^2 - 5 = 3x$ is *not* a linear equation, because it involves the term x^2. $\sqrt{x} = 5$ is not a linear equation, because it involves a square root. $(x - 1)^2 = 4$ is not a linear equation because even though there's no exponent on the x directly, it appears as part of an expression that is squared. The two-variable equation $x + xy - y = 5$ is not a linear equation because it includes the term xy, where two variables are multiplied together.

Linear equations can always be solved (or shown to have no solution) by combining like terms and performing simple operations on both sides of the equation. Some non-linear equations can be solved by similar methods, but others may require more advanced methods of solution, if they can be solved analytically at all.

SOLVING EQUATIONS INVOLVING ROOTS

In an equation involving roots, the first step is to isolate the term with the root, if possible, and then raise both sides of the equation to the appropriate power to eliminate it. Consider an example equation, $2\sqrt{x + 1} - 1 = 3$. In this case, begin by adding 1 to both sides, yielding $2\sqrt{x + 1} = 4$, and then dividing both sides by 2, yielding $\sqrt{x + 1} = 2$. Now square both sides, yielding $x + 1 = 4$. Finally, subtracting 1 from both sides yields $x = 3$.

Squaring both sides of an equation may, however, yield a spurious solution—a solution to the squared equation that is *not* a solution of the original equation. It's therefore necessary to plug the solution back into the original equation to make sure it works. In this case, it does: $2\sqrt{3 + 1} - 1 = 2\sqrt{4} - 1 = 2(2) - 1 = 4 - 1 = 3$.

The same procedure applies for other roots as well. For example, given the equation $3 + \sqrt[3]{2x} = 5$, we can first subtract 3 from both sides, yielding $\sqrt[3]{2x} = 2$ and isolating the root. Raising both sides to the third power yields $2x = 2^3$; i.e., $2x = 8$. We can now divide both sides by 2 to get $x = 4$.

SOLVING EQUATIONS WITH EXPONENTS

To solve an equation involving an exponent, the first step is to isolate the variable with the exponent. We can then take the appropriate root of both sides to eliminate the exponent. For instance, for the equation $2x^3 + 17 = 5x^3 - 7$, we can subtract $5x^3$ from both sides to get $-3x^3 + 17 = -7$, and then subtract 17 from both sides to get $-3x^3 = -24$. Finally, we can divide both sides by –3 to get $x^3 = 8$. Finally, we can take the cube root of both sides to get $x = \sqrt[3]{8} = 2$.

One important but often overlooked point is that equations with an exponent greater than 1 may have more than one answer. The solution to $x^2 = 9$ isn't simply $x = 3$; it's $x = \pm 3$ (that is, $x = 3$ or $x = -3$). For a slightly more complicated example, consider the equation $(x - 1)^2 - 1 = 3$. Adding 1 to both sides yields $(x - 1)^2 = 4$; taking the square root of both sides yields $x - 1 = 2$. We can then add 1 to both sides to get $x = 3$. However, there's a second solution. We also have the possibility that $x - 1 = -2$, in which case $x = -1$. Both $x = 3$ and $x = -1$ are valid solutions, as can be verified by substituting them both into the original equation.

> **Review Video: <u>Solving Equations with Exponents</u>**
> Visit mometrix.com/academy and enter code: 514557

SOLVING EQUATIONS WITH ABSOLUTE VALUES

When solving an equation with an absolute value, the first step is to isolate the absolute value term. We then consider two possibilities: when the expression inside the absolute value is positive or when it is negative. In the former case, the expression in the absolute value equals the expression on the other side of the equation; in the latter, it equals the additive inverse of that expression—the expression times negative one. We consider each case separately and finally check for spurious solutions.

For instance, consider solving $|2x - 1| + x = 5$ for x. We can first isolate the absolute value by moving the x to the other side: $|2x - 1| = -x + 5$. Now, we have two possibilities. First, that $2x - 1$ is positive, and hence $2x - 1 = -x + 5$. Rearranging and combining like terms yields $3x = 6$, and hence $x = 2$. The other possibility is that $2x - 1$ is negative, and hence $2x - 1 = -(-x + 5) = x - 5$. In this case, rearranging and combining like terms yields $x = -4$. Substituting $x = 2$ and $x = -4$ back into the original equation, we see that they are both valid solutions.

Note that the absolute value of a sum or difference applies to the sum or difference as a whole, not to the individual terms; in general, $|2x - 1|$ is not equal to $|2x + 1|$ or to $|2x| - 1$.

SPURIOUS SOLUTIONS

A **spurious solution** may arise when we square both sides of an equation as a step in solving it or under certain other operations on the equation. It is a solution to the squared or otherwise modified equation that is *not* a solution of the original equation. To identify a spurious solution, it's useful when you solve an equation involving roots or absolute values to plug the solution back into the original equation to make sure it's valid.

CHOOSING WHICH VARIABLE TO ISOLATE IN TWO-VARIABLE EQUATIONS

Similar to methods for a one-variable equation, solving a two-variable equation involves isolating a variable: manipulating the equation so that a variable appears by itself on one side of the equation, and not at all on the other side. However, in a two-variable equation, you will usually only be able to isolate one of the variables; the other variable may appear on the other side along with constant terms, or with exponents or other functions.

Often one variable will be much more easily isolated than the other, and therefore that's the variable you should choose. If one variable appears with various exponents, and the other is only raised to the first power, the latter variable is the one to isolate: given the equation $a^2 + 2b = a^3 + b + 3$, the b only appears to the first power, whereas a appears squared and cubed, so b is the variable that can be solved for: combining like terms and isolating the b on the left side of the equation, we get $b = a^3 - a^2 + 3$. If both variables are equally easy to isolate, then it's best to isolate the dependent variable, if one is defined; if the two variables are x and y, the convention is that y is the dependent variable.

> **Review Video: <u>Solving Equations with Variables on Both Sides</u>**
> Visit mometrix.com/academy and enter code: 402497

GRAPHING EQUATIONS
GRAPHICAL SOLUTIONS TO EQUATIONS

When equations are shown graphically, they are usually shown on a **Cartesian coordinate plane**. The Cartesian coordinate plane consists of two number lines placed perpendicular to each other and intersecting at the zero point, also known as the origin. The horizontal number line is known as the x-axis, with positive values to the right of the origin, and negative values to the left of the origin. The vertical number line is known as the y-axis, with positive values above the origin, and negative values below the origin. Any point on the plane can be identified by an ordered pair in the form (x, y), called coordinates. The x-value of the coordinate is called the abscissa, and the y-value of the coordinate is called the ordinate. The two number lines divide the plane into **four quadrants**: I, II, III, and IV.

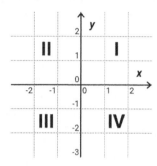

Note that in quadrant I $x > 0$ and $y > 0$, in quadrant II $x < 0$ and $y > 0$, in quadrant III $x < 0$ and $y < 0$, and in quadrant IV $x > 0$ and $y < 0$.

Recall that if the value of the slope of a line is positive, the line slopes upward from left to right. If the value of the slope is negative, the line slopes downward from left to right. If the y-coordinates are the same for two points on a line, the slope is 0 and the line is a **horizontal line**. If the x-coordinates are the same for two points on a line, there is no slope and the line is a **vertical line**. Two or more lines that have equivalent slopes are **parallel lines**. **Perpendicular lines** have slopes that are negative reciprocals of each other, such as $\frac{a}{b}$ and $\frac{-b}{a}$.

> **Review Video: Cartesian Coordinate Plane and Graphing**
> Visit mometrix.com/academy and enter code: 115173

GRAPHING EQUATIONS IN TWO VARIABLES

One way of graphing an equation in two variables is to plot enough points to get an idea for its shape and then draw the appropriate curve through those points. A point can be plotted by substituting in a value for one variable and solving for the other. If the equation is linear, we only need two points and can then draw a straight line between them.

For example, consider the equation $y = 2x - 1$. This is a linear equation—both variables only appear raised to the first power—so we only need two points. When $x = 0$, $y = 2(0) - 1 = -1$. When $x = 2$, $y = 2(2) - 1 = 3$. We can therefore choose the points $(0, -1)$ and $(2, 3)$, and draw a line between them:

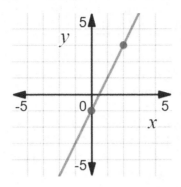

INEQUALITIES

WORKING WITH INEQUALITIES

Commonly in algebra and other upper-level fields of math you find yourself working with mathematical expressions that do not equal each other. The statement comparing such expressions with symbols such as $<$ (less than) or $>$ (greater than) is called an *inequality*. An example of an inequality is $7x > 5$. To solve for x, simply divide both sides by 7 and the solution is shown to be $x > \frac{5}{7}$. Graphs of the solution set of inequalities are represented on a number line. Open circles are used to show that an expression approaches a number but is never quite equal to that number.

> **Review Video: Solving Multi-Step Inequalities**
> Visit mometrix.com/academy and enter code: 347842
>
> **Review Video: Solving Inequalities Using All 4 Basic Operations**
> Visit mometrix.com/academy and enter code: 401111

Conditional inequalities are those with certain values for the variable that will make the condition true and other values for the variable where the condition will be false. **Absolute inequalities** can have any real number as the value for the variable to make the condition true, while there is no real number value for the variable that will make the condition false. Solving inequalities is done by following the same rules for solving equations with the exception that when multiplying or dividing by a negative number the direction of the inequality sign must be flipped or reversed. **Double inequalities** are situations where two inequality statements apply to the same variable expression. Example: $-c < ax + b < c$.

> **Review Video: Conditional and Absolute Inequalities**
> Visit mometrix.com/academy and enter code: 980164

DETERMINING SOLUTIONS TO INEQUALITIES

To determine whether a coordinate is a solution of an inequality, you can substitute the values of the coordinate into the inequality, simplify, and check whether the resulting statement holds true. For instance, to determine whether $(-2,4)$ is a solution of the inequality $y \geq -2x + 3$, substitute the values into the inequality, $4 \geq -2(-2) + 3$. Simplify the right side of the inequality and the result is $4 \geq 7$, which is a false statement. Therefore, the coordinate is not a solution of the inequality. You can also use this method to determine which part of the graph of an inequality is shaded. The graph of $y \geq -2x + 3$ includes the solid line $y = -2x + 3$ and, since it excludes the point $(-2,4)$ to the left of the line, it is shaded to the right of the line.

FLIPPING INEQUALITY SIGNS

When given an inequality, we can always turn the entire inequality around, swapping the two sides of the inequality and changing the inequality sign. For instance, $x + 2 > 2x - 3$ is equivalent to $2x - 3 < x + 2$. Aside from that, normally the inequality does not change if we carry out the same operation on both sides of the inequality. There is, however, one principal exception: if we *multiply* or *divide* both sides of the inequality by a *negative number*, the inequality is flipped. For example, if we take the inequality $-2x < 6$ and divide both sides by –2, the inequality flips and we are left with $x > -3$. This *only* applies to multiplication and division, and only with negative numbers. Multiplying or dividing both sides by a positive number, or adding or subtracting any number regardless of sign, does not flip the inequality. Another special case that flips the inequality sign is when reciprocals are used. For instance, $3 > 2$ but the relation of the reciprocals is $\frac{1}{2} < \frac{1}{3}$.

COMPOUND INEQUALITIES

A **compound inequality** is an equality that consists of two inequalities combined with *and* or *or*. The two components of a proper compound inequality must be of opposite type: that is, one must be greater than (or greater than or equal to), the other less than (or less than or equal to). For instance, "$x + 1 < 2$ or $x + 1 > 3$" is a compound inequality, as is "$2x \geq 4$ and $2x \leq 6$." An *and* inequality can be written more compactly by having one inequality on each side of the common part: "$2x \geq 1$ and $2x \leq 6$," can also be written as $1 \leq 2x \leq 6$.

In order for the compound inequality to be meaningful, the two parts of an *and* inequality must overlap; otherwise, no numbers satisfy the inequality. On the other hand, if the two parts of an *or* inequality overlap, then *all* numbers satisfy the inequality and as such the inequality is usually not meaningful.

Solving a compound inequality requires solving each part separately. For example, given the compound inequality "$x + 1 < 2$ or $x + 1 > 3$," the first inequality, $x + 1 < 2$, reduces to $x < 1$, and the second part, $x + 1 > 3$, reduces to $x > 2$, so the whole compound inequality can be written as "$x < 1$ or $x > 2$." Similarly, $1 \leq 2x \leq 6$ can be solved by dividing each term by 2, yielding $\frac{1}{2} \leq x \leq 3$.

SOLVING INEQUALITIES INVOLVING ABSOLUTE VALUES

To solve an inequality involving an absolute value, first isolate the term with the absolute value. Then proceed to treat the two cases separately as with an absolute value equation, but flipping the inequality in the case where the expression in the absolute value is negative (since that essentially involves multiplying both sides by –1.) The two cases are then combined into a compound inequality; if the absolute value is on the greater side of the inequality, then it is an *or* compound inequality, if on the lesser side, then it's an *and*.

Consider the inequality $2 + |x - 1| \geq 3$. We can isolate the absolute value term by subtracting 2 from both sides: $|x - 1| \geq 1$. Now, we're left with the two cases $x - 1 \geq 1$ or $x - 1 \leq -1$: note that in the latter, negative case, the inequality is flipped. $x - 1 \geq 1$ reduces to $x \geq 2$, and $x - 1 \leq -1$ reduces to $x \leq 0$. Since in the inequality $|x - 1| \geq 1$ the absolute value is on the greater side, the two cases combine into an *or* compound inequality, so the final, solved inequality is "$x \leq 0$ or $x \geq 2$."

SOLVING INEQUALITIES INVOLVING SQUARE ROOTS

Solving an inequality with a square root involves two parts. First, we solve the inequality as if it were an equation, isolating the square root and then squaring both sides of the equation. Second, we restrict the solution to the set of values of x for which the value inside the square root sign is non-negative.

For example, in the inequality, $\sqrt{x - 2} + 1 < 5$, we can isolate the square root by subtracting 1 from both sides, yielding $\sqrt{x - 2} < 4$. Squaring both sides of the inequality yields $x - 2 < 16$, so $x < 18$. Since we can't take the square root of a negative number, we also require the part inside the square root to be non-negative. In this case, that means $x - 2 \geq 0$. Adding 2 to both sides of the inequality yields $x \geq 2$. Our final answer is a compound inequality combining the two simple inequalities: $x \geq 2$ and $x < 18$, or $2 \leq x < 18$.

Note that we only get a compound inequality if the two simple inequalities are in opposite directions; otherwise, we take the one that is more restrictive.

The same technique can be used for other even roots, such as fourth roots. It is *not*, however, used for cube roots or other odd roots—negative numbers *do* have cube roots, so the condition that the quantity inside the root sign cannot be negative does not apply.

> **Review Video: <u>Solving Inequalities Involving Square Roots</u>**
> Visit mometrix.com/academy and enter code: 800288

SPECIAL CIRCUMSTANCES

Sometimes an inequality involving an absolute value or an even exponent is true for all values of x, and we don't need to do any further work to solve it. This is true if the inequality, once the absolute value or exponent term is isolated, says that term is greater than a negative number (or greater than or equal to zero). Since an absolute value or a number raised to an even exponent is *always* non-negative, this inequality is always true.

GRAPHICAL SOLUTIONS TO INEQUALITIES

GRAPHING SIMPLE INEQUALITIES

To graph a simple inequality, we first mark on the number line the value that signifies the end point of the inequality. If the inequality is strict (involves a less than or greater than), we use a hollow circle; if it is not strict (less than or equal to or greater than or equal to), we use a solid circle. We then fill in the part of the number line that satisfies the inequality: to the left of the marked point for less than (or less than or equal to), to the right for greater than (or greater than or equal to).

For example, we would graph the inequality $x < 5$ by putting a hollow circle at 5 and filling in the part of the line to the left:

GRAPHING COMPOUND INEQUALITIES

To graph a compound inequality, we fill in both parts of the inequality for an *or* inequality, or the overlap between them for an *and* inequality. More specifically, we start by plotting the endpoints of each inequality on the number line. For an *or* inequality, we then fill in the appropriate side of the line for each inequality. Typically, the two component inequalities do not overlap, which means the shaded part is *outside* the two points. For an *and* inequality, we instead fill in the part of the line that meets both inequalities.

For the inequality "$x \leq -3$ or $x > 4$," we first put a solid circle at –3 and a hollow circle at 4. We then fill the parts of the line *outside* these circles:

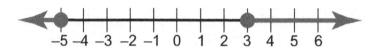

GRAPHING INEQUALITIES INCLUDING ABSOLUTE VALUES

An inequality with an absolute value can be converted to a compound inequality. To graph the inequality, first convert it to a compound inequality, and then graph that normally. If the absolute value is on the greater side of the inequality, we end up with an *or* inequality; we plot the endpoints of the inequality on the number line and fill in the part of the line *outside* those points. If the absolute value is on the smaller side of the inequality, we end up with an *and* inequality; we plot the endpoints of the inequality on the number line and fill in the part of the line *between* those points.

For example, the inequality $|x + 1| \geq 4$ can be rewritten as $x \geq 3$ or $x \leq -5$. We place solid circles at the points 3 and –5 and fill in the part of the line *outside* them:

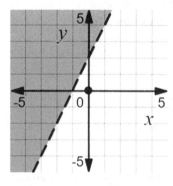

GRAPHING INEQUALITIES IN TWO VARIABLES

To graph an inequality in two variables, we first graph the border of the inequality. This means graphing the equation that we get if we replace the inequality sign with an equals sign. If the inequality is strict ($>$ or $<$), we graph the border with a dashed or dotted line; if it is not strict ($\geq$ or $\leq$), we use a solid line. We can then test any point not on the border to see if it satisfies the inequality. If it does, we shade in that side of the border; if not, we shade in the other side. As an example, consider $y > 2x + 2$. To graph this inequality, we first graph the border, $y = 2x + 2$. Since it is a strict inequality, we use a dashed line. Then, we choose a test point. This can be any point not on the border; in this case, we will choose the origin, (0,0). (This makes the calculation easy and is generally a good choice unless the border passes through the origin.) Putting this into the original inequality, we get $0 > 2(0) + 2$, i.e., $0 > 2$. This is *not* true, so we shade in the side of the border that does *not* include the point (0,0):

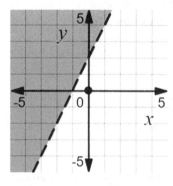

GRAPHING COMPOUND INEQUALITIES IN TWO VARIABLES

One way to graph a compound inequality in two variables is to first graph each of the component inequalities. For an *and* inequality, we then shade in only the parts where the two graphs overlap; for an *or* inequality, we shade in any region that pertains to either of the individual inequalities.

Consider the graph of "$y \geq x - 1$ and $y \leq -x$":

We first shade in the individual inequalities:

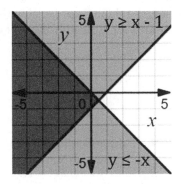

Now, since the compound inequality has an *and*, we only leave shaded the overlap—the part that pertains to *both* inequalities:

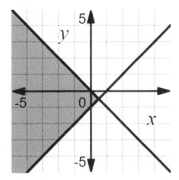

If instead the inequality had been "$y \geq x - 1$ or $y \leq -x$," our final graph would involve the *total* shaded area:

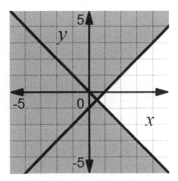

> **Review Video: Graphing Solutions to Inequalities**
> Visit mometrix.com/academy and enter code: 391281

SYSTEMS OF EQUATIONS
SOLVING SYSTEMS OF EQUATIONS

A **system of equations** is a set of simultaneous equations that all use the same variables. A solution to a system of equations must be true for each equation in the system. **Consistent systems** are those with at least one solution. **Inconsistent systems** are systems of equations that have no solution.

> **Review Video: Solving Systems of Linear Equations**
> Visit mometrix.com/academy and enter code: 746745

SUBSTITUTION

To solve a system of linear equations by **substitution**, start with the easier equation and solve for one of the variables. Express this variable in terms of the other variable. Substitute this expression in the other equation and solve for the other variable. The solution should be expressed in the form (x, y). Substitute the values into both of the original equations to check your answer. Consider the following system of equations:

$$x + 6y = 15$$
$$3x - 12y = 18$$

Solving the first equation for x: $x = 15 - 6y$

Substitute this value in place of x in the second equation, and solve for y:

$$3(15 - 6y) - 12y = 18$$
$$45 - 18y - 12y = 18$$
$$30y = 27$$
$$y = \frac{27}{30} = \frac{9}{10} = 0.9$$

Plug this value for y back into the first equation to solve for x:

$$x = 15 - 6(0.9) = 15 - 5.4 = 9.6$$

Check both equations if you have time:

$$9.6 + 6(0.9) = 15 \qquad 3(9.6) - 12(0.9) = 18$$
$$9.6 + 5.4 = 15 \qquad 28.8 - 10.8 = 18$$
$$15 = 15 \qquad 18 = 18$$

Therefore, the solution is (9.6, 0.9).

> **Review Video: The Substitution Method**
> Visit mometrix.com/academy and enter code: 565151
>
> **Review Video: Substitution and Elimination**
> Visit mometrix.com/academy and enter code: 958611

ELIMINATION

To solve a system of equations using **elimination**, begin by rewriting both equations in standard form $Ax + By = C$. Check to see if the coefficients of one pair of like variables add to zero. If not, multiply one or both of the equations by a non-zero number to make one set of like variables add to zero. Add the two equations to solve for one of the variables. Substitute this value into one of the original equations to solve for the other variable. Check your work by substituting into the other equation. Now, let's look at solving the following system using the elimination method:

$$5x + 6y = 4$$
$$x + 2y = 4$$

If we multiply the second equation by -3, we can eliminate the y-terms:

$$5x + 6y = 4$$
$$-3x - 6y = -12$$

Add the equations together and solve for x:

$$2x = -8$$
$$x = \frac{-8}{2} = -4$$

Plug the value for x back in to either of the original equations and solve for y:

$$-4 + 2y = 4$$
$$y = \frac{4 + 4}{2} = 4$$

Check both equations if you have time:

$$5(-4) + 6(4) = 4 \qquad\qquad -4 + 2(4) = 4$$
$$-20 + 24 = 4 \qquad\qquad -4 + 8 = 4$$
$$4 = 4 \qquad\qquad 4 = 4$$

Therefore, the solution is $(-4, 4)$.

> **Review Video: The Elimination Method**
> Visit mometrix.com/academy and enter code: 449121

GRAPHICALLY

To solve a system of linear equations **graphically**, plot both equations on the same graph. The solution of the equations is the point where both lines cross. If the lines do not cross (are parallel), then there is **no solution**.

For example, consider the following system of equations:

$$y = 2x + 7$$
$$y = -x + 1$$

Since these equations are given in slope-intercept form, they are easy to graph; the y-intercepts of the lines are $(0,7)$ and $(0,1)$. The respective slopes are 2 and -1, thus the graphs look like this:

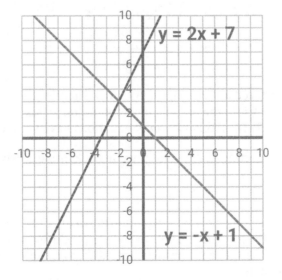

The two lines intersect at the point $(-2, 3)$, thus this is the solution to the system of equations.

Solving a system graphically is generally only practical if both coordinates of the solution are integers; otherwise the intersection will lie between gridlines on the graph and the coordinates will be difficult or impossible to determine exactly. It also helps if, as in this example, the equations are in slope-intercept form or some other form that makes them easy to graph. Otherwise, another method of solution (by substitution or elimination) is likely to be more useful.

> **Review Video: Solving Systems by Graphing**
> Visit mometrix.com/academy and enter code: 634812

SOLVING SYSTEMS OF EQUATIONS USING THE TRACE FEATURE

Using the trace feature on a calculator requires that you rewrite each equation, isolating the y-variable on one side of the equal sign. Enter both equations in the graphing calculator and plot the graphs simultaneously. Use the trace cursor to find where the two lines cross. Use the zoom feature if necessary to obtain more accurate results. Always check your answer by substituting into the original equations. The trace method is likely to be less accurate than other methods due to the resolution of graphing calculators but is a useful tool to provide an approximate answer.

ADVANCED SYSTEMS OF EQUATIONS

SOLVING A SYSTEM OF EQUATIONS CONSISTING OF A LINEAR EQUATION AND A QUADRATIC EQUATION

ALGEBRAICALLY

Generally, the simplest way to solve a system of equations consisting of a linear equation and a quadratic equation algebraically is through the method of substitution. One possible strategy is to solve the linear equation for y and then substitute that expression into the quadratic equation. After expansion and combining like terms, this will result in a new quadratic equation for x, which, like all quadratic equations, may have zero, one, or two solutions. Plugging each solution for x back into one of the original equations will then produce the corresponding value of y.

For example, consider the following system of equations:

$$x + y = 1$$
$$y = (x + 3)^2 - 2$$

We can solve the linear equation for y to yield $y = -x + 1$. Substituting this expression into the quadratic equation produces $-x + 1 = (x + 3)^2 - 2$. We can simplify this equation:

$$-x + 1 = (x + 3)^2 - 2$$
$$-x + 1 = x^2 + 6x + 9 - 2$$
$$-x + 1 = x^2 + 6x + 7$$
$$0 = x^2 + 7x + 6$$

This quadratic equation can be factored as $(x + 1)(x + 6) = 0$. It therefore has two solutions: $x_1 = -1$ and $x_2 = -6$. Plugging each of these back into the original linear equation yields $y_1 = -x_1 + 1 = -(-1) + 1 = 2$ and $y_2 = -x_2 + 1 = -(-6) + 1 = 7$. Thus, this system of equations has two solutions, $(-1,2)$ and $(-6,7)$.

It may help to check your work by putting each x- and y-value back into the original equations and verifying that they do provide a solution.

GRAPHICALLY

To solve a system of equations consisting of a linear equation and a quadratic equation graphically, plot both equations on the same graph. The linear equation will, of course, produce a straight line, while the quadratic equation will produce a parabola. These two graphs will intersect at zero, one, or two points; each point of intersection is a solution of the system.

For example, consider the following system of equations:

$$y = -2x + 2$$
$$y = -2x^2 + 4x + 2$$

The linear equation describes a line with a y-intercept of $(0,2)$ and a slope of -2.

To graph the quadratic equation, we can first find the vertex of the parabola: the x-coordinate of the vertex is $h = -\frac{b}{2a} = -\frac{4}{2(-2)} = 1$, and the y-coordinate is $k = -2(1)^2 + 4(1) + 2 = 4$. Thus, the vertex lies at $(1,4)$. To get a feel for the rest of the parabola, we can plug in a few more values of x to find more points; by putting in $x = 2$ and $x = 3$ in the quadratic equation, we find that the points $(2,2)$ and $(3,-4)$ lie on the parabola; by symmetry, so must $(0,2)$ and $(-1,-4)$. We can now plot both equations:

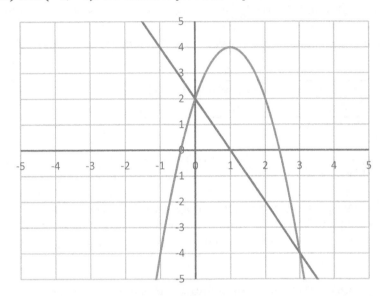

These two curves intersect at the points $(0,2)$ and $(3,-4)$, thus these are the solutions of the equation.

> **Review Video: Solving a System of Equations Consisting of a Linear Equation and Quadratic Equations**
> Visit mometrix.com/academy and enter code: 194870

CALCULATIONS USING POINTS

Sometimes you need to perform calculations using only points on a graph as input data. Using points, you can determine what the **midpoint** and **distance** are. If you know the equation for a line, you can calculate the distance between the line and the point.

To find the **midpoint** of two points (x_1, y_1) and (x_2, y_2), average the x-coordinates to get the x-coordinate of the midpoint, and average the y-coordinates to get the y-coordinate of the midpoint. The formula is: $\left(\frac{x_1+x_2}{2}, \frac{y_1+y_2}{2}\right)$.

The **distance** between two points is the same as the length of the hypotenuse of a right triangle with the two given points as endpoints, and the two sides of the right triangle parallel to the x-axis and y-axis, respectively. The length of the segment parallel to the x-axis is the difference between the x-coordinates of the two points. The length of the segment parallel to the y-axis is the difference between the y-coordinates of the two points. Use the Pythagorean theorem $a^2 + b^2 = c^2$ or $c = \sqrt{a^2 + b^2}$ to find the distance. The formula is $d = \sqrt{(x_2 - x_1)^2 + (y_2 - y_1)^2}$.

When a line is in the format $Ax + By + C = 0$, where A, B, and C are coefficients, you can use a point (x_1, y_1) not on the line and apply the formula $d = \frac{|Ax_1 + By_1 + C|}{\sqrt{A^2 + B^2}}$ to find the distance between the line and the point (x_1, y_1).

POLYNOMIALS

MONOMIALS AND POLYNOMIALS

A **monomial** is a single constant, variable, or product of constants and variables, such as 7, x, $2x$, or x^3y. There will never be addition or subtraction symbols in a monomial. Like monomials have like variables, but they may have different coefficients. **Polynomials** are algebraic expressions that use addition and subtraction to combine two or more monomials. Two terms make a **binomial**, three terms make a **trinomial**, etc. The **degree of a monomial** is the sum of the exponents of the variables. The **degree of a polynomial** is the highest degree of any individual term.

SIMPLIFYING POLYNOMIALS

Simplifying polynomials requires combining like terms. The like terms in a polynomial expression are those that have the same variable raised to the same power. It is often helpful to connect the like terms with arrows or lines in order to separate them from the other monomials. Once you have determined the like terms, you can rearrange the polynomial by placing them together. Remember to include the sign that is in front of each term. Once the like terms are placed together, you can apply each operation and simplify. When adding and subtracting polynomials, only add and subtract the **coefficient**, or the number part; the variable and exponent stay the same.

THE FOIL METHOD

In general, multiplying polynomials is done by multiplying each term in one polynomial by each term in the other and adding the results. In the specific case for multiplying binomials, there is a useful acronym, FOIL, that can help you make sure to cover each combination of terms. The **FOIL method** for $(Ax + By)(Cx + Dy)$ would be:

F	Multiply the *first* terms of each binomial	$(\overset{first}{Ax} + By)(\overset{first}{Cx} + Dy)$	ACx^2
O	Multiply the *outer* terms	$(\overset{outer}{Ax} + By)(Cx + \overset{outer}{Dy})$	$ADxy$
I	Multiply the *inner* terms	$(Ax + \overset{inner}{By})(\overset{inner}{Cx} + Dy)$	$BCxy$
L	Multiply the *last* terms of each binomial	$(Ax + \overset{last}{By})(Cx + \overset{last}{Dy})$	BDy^2

Then, add up the result of each and combine like terms: $ACx^2 + (AD + BC)xy + BDy^2$.

For example, using the FOIL method on binomials $(x + 2)$ and $(x - 3)$:

First: $(\boxed{x} + 2)(\boxed{x} + (-3)) \rightarrow (x)(x) = x^2$

Outer: $(\boxed{x} + 2)(x + \boxed{(-3)}) \rightarrow (x)(-3) = -3x$

Inner: $(x + \boxed{2})(\boxed{x} + (-3)) \rightarrow (2)(x) = 2x$

Last: $(x + \boxed{2})(x + \boxed{(-3)}) \rightarrow (2)(-3) = -6$

This results in: $(x^2) + (-3x) + (2x) + (-6)$

Combine like terms: $x^2 + (-3 + 2)x + (-6) = x^2 - x - 6$

Review Video: **Multiplying Terms Using the FOIL Method**
Visit mometrix.com/academy and enter code: 854792

DIVIDING POLYNOMIALS

Use long division to divide a polynomial by either a monomial or another polynomial of equal or lesser degree.

When **dividing by a monomial**, divide each term of the polynomial by the monomial.

When **dividing by a polynomial**, begin by arranging the terms of each polynomial in order of one variable. You may arrange in ascending or descending order, but be consistent with both polynomials. To get the first term of the quotient, divide the first term of the dividend by the first term of the divisor. Multiply the first term of the quotient by the entire divisor and subtract that product from the dividend. Repeat for the second and successive terms until you either get a remainder of zero or a remainder whose degree is less than the degree of the divisor. If the quotient has a remainder, write the answer as a mixed expression in the form:

$$\text{quotient} + \frac{\text{remainder}}{\text{divisor}}$$

For example, we can evaluate the following expression in the same way as long division:

$$\frac{x^3 - 3x^2 - 2x + 5}{x - 5}$$

$$
\begin{array}{r}
x^2 + 2x + 8 \\
x - 5 \overline{\smash{)} x^3 - 3x^2 - 2x + 5} \\
-(x^3 - 5x^2) \\
\hline
2x^2 - 2x \\
-(2x^2 - 10x) \\
\hline
8x + 5 \\
-(8x - 40) \\
\hline
45
\end{array}
$$

$$\frac{x^3 - 3x^2 - 2x + 5}{x - 5} = x^2 + 2x + 8 + \frac{45}{x - 5}$$

When **factoring** a polynomial, first check for a common monomial factor, that is, look to see if each coefficient has a common factor or if each term has an x in it. If the factor is a trinomial but not a perfect trinomial square, look for a factorable form, such as one of these:

$$x^2 + (a + b)x + ab = (x + a)(x + b)$$
$$(ac)x^2 + (ad + bc)x + bd = (ax + b)(cx + d)$$

For factors with four terms, look for groups to factor. Once you have found the factors, write the original polynomial as the product of all the factors. Make sure all of the polynomial factors are prime. Monomial factors may be *prime* or *composite*. Check your work by multiplying the factors to make sure you get the original polynomial.

Below are patterns of some special products to remember to help make factoring easier:

- Perfect trinomial squares: $x^2 + 2xy + y^2 = (x + y)^2$ or $x^2 - 2xy + y^2 = (x - y)^2$
- Difference between two squares: $x^2 - y^2 = (x + y)(x - y)$
- Sum of two cubes: $x^3 + y^3 = (x + y)(x^2 - xy + y^2)$
  - Note: the second factor is *not* the same as a perfect trinomial square, so do not try to factor it further.
- Difference between two cubes: $x^3 - y^3 = (x - y)(x^2 + xy + y^2)$
  - Again, the second factor is *not* the same as a perfect trinomial square.
- Perfect cubes: $x^3 + 3x^2y + 3xy^2 + y^3 = (x + y)^3$ and $x^3 - 3x^2y + 3xy^2 - y^3 = (x - y)^3$

RATIONAL EXPRESSIONS

Rational expressions are fractions with polynomials in both the numerator and the denominator; the value of the polynomial in the denominator cannot be equal to zero. Be sure to keep track of values that make the denominator of the original expression zero as the final result inherits the same restrictions. For example, a denominator of $x - 3$ indicates that the expression is not defined when $x = 3$ and, as such, regardless of any operations done to the expression, it remains undefined there.

To **add or subtract** rational expressions, first find the common denominator, then rewrite each fraction as an equivalent fraction with the common denominator. Finally, add or subtract the numerators to get the numerator of the answer, and keep the common denominator as the denominator of the answer.

When **multiplying** rational expressions, factor each polynomial and cancel like factors (a factor which appears in both the numerator and the denominator). Then, multiply all remaining factors in the numerator to get the numerator of the product, and multiply the remaining factors in the denominator to get the denominator of the product. Remember: cancel entire factors, not individual terms.

To **divide** rational expressions, take the reciprocal of the divisor (the rational expression you are dividing by) and multiply by the dividend.

> **Review Video: Rational Expressions**
> Visit mometrix.com/academy and enter code: 415183

SIMPLIFYING RATIONAL EXPRESSIONS

To simplify a rational expression, factor the numerator and denominator completely. Factors that are the same and appear in the numerator and denominator have a ratio of 1. For example, look at the following expression:

$$\frac{x - 1}{1 - x^2}$$

The denominator, $(1 - x^2)$, is a difference of squares. It can be factored as $(1 - x)(1 + x)$. The factor $1 - x$ and the numerator $x - 1$ are opposites and have a ratio of –1. Rewrite the numerator as $-1(1 - x)$. So, the rational expression can be simplified as follows:

$$\frac{x - 1}{1 - x^2} = \frac{-1(1 - x)}{(1 - x)(1 + x)} = \frac{-1}{1 + x}$$

Note that since the original expression is only defined for $x \neq \{-1, 1\}$, the simplified expression has the same restrictions.

> **Review Video: <u>Reducing Rational Expressions</u>**
> Visit mometrix.com/academy and enter code: 788868

ALGEBRAIC THEOREMS

According to the **fundamental theorem of algebra**, every non-constant, single-variable polynomial has exactly as many roots as the polynomial's highest exponent. For example, if x^4 is the largest exponent of a term, the polynomial will have exactly 4 roots. However, some of these roots may have multiplicity or be complex numbers. For instance, in the polynomial function $f(x) = x^4 - 4x + 3$, the only real root is 1, though it has multiplicity of 2 – that is, it occurs twice. The other two roots, $(-1 - i\sqrt{2})$ and $(-1 + i\sqrt{2})$, are complex, consisting of both real and non-real components.

The **remainder theorem** is useful for determining the remainder when a polynomial is divided by a binomial. The remainder theorem states that if a polynomial function $f(x)$ is divided by a binomial $x - a$, where a is a real number, the remainder of the division will be the value of $f(a)$. If $f(a) = 0$, then a is a root of the polynomial.

The **factor theorem** is related to the remainder theorem and states that if $f(a) = 0$ then $(x - a)$ is a factor of the function.

According to the **rational root theorem,** any rational root of a polynomial function $f(x) = a_n x^n + a_{n-1} x^{n-1} + \cdots + a_1 x + a_0$ with integer coefficients will, when reduced to its lowest terms, be a positive or negative fraction such that the numerator is a factor of a_0 and the denominator is a factor of a_n. For instance, if the polynomial function $f(x) = x^3 + 3x^2 - 4$ has any rational roots, the numerators of those roots can only be factors of 4 (1, 2, 4), and the denominators can only be factors of 1 (1). The function in this example has roots of 1 (or $\frac{1}{1}$) and –2 (or $\frac{-2}{1}$).

QUADRATICS
SOLVING QUADRATIC EQUATIONS

Quadratic equations are a special set of trinomials of the form $y = ax^2 + bx + c$ that occur commonly in math and real-world applications. The **roots** of a quadratic equation are the solutions that satisfy the equation when $y = 0$; in other words, where the graph touches the x-axis. There are several ways to determine these solutions including using the quadratic formula, factoring, completing the square, and graphing the function.

> **Review Video: <u>Quadratic Equations Overview</u>**
> Visit mometrix.com/academy and enter code: 476276
>
> **Review Video: <u>Solutions of a Quadratic Equation on a Graph</u>**
> Visit mometrix.com/academy and enter code: 328231

QUADRATIC FORMULA

The **quadratic formula** is used to solve quadratic equations when other methods are more difficult. To use the quadratic formula to solve a quadratic equation, begin by rewriting the equation in standard form $ax^2 + bx +$

$c = 0$, where a, b, and c are coefficients. Once you have identified the values of the coefficients, substitute those values into the quadratic formula

$$x = \frac{-b \pm \sqrt{b^2 - 4ac}}{2a}$$

Evaluate the equation and simplify the expression. Again, check each root by substituting into the original equation. In the quadratic formula, the portion of the formula under the radical ($b^2 - 4ac$) is called the **discriminant**. If the discriminant is zero, there is only one root: $-\frac{b}{2a}$. If the discriminant is positive, there are two different real roots. If the discriminant is negative, there are no real roots; you will instead find complex roots. Often these solutions don't make sense in context and are ignored.

Review Video: Using the Quadratic Formula
Visit mometrix.com/academy and enter code: 163102

FACTORING

To solve a quadratic equation by factoring, begin by rewriting the equation in standard form, $x^2 + bx + c = 0$. Remember that the goal of factoring is to find numbers f and g such that $(x + f)(x + g) = x^2 + (f + g)x + fg$, in other words $(f + g) = b$ and $fg = c$. This can be a really useful method when b and c are integers. Determine the factors of c and look for pairs that could sum to b.

For example, consider finding the roots of $x^2 + 6x - 16 = 0$. The factors of -16 include, -4 and 4, -8 and 2, -2 and 8, -1 and 16, and 1 and -16. The factors that sum to 6 are -2 and 8. Write these factors as the product of two binomials, $0 = (x - 2)(x + 8)$. Finally, since these binomials multiply together to equal zero, set them each equal to zero and solve each for x. This results in $x - 2 = 0$, which simplifies to $x = 2$ and $x + 8 = 0$, which simplifies to $x = -8$. Therefore, the roots of the equation are 2 and -8.

Review Video: Factoring Quadratic Equations
Visit mometrix.com/academy and enter code: 336566

COMPLETING THE SQUARE

One way to find the roots of a quadratic equation is to find a way to manipulate it such that it follows the form of a perfect square ($x^2 + 2px + p^2$) by adding and subtracting a constant. This process is called **completing the square**. In other words, if you are given a quadratic that is not a perfect square, $x^2 + bx + c = 0$, you can find a constant d that could be added in to make it a perfect square:

$$x^2 + bx + c + (d - d) = 0; \; \{\text{Let } b = 2p \text{ and } c + d = p^2\}$$

then:

$$x^2 + 2px + p^2 - d = 0 \text{ and } d = \frac{b^2}{4} - c$$

Once you have completed the square you can find the roots of the resulting equation:

$$x^2 + 2px + p^2 - d = 0$$
$$(x + p)^2 = d$$
$$x + p = \pm\sqrt{d}$$
$$x = -p \pm \sqrt{d}$$

It is worth noting that substituting the original expressions into this solution gives the same result as the quadratic formula where $a = 1$:

$$x = -p \pm \sqrt{d} = -\frac{b}{2} \pm \sqrt{\frac{b^2}{4} - c} = -\frac{b}{2} \pm \frac{\sqrt{b^2 - 4c}}{2} = \frac{-b \pm \sqrt{b^2 - 4c}}{2}$$

Completing the square can be seen as arranging block representations of each of the terms to be as close to a square as possible and then filling in the gaps. For example, consider the quadratic expression $x^2 + 6x + 2$:

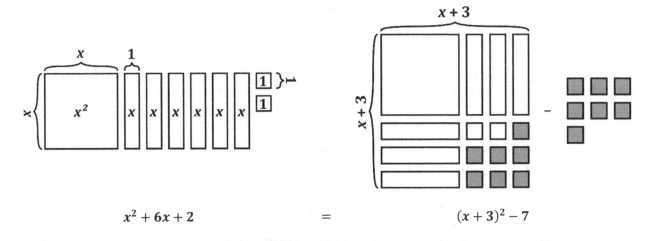

$$x^2 + 6x + 2 \qquad = \qquad (x + 3)^2 - 7$$

Review Video: Completing the Square
Visit mometrix.com/academy and enter code: 982479

USING GIVEN ROOTS TO FIND QUADRATIC EQUATION

One way to find the roots of a quadratic equation is to factor the equation and use the **zero product property**, setting each factor of the equation equal to zero to find the corresponding root. We can use this technique in reverse to find an equation given its roots. Each root corresponds to a linear equation which in turn corresponds to a factor of the quadratic equation.

For example, we can find a quadratic equation whose roots are $x = 2$ and $x = -1$. The root $x = 2$ corresponds to the equation $x - 2 = 0$, and the root $x = -1$ corresponds to the equation $x + 1 = 0$.

These two equations correspond to the factors $(x - 2)$ and $(x + 1)$, from which we can derive the equation $(x - 2)(x + 1) = 0$, or $x^2 - x - 2 = 0$.

Any integer multiple of this entire equation will also yield the same roots, as the integer will simply cancel out when the equation is factored. For example, $2x^2 - 2x - 4 = 0$ factors as $2(x - 2)(x + 1) = 0$.

BASIC FUNCTIONS

FUNCTION AND RELATION

When expressing functional relationships, the **variables** x and y are typically used. These values are often written as the **coordinates** (x, y). The x-value is the independent variable and the y-value is the dependent variable. A **relation** is a set of data in which there is not a unique y-value for each x-value in the dataset. This means that there can be two of the same x-values assigned to different y-values. A relation is simply a relationship between the x- and y-values in each coordinate but does not apply to the relationship between the values of x and y in the data set. A **function** is a relation where one quantity depends on the other. For example, the amount of money that you make depends on the number of hours that you work. In a function, each x-value in the data set has one unique y-value because the y-value depends on the x-value.

FUNCTIONS

A function has exactly one value of **output variable** (dependent variable) for each value of the **input variable** (independent variable). The set of all values for the input variable (here assumed to be x) is the domain of the function, and the set of all corresponding values of the output variable (here assumed to be y) is the range of the function. When looking at a graph of an equation, the easiest way to determine if the equation is a function or not is to conduct the vertical line test. If a vertical line drawn through any value of x crosses the graph in more than one place, the equation is not a function.

DETERMINING A FUNCTION

You can determine whether an equation is a **function** by substituting different values into the equation for x. You can display and organize these numbers in a data table. A **data table** contains the values for x and y, which you can also list as coordinates. In order for a function to exist, the table cannot contain any repeating x-values that correspond with different y-values. If each x-coordinate has a unique y-coordinate, the table contains a function. However, there can be repeating y-values that correspond with different x-values. An example of this is when the function contains an exponent. Example: if $x^2 = y$, $2^2 = 4$, and $(-2)^2 = 4$.

> **Review Video: Definition of a Function**
> Visit mometrix.com/academy and enter code: 784611

FINDING THE DOMAIN AND RANGE OF A FUNCTION

The **domain** of a function $f(x)$ is the set of all input values for which the function is defined. The **range** of a function $f(x)$ is the set of all possible output values of the function—that is, of every possible value of $f(x)$, for any value of x in the function's domain. For a function expressed in a table, every input-output pair is given explicitly. To find the domain, we just list all the x-values and to find the range, we just list all the values of $f(x)$. Consider the following example:

x	−1	4	2	1	0	3	8	6
$f(x)$	3	0	3	−1	−1	2	4	6

In this case, the domain would be $\{-1, 4, 2, 1, 0, 3, 8, 6\}$ or, putting them in ascending order, $\{-1, 0, 1, 2, 3, 4, 6, 8\}$. (Putting the values in ascending order isn't strictly necessary, but generally makes the set easier to read.) The range would be $\{3, 0, 3, -1, -1, 2, 4, 6\}$. Note that some of these values appear more than once. This is entirely permissible for a function; while each value of x must be matched to a unique value of $f(x)$, the converse is not true. We don't need to list each value more than once, so eliminating duplicates, the range is $\{3, 0, -1, 2, 4, 6\}$, or, putting them in ascending order, $\{-1, 0, 2, 3, 4, 6\}$.

Note that by definition of a function, no input value can be matched to more than one output value. It is good to double-check to make sure that the data given follows this and is therefore actually a function.

> **Review Video: Domain and Range**
> Visit mometrix.com/academy and enter code: 778133
>
> **Review Video: Domain and Range of Quadratic Functions**
> Visit mometrix.com/academy and enter code: 331768

WRITING A FUNCTION RULE USING A TABLE

If given a set of data, place the corresponding x- and y-values into a table and analyze the relationship between them. Consider what you can do to each x-value to obtain the corresponding y-value. Try adding or subtracting different numbers to and from x and then try multiplying or dividing different numbers to and from x. If none of these **operations** give you the y-value, try combining the operations. Once you find a rule that works for one pair, make sure to try it with each additional set of ordered pairs in the table. If the same operation or combination of operations satisfies each set of coordinates, then the table contains a function. The rule is then used to write the equation of the function in "$y = f(x)$" form.

DIRECT AND INVERSE VARIATIONS OF VARIABLES

Variables that vary directly are those that either both increase at the same rate or both decrease at the same rate. For example, in the functions $y = kx$ or $y = kx^n$, where k and n are positive, the value of y increases as the value of x increases and decreases as the value of x decreases.

Variables that vary inversely are those where one increases while the other decreases. For example, in the functions $y = \frac{k}{x}$ or $y = \frac{k}{x^n}$ where k and n are positive, the value of y increases as the value of x decreases and decreases as the value of x increases.

In both cases, k is the constant of variation.

PROPERTIES OF FUNCTIONS

There are many different ways to classify functions based on their structure or behavior. Important features of functions include:

- **End behavior**: the behavior of the function at extreme values ($f(x)$ as $x \to \pm\infty$)
- **y-intercept**: the value of the function at $f(0)$
- **Roots**: the values of x where the function equals zero ($f(x) = 0$)
- **Extrema**: minimum or maximum values of the function or where the function changes direction ($f(x) \geq k$ or $f(x) \leq k$)

CLASSIFICATION OF FUNCTIONS

An **invertible function** is defined as a function, $f(x)$, for which there is another function, $f^{-1}(x)$, such that $f^{-1}(f(x)) = x$. For example, if $f(x) = 3x - 2$ the inverse function, $f^{-1}(x)$, can be found:

$$x = 3(f^{-1}(x)) - 2$$
$$\frac{x + 2}{3} = f^{-1}(x)$$

$$f^{-1}(f(x)) = \frac{3x - 2 + 2}{3}$$
$$= \frac{3x}{3}$$
$$= x$$

Note that $f^{-1}(x)$ is a valid function over all values of x.

In a **one-to-one function**, each value of x has exactly one value for y on the coordinate plane (this is the definition of a function) and each value of y has exactly one value for x. While the vertical line test will determine if a graph is that of a function, the horizontal line test will determine if a function is a one-to-one function. If a horizontal line drawn at any value of y intersects the graph in more than one place, the graph is not that of a one-to-one function. Do not make the mistake of using the horizontal line test exclusively in determining if a graph is that of a one-to-one function. A one-to-one function must pass both the vertical line test and the horizontal line test. As such, one-to-one functions are invertible functions.

A **many-to-one function** is a function whereby the relation is a function, but the inverse of the function is not a function. In other words, each element in the domain is mapped to one and only one element in the range. However, one or more elements in the range may be mapped to the same element in the domain. A graph of a many-to-one function would pass the vertical line test, but not the horizontal line test. This is why many-to-one functions are not invertible.

A **monotone function** is a function whose graph either constantly increases or constantly decreases. Examples include the functions $f(x) = x$, $f(x) = -x$, or $f(x) = x^3$.

An **even function** has a graph that is symmetric with respect to the y-axis and satisfies the equation $f(x) = f(-x)$. Examples include the functions $f(x) = x^2$ and $f(x) = ax^n$, where a is any real number and n is a positive even integer.

An **odd function** has a graph that is symmetric with respect to the origin and satisfies the equation $f(x) = -f(-x)$. Examples include the functions $f(x) = x^3$ and $f(x) = ax^n$, where a is any real number and n is a positive odd integer.

> **Review Video: Even and Odd Functions**
> Visit mometrix.com/academy and enter code: 278985

Constant functions are given by the equation $f(x) = b$, where b is a real number. There is no independent variable present in the equation, so the function has a constant value for all x. The graph of a constant function is a horizontal line of slope 0 that is positioned b units from the x-axis. If b is positive, the line is above the x-axis; if b is negative, the line is below the x-axis.

Identity functions are identified by the equation $f(x) = x$, where every value of the function is equal to its corresponding value of x. The only zero is the point $(0,0)$. The graph is a line with a slope of 1.

In **linear functions**, the value of the function changes in direct proportion to x. The rate of change, represented by the slope on its graph, is constant throughout. The standard form of a linear equation is $ax + cy = d$, where a, c, and d are real numbers. As a function, this equation is commonly in the form $y = mx + b$ or $f(x) = mx + b$ where $m = -\frac{a}{c}$ and $b = \frac{d}{c}$. This is known as the slope-intercept form, because the coefficients give the slope of the graphed function (m) and its y-intercept (b). Solve the equation $mx + b = 0$ for x to get $x = -\frac{b}{m}$, which is the only zero of the function. The domain and range are both the set of all real numbers.

> **Review Video: Graphing Linear Functions**
> Visit mometrix.com/academy and enter code: 699478

Algebraic functions are those that exclusively use polynomials and roots. These would include polynomial functions, rational functions, square root functions, and all combinations of these functions, such as polynomials as the radicand. These combinations may be joined by addition, subtraction, multiplication, or division, but may not include variables as exponents.

> **Review Video: Common Functions**
> Visit mometrix.com/academy and enter code: 629798

ABSOLUTE VALUE FUNCTIONS

An **absolute value function** is in the format $f(x) = |ax + b|$. Like other functions, the domain is the set of all real numbers. However, because absolute value indicates positive numbers, the range is limited to positive real numbers. To find the zero of an absolute value function, set the portion inside the absolute value sign equal to zero and solve for x. An absolute value function is also known as a piecewise function because it must be solved in pieces—one for if the value inside the absolute value sign is positive, and one for if the value is negative. The function can be expressed as:

$$f(x) = \begin{cases} ax + b \text{ if } ax + b \geq 0 \\ -(ax + b) \text{ if } ax + b < 0 \end{cases}$$

This will allow for an accurate statement of the range. The graph of an example absolute value function, $f(x) = |2x - 1|$, is below:

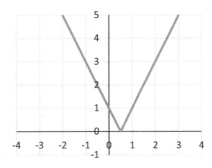

PIECEWISE FUNCTIONS

A **piecewise function** is a function that has different definitions on two or more different intervals. The following, for instance, is one example of a piecewise-defined function:

$$f(x) = \begin{cases} x^2, & x < 0 \\ x, & 0 \le x \le 2 \\ (x-2)^2, & x > 2 \end{cases}$$

To graph this function, you would simply graph each part separately in the appropriate domain. The final graph would look like this:

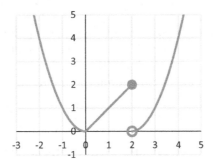

Note the filled and hollow dots at the discontinuity at $x = 2$. This is important to show which side of the graph that point corresponds to. Because $f(x) = x$ on the closed interval $0 \le x \le 2$, $f(2) = 2$. The point $(2, 2)$ is therefore marked with a filled circle, and the point $(2, 0)$, which is the endpoint of the rightmost $(x - 2)^2$ part of the graph but *not actually part of the function*, is marked with a hollow dot to indicate this.

> **Review Video: <u>Piecewise Functions</u>**
> Visit mometrix.com/academy and enter code: 707921

QUADRATIC FUNCTIONS

A **quadratic function** is a function in the form $y = ax^2 + bx + c$, where a does not equal 0. While a linear function forms a line, a quadratic function forms a **parabola**, which is a u-shaped figure that either opens upward or downward. A parabola that opens upward is said to be a **positive quadratic function**, and a parabola that opens downward is said to be a **negative quadratic function**. The shape of a parabola can differ, depending on the values of a, b, and c. All parabolas contain a **vertex**, which is the highest possible point, the **maximum**, or the lowest possible point, the **minimum**. This is the point where the graph begins moving in the opposite direction. A quadratic function can have zero, one, or two solutions, and therefore zero, one, or two x-intercepts. Recall that the x-intercepts are referred to as the zeros, or roots, of a function. A quadratic function

171

will have only one y-intercept. Understanding the basic components of a quadratic function can give you an idea of the shape of its graph.

Example graph of a positive quadratic function, $x^2 + 2x - 3$:

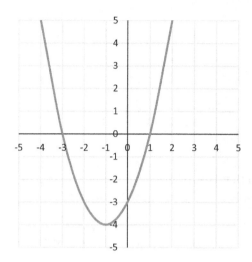

POLYNOMIAL FUNCTIONS

A **polynomial function** is a function with multiple terms and multiple powers of x, such as:

$$f(x) = a_n x^n + a_{n-1} x^{n-1} + a_{n-2} x^{n-2} + \cdots + a_1 x + a_0$$

where n is a non-negative integer that is the highest exponent in the polynomial and $a_n \neq 0$. The domain of a polynomial function is the set of all real numbers. If the greatest exponent in the polynomial is even, the polynomial is said to be of even degree and the range is the set of real numbers that satisfy the function. If the greatest exponent in the polynomial is odd, the polynomial is said to be odd and the range, like the domain, is the set of all real numbers.

RATIONAL FUNCTIONS

A **rational function** is a function that can be constructed as a ratio of two polynomial expressions: $f(x) = \frac{p(x)}{q(x)}$, where $p(x)$ and $q(x)$ are both polynomial expressions and $q(x) \neq 0$. The domain is the set of all real numbers, except any values for which $q(x) = 0$. The range is the set of real numbers that satisfies the function when the domain is applied. When you graph a rational function, you will have vertical asymptotes wherever $q(x) = 0$. If the polynomial in the numerator is of lesser degree than the polynomial in the denominator, the x-axis will also be a horizontal asymptote. If the numerator and denominator have equal degrees, there will be a horizontal asymptote not on the x-axis. If the degree of the numerator is exactly one greater than the degree of the denominator, the graph will have an oblique, or diagonal, asymptote. The asymptote will be along the line $y = \frac{p_n}{q_{n-1}} x + \frac{p_{n-1}}{q_{n-1}}$, where p_n and q_{n-1} are the coefficients of the highest degree terms in their respective polynomials.

SQUARE ROOT FUNCTIONS

A **square root function** is a function that contains a radical and is in the format $f(x) = \sqrt{ax + b}$. The domain is the set of all real numbers that yields a positive radicand or a radicand equal to zero. Because square root values are assumed to be positive unless otherwise identified, the range is all real numbers from zero to infinity. To find the zero of a square root function, set the radicand equal to zero and solve for x. The graph of a square root function is always to the right of the zero and always above the x-axis.

Example graph of a square root function, $f(x) = \sqrt{2x + 1}$:

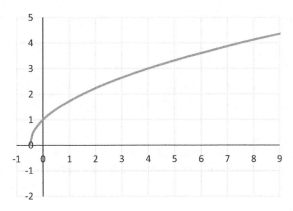

WORKING WITH FUNCTIONS

MANIPULATION OF FUNCTIONS

Translation occurs when values are added to or subtracted from the x- or y-values. If a constant is added to the y-portion of each point, the graph shifts up. If a constant is subtracted from the y-portion of each point, the graph shifts down. This is represented by the expression $f(x) \pm k$, where k is a constant. If a constant is added to the x-portion of each point, the graph shifts left. If a constant is subtracted from the x-portion of each point, the graph shifts right. This is represented by the expression $f(x \pm k)$, where k is a constant.

Stretching, compression, and reflection occur when different parts of a function are multiplied by different groups of constants. If the function as a whole is multiplied by a real number constant greater than 1, $(k \times f(x))$, the graph is stretched vertically. If k in the previous equation is greater than zero but less than 1, the graph is compressed vertically. If k is less than zero, the graph is reflected about the x-axis, in addition to being either stretched or compressed vertically if k is less than or greater than –1, respectively. If instead, just the x-term is multiplied by a constant greater than 1 $(f(k \times x))$, the graph is compressed horizontally. If k in the previous equation is greater than zero but less than 1, the graph is stretched horizontally. If k is less than zero, the graph is reflected about the y-axis, in addition to being either stretched or compressed horizontally if k is greater than or less than –1, respectively.

> **Review Video: Manipulation of Functions**
> Visit mometrix.com/academy and enter code: 669117

APPLYING THE BASIC OPERATIONS TO FUNCTIONS

For each of the basic operations, we will use these functions as examples: $f(x) = x^2$ and $g(x) = x$.

To find the sum of two functions f and g, assuming the domains are compatible, simply add the two functions together: $(f + g)(x) = f(x) + g(x) = x^2 + x$.

To find the difference of two functions f and g, assuming the domains are compatible, simply subtract the second function from the first: $(f - g)(x) = f(x) - g(x) = x^2 - x$.

To find the product of two functions f and g, assuming the domains are compatible, multiply the two functions together: $(f \times g)(x) = f(x) \times g(x) = x^2 \times x = x^3$.

To find the quotient of two functions f and g, assuming the domains are compatible, divide the first function by the second: $\frac{f}{g}(x) = \frac{f(x)}{g(x)} = \frac{x^2}{x} = x \, ; x \neq 0$.

The example given in each case is fairly simple, but on a given problem, if you are looking only for the value of the sum, difference, product, or quotient of two functions at a particular x-value, it may be simpler to solve the functions individually and then perform the given operation using those values.

The composite of two functions f and g, written as $(f \circ g)(x)$ simply means that the output of the second function is used as the input of the first. This can also be written as $f\big(g(x)\big)$. In general, this can be solved by substituting $g(x)$ for all instances of x in $f(x)$ and simplifying. Using the example functions $f(x) = x^2 - x + 2$ and $g(x) = x + 1$, we can find that $(f \circ g)(x)$ or $f\big(g(x)\big)$ is equal to $f(x + 1) = (x + 1)^2 - (x + 1) + 2$, which simplifies to $x^2 + x + 2$.

It is important to note that $(f \circ g)(x)$ is not necessarily the same as $(g \circ f)(x)$. The process is not always commutative like addition or multiplication expressions. It *can* be commutative, but most often this is not the case.

EVALUATING LINEAR FUNCTIONS

A **function** can be expressed as an equation that relates an input to an output where each input corresponds to exactly one output. The input of a function is defined by the x-variable, and the output is defined by the y-variable. For example, consider the function $y = 2x + 6$. The value of y, the output, is determined by the value of the x, the input. If the value of x is 3, the value of y is $y = 2(3) + 6 = 6 + 6 = 12$. This means that when $x = 3$, $y = 12$. This can be expressed as the ordered pair $(3,12)$.

It is common for function equations to use the form $f(x) =$ instead of $y =$. However, $f(x)$ and y represent the same thing. We read $f(x)$ as "f of x." "f of x" implies that the value of f depends on the value of x. The function used in the example above could be expressed as $y = 2x + 6$ or $f(x) = 2x + 6$. Both functions represent the same line when graphed.

Functions that are expressed in the form $f(x) =$ are evaluated in the same way the equations are evaluated in the form $y =$. For example, when evaluating the function $f(x) = 3x - 2$ for $f(6)$, substitute 6 in for x, and simplify. $f(x) = 3x - 2$ becomes $f(6) = 3(6) - 2 = 18 - 2 = 16$. When x is 6, $f(x)$ is 16.

Find the value of $f(8)$.

$$f(x) = 3x - 2$$
$$f(8) = 3(8) - 2$$
$$f(8) = 22$$

ADVANCED FUNCTIONS

STEP FUNCTIONS

The double brackets indicate a step function. For a step function, the value inside the double brackets is rounded down to the nearest integer. The graph of the function $f_0(x) = [\![x]\!]$ appears on the left graph. In comparison $f(x) = 2 \left[\!\left[\frac{1}{3}(x - 1) \right]\!\right]$ is on the right graph. The coefficient of 2 shows that it's stretched vertically by a factor of 2 (so there's a vertical distance of 2 units between successive "steps"). The coefficient of $\frac{1}{3}$ in front

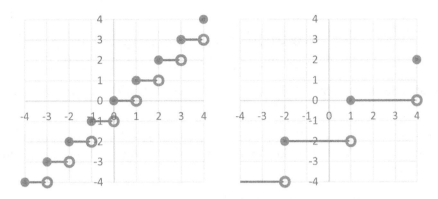

of the x shows that it's stretched horizontally by a factor of 3 (so each "step" is three units long), and the $x - 1$ shows that it's displaced one unit to the right.

TRANSCENDENTAL FUNCTIONS

Transcendental functions are all functions that are non-algebraic. Any function that includes logarithms, trigonometric functions, variables as exponents, or any combination that includes any of these is not algebraic in nature, even if the function includes polynomials or roots.

EXPONENTIAL FUNCTIONS

Exponential functions are equations that have the format $y = b^x$, where base $b > 0$ and $b \neq 1$. The exponential function can also be written $f(x) = b^x$. Recall the properties of exponents, like the product of terms with the same base is equal to the base raised to the sum of the exponents ($a^x \times a^y = a^{x+y}$) and a term with an exponent that is raised to an exponent is equal to the base of the original term raised to the product of the exponents: ($(a^x)^y = a^{xy}$). The graph of an example exponential function, $f(x) = 2^x$, is below:

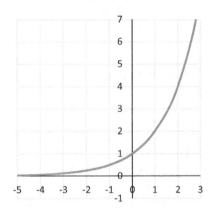

Note in the graph that the y-value approaches zero to the left and infinity to the right. One of the key features of an exponential function is that there will be one end that goes off to infinity and another that asymptotically approaches a lower bound. Common forms of exponential functions include:

Geometric sequences: $a_n = a_1 \times r^{n-1}$, where a_n is the value of the nth term, a_1 is the initial value, r is the common ratio, and n is the number of terms. Note that $a_1 \times r^{1-1} = a_1 \times r^0 = a_1 \times 1 = a_1$.

Population growth: $f(t) = ae^{rt}$, where $f(t)$ is the population at time $t \geq 0$, a is the initial population, e is the mathematical constant known as Euler's number, and r is the growth rate.

Review Video: Population Growth
Visit mometrix.com/academy and enter code: 109278

175

Compound interest: $f(t) = P\left(1 + \frac{r}{n}\right)^{nt}$, where $f(t)$ is the account value at a certain number of time periods $t \geq 0$, P is the initial principal balance, r is the interest rate, and n is the number of times the interest is applied per time period.

> **Review Video: Interest Functions**
> Visit mometrix.com/academy and enter code: 559176

General exponential growth or decay: $f(t) = a(1 + r)^t$, where $f(t)$ is the future count, a is the current or initial count, r is the growth or decay rate, and t is the time.

For example, suppose the initial population of a town was 1,200 people. The annual population growth is 5%. The current population is 2,400. To find out how much time has passed since the town was founded, we can use the following function:

$$2{,}400 = 1{,}200e^{0.05t}.$$

The general form for population growth may be represented as $f(t) = ae^{rt}$, where $f(t)$ represents the current population, a represents the initial population, r represents the growth rate, and t represents the time. Thus, substituting the initial population, current population, and rate into this form gives the equation above.

The number of years that have passed were found by first dividing both sides of the equation by 1,200. Doing so gives $2 = e^{0.05t}$. Taking the natural logarithm of both sides gives $\ln(2) = ln(e^{0.05t})$. Applying the power property of logarithms, the equation may be rewritten as $\ln(2) = 0.05t \times \ln(e)$, which simplifies as $\ln(2) = 0.05t$. Dividing both sides of this equation by 0.05 gives $t \approx 13.86$. Thus, approximately 13.86 years passed.

LOGARITHMIC FUNCTIONS

Logarithmic functions are equations that have the format $y = \log_b x$ or $f(x) = \log_b x$. The base b may be any number except one; however, the most common bases for logarithms are base 10 and base e. The log base e is the natural logarithm, or ln, expressed by the function $f(x) = \ln x$.

Any logarithm that does not have an assigned value of b is assumed to be base 10: $\log x = \log_{10} x$. Exponential functions and logarithmic functions are related in that one is the inverse of the other. If $f(x) = b^x$, then $f^{-1}(x) = \log_b x$. This can perhaps be expressed more clearly by the two equations: $y = b^x$ and $x = \log_b y$.

The following properties apply to logarithmic expressions:

Property	Description
$\log_b 1 = 0$	The log of 1 is equal to 0 for any base
$\log_b b = 1$	The log of the base is equal to 1
$\log_b b^p = p$	The log of the base raised to a power is equal to that power
$\log_b MN = \log_b M + \log_b N$	The log of a product is the sum of the log of each factor
$\log_b \frac{M}{N} = \log_b M - \log_b N$	The log of a quotient is equal to the log of the dividend minus the log of the divisor
$\log_b M^p = p \log_b M$	The log of a value raised to a power is equal to the power times the log of the value

The graph of an example logarithmic function, $f(x) = \log_2(x + 2)$, is below:

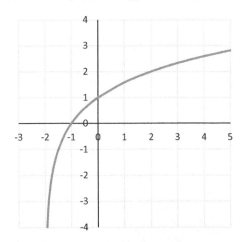

TRIGONOMETRIC FUNCTIONS

Trigonometric functions are periodic, meaning that they repeat the same form over and over. The basic trigonometric functions are sine (abbreviated 'sin'), cosine (abbreviated 'cos'), and tangent (abbreviated 'tan'). The simplest way to think of them is as describing the ratio of the side lengths of a right triangle in relation to the angles of the triangle.

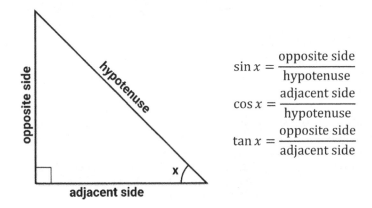

$$\sin x = \frac{\text{opposite side}}{\text{hypotenuse}}$$

$$\cos x = \frac{\text{adjacent side}}{\text{hypotenuse}}$$

$$\tan x = \frac{\text{opposite side}}{\text{adjacent side}}$$

Using sine as an example, trigonometric functions take the form $f(x) = A\sin(Bx + C) + D$, where the **amplitude** is simply equal to A. The **period** is the distance between successive peaks or troughs, essentially the length of the repeated pattern. In this form, the period is equal to $\frac{2\pi}{B}$. As for C, this is the **phase shift** or the horizontal shift of the function. The last term, D, is the vertical shift and determines the **midline** as $y = D$.

For instance, consider the function $f(x) = 2 + \frac{3}{2}\sin\left(\pi x + \frac{\pi}{2}\right)$. Here, $A = \frac{3}{2}$, $B = \pi$, $C = \frac{\pi}{2}$, and $D = 2$, so the midline is at $y = 2$, the amplitude is $\frac{3}{2}$, and the period is $\frac{2\pi}{\pi} = 2$. To graph this function, we center the sine wave on the midline and extend it to a height above and below the midline equal to the amplitude—so this graph

177

would have a minimum value of $2 - \frac{3}{2} = \frac{1}{2}$ and a maximum of $2 + \frac{3}{2} = \frac{7}{2}$. So, the function would be graphed as follows:

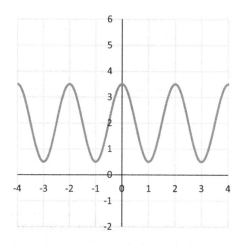

MATRIX BASICS

A **matrix** (plural: matrices) is a rectangular array of numbers or variables, often called **elements**, which are arranged in columns and rows. A matrix is generally represented by a capital letter, with its elements represented by the corresponding lowercase letter with two subscripts indicating the row and column of the element. For example, n_{ab} represents the element in row a column b of matrix N.

$$N = \begin{bmatrix} n_{11} & n_{12} & n_{13} \\ n_{21} & n_{22} & n_{23} \end{bmatrix}$$

A matrix can be described in terms of the number of rows and columns it contains in the format $a \times b$, where a is the number of rows and b is the number of columns. The matrix shown above is a 2×3 matrix. Any $a \times b$ matrix where $a = b$ is a square matrix. A **vector** is a matrix that has exactly one column (**column vector**) or exactly one row (**row vector**).

The **main diagonal** of a matrix is the set of elements on the diagonal from the top left to the bottom right of a matrix. Because of the way it is defined, only square matrices will have a main diagonal. For the matrix shown below, the main diagonal consists of the elements $n_{11}, n_{22}, n_{33}, n_{44}$.

$$\begin{bmatrix} n_{11} & n_{12} & n_{13} & n_{14} \\ n_{21} & n_{22} & n_{23} & n_{24} \\ n_{31} & n_{32} & n_{33} & n_{34} \\ n_{41} & n_{42} & n_{43} & n_{44} \end{bmatrix}$$

A 3×4 matrix such as the one shown below would not have a main diagonal because there is no straight line of elements between the top left corner and the bottom right corner that joins the elements.

$$\begin{bmatrix} n_{11} & n_{12} & n_{13} & n_{14} \\ n_{21} & n_{22} & n_{23} & n_{24} \\ n_{31} & n_{32} & n_{33} & n_{34} \end{bmatrix}$$

A **diagonal matrix** is a square matrix that has a zero for every element in the matrix except the elements on the main diagonal. All the elements on the main diagonal must be nonzero numbers.

$$\begin{bmatrix} n_{11} & 0 & 0 & 0 \\ 0 & n_{22} & 0 & 0 \\ 0 & 0 & n_{33} & 0 \\ 0 & 0 & 0 & n_{44} \end{bmatrix}$$

If every element on the main diagonal of a diagonal matrix is equal to one, the matrix is called an **identity matrix**. The identity matrix is often represented by the letter I.

$$I = \begin{bmatrix} 1 & 0 & 0 & 0 \\ 0 & 1 & 0 & 0 \\ 0 & 0 & 1 & 0 \\ 0 & 0 & 0 & 1 \end{bmatrix}$$

A **zero matrix** is a matrix that has zero as the value for every element in the matrix.

$$\begin{bmatrix} 0 & 0 & 0 & 0 \\ 0 & 0 & 0 & 0 \\ 0 & 0 & 0 & 0 \\ 0 & 0 & 0 & 0 \end{bmatrix}$$

The zero matrix is the *identity for matrix addition*. Do not confuse the zero matrix with the identity matrix.

The **negative of a matrix** is also known as the additive inverse of a matrix. If matrix N is the given matrix, then matrix $-N$ is its negative. This means that every element n_{ab} is equal to $-n_{ab}$ in the negative. To find the negative of a given matrix, change the sign of every element in the matrix and keep all elements in their original corresponding positions in the matrix.

If two matrices have the same order and all corresponding elements in the two matrices are the same, then the two matrices are **equal matrices**.

A matrix N may be **transposed** to matrix N^T by changing all rows into columns and changing all columns into rows. The easiest way to accomplish this is to swap the positions of the row and column notations for each element. For example, suppose the element in the second row of the third column of matrix N is $n_{23} = 6$. In the transposed matrix N^T, the transposed element would be $n_{32} = 6$, and it would be placed in the third row of the second column.

$$N = \begin{bmatrix} 1 & 2 & 3 \\ 4 & 5 & 6 \end{bmatrix}; \ N^T = \begin{bmatrix} 1 & 4 \\ 2 & 5 \\ 3 & 6 \end{bmatrix}$$

To quickly transpose a matrix by hand, begin with the first column and rewrite a new matrix with those same elements in the same order in the first row. Write the elements from the second column of the original matrix in the second row of the transposed matrix. Continue this process until all columns have been completed. If the original matrix is identical to the transposed matrix, the matrices are symmetric.

BASIC OPERATIONS WITH MATRICES

There are two categories of basic operations with regard to matrices: operations between a matrix and a scalar, and operations between two matrices.

SCALAR OPERATIONS

A scalar being added to a matrix is treated as though it were being added to each element of the matrix. The same is true for subtraction, multiplication and division:

$$M + k = \begin{bmatrix} m_{11} + k & m_{12} + k \\ m_{21} + k & m_{22} + k \end{bmatrix}$$

$$M - k = \begin{bmatrix} m_{11} - k & m_{12} - k \\ m_{21} - k & m_{22} - k \end{bmatrix}$$

$$M \times k = \begin{bmatrix} m_{11} \times k & m_{12} \times k \\ m_{21} \times k & m_{22} \times k \end{bmatrix}$$

$$M \div k = \begin{bmatrix} m_{11} \div k & m_{12} \div k \\ m_{21} \div k & m_{22} \div k \end{bmatrix}$$

MATRIX ADDITION AND SUBTRACTION

All four of the basic operations can be used with operations between matrices (although division is usually discarded in favor of multiplication by the inverse), but there are restrictions on the situations in which they can be used. Matrices that meet all the qualifications for a given operation are called **conformable matrices**. However, conformability is specific to the operation; two matrices that are conformable for addition are not necessarily conformable for multiplication.

For two matrices to be conformable for addition or subtraction, they must be of the same dimension; otherwise, the operation is not defined. If matrix M is a 3×2 matrix and matrix N is a 2×3 matrix, the operations $M + N$ and $M - N$ are meaningless. If matrices M and N are the same size, the operation is as simple as adding or subtracting all of the corresponding elements:

$$\begin{bmatrix} m_{11} & m_{12} \\ m_{21} & m_{22} \end{bmatrix} + \begin{bmatrix} n_{11} & n_{12} \\ n_{21} & n_{22} \end{bmatrix} = \begin{bmatrix} m_{11} + n_{11} & m_{12} + n_{12} \\ m_{21} + n_{21} & m_{22} + n_{22} \end{bmatrix}$$

$$\begin{bmatrix} m_{11} & m_{12} \\ m_{21} & m_{22} \end{bmatrix} - \begin{bmatrix} n_{11} & n_{12} \\ n_{21} & n_{22} \end{bmatrix} = \begin{bmatrix} m_{11} - n_{11} & m_{12} - n_{12} \\ m_{21} - n_{21} & m_{22} - n_{22} \end{bmatrix}$$

The result of addition or subtraction is a matrix of the same dimension as the two original matrices involved in the operation.

MATRIX MULTIPLICATION

The first thing it is necessary to understand about matrix multiplication is that it is not commutative. In scalar multiplication, the operation is commutative, meaning that $a \times b = b \times a$. For matrix multiplication, this is not the case: $A \times B \neq B \times A$. The terminology must be specific when describing matrix multiplication. The operation $A \times B$ can be described as A multiplied (or **post-multiplied**) by B, or B **pre-multiplied** by A.

For two matrices to be conformable for multiplication, they need not be of the same dimension, but specific dimensions must correspond. Taking the example of two matrices M and N to be multiplied $M \times N$, matrix M must have the same number of columns as matrix N has rows. Put another way, if matrix M has the dimensions $a \times b$ and matrix N has the dimensions $c \times d$, b must equal c if the two matrices are to be conformable for this multiplication. The matrix that results from the multiplication will have the dimensions $a \times d$. If a and d are both equal to 1, the product is simply a scalar. Square matrices of the same dimensions are always conformable for multiplication, and their product is always a matrix of the same size.

The simplest type of matrix multiplication is a 1×2 matrix (a row vector) times a 2×1 matrix (a column vector). These will multiply in the following way:

$$\begin{bmatrix} m_{11} & m_{12} \end{bmatrix} \times \begin{bmatrix} n_{11} \\ n_{21} \end{bmatrix} = m_{11}n_{11} + m_{12}n_{21}$$

The two matrices are conformable for multiplication because matrix M has the same number of columns as matrix N has rows. Because the other dimensions are both 1, the result is a scalar. Expanding our matrices to 1×3 and 3×1, the process is the same:

$$[m_{11} \quad m_{12} \quad m_{13}] \times \begin{bmatrix} n_{11} \\ n_{21} \\ n_{31} \end{bmatrix} = m_{11}n_{11} + m_{12}n_{21} + m_{13}n_{31}$$

Once again, the result is a scalar. This type of basic matrix multiplication is the building block for the multiplication of larger matrices.

To multiply larger matrices, treat each **row from the first matrix** and each **column from the second matrix** as individual vectors and follow the pattern for multiplying vectors. The scalar value found from multiplying the first-row vector by the first column vector is placed in the first row, first column of the new matrix. The scalar value found from multiplying the second-row vector by the first column vector is placed in the second row, first column of the new matrix. Continue this pattern until each row of the first matrix has been multiplied by each column of the second matrix.

Below is an example of the multiplication of a 3×2 matrix and a 2×3 matrix.

$$\begin{bmatrix} m_{11} & m_{12} \\ m_{21} & m_{22} \\ m_{31} & m_{32} \end{bmatrix} \times \begin{bmatrix} n_{11} & n_{12} & n_{13} \\ n_{21} & n_{22} & n_{23} \end{bmatrix} = \begin{bmatrix} m_{11}n_{11} + m_{12}n_{21} & m_{11}n_{12} + m_{12}n_{22} & m_{11}n_{13} + m_{12}n_{23} \\ m_{21}n_{11} + m_{22}n_{21} & m_{21}n_{12} + m_{22}n_{22} & m_{21}n_{13} + m_{22}n_{23} \\ m_{31}n_{11} + m_{32}n_{21} & m_{31}n_{12} + m_{32}n_{22} & m_{31}n_{13} + m_{32}n_{23} \end{bmatrix}$$

This process starts by taking the first column of the second matrix and running it through each row of the first matrix. Removing all but the first M row and first N column, we would see only the following:

$$[m_{11} \quad m_{12}] \times \begin{bmatrix} n_{11} \\ n_{21} \end{bmatrix} = m_{11}n_{11} + m_{12}n_{21}$$

The first product would then be $m_{11}n_{11} + m_{12}n_{21}$. This process will be continued for each column of the N matrix to find the first full row of the product matrix, as shown below.

$$[m_{11}n_{11} + m_{12}n_{21} \quad m_{11}n_{12} + m_{12}n_{22} \quad m_{11}n_{13} + m_{12}n_{23}]$$

After completing the first row, the next step would be to simply move to the second row of the M matrix and repeat the process until all of the rows have been finished. The result is a 3×3 matrix.

$$\begin{bmatrix} m_{11} & m_{12} \\ m_{21} & m_{22} \\ m_{31} & m_{32} \end{bmatrix} \times \begin{bmatrix} n_{11} & n_{12} & n_{13} \\ n_{21} & n_{22} & n_{23} \end{bmatrix} = \begin{bmatrix} m_{11}n_{11} + m_{12}n_{21} & m_{11}n_{12} + m_{12}n_{22} & m_{11}n_{13} + m_{12}n_{23} \\ m_{21}n_{11} + m_{22}n_{21} & m_{21}n_{12} + m_{22}n_{22} & m_{21}n_{13} + m_{22}n_{23} \\ m_{31}n_{11} + m_{32}n_{21} & m_{31}n_{12} + m_{32}n_{22} & m_{31}n_{13} + m_{32}n_{23} \end{bmatrix}$$

If the operation were done in reverse ($N \times M$), the result would be a 2×2 matrix.

$$\begin{bmatrix} n_{11} & n_{12} & n_{13} \\ n_{21} & n_{22} & n_{23} \end{bmatrix} \times \begin{bmatrix} m_{11} & m_{12} \\ m_{21} & m_{22} \\ m_{31} & m_{32} \end{bmatrix} = \begin{bmatrix} m_{11}n_{11} + m_{21}n_{12} + m_{31}n_{13} & m_{12}n_{11} + m_{22}n_{12} + m_{32}n_{13} \\ m_{11}n_{21} + m_{21}n_{22} + m_{31}n_{23} & m_{12}n_{21} + m_{22}n_{22} + m_{32}n_{23} \end{bmatrix}$$

> **Review Video: Matrices: The Basics**
> Visit mometrix.com/academy and enter code: 516658

ADVANCED MATRICES

ELEMENTARY ROW OPERATIONS

Elementary row operations include multiplying a row by a non-zero scalar, adding scalar multiples of two rows, and switching rows. These operations can be done using matrix multiplication with specialized transformation matrices. Elementary row operations are left multiplied, $A' = MA$. To do the same type of operations on the columns, then the transformation matrix is right multiplied, $A' = AM$. **Row switching** is achieved by swapping the corresponding rows in the identity matrix. For example, consider switching row 2 and row 3 in a 3×3 matrix:

$$M_{R_2 \leftrightarrow R_3} = \begin{bmatrix} 1 & 0 & 0 \\ 0 & 0 & 1 \\ 0 & 1 & 0 \end{bmatrix}$$

The transformation matrix for **row multiplication** is also based on the identity matrix with the scalar multiplication factor in place of the 1 in the corresponding row. Multiplying row 1 by –4 in a 3×3 matrix:

$$M_{-4R_1 \rightarrow R_1} = \begin{bmatrix} -4 & 0 & 0 \\ 0 & 1 & 0 \\ 0 & 0 & 1 \end{bmatrix}$$

The transformation matrix for **row addition** consists of the identity matrix with a 1 in the element corresponding to the two rows being added in the column where you want the result to go. Adding row 2 to row 1 in a 3×3 matrix:

$$M_{R_1 + R_2 \rightarrow R_1} = \begin{bmatrix} 1 & 1 & 0 \\ 0 & 1 & 0 \\ 0 & 0 & 1 \end{bmatrix}$$

> **Review Video: <u>Matrices: Elementary Row Operations</u>**
> Visit mometrix.com/academy and enter code: 493170

DETERMINANTS AND INVERSES OF MATRICES

The **determinant** of a matrix is a scalar value that is calculated by taking into account all the elements of a square matrix. A determinant only exists for square matrices. Finding the determinant of a 2×2 matrix is as simple as remembering a simple equation. For a 2×2 matrix $M = \begin{bmatrix} m_{11} & m_{12} \\ m_{21} & m_{22} \end{bmatrix}$, the determinant is obtained by the equation $|M| = m_{11}m_{22} - m_{12}m_{21}$. Anything larger than 2×2 requires multiple steps. Take matrix $N = \begin{bmatrix} a & b & c \\ d & e & f \\ g & h & j \end{bmatrix}$. The determinant of N is calculated as $|N| = a \begin{vmatrix} e & f \\ h & j \end{vmatrix} - b \begin{vmatrix} d & f \\ g & j \end{vmatrix} + c \begin{vmatrix} d & e \\ g & h \end{vmatrix}$ or $|N| = a(ej - fh) - b(dj - fg) + c(dh - eg)$.

There is a shortcut for 3×3 matrices: add the products of each unique set of elements diagonally left-to-right and subtract the products of each unique set of elements diagonally right-to-left. In matrix N, the left-to-right diagonal elements are (a, e, j), (b, f, g), and (c, d, h). The right-to-left diagonal elements are (a, f, h), (b, d, j), and (c, e, g). $\det(N) = aej + bfg + cdh - afh - bdj - ceg$.

Calculating the determinants of matrices larger than 3×3 is rarely, if ever, done by hand.

The **inverse** of a matrix M is the matrix that, when multiplied by matrix M, yields a product that is the identity matrix. Multiplication of matrices will be explained in greater detail shortly. Not all matrices have inverses. Only a square matrix whose determinant is not zero has an inverse. If a matrix has an inverse, that inverse is unique to that matrix. For any matrix M that has an inverse, the inverse is represented by the symbol M^{-1}. To calculate the inverse of a 2×2 square matrix, use the following pattern:

$$M = \begin{bmatrix} m_{11} & m_{12} \\ m_{21} & m_{22} \end{bmatrix}; M^{-1} = \begin{bmatrix} \dfrac{m_{22}}{|M|} & \dfrac{-m_{12}}{|M|} \\ \dfrac{-m_{21}}{|M|} & \dfrac{m_{11}}{|M|} \end{bmatrix}$$

Another way to find the inverse of a matrix by hand is use an augmented matrix and elementary row operations. An **augmented matrix** is formed by appending the entries from one matrix onto the end of another. For example, given a 2×2 invertible matrix $N = \begin{bmatrix} a & b \\ c & d \end{bmatrix}$, you can find the inverse N^{-1} by creating an augmented matrix by appending a 2×2 identity matrix: $\begin{bmatrix} a & b & 1 & 0 \\ c & d & 0 & 1 \end{bmatrix}$. To find the inverse of the original 2×2 matrix, perform elementary row operations to convert the original matrix on the left to an identity matrix: $\begin{bmatrix} 1 & 0 & e & f \\ 0 & 1 & g & h \end{bmatrix}$. For instance, the first step might be to multiply the second row by $\frac{b}{d}$ and then subtract it from the first row to make its second column a zero. The end result is that the 2×2 section on the right will become the inverse of the original matrix: $N^{-1} = \begin{bmatrix} e & f \\ g & h \end{bmatrix}$.

> **Review Video: Matrices: Transposition, Determinants, and Augmentation**
> Visit mometrix.com/academy and enter code: 521365

REDUCED ROW-ECHELON FORMS

When a system of equations has a solution, finding the transformation of the augmented matrix will result in one of three reduced row-echelon forms. Only one of these forms will give a unique solution to the system of equations, however. The following examples show the solutions indicated by particular results:

$\begin{bmatrix} 1 & 0 & 0 & x_0 \\ 0 & 1 & 0 & y_0 \\ 0 & 0 & 1 & z_0 \end{bmatrix}$ gives the unique solution $x = x_0$; $y = y_0$; $z = z_0$

$\begin{bmatrix} 1 & 0 & k_1 & x_0 \\ 0 & 1 & k_2 & y_0 \\ 0 & 0 & 0 & 0 \end{bmatrix}$ gives a non-unique solution $x = x_0 - k_1 z$; $y = y_0 - k_2 z$

$\begin{bmatrix} 1 & j_1 & k_1 & x_0 \\ 0 & 0 & 0 & 0 \\ 0 & 0 & 0 & 0 \end{bmatrix}$ gives a non-unique solution $x = x_0 - j_1 y - k_1 z$

GEOMETRIC TRANSFORMATIONS

The four *geometric transformations* are **translations, reflections, rotations,** and **dilations**. When geometric transformations are expressed as matrices, the process of performing the transformations is simplified. For calculations of the geometric transformations of a planar figure, make a $2 \times n$ matrix, where n is the number of vertices in the planar figure. Each column represents the rectangular coordinates of one vertex of the figure, with the top row containing the values of the x-coordinates and the bottom row containing the values of the y-coordinates. For example, given a planar triangular figure with coordinates (x_1, y_1), (x_2, y_2), and (x_3, y_3), the corresponding matrix is $\begin{bmatrix} x_1 & x_2 & x_3 \\ y_1 & y_2 & y_3 \end{bmatrix}$. You can then perform the necessary transformations on this matrix to determine the coordinates of the resulting figure.

> **Review Video: Matrices: Geometric Transformations**
> Visit mometrix.com/academy and enter code: 612781

TRANSLATION

A **translation** moves a figure along the x-axis, the y-axis, or both axes without changing the size or shape of the figure. To calculate the new coordinates of a planar figure following a translation, set up a matrix of the coordinates and a matrix of the translation values and add the two matrices.

$$\begin{bmatrix} h & h & h \\ v & v & v \end{bmatrix} + \begin{bmatrix} x_1 & x_2 & x_3 \\ y_1 & y_2 & y_3 \end{bmatrix} = \begin{bmatrix} h + x_1 & h + x_2 & h + x_3 \\ v + y_1 & v + y_2 & v + y_3 \end{bmatrix}$$

where h is the number of units the figure is moved along the x-axis (horizontally) and v is the number of units the figure is moved along the y-axis (vertically).

REFLECTION

To find the **reflection** of a planar figure over the x-axis, set up a matrix of the coordinates of the vertices and pre-multiply the matrix by the 2×2 matrix $\begin{bmatrix} 1 & 0 \\ 0 & -1 \end{bmatrix}$ so that $\begin{bmatrix} 1 & 0 \\ 0 & -1 \end{bmatrix}\begin{bmatrix} x_1 & x_2 & x_3 \\ y_1 & y_2 & y_3 \end{bmatrix} = \begin{bmatrix} x_1 & x_2 & x_3 \\ -y_1 & -y_2 & -y_3 \end{bmatrix}$. To find the reflection of a planar figure over the y-axis, set up a matrix of the coordinates of the vertices and pre-multiply the matrix by the 2×2 matrix $\begin{bmatrix} -1 & 0 \\ 0 & 1 \end{bmatrix}$ so that $\begin{bmatrix} -1 & 0 \\ 0 & 1 \end{bmatrix}\begin{bmatrix} x_1 & x_2 & x_3 \\ y_1 & y_2 & y_3 \end{bmatrix} = \begin{bmatrix} -x_1 & -x_2 & -x_3 \\ y_1 & y_2 & y_3 \end{bmatrix}$. To find the reflection of a planar figure over the line $y = x$, set up a matrix of the coordinates of the vertices and pre-multiply the matrix by the 2×2 matrix $\begin{bmatrix} 0 & 1 \\ 1 & 0 \end{bmatrix}$ so that $\begin{bmatrix} 0 & 1 \\ 1 & 0 \end{bmatrix}\begin{bmatrix} x_1 & x_2 & x_3 \\ y_1 & y_2 & y_3 \end{bmatrix} = \begin{bmatrix} y_1 & y_2 & y_3 \\ x_1 & x_2 & x_3 \end{bmatrix}$. Remember that the order of multiplication is important when multiplying matrices. The commutative property does not apply.

ROTATION

To find the coordinates of the figure formed by rotating a planar figure about the origin θ degrees in a counterclockwise direction, set up a matrix of the coordinates of the vertices and pre-multiply the matrix by the 2×2 matrix $\begin{bmatrix} \cos\theta & \sin\theta \\ -\sin\theta & \cos\theta \end{bmatrix}$. For example, if you want to rotate a figure $90°$ clockwise around the origin, you would have to convert the degree measure to $270°$ counterclockwise and solve the 2×2 matrix you have set as the pre-multiplier: $\begin{bmatrix} \cos 270° & \sin 270° \\ -\sin 270° & \cos 270° \end{bmatrix} = \begin{bmatrix} 0 & -1 \\ 1 & 0 \end{bmatrix}$. Use this as the pre-multiplier for the matrix $\begin{bmatrix} x_1 & x_2 & x_3 \\ y_1 & y_2 & y_3 \end{bmatrix}$ and solve to find the new coordinates.

DILATION

To find the **dilation** of a planar figure by a scale factor of k, set up a matrix of the coordinates of the vertices of the planar figure and pre-multiply the matrix by the 2×2 matrix $\begin{bmatrix} k & 0 \\ 0 & k \end{bmatrix}$ so that $\begin{bmatrix} k & 0 \\ 0 & k \end{bmatrix}\begin{bmatrix} x_1 & x_2 & x_3 \\ y_1 & y_2 & y_3 \end{bmatrix} = \begin{bmatrix} kx_1 & kx_2 & kx_3 \\ ky_1 & ky_2 & ky_3 \end{bmatrix}$. This is effectively the same as multiplying the matrix by the scalar k, but the matrix equation would still be necessary if the figure were being dilated by different factors in vertical and horizontal directions. The scale factor k will be greater than 1 if the figure is being enlarged, and between 0 and 1 if the figure is being shrunk. Again, remember that when multiplying matrices, the order of the matrices is important. The commutative property does not apply, and the matrix with the coordinates of the figure must be the second matrix.

MATRIX SYSTEMS

SOLVING SYSTEMS OF EQUATIONS

Matrices can be used to represent the coefficients of a system of linear equations and can be very useful in solving those systems. Take for instance three equations with three variables where all a, b, c, and d are known constants:

$$a_1x + b_1y + c_1z = d_1$$
$$a_2x + b_2y + c_2z = d_2$$
$$a_3x + b_3y + c_3z = d_3$$

To solve this system, define three matrices:

$$A = \begin{bmatrix} a_1 & b_1 & c_1 \\ a_2 & b_2 & c_2 \\ a_3 & b_3 & c_3 \end{bmatrix}; D = \begin{bmatrix} d_1 \\ d_2 \\ d_3 \end{bmatrix}; X = \begin{bmatrix} x \\ y \\ z \end{bmatrix}$$

The three equations in our system can be fully represented by a single matrix equation:

$$AX = D$$

We know that the identity matrix times X is equal to X, and we know that any matrix multiplied by its inverse is equal to the identity matrix.

$$A^{-1}AX = IX = X; \text{ thus } X = A^{-1}D$$

Our goal then is to find the inverse of A, or A^{-1}. Once we have that, we can pre-multiply matrix D by A^{-1} (post-multiplying here is an undefined operation) to find matrix X.

Systems of equations can also be solved using the transformation of an augmented matrix in a process similar to that for finding a matrix inverse. Begin by arranging each equation of the system in the following format:

$$a_1x + b_1y + c_1z = d_1$$
$$a_2x + b_2y + c_2z = d_2$$
$$a_3x + b_3y + c_3z = d_3$$

Define matrices A and D and combine them into augmented matrix A_a:

$$A = \begin{bmatrix} a_1 & b_1 & c_1 \\ a_2 & b_2 & c_2 \\ a_3 & b_3 & c_3 \end{bmatrix}; D = \begin{bmatrix} d_1 \\ d_2 \\ d_3 \end{bmatrix}; A_a = \begin{bmatrix} a_1 & b_1 & c_1 & d_1 \\ a_2 & b_2 & c_2 & d_2 \\ a_3 & b_3 & c_3 & d_3 \end{bmatrix}$$

To solve the augmented matrix and the system of equations, use elementary row operations to form an identity matrix in the first 3×3 section. When this is complete, the values in the last column are the solutions to the system of equations:

$$\begin{bmatrix} 1 & 0 & 0 & x \\ 0 & 1 & 0 & y \\ 0 & 0 & 1 & z \end{bmatrix}$$

If an identity matrix is not possible, the system of equations has no unique solution. Sometimes only a partial solution will be possible. The following are partial solutions you may find:

$$\begin{bmatrix} 1 & 0 & k_1 & x_0 \\ 0 & 1 & k_2 & y_0 \\ 0 & 0 & 0 & 0 \end{bmatrix}$$ gives the non-unique solution $x = x_0 - k_1z$; $y = y_0 - k_2z$

$$\begin{bmatrix} 1 & j_1 & k_1 & x_0 \\ 0 & 0 & 0 & 0 \\ 0 & 0 & 0 & 0 \end{bmatrix}$$ gives the non-unique solution $x = x_0 - j_1 y - k_1 z$

This process can be used to solve systems of equations with any number of variables, but three is the upper limit for practical purposes. Anything more ought to be done with a graphing calculator.

> **Review Video: Matrices: Data Systems**
> Visit mometrix.com/academy and enter code: 579763

Geometry

ROUNDING AND ESTIMATION

Rounding is reducing the digits in a number while still trying to keep the value similar. The result will be less accurate but in a simpler form and easier to use. Whole numbers can be rounded to the nearest ten, hundred, or thousand.

When you are asked to estimate the solution to a problem, you will need to provide only an approximate figure or **estimation** for your answer. In this situation, you will need to round each number in the calculation to the level indicated (nearest hundred, nearest thousand, etc.) or to a level that makes sense for the numbers involved. When estimating a sum **all numbers must be rounded to the same level**. You cannot round one number to the nearest thousand while rounding another to the nearest hundred.

> **Review Video: Rounding and Estimation**
> Visit mometrix.com/academy and enter code: 126243

SCIENTIFIC NOTATION

Scientific notation is a way of writing large numbers in a shorter form. The form $a \times 10^n$ is used in scientific notation, where a is greater than or equal to 1 but less than 10, and n is the number of places the decimal must move to get from the original number to a. Example: The number 230,400,000 is cumbersome to write. To write the value in scientific notation, place a decimal point between the first and second numbers, and include all digits through the last non-zero digit ($a = 2.304$). To find the appropriate power of 10, count the number of places the decimal point had to move ($n = 8$). The number is positive if the decimal moved to the left, and negative if it moved to the right. We can then write 230,400,000 as 2.304×10^8. If we look instead at the number 0.00002304, we have the same value for a, but this time the decimal moved 5 places to the right ($n = -5$). Thus, 0.00002304 can be written as 2.304×10^{-5}. Using this notation makes it simple to compare very large or very small numbers. By comparing exponents, it is easy to see that 3.28×10^4 is smaller than 1.51×10^5, because 4 is less than 5.

> **Review Video: Scientific Notation**
> Visit mometrix.com/academy and enter code: 976454

PRECISION, ACCURACY, AND ERROR

Precision: How reliable and repeatable a measurement is. The more consistent the data is with repeated testing, the more precise it is. For example, hitting a target consistently in the same spot, which may or may not be the center of the target, is precision.

Accuracy: How close the data is to the correct data. For example, hitting a target consistently in the center area of the target, whether or not the hits are all in the same spot, is accuracy.

Note: it is possible for data to be precise without being accurate. If a scale is off balance, the data will be precise, but will not be accurate. For data to have precision and accuracy, it must be repeatable and correct.

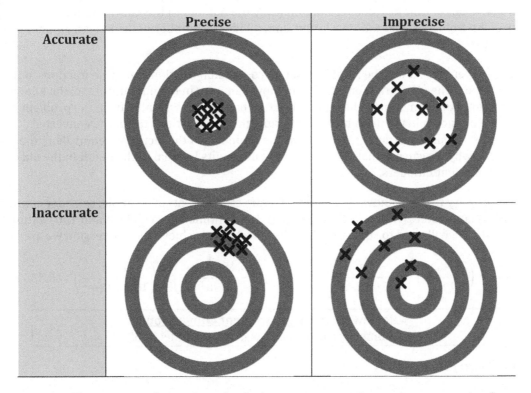

Approximate error: The amount of error in a physical measurement. Approximate error is often reported as the measurement, followed by the $\pm$ symbol and the amount of the approximate error.

Maximum possible error: Half the magnitude of the smallest unit used in the measurement. For example, if the unit of measurement is 1 centimeter, the maximum possible error is $\frac{1}{2}$ cm, written as ± 0.5 cm following the measurement. It is important to apply significant figures in reporting maximum possible error. Do not make the answer appear more accurate than the least accurate of your measurements.

> **Review Video: Precision, Accuracy, and Error**
> Visit mometrix.com/academy and enter code: 520377

METRIC AND CUSTOMARY MEASUREMENTS
METRIC MEASUREMENT PREFIXES

Giga-	One billion	1 *giga*watt is one billion watts
Mega-	One million	1 *mega*hertz is one million hertz
Kilo-	One thousand	1 *kilo*gram is one thousand grams
Deci-	One-tenth	1 *deci*meter is one-tenth of a meter
Centi-	One-hundredth	1 *centi*meter is one-hundredth of a meter
Milli-	One-thousandth	1 *milli*liter is one-thousandth of a liter
Micro-	One-millionth	1 *micro*gram is one-millionth of a gram

> **Review Video: Metric System Conversion - How the Metric System Works**
> Visit mometrix.com/academy and enter code: 163709

MEASUREMENT CONVERSION

When converting between units, the goal is to maintain the same meaning but change the way it is displayed. In order to go from a larger unit to a smaller unit, multiply the number of the known amount by the equivalent amount. When going from a smaller unit to a larger unit, divide the number of the known amount by the equivalent amount.

For complicated conversions, it may be helpful to set up conversion fractions. In these fractions, one fraction is the **conversion factor**. The other fraction has the unknown amount in the numerator. So, the known value is placed in the denominator. Sometimes, the second fraction has the known value from the problem in the numerator and the unknown in the denominator. Multiply the two fractions to get the converted measurement. Note that since the numerator and the denominator of the factor are equivalent, the value of the fraction is 1. That is why we can say that the result in the new units is equal to the result in the old units even though they have different numbers.

It can often be necessary to chain known conversion factors together. As an example, consider converting 512 square inches to square meters. We know that there are 2.54 centimeters in an inch and 100 centimeters in a meter, and we know we will need to square each of these factors to achieve the conversion we are looking for.

$$\frac{512 \text{ in}^2}{1} \times \left(\frac{2.54 \text{ cm}}{1 \text{ in}}\right)^2 \times \left(\frac{1 \text{ m}}{100 \text{ cm}}\right)^2 = \frac{512 \text{ in}^2}{1} \times \left(\frac{6.4516 \text{ cm}^2}{1 \text{ in}^2}\right) \times \left(\frac{1 \text{ m}^2}{10,000 \text{ cm}^2}\right) = 0.330 \text{ m}^2$$

> **Review Video: Measurement Conversions**
> Visit mometrix.com/academy and enter code: 316703

COMMON UNITS AND EQUIVALENTS
METRIC EQUIVALENTS

1000 µg (microgram)	1 mg
1000 mg (milligram)	1 g
1000 g (gram)	1 kg
1000 kg (kilogram)	1 metric ton
1000 mL (milliliter)	1 L
1000 µm (micrometer)	1 mm
1000 mm (millimeter)	1 m
100 cm (centimeter)	1 m
1000 m (meter)	1 km

DISTANCE AND AREA MEASUREMENT

Unit	Abbreviation	US equivalent	Metric equivalent
Inch	in	1 inch	2.54 centimeters
Foot	ft	12 inches	0.305 meters
Yard	yd	3 feet	0.914 meters
Mile	mi	5280 feet	1.609 kilometers
Acre	ac	4840 square yards	0.405 hectares
Square Mile	sq. mi. or mi.²	640 acres	2.590 square kilometers

CAPACITY MEASUREMENTS

Unit	Abbreviation	US equivalent	Metric equivalent
Fluid Ounce	fl oz	8 fluid drams	29.573 milliliters
Cup	c	8 fluid ounces	0.237 liter
Pint	pt.	16 fluid ounces	0.473 liter
Quart	qt.	2 pints	0.946 liter
Gallon	gal.	4 quarts	3.785 liters
Teaspoon	t or tsp.	1 fluid dram	5 milliliters
Tablespoon	T or tbsp.	4 fluid drams	15 or 16 milliliters
Cubic Centimeter	cc or cm^3	0.271 drams	1 milliliter

WEIGHT MEASUREMENTS

Unit	Abbreviation	US equivalent	Metric equivalent
Ounce	oz	16 drams	28.35 grams
Pound	lb	16 ounces	453.6 grams
Ton	tn.	2,000 pounds	907.2 kilograms

VOLUME AND WEIGHT MEASUREMENT CLARIFICATIONS

Always be careful when using ounces and fluid ounces. They are not equivalent.

1 pint = 16 fluid ounces	1 fluid ounce ≠ 1 ounce
1 pound = 16 ounces	1 pint ≠ 1 pound

Having one pint of something does not mean you have one pound of it. In the same way, just because something weighs one pound does not mean that its volume is one pint.

In the United States, the word "ton" by itself refers to a short ton or a net ton. Do not confuse this with a long ton (also called a gross ton) or a metric ton (also spelled *tonne*), which have different measurement equivalents.

$$1 \text{ US ton} = 2000 \text{ pounds} \quad \neq \quad 1 \text{ metric ton} = 1000 \text{ kilograms}$$

POINTS, LINES, AND PLANES

POINTS AND LINES

A **point** is a fixed location in space, has no size or dimensions, and is commonly represented by a dot. A **line** is a set of points that extends infinitely in two opposite directions. It has length, but no width or depth. A line can be defined by any two distinct points that it contains. A **line segment** is a portion of a line that has definite endpoints. A **ray** is a portion of a line that extends from a single point on that line in one direction along the line. It has a definite beginning, but no ending.

INTERACTIONS BETWEEN LINES

Intersecting lines are lines that have exactly one point in common. **Concurrent lines** are multiple lines that intersect at a single point. **Perpendicular lines** are lines that intersect at right angles. They are represented by the symbol ⊥. The shortest distance from a line to a point not on the line is a perpendicular segment from the point to the line. **Parallel lines** are lines in the same plane that have no points in common and never meet. It is possible for lines to be in different planes, have no points in common, and never meet, but they are not parallel because they are in different planes.

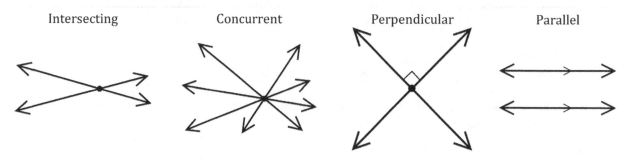

| Intersecting | Concurrent | Perpendicular | Parallel |

> **Review Video: <u>Parallel and Perpendicular Lines</u>**
> Visit mometrix.com/academy and enter code: 815923

A **transversal** is a line that intersects at least two other lines, which may or may not be parallel to one another. A transversal that intersects parallel lines is a common occurrence in geometry. A **bisector** is a line or line segment that divides another line segment into two equal lengths. A **perpendicular bisector** of a line segment is composed of points that are equidistant from the endpoints of the segment it is dividing.

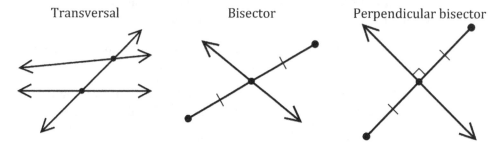

| Transversal | Bisector | Perpendicular bisector |

The **projection of a point on a line** is the point at which a perpendicular line drawn from the given point to the given line intersects the line. This is also the shortest distance from the given point to the line. The **projection of a segment on a line** is a segment whose endpoints are the points formed when perpendicular lines are drawn from the endpoints of the given segment to the given line. This is similar to the length a diagonal line appears to be when viewed from above.

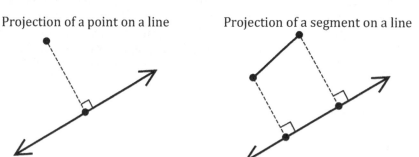

| Projection of a point on a line | Projection of a segment on a line |

PLANES

A **plane** is a two-dimensional flat surface defined by three non-collinear points. A plane extends an infinite distance in all directions in those two dimensions. It contains an infinite number of points, parallel lines and segments, intersecting lines and segments, as well as parallel or intersecting rays. A plane will never contain a three-dimensional figure or skew lines, which are lines that don't intersect and are not parallel. Two given planes are either parallel or they intersect at a line. A plane may intersect a circular conic surface to form **conic sections**, such as a parabola, hyperbola, circle or ellipse.

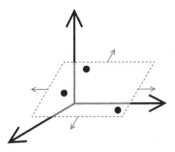

ANGLES

ANGLES AND VERTICES

An **angle** is formed when two lines or line segments meet at a common point. It may be a common starting point for a pair of segments or rays, or it may be the intersection of lines. Angles are represented by the symbol ∠.

The **vertex** is the point at which two segments or rays meet to form an angle. If the angle is formed by intersecting rays, lines, and/or line segments, the vertex is the point at which four angles are formed. The pairs of angles opposite one another are called vertical angles, and their measures are equal.

- An **acute** angle is an angle with a degree measure less than 90°.
- A **right** angle is an angle with a degree measure of exactly 90°.
- An **obtuse** angle is an angle with a degree measure greater than 90° but less than 180°.
- A **straight angle** is an angle with a degree measure of exactly 180°. This is also a semicircle.
- A **reflex angle** is an angle with a degree measure greater than 180° but less than 360°.
- A **full angle** is an angle with a degree measure of exactly 360°. This is also a circle.

RELATIONSHIPS BETWEEN ANGLES

Two angles whose sum is exactly 90° are said to be **complementary**. The two angles may or may not be adjacent. In a right triangle, the two acute angles are complementary.

Two angles whose sum is exactly 180° are said to be **supplementary**. The two angles may or may not be adjacent. Two intersecting lines always form two pairs of supplementary angles. Adjacent supplementary angles will always form a straight line.

Two angles that have the same vertex and share a side are said to be **adjacent**. Vertical angles are not adjacent because they share a vertex but no common side.

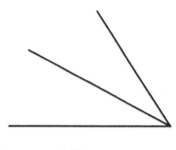

Adjacent
Share vertex and side

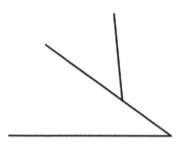

Not adjacent
Share part of a side, but not vertex

When two parallel lines are cut by a transversal, the angles that are between the two parallel lines are **interior angles**. In the diagram below, angles 3, 4, 5, and 6 are interior angles.

When two parallel lines are cut by a transversal, the angles that are outside the parallel lines are **exterior angles**. In the diagram below, angles 1, 2, 7, and 8 are exterior angles.

When two parallel lines are cut by a transversal, the angles that are in the same position relative to the transversal and a parallel line are **corresponding angles**. The diagram below has four pairs of corresponding angles: angles 1 and 5, angles 2 and 6, angles 3 and 7, and angles 4 and 8. Corresponding angles formed by parallel lines are congruent.

When two parallel lines are cut by a transversal, the two interior angles that are on opposite sides of the transversal are called **alternate interior angles**. In the diagram below, there are two pairs of alternate interior angles: angles 3 and 6, and angles 4 and 5. Alternate interior angles formed by parallel lines are congruent.

When two parallel lines are cut by a transversal, the two exterior angles that are on opposite sides of the transversal are called **alternate exterior angles**.

In the diagram below, there are two pairs of alternate exterior angles: angles 1 and 8, and angles 2 and 7. Alternate exterior angles formed by parallel lines are congruent.

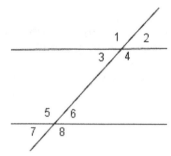

192

When two lines intersect, four angles are formed. The non-adjacent angles at this vertex are called vertical angles. Vertical angles are congruent. In the diagram, $\angle ABD \cong \angle CBE$ and $\angle ABC \cong \angle DBE$. The other pairs of angles, $(\angle ABC, \angle CBE)$ and $(\angle ABD, \angle DBE)$, are supplementary, meaning the pairs sum to 180°.

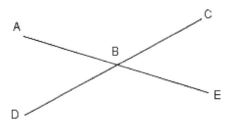

POLYGONS

A **polygon** is a closed, two-dimensional figure with three or more straight line segments called **sides**. The point at which two sides of a polygon intersect is called the **vertex**. In a polygon, the number of sides is always equal to the number of vertices. A polygon with all sides congruent and all angles equal is called a **regular polygon**. Common polygons are:

Triangle = 3 sides
Quadrilateral = 4 sides
Pentagon = 5 sides
Hexagon = 6 sides
Heptagon = 7 sides
Octagon = 8 sides
Nonagon = 9 sides
Decagon = 10 sides
Dodecagon = 12 sides

More generally, an n-gon is a polygon that has n angles and n sides.

Review Video: Intro to Polygons
Visit mometrix.com/academy and enter code: 271869

The sum of the interior angles of an n-sided polygon is $(n-2) \times 180°$. For example, in a triangle $n = 3$. So the sum of the interior angles is $(3-2) \times 180° = 180°$. In a quadrilateral, $n = 4$, and the sum of the angles is $(4-2) \times 180° = 360°$.

Review Video: Sum of Interior Angles
Visit mometrix.com/academy and enter code: 984991

CONVEX AND CONCAVE POLYGONS

A **convex polygon** is a polygon whose diagonals all lie within the interior of the polygon. A **concave polygon** is a polygon with a least one diagonal that is outside the polygon. In the diagram below, quadrilateral *ABCD* is concave because diagonal $\overline{AC}$ lies outside the polygon and quadrilateral $EFGH$ is convex because both diagonals lie inside the polygon.

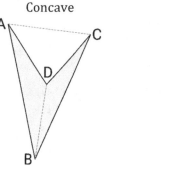
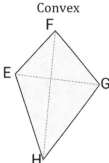

Concave

Convex

APOTHEM AND RADIUS

A line segment from the center of a polygon that is perpendicular to a side of the polygon is called the **apothem**. A line segment from the center of a polygon to a vertex of the polygon is called a **radius**. In a regular polygon, the apothem can be used to find the area of the polygon using the formula $A = \frac{1}{2}ap$, where a is the apothem, and p is the perimeter.

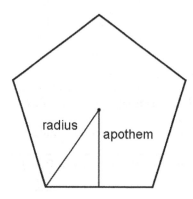

A **diagonal** is a line segment that joins two non-adjacent vertices of a polygon. The number of diagonals a polygon has can be found by using the formula:

$$\text{number of diagonals} = \frac{n(n-3)}{2}$$

Note that n is the number of sides in the polygon. This formula works for all polygons, not just regular polygons.

CONGRUENCE AND SIMILARITY

Congruent figures are geometric figures that have the same size and shape. All corresponding angles are equal, and all corresponding sides are equal. Congruence is indicated by the symbol ≅.

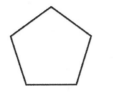

Congruent polygons

Similar figures are geometric figures that have the same shape, but do not necessarily have the same size. All corresponding angles are equal, and all corresponding sides are proportional, but they do not have to be equal. It is indicated by the symbol ~.

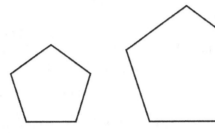

Similar polygons

Note that all congruent figures are also similar, but not all similar figures are congruent.

> **Review Video: Congruent Shapes**
> Visit mometrix.com/academy and enter code: 492281

LINE OF SYMMETRY

A line that divides a figure or object into congruent parts is called a **line of symmetry**. An object may have no lines of symmetry, one line of symmetry, or multiple (i.e., more than one) lines of symmetry.

None   One   Multiple

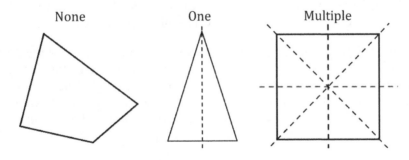

> **Review Video: Symmetry**
> Visit mometrix.com/academy and enter code: 528106

195

TRIANGLES

A triangle is a three-sided figure with the sum of its interior angles being 180°. The **perimeter of any triangle** is found by summing the three side lengths; $P = a + b + c$. For an equilateral triangle, this is the same as $P = 3a$, where a is any side length, since all three sides are the same length.

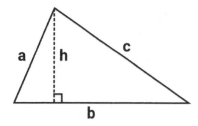

The **area of any triangle** can be found by taking half the product of one side length referred to as the base, often given the variable b and the perpendicular distance from that side to the opposite vertex called the altitude or height and given the variable h. In equation form that is $A = \frac{1}{2}bh$. Another formula that works for any triangle is $A = \sqrt{s(s-a)(s-b)(s-c)}$, where s is the semiperimeter: $\frac{a+b+c}{2}$, and a, b, and c are the lengths of the three sides. Special cases include isosceles triangles, $A = \frac{1}{2}b\sqrt{a^2 - \frac{b^2}{4}}$, where b is the unique side and a is the length of one of the two congruent sides, and equilateral triangles, $A = \frac{\sqrt{3}}{4}a^2$, where a is the length of a side.

PARTS OF A TRIANGLE

An **altitude** of a triangle is a line segment drawn from one vertex perpendicular to the opposite side. In the diagram that follows, $\overline{BE}$, $\overline{AD}$, and $\overline{CF}$ are altitudes. The length of an altitude is also called the height of the triangle. The three altitudes in a triangle are always concurrent. The point of concurrency of the altitudes of a triangle, O, is called the **orthocenter**. Note that in an obtuse triangle, the orthocenter will be outside the triangle, and in a right triangle, the orthocenter is the vertex of the right angle.

A **median** of a triangle is a line segment drawn from one vertex to the midpoint of the opposite side. In the diagram that follows, $\overline{BH}$, $\overline{AG}$, and $\overline{CI}$ are medians. This is not the same as the altitude, except the altitude to the base of an isosceles triangle and all three altitudes of an equilateral triangle. The point of concurrency of the medians of a triangle, T, is called the **centroid**. This is the same point as the orthocenter only in an equilateral triangle. Unlike the orthocenter, the centroid is always inside the triangle. The centroid can also be considered the exact center of the triangle. Any shape triangle can be perfectly balanced on a tip placed at the centroid. The centroid is also the point that is two-thirds the distance from the vertex to the opposite side.

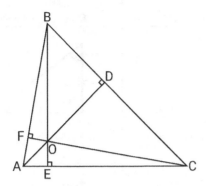 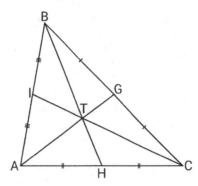

Review Video: Centroid, Incenter, Circumcenter, and Orthocenter
Visit mometrix.com/academy and enter code: 598260

TRIANGLE PROPERTIES
CLASSIFICATIONS OF TRIANGLES

A **scalene triangle** is a triangle with no congruent sides. A scalene triangle will also have three angles of different measures. The angle with the largest measure is opposite the longest side, and the angle with the smallest measure is opposite the shortest side. An **acute triangle** is a triangle whose three angles are all less than 90°. If two of the angles are equal, the acute triangle is also an **isosceles triangle**. An isosceles triangle will also have two congruent angles opposite the two congruent sides. If the three angles are all equal, the acute triangle is also an **equilateral triangle**. An equilateral triangle will also have three congruent angles, each 60°. All equilateral triangles are also acute triangles. An **obtuse triangle** is a triangle with exactly one angle greater than 90°. The other two angles may or may not be equal. If the two remaining angles are equal, the obtuse triangle is also an isosceles triangle. A **right triangle** is a triangle with exactly one angle equal to 90°. All right triangles follow the Pythagorean theorem. A right triangle can never be acute or obtuse.

The table below illustrates how each descriptor places a different restriction on the triangle:

Angles / Sides	Acute: All angles < 90°	Obtuse: One angle > 90°	Right: One angle = 90°
Scalene: No equal side lengths	$90° > \angle a > \angle b > \angle c$ $x > y > z$	$\angle a > 90° > \angle b > \angle c$ $x > y > z$	$90° = \angle a > \angle b > \angle c$ $x > y > z$
Isosceles: Two equal side lengths	$90° > \angle a, \angle b, or \angle c$ $\angle b = \angle c, \qquad y = z$	$\angle a > 90° > \angle b = \angle c$ $x > y = z$	$\angle a = 90°$ $\angle b = \angle c = 45°$ $x > y = z$
Equilateral: Three equal side lengths	$60° = \angle a = \angle b = \angle c$ $x = y = z$		

> **Review Video: Introduction to Types of Triangles**
> Visit mometrix.com/academy and enter code: 511711

GENERAL RULES FOR TRIANGLES

The **triangle inequality theorem** states that the sum of the measures of any two sides of a triangle is always greater than the measure of the third side. If the sum of the measures of two sides were equal to the third side, a triangle would be impossible because the two sides would lie flat across the third side and there would be no vertex. If the sum of the measures of two of the sides was less than the third side, a closed figure would be impossible because the two shortest sides would never meet. In other words, for a triangle with sides lengths $A, B,$ and C: $A + B > C, B + C > A,$ and $A + C > B$.

The sum of the measures of the interior angles of a triangle is always 180°. Therefore, a triangle can never have more than one angle greater than or equal to 90°.

In any triangle, the angles opposite congruent sides are congruent, and the sides opposite congruent angles are congruent. The largest angle is always opposite the longest side, and the smallest angle is always opposite the shortest side.

The line segment that joins the midpoints of any two sides of a triangle is always parallel to the third side and exactly half the length of the third side.

SIMILARITY AND CONGRUENCE RULES

Similar triangles are triangles whose corresponding angles are equal and whose corresponding sides are proportional. Represented by AAA. Similar triangles whose corresponding sides are congruent are also congruent triangles.

Triangles can be shown to be **congruent** in 5 ways:

- **SSS**: Three sides of one triangle are congruent to the three corresponding sides of the second triangle.
- **SAS**: Two sides and the included angle (the angle formed by those two sides) of one triangle are congruent to the corresponding two sides and included angle of the second triangle.
- **ASA**: Two angles and the included side (the side that joins the two angles) of one triangle are congruent to the corresponding two angles and included side of the second triangle.
- **AAS**: Two angles and a non-included side of one triangle are congruent to the corresponding two angles and non-included side of the second triangle.
- **HL**: The hypotenuse and leg of one right triangle are congruent to the corresponding hypotenuse and leg of the second right triangle.

TRANSFORMATIONS

ROTATION

A **rotation** is a transformation that turns a figure around a point called the **center of rotation**, which can lie anywhere in the plane. If a line is drawn from a point on a figure to the center of rotation, and another line is drawn from the center to the rotated image of that point, the angle between the two lines is the **angle of rotation**. The vertex of the angle of rotation is the center of rotation.

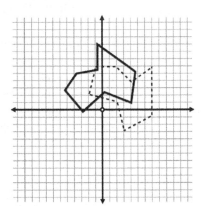

TRANSLATION AND DILATION

A **translation** is a transformation which slides a figure from one position in the plane to another position in the plane. The original figure and the translated figure have the same size, shape, and orientation. A **dilation** is a transformation which proportionally stretches or shrinks a figure by a **scale factor**. The dilated image is the same shape and orientation as the original image but a different size. A polygon and its dilated image are similar.

Translation

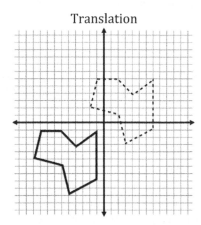

Dilation

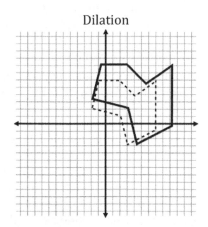

Review Video: Translation
Visit mometrix.com/academy and enter code: 718628

Review Video: Dilation
Visit mometrix.com/academy and enter code: 471630

A **reflection of a figure over a line** (a "flip") creates a congruent image that is the same distance from the line as the original figure but on the opposite side. The **line of reflection** is the perpendicular bisector of any line segment drawn from a point on the original figure to its reflected image (unless the point and its reflected image happen to be the same point, which happens when a figure is reflected over one of its own sides). A **reflection of a figure over a point** (an inversion) in two dimensions is the same as the rotation of the figure 180° about that point. The image of the figure is congruent to the original figure. The **point of reflection** is the midpoint of a line segment which connects a point in the figure to its image (unless the point and its reflected image happen to be the same point, which happens when a figure is reflected in one of its own points).

Reflection of a figure over a line

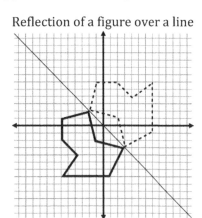

Reflection of a figure over a point

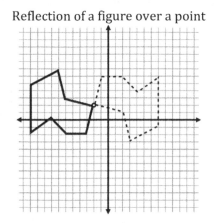

Review Video: Reflection
Visit mometrix.com/academy and enter code: 955068

200

PYTHAGOREAN THEOREM

The side of a triangle opposite the right angle is called the **hypotenuse**. The other two sides are called the legs. The Pythagorean theorem states a relationship among the legs and hypotenuse of a right triangle: $(a^2 + b^2 = c^2)$, where a and b are the lengths of the legs of a right triangle, and c is the length of the hypotenuse. Note that this formula will only work with right triangles.

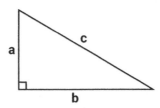

TRIGONOMETRIC FORMULAS

In the diagram below, angle C is the right angle, and side c is the hypotenuse. Side a is the side opposite to angle A and side b is the side opposite to angle B. Using ratios of side lengths as a means to calculate the sine, cosine, and tangent of an acute angle only works for right triangles.

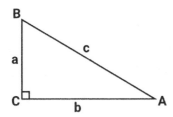

$$\sin A = \frac{\text{opposite side}}{\text{hypotenuse}} = \frac{a}{c} \qquad \csc A = \frac{1}{\sin A} = \frac{\text{hypotenuse}}{\text{opposite side}} = \frac{c}{a}$$

$$\cos A = \frac{\text{adjacent side}}{\text{hypotenuse}} = \frac{b}{c} \qquad \sec A = \frac{1}{\cos A} = \frac{\text{hypotenuse}}{\text{adjacent side}} = \frac{c}{b}$$

$$\tan A = \frac{\text{opposite side}}{\text{adjacent side}} = \frac{a}{b} \qquad \cot A = \frac{1}{\tan A} = \frac{\text{adjacent side}}{\text{opposite side}} = \frac{b}{a}$$

LAWS OF SINES AND COSINES

The **law of sines** states that $\frac{\sin A}{a} = \frac{\sin B}{b} = \frac{\sin C}{c}$, where A, B, and C are the angles of a triangle, and a, b, and c are the sides opposite their respective angles. This formula will work with all triangles, not just right triangles.

The **law of cosines** is given by the formula $c^2 = a^2 + b^2 - 2ab(\cos C)$, where a, b, and c are the sides of a triangle, and C is the angle opposite side c. This is a generalized form of the Pythagorean theorem that can be used on any triangle.

QUADRILATERALS

A **quadrilateral** is a closed two-dimensional geometric figure that has four straight sides. The sum of the interior angles of any quadrilateral is 360°.

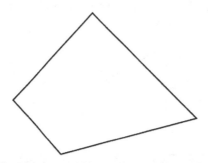

> **Review Video: Diagonals of Parallelograms, Rectangles, and Rhombi**
> Visit mometrix.com/academy and enter code: 320040

KITE

A **kite** is a quadrilateral with two pairs of adjacent sides that are congruent. A result of this is perpendicular diagonals. A kite can be concave or convex and has one line of symmetry.

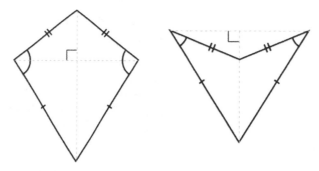

TRAPEZOID

Trapezoid: A trapezoid is defined as a quadrilateral that has at least one pair of parallel sides. There are no rules for the second pair of sides. So, there are no rules for the diagonals and no lines of symmetry for a trapezoid.

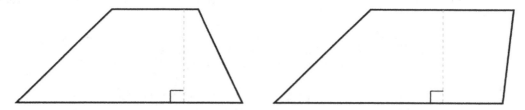

The **area of a trapezoid** is found by the formula $A = \frac{1}{2}h(b_1 + b_2)$, where h is the height (segment joining and perpendicular to the parallel bases), and b_1 and b_2 are the two parallel sides (bases). Do not use one of the other two sides as the height unless that side is also perpendicular to the parallel bases.

The **perimeter of a trapezoid** is found by the formula $P = a + b_1 + c + b_2$, where a, b_1, c, and b_2 are the four sides of the trapezoid.

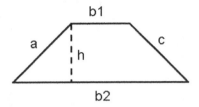

Isosceles trapezoid: A trapezoid with equal base angles. This gives rise to other properties including: the two nonparallel sides have the same length, the two non-base angles are also equal, and there is one line of symmetry through the midpoints of the parallel sides.

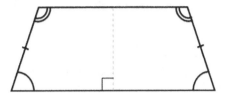

PARALLELOGRAM

A **parallelogram** is a quadrilateral that has two pairs of opposite parallel sides. As such it is a special type of trapezoid. The sides that are parallel are also congruent. The opposite interior angles are always congruent, and the consecutive interior angles are supplementary. The diagonals of a parallelogram divide each other. Each diagonal divides the parallelogram into two congruent triangles. A parallelogram has no line of symmetry, but does have 180-degree rotational symmetry about the midpoint.

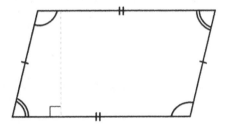

The **area of a parallelogram** is found by the formula $A = bh$, where b is the length of the base, and h is the height. Note that the base and height correspond to the length and width in a rectangle, so this formula would apply to rectangles as well. Do not confuse the height of a parallelogram with the length of the second side. The two are only the same measure in the case of a rectangle.

The **perimeter of a parallelogram** is found by the formula $P = 2a + 2b$ or $P = 2(a + b)$, where a and b are the lengths of the two sides.

RECTANGLE

A **rectangle** is a quadrilateral with four right angles. All rectangles are parallelograms and trapezoids, but not all parallelograms or trapezoids are rectangles. The diagonals of a rectangle are congruent. Rectangles have two lines of symmetry (through each pair of opposing midpoints) and 180-degree rotational symmetry about the midpoint.

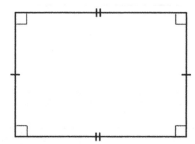

The **area of a rectangle** is found by the formula $A = lw$, where A is the area of the rectangle, l is the length (usually considered to be the longer side) and w is the width (usually considered to be the shorter side). The numbers for l and w are interchangeable.

The **perimeter of a rectangle** is found by the formula $P = 2l + 2w$ or $P = 2(l + w)$, where l is the length, and w is the width. It may be easier to add the length and width first and then double the result, as in the second formula.

RHOMBUS

A **rhombus** is a quadrilateral with four congruent sides. All rhombuses are parallelograms and kites; thus, they inherit all the properties of both types of quadrilaterals. The diagonals of a rhombus are perpendicular to each other. Rhombi have two lines of symmetry (along each of the diagonals) and 180° rotational symmetry. The **area of a rhombus** is half the product of the diagonals: $A = \frac{d_1 d_2}{2}$ and the perimeter of a rhombus is: $P = 2\sqrt{(d_1)^2 + (d_2)^2}$.

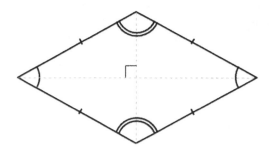

SQUARE

A **square** is a quadrilateral with four right angles and four congruent sides. Squares satisfy the criteria of all other types of quadrilaterals. The diagonals of a square are congruent and perpendicular to each other. Squares have four lines of symmetry (through each pair of opposing midpoints and along each of the diagonals) as well as 90° rotational symmetry about the midpoint.

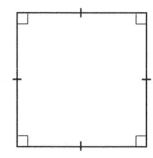

The **area of a square** is found by using the formula $A = s^2$, where s is the length of one side. The **perimeter of a square** is found by using the formula $P = 4s$, where s is the length of one side. Because all four sides are equal in a square, it is faster to multiply the length of one side by 4 than to add the same number four times. You could use the formulas for rectangles and get the same answer.

> **Review Video: <u>Area and Perimeter of Rectangles and Squares</u>**
> Visit mometrix.com/academy and enter code: 428109

HIERARCHY OF QUADRILATERALS

The hierarchy of quadrilaterals is as follows:

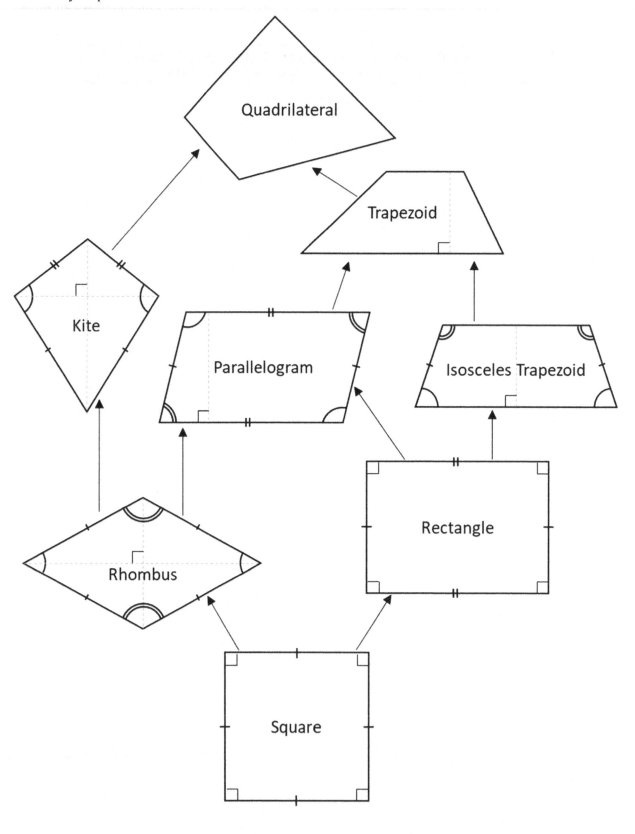

CIRCLES

The **center** of a circle is the single point from which every point on the circle is **equidistant**. The **radius** is a line segment that joins the center of the circle and any one point on the circle. All radii of a circle are equal. Circles that have the same center but not the same length of radii are **concentric**. The **diameter** is a line segment that passes through the center of the circle and has both endpoints on the circle. The length of the diameter is exactly twice the length of the radius. Point O in the diagram below is the center of the circle, segments $\overline{OX}$, $\overline{OY}$, and $\overline{OZ}$ are radii; and segment $\overline{XZ}$ is a diameter.

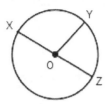

Review Video: **Points of a Circle**
Visit mometrix.com/academy and enter code: 420746
Review Video: **The Diameter, Radius, and Circumference of Circles**
Visit mometrix.com/academy and enter code: 448988

The **area of a circle** is found by the formula $A = \pi r^2$, where r is the length of the radius. If the diameter of the circle is given, remember to divide it in half to get the length of the radius before proceeding.

The **circumference** of a circle is found by the formula $C = 2\pi r$, where r is the radius. Again, remember to convert the diameter if you are given that measure rather than the radius.

Review Video: **Area and Circumference of a Circle**
Visit mometrix.com/academy and enter code: 243015

INSCRIBED AND CIRCUMSCRIBED FIGURES

These terms can both be used to describe a given arrangement of figures, depending on perspective. If each of the vertices of figure A lie on figure B, then it can be said that figure A is **inscribed** in figure B, but it can also be said that figure B is **circumscribed** about figure A. The following table and examples help to illustrate the concept. Note that the figures cannot both be circles, as they would be completely overlapping and neither would be inscribed or circumscribed.

Given	Description	Equivalent Description	Figures
Each of the sides of a pentagon is tangent to a circle	The circle is inscribed in the pentagon	The pentagon is circumscribed about the circle	
Each of the vertices of a pentagon lie on a circle	The pentagon is inscribed in the circle	The circle is circumscribed about the pentagon	

Praxis Practice Test #1

Want to take this practice test in an online interactive format?
Check out the bonus page, which includes interactive practice questions and much more: **mometrix.com/bonus948/praxcore**

Reading

Refer to the following for questions 1 - 2:

For lunch, she likes ham and cheese (torn into bites), yogurt, raisins, applesauce, peanut butter sandwiches in the fridge drawer, or any combo of these. She's not a huge eater. Help yourself too. Bread is on counter if you want to make a sandwich.

It's fine if you want to go somewhere, just leave us a note of where you are. Make sure she's buckled and drive carefully! Certain fast-food places are fun if they have playgrounds and are indoors. It's probably too hot for the playground, but whatever you want to do is fine. Take a sippy cup of water and a diaper wherever you go. There's some money here for you in case you decide to go out for lunch with her.

As for nap, try after lunch. She may not sleep, but try anyway. Read her a couple of books first, put cream on her mosquito bites (it's in the den on the buffet), then maybe rock in her chair. Give her a bottle of milk, and refill as needed, but don't let her drink more than $2\frac{1}{2}$ bottles of milk or she'll throw up. Turn on music in her room, leave her in her crib with a dry diaper and bottle to try to sleep. She likes a stuffed animal too. Try for 30–45 minutes. You may have to start the tape again. If she won't sleep, that's fine. We just call it "rest time" on those days that naps won't happen.

1. To whom is this passage probably being written?

    a. a mother
    b. a father
    c. a babysitter
    d. a nurse
    e. The question cannot be answered from the information given.

2. You can assume the writer of the passage is:

    a. a mom
    b. a dad
    c. a teacher
    d. a parent
    e. a nurse

Refer to the following for questions 3 - 12:

In 1603, Queen Elizabeth I of England died. She had never married and had no heir, so the throne passed to a distant relative: James Stuart, the son of Elizabeth's cousin and one-time rival for the throne, Mary, Queen of Scots. James was crowned King James I of England. At the time, he was also

208

King James VI of Scotland, and the combination of roles would create a spirit of conflict that haunted the two nations for generations to come.

The conflict developed as a result of rising tensions among the people within the nations, as well as between them. Scholars in the 21st century are far too hasty in dismissing the role of religion in political disputes, but religion undoubtedly played a role in the problems that faced England and Scotland. By the time of James Stuart's succession to the English throne, the English people had firmly embraced the teachings of Protestant theology. Similarly, the Scottish Lowlands was decisively Protestant. In the Scottish Highlands, however, the clans retained their Catholic faith. James acknowledged the Church of England and still sanctioned the largely Protestant translation of the Bible that still bears his name.

James's son King Charles I proved himself to be less committed to the Protestant Church of England. Charles married the Catholic Princess Henrietta Maria of France, and there were suspicions among the English and the Lowland Scots that Charles was quietly a Catholic. Charles's own political troubles extended beyond religion in this case, and he was beheaded in 1649. Eventually, his son King Charles II would be crowned, and this Charles is believed to have converted secretly to the Catholic Church. Charles II died without a legitimate heir, and his brother James ascended to the throne as King James II.

James was recognized to be a practicing Catholic, and his commitment to Catholicism would prove to be his downfall. James's wife Mary Beatrice lost a number of children during their infancy, and when she became pregnant again in 1687 the public became concerned. If James had a son, that son would undoubtedly be raised a Catholic, and the English people would not stand for this. Mary gave birth to a son, but the story quickly circulated that the royal child had died and the child named James's heir was a foundling smuggled in. James, his wife, and his infant son were forced to flee; and James's Protestant daughter Mary was crowned the queen.

In spite of a strong resemblance to the king, the young James II was generally rejected among the English and the Lowland Scots, who referred to him as "the Pretender." But in the Highlands the Catholic princeling was welcomed. He inspired a group known as *Jacobites*, to reflect the Latin version of his name. His own son Charles, known affectionately as Bonnie Prince Charlie, would eventually raise an army and attempt to recapture what he believed to be his throne. The movement was soundly defeated at the Battle of Culloden in 1746, and England and Scotland have remained ostensibly Protestant ever since.

3. According to the author, the tension between England and Scotland stemmed from what issue?
   a. Politics
   b. Rivalry within the royal families
   c. Religion
   d. Boundary disputes
   e. Economics

4. According to the text, who was the successor of Queen Elizabeth I?
   a. King Charles I
   b. James Stuart
   c. King James II
   d. Queen Mary
   e. King Charles II

5. Which of the following best summarizes paragraph 4?

a. The English were determined to convince the son of King James to bring Catholicism to England.
b. The son of King James died tragically as an infant, leaving no heir to the throne.
c. James and his wife had only one surviving child, a daughter named Mary.
d. The English feared that the son of King James would be raised Catholic, causing them to fabricate a story of his death and create a rumor of an illegitimate heir to the throne.
e. Mary became the queen because she was a Protestant, unlike her parents and siblings.

6. Which of the following best compares the religious beliefs of the Scottish Highlands and Lowlands?

a. Scotland was devoutly Protestant in both the Highlands and Lowlands.
b. The Highlands were devoutly Protestant, while the Lowlands embraced Catholicism.
c. The Highlands were devoutly Catholic, and the Lowlands were accepting of either religion.
d. Scotland embraced Catholicism in both the Highlands and the Lowlands.
e. The Highlands were accepting of Catholicism, while the Lowlands were devoutly Protestant.

7. Which of the following choices best describes the relationship between King James I of England and King James VI of Scotland?

a. They were cousins.
b. They were brothers.
c. King James VI was the successor of King James I.
d. King James I was the father of King James VI.
e. They were the same person.

8. Which of the following is a synonym for the term "foundling" as used in paragraph 4?

a. Orphan
b. Distant relative
c. Son
d. Foreigner
e. Impersonator

9. What can we infer from the text?

a. Queen Elizabeth I died at a young age.
b. King Charles I was not a devout Protestant.
c. King James II was committed to his family.
d. King James II was crowned after his brother, King Charles II, died.
e. James Stuart supported the Protestant faith in England.

10. According to the text, which statement best supports the author's claim that the downfall of King James II was due to his belief in Catholicism?

a. He was beheaded for forming the group known as the "Jacobites."
b. The fear of a Catholic king caused the English to create rumors of an illegitimate son, forcing James to flee England.
c. He was killed in the Battle of Culloden in 1746.
d. His wife lost a number of infants, causing a strain in their relationship.
e. He was the first in his family to embrace Catholicism, so he was forced to flee England.

11. Which of the following best describes the term "Jacobites"?

a. A group of Catholics inspired by the young King James II
b. A group of Protestants inspired by the young King James II
c. A group of Protestants inspired by the young Bonnie Prince Charlie
d. A group of Catholics inspired by the young King Charles II
e. A group of Protestants inspired by the daughter of King James II

12. Choose the option that best describes the central idea of the passage.

   a.   King James II tried to fool the English with an illegitimate son as heir to the throne.

   b.   The troubles between England and Scotland were largely due to a clash in religious beliefs.

   c.   Queen Elizabeth I was the head of a troubled royal family.

   d.   James's wife, Mary Beatrice, suffered the loss of many infants.

   e.   James II's daughter, Mary, facilitated a resurgence of the Protestant religion in England.

Refer to the following for question 13:

> The US Department of State is a part of the executive branch of the federal government. Commonly referred to as the State Department, it is headed by the Secretary of State who is appointed by the president. The State Department's chief responsibility is United States foreign policy with some of the duties of the department being to confer with foreign government leaders, maintain a good relationship with America's allies, negotiate treaties, and provide aid to countries in need of help after a disaster, war, or other catastrophic occurrence. Such help may be in the form of economic aid or food.

13. According to the passage, what is the main role of the State Department?

   a.   Economic aid

   b.   Food

   c.   Disaster help

   d.   Foreign policy

   e.   Treaty negotiation

Refer to the following for questions 14 - 15:

> The concept of gravity intrigued great thinkers even in the earliest of times. Although Aristotle did not accurately determine why objects fall down toward the
> 5 earth, he did give those researchers who came after him an excellent starting point to move from.
>
> Galileo was especially influenced by the idea of gravity and its relevance to the world.
> 10 He was able to show not only that the earth is subject to the pull of gravity, but also that other planets are as well. Galileo confirmed that Earth is not a solitary celestial entity, as there are other large bodies in the solar
> 15 system that also experienced the same type of gravitational forces. Although parts of his findings were eventually disproven, Galileo's work nevertheless advanced the scientific world's understanding of gravity.
>
> 20 Taking the ideas of Aristotle and Galileo into account, Isaac Newton continued to study the forces, properties, and principles that rule Earth. His First and Second Laws of Motion were the result of many years of
> 25 study.

14. Based on the information given, what is a celestial entity?

   a.   A body in space

   b.   A star grouping

   c.   A cosmic alien

   d.   A solar flare

   e.   A star unit

15. Based on the information in the passage, which statement is true?

    a.   Galileo's work was proven to be entirely false by later scientists and researchers.

    b.   Aristotle and Galileo may have known each other.

    c.   The First and Second Laws of Motion were influenced by Galileo's studies.

    d.   Galileo's ideas are not relevant in the modern world.

    e.   The earth is the only large body that experiences gravitational pulls.

Refer to the following for question 16:

       Writing an online journal is a difficult way to make money. Money is certainly not the goal of every blogger, but a good blog with a large audience can provide an extra income to those who work at it.

       If a blogger is able to prove that he or she consistently has a large number of readers who check the blog every few days, the blogger may be able to attract advertisers. These advertisers can be a valuable source of income for the blogger since the online ads will be seen by many people each day.

16. According to the passage, which of the following statements is true?

    a.   All blogs make money.

    b.   Popular blogs can make money for the blogger.

    c.   All bloggers want to earn an income by blogging.

    d.   Online advertisements are not income producers.

    e.   Companies can be easily convinced to advertise on a blog.

Refer to the following for questions 17 - 20:

       Swiss psychologist Carl Jung coined the terms "extrovert" and "introvert" to describe characteristics he identified and classified in people's personalities.

5   Imagine a restaurant buffet table full of a variety of breakfast food selections. One woman walks over to the table and immediately talks with a chef creating omelets to order. After she orders her omelet,
10 the woman turns and talks with another stranger on her left and then to one on her right. She loudly thanks the chef after he slides the omelet onto her plate. Another woman slips into the buffet line and observes
15 those ahead of her as they lift the lids from the food warmers. She moves through the line silently and then takes her seat with her group.

       Jung described an extrovert, such as the
20 woman who talked to people she did not

know, as one whose actions are external and apparent. He said that in general, extroverts tend to make friends and establish connections with other people with relative
25 ease. Extroverts are able to assess social situations and make an easy adjustment to being with groups of people. They typically demonstrate an obvious interest in their surroundings and often act without much
30 forethought.

       Introverts tend to be more thoughtful than extroverts, and many of their decisions are processed internal without outwardly apparent signs. Introverts will think of what
35 to do in certain situations before they act. Most introverts are more comfortable keeping to themselves than socializing with other people.

17. Which profession is most likely to be chosen by an introvert?

    a. A stand-up comedian
    b. An event organizer
    c. A Master of Ceremonies
    d. A painter
    e. A street musician

18. According to the passage, which is a true statement?

    a. Introverts rarely have friends.
    b. Extroverts are bored without people around.
    c. Introverts and extroverts do not get along.
    d. Extroverts are insensitive people.
    e. Introverts like solitary tasks.

19. What do the words "extrovert" and "introvert" describe?

    a. Degrees of personal happiness
    b. Personality characteristics
    c. Demographic classifications
    d. Cultural differences
    e. Perceived intelligence

20. According to the passage, what is true about an extrovert's actions?

    a. They are apparent.
    b. They are completely subconscious.
    c. They are secretive.
    d. They are admired by everyone around them.
    e. They are kind and caring.

Refer to the following for questions 21 - 30:

"So that Nobody Has to Go to School if They Don't Want to"

An Excerpt by Roger Sipher

A decline in standardized test scores is but the most recent indicator that American education is in trouble. One reason for the crisis is that present mandatory-attendance laws force many to attend school that have no wish to be there. Such children have little desire to learn and are so antagonistic to school that neither they nor more highly motivated students receive the quality education that is the birthright of every American. The solution to this problem is simple: Abolish compulsory-attendance laws and allow only those who are committed to getting an education to attend.

Most parents want a high school education for their children. Unfortunately, compulsory attendance hampers the ability of public school officials to enforce legitimate educational and disciplinary policies and thereby make the education a good one. Private schools have no such problem. They can fail or dismiss students, knowing such students can attend public school. Without compulsory attendance, public schools would be freer to oust students whose academic or personal behavior undermines the educational mission of the institution.

Abolition of archaic attendance laws would produce enormous dividends:

- First, it would alert everyone that school is a serious place where one goes to learn. Schools are neither day-care centers nor indoor street corners. Young people who resist learning should stay away; indeed, an end to compulsory schooling would require them to stay away.

- Second, students opposed to learning would not be able to pollute the educational atmosphere for those who want to learn. Teachers could stop policing recalcitrant students and start educating.
- Third, grades would show what they are supposed to: how well a student is learning. Parents could again read report cards and know if their children were making progress.
- Fourth, public esteem for schools would increase. People would stop regarding them as way stations for adolescents and start thinking of them as institutions for educating America's youth.
- Fifth, elementary schools would change because students would find out early they had better learn something or risk flunking out later. Elementary teachers would no longer have to pass their failures on to junior high and high school.
- Sixth, the cost of enforcing compulsory education would be eliminated. Despite enforcement efforts, nearly 15 percent of the school-age children in our largest cities are almost permanently absent from school.

Communities could use these savings to support institutions to deal with young people not in school. If, in the long run, these institutions prove more costly, at least we would not confuse their mission with that of schools. Schools should be for education. At present, they are only tangentially so. They have attempted to serve an all-encompassing social function, trying to be all things to all people. In the process they have failed miserably at what they were originally formed to accomplish.

21. Which of the following statements supports the conclusion that abolishing mandatory attendance laws would prove economical for school districts?
   a. It would eliminate the misconception that schools are day-care centers or indoor street corners.
   b. Public esteem for schools would increase.
   c. The cost of enforcing compulsory education would be eliminated.
   d. Report cards would reflect how well a student is learning.
   e. Students who are motivated to learn would receive a more fulfilling education.

22. Which of the following statements would the author most likely agree with?
   a. The longer students attend school, the more productive the community will be.
   b. Schools should be responsible for providing students with extracurricular opportunities.
   c. Truancy officers should be doubled in districts with low attendance rates.
   d. Report cards should reflect the effort of a student, rather than the ability of that student.
   e. Students should not be forced or entitled to an education.

23. According to the author, abolishing attendance laws would allow school districts the freedom to _____.
   a. provide counseling to students with poor attendance
   b. fail or dismiss students who have attendance or discipline issues, which disrupt the education of others
   c. provide transportation to students unwilling to attend school
   d. move students from elementary to middle school without proof that learning has occurred
   e. provide scholarships for the highest performing students

24. Which of the following is an assumption made by the author?
   a. Private schools can choose to fail or dismiss students.
   b. Nearly 15 percent of the school-age children in our largest cities are almost permanently absent from school.
   c. If we can improve student attendance, we can improve standardized test scores.
   d. Most parents want a high school education for their children.
   e. Schools were originally formed to serve all adolescents.

25. Choose the option that best describes the central idea of the passage.

    a. Standardized test scores would increase if teachers could fail or dismiss students.

    b. Schools are intended to educate adolescents, not replace day-care centers or give adolescents a place to socialize.

    c. Report cards should communicate with parents how well a student is learning.

    d. Private schools have an easier time with absenteeism than public schools.

    e. Abolishing mandatory attendance laws would create better school environments for the students with a genuine desire to learn.

26. Which of the following best summarizes the first paragraph?

    a. American education is in trouble.

    b. Students with little desire to learn are often absent.

    c. Abolishing the mandatory attendance laws would improve the quality of education in schools.

    d. Standardized test scores are the best indicator of student success.

    e. Neither highly motivated students or highly unmotivated students are properly educated.

27. Which of the following statements LEAST supports the main idea of the passage?

    a. School is a serious place where one goes to learn.

    b. Students opposed to learning would not be able to pollute the educational atmosphere for those who want to learn.

    c. Grades would show what they are supposed to: how well a student is learning.

    d. Public esteem for schools would increase.

    e. Current truancy laws do not promote the original purpose of public education.

28. According to the text, what effect do mandatory attendance laws have on the esteem of schools?

    a. These laws prove that schools have the right to force education on all minors.

    b. These laws undermine the integrity of schools.

    c. These laws allow students to choose their own path of education.

    d. These laws provide teachers with freedom to grade and dismiss as they see fit.

    e. These laws allow promote every student's opportunity for quality education.

29. What can we infer from the text?

    a. The author believes that school districts should reexamine their procedures for standardized testing.

    b. The author believes that all students deserve an equal amount of attention from the teacher.

    c. The author believes that stricter attendance laws would improve classroom dynamics.

    d. The author believes that education is a privilege, not a right.

    e. The author believes that current truancy laws are effective and should not change.

30. Which of the following is a synonym of the word, "recalcitrant," as used in Paragraph 3?

    a. Absent

    b. Organized

    c. Disobedient

    d. Responsible

    e. Unintelligent

Refer to the following for questions 31 - 33:

During difficult economic times, a company may apply to the court for Chapter 11 bankruptcy. This legal filing, a part of the United States bankruptcy law, protects the firm from all creditors while it attempts to reorganize its business and then repay its debts.

By filing Chapter 11, a company will not be closed down due to the outstanding funds it owes to a creditor. While the firm is under the protection of Chapter 11, it will usually make sweeping changes throughout the company. Employees may be laid off or fired, management may be consolidated, buildings may be sold off, and employee benefits may be affected. All changes within the company are designed to return it to profitability, repay creditors, and continue to remain viable.

31. What is the main idea of the passage?
a. An overview of Chapter 11
b. Why a company will file for Chapter 11
c. Legal rules associated with filing Chapter 11
d. What happens after a Chapter 11 filing
e. Creditors' rights with Chapter 11

32. When a company is in Chapter 11, executives will make changes mainly:
a. To work toward solvency
b. To save money
c. To ensure their salaries remain intact
d. To keep creditors at bay
e. To create a smaller company

33. Which statement about the passage is NOT true?
a. Creditors do not get paid during Chapter 11 proceedings.
b. Chapter 11 is a legal filing.
c. After a business reorganizes, most debts will be repaid.
d. Management is often changed during reorganization.
e. Employee benefits are usually unaffected during Chapter 11.

Refer to the following for questions 34 - 35:

To "take the Fifth" means to refuse to testify against oneself in court. A person cannot be forced to testify in court if that testimony will be self-incriminating. The Fifth Amendment of the Constitution states this basic principle of United States law.

The Miranda decision, a 1966 Supreme Court ruling, states that under the Fifth Amendment, a suspect in police custody has the right to remain silent and to consult an attorney and that anything the person says can be used against him or her in court. This information is recited to suspects before police officers ask them any questions.

Aside from protecting a person in custody and in a court of law, prohibiting self-incrimination ensures that the prosecution is responsible for the burden of proof.

216

34. According to the passage, which of the following is true?

a. People cannot be forced to testify in court.
b. Suspects in police custody must answer police questions.
c. The Miranda decision and "take the fifth" are the same thing.
d. The Fifth Amendment was added in 1966.
e. The Miranda decision protects suspects in police custody.

35. What is the main purpose of this passage?

a. To explain self-incrimination
b. To discuss our legal system
c. To explain how the Miranda decision came from the Fifth Amendment
d. To provide details of the 1966 Supreme Court case
e. To discuss suspects' rights

Refer to the following for question 36:

A topographic map is designed to showcase the surface features of a specific land area. These types of maps feature the area's geography and highlight political boundaries, roads, highways, railroads, bodies of water, and some buildings. The maps show the relative positions and elevations of the natural and manmade features of the area.

36. Which of the following would be the best introductory sentence for this passage?

a. Many maps include typographic details.
b. Use a topographic map if you plan to hike in a new area.
c. Comparing two areas is easy with a topographic map.
d. Topographic maps are usually the most inclusive of all map types.
e. Most topographic maps are made using computers.

Refer to the following for question 37:

The classic opera *Madame Butterfly* was written by Giacomo Puccini. In the opus, an American naval officer stationed in Japan falls in love with Butterfly, a Japanese woman. He returns to America but promises to come back to marry her. When the soldier does return to Japan three years later, he is accompanied by his American wife. Shocked and humiliated, Butterfly stabs herself. She dies in the soldier's arms as he begs her to forgive him.

37. This passage describes characters' feelings in *Madame Butterfly* as all of the following EXCEPT:

a. Romantic
b. Poignant
c. Crushing
d. Musical
e. Tragic

Refer to the following for questions 38 - 39:

De facto segregation, which literally means segregation "by fact," occurs when a specific socioeconomic group resides in an area with other families of that same demographic. Students living in those areas will typically end up going to neighborhood schools comprised of children of one minority group or one income level. Because it was not considered direct discrimination, de facto segregation was not considered unconstitutional.

De facto segregation was a particularly serious problem in the racially-charged 1960s. Many elementary schools were completely racially segregated, especially in the South, with

African Americans attending all-black schools, while white students attended all-white schools. Most people agreed that these schools had vast differences in buildings, materials, and staff, with students from higher-income neighborhoods enjoying an education in what can be described as a higher quality setting than their less-affluent peers at other schools. Although not often discussed, de facto segregation can still be found in our country.

38. According to the passage, which of the following is an example of de facto segregation?

- a. Large schools
- b. Separate schools
- c. Diverse schools
- d. Integrated schools
- e. Heterogeneous schools

39. According to the passage, which of the following is true?

- a. De facto segregation happens today.
- b. De facto segregation was never a serious problem.
- c. De facto segregation was a problem only for high income students.
- d. De facto segregation is always characterized by race.
- e. De facto segregation creates equality.

Refer to the following for question 40:

Corrosion is the deterioration of a metal. This decay can be easily seen on pots, pans, jewelry, and silverware. Iron corrodes when it comes into contact with water and oxygen, with the decomposition present as rust. Copper corrodes when it is exposed to the elements, and the decay is present as a green sheen. Silver tarnishes, or corrodes after a period of time, with its deterioration apparent in a dull black covering of the silver surface.

40. Which of the following is NOT stated as a reason for corrosion?

- a. Exposure to elements
- b. Passage of time
- c. Deterioration from heat
- d. Contact with water
- e. Contact with air

Refer to the following for question 41:

A market economy, also called a "free economy," is one in which individuals and corporations control the production, marketing, and distribution of goods and services within a society. There is a minimum of government interference in a market economy. Competition between markets keeps prices at a particular level. When prices become too high, consumers will not purchase goods, which forces sellers to adjust prices to a level where consumers will buy.

Market economies have minimal government involvement; this type of economic system still requires some federal regulation. A complete market economy would mean there would be no government regulation or taxation, two components necessary to ensure that the economy keeps running.

41. Which is a true statement about a market economy?

a. Sellers determine price.
b. Government determines price.
c. Corporations determine price.
d. Individuals determine price.
e. Competition determines price.

Refer to the following for questions 42 - 43:

In literature, the problem, usually referred to as the conflict, should be introduced in the early paragraphs of a story and should directly involve the main character. Throughout the story, the main character should seek to determine how the conflict will be resolved. The conflict resolution should not be obvious to the reader; instead, the reader should wonder how things are going to work out and should be connected enough with the main character so that the character's actions matter.

By the end of the story, the main character should have somehow grown or changed, even just a little, from the experience. Stories in which the main character experiences the same lesson over and over again are not as effective as stories in which the character experiences real change. Most readers enjoy thinking about the way a conflict has been resolved and come to their own conclusions after mulling it over for a period of time. When the resolution is simply stated at the end of a story, the reader often ends up with little or nothing to think about.

42. What is the best way to describe conflict?

a. It is a story situation.
b. It is a story problem.
c. It is a resolution.
d. It is the character's growth process.
e. It is an experience.

43. According to the passage, what is one important element of a good story?

a. A story in which the lesson learned is narrated by the main character
b. A story with a problem embedded in the middle
c. A story with a few different conflicts
d. A story with a predictable resolution
e. A story in which the main character matters to the reader

Refer to the following for questions 44 - 48:

Journalists often use a recording device to capture the audio transcript of an interview with a subject. The recording device is thought of as a reliable and efficient way to ensure that all important parts of the interview have been archived, which is something that may be complicated for a journalist to do by hand. Besides being difficult to execute quickly, legibly, and efficiently, taking notes by hand can distract the journalist from the interview subject's body language, verbal cues, or other subtle information that can go unnoticed when the journalist is not fully concentrating on the person talking. These missed cues, for example, noticing that the tough-guy interview subject closed his eyes and trembled slightly when he talked about his recently departed mother, could add an interesting perspective to the article.

Relying on a recording device is not without troubles; however, most journalists can quickly relate stories of disappointments they or co-workers have endured due to problems with equipment. For instance, a journalist may not notice low batteries until it is too late. As a result, a portion of an interview can be lost without any way to reclaim it. The machine's volume can be accidentally left too low to hear the subject on later playback, the recorder may be accidentally switched off during the interview, and any number of other unplanned and unexpected electronic malfunctions can occur to sabotage the recording. While recording device problems may not occur often, even a rate of once a year can be extremely problematic for a writer. Some glitches may be unrealized until hours later when the journalist is prepared to work with the recording.

Most experienced journalists do not rely solely on technology when they are interviewing a subject for an article. Instead, as the recording device creates an audio record of the interview, journalists will simultaneously record their own notes by hand. This dual-note method means that most of the time, a wise journalist has two good resources to use as he or she writes the article draft.

44. According to the passage, which of the following is NOT a reason a recording device can be superior to taking notes by hand?
   a. Note taking can be slow.
   b. Note taking is unreliable.
   c. Note taking forces the writer to look away from the subject.
   d. Note taking can cause body language to go unnoticed.
   e. Note taking can be difficult to read later.

45. Which of the following is NOT an example of body language?
   a. A quiet answer
   b. Shocked look
   c. Wringing hands
   d. Blinking eyes
   e. A glance to the side

46. What is the best way journalists can ensure that all interview notes will be available to them when they need them?
   a. Taking notes by hand and also recording them
   b. Bringing recorder batteries regularly
   c. Bringing an extra tape for the recorder
   d. Making sure the volume is set on high
   e. Taping the recorder switch to the *On* position

47. Which title is the best choice for this passage?
   a. The Art of Writing Notes
   b. Conducting an Interview
   c. Tape Recording an Interview
   d. Body Language is Important
   e. Problems with Interviews

48. According to the passage, which of the following are reasons an audio recording device can be superior to taking notes by hand during an interview? (Select all that apply.)
   a. A recording device may be low on batteries without the journalist noticing.
   b. Efficient, legible note-taking is a difficult skill to master.
   c. The journalist has to look away from the interview subject to write notes.
   d. Recording devices capture only what is said, ignoring non-verbal cues.
   e. Taking notes by hand does not require any advanced technology.

Refer to the following for questions 49 - 50:

Florence is not the capital of Italy, but from the fourteenth to the sixteenth centuries, it was the heart of the Italian Renaissance. During those years, the city burgeoned with creativity, and great artists and writers whose works came to be considered classics were active in Florence. Michelangelo, Botticelli, Raphael, da Vinci, and the Medici family called the city their home and were among those responsible for its cultural dominance at the time.

Today, tourists still flock to Florence, which is located in the center of Italy on the Arno River, to view the cathedrals, buildings, and other works of architecture that have been preserved largely in excellent condition. Artists of all kinds continue to be attracted to Florence as an inspirational place to practice their craft.

49. What is NOT true about Florence?
   a. It has a rich cultural history.
   b. It is an artistic center.
   c. It is centrally located.
   d. It is the capital of Italy.
   e. It is still relevant.

50. As it is used in the passage, what does *burgeoned* most nearly mean?
   a. Dwindled
   b. Stagnated
   c. Originated
   d. Deteriorated
   e. Exploded

Refer to the following for question 51:

Scaffolding is a tactical support method used by teachers to assist students so that they are able to successfully accomplish a particular task they would not be able to complete independently. As they scaffold, teachers assess the type and amount of assistance individual students will need to correctly perform a task or respond to a question. The goal is not simply for the student to accomplish the single task, but to internalize the skills needed to complete comparable tasks in the future. Scaffolding may entail cues, comments, or other directives designed to guide the student to a particular response.

51. Which of the following sentences would be a relevant detail to add as the second sentence to the paragraph above?
   a. Scaffolding is individual instruction for the weakest students.
   b. Students will want to use scaffolding methods in all their learning.
   c. Teachers are able to assess students' needs individually when scaffolding.
   d. Students appreciate the help.
   e. Scaffolding is done quietly and is unnoticed by many students.

Refer to the following for question 52:

Conflicts between students occur every day in most schools across the country. Because the conflicts can vary in severity, some do not necessarily require someone in authority to intercede. However, some conflicts can be quite violent and conflict mediation is necessary to arbitrate the problem.

52. Which statement is most likely to appear next in the text?

a. Some students get hurt in school fights.
b. Conflict mediation can stop all school disputes.
c. Teachers should not have to deal with these problems.
d. Students get themselves into all kinds of scuffles with their peers.
e. Conflict mediation is an effective method of solving school disputes.

Refer to the following for questions 53 - 54:

Today, most everyone with a cell phone has the capability to send and receive text messages. High school students may be the biggest users of this technology. Some parents have had to impose limits on their teen, which oftentimes easily exceeds the three to five hundred text messages allotted to many family plans each month. A flat fee will usually cover this set number of messages, but each additional message may cost twenty or twenty-five cents, an amount that can add up to a staggering figure in a short period of time if a user is texting with wild abandon.

These days, most high school teachers do not permit students to bring cell phones into the classroom. Students may spend more time texting friends than paying attention to what is happening in class. Some savvy students have figured out ways to text-message peers inconspicuously and share test answers. Most students would probably agree that there is no reason to have their cell phones with them during the school day; however, most are reluctant to leave their phones in their lockers.

Typing a message into a phone was an unheard-of communication method even two decades ago. Today, many young users may not remember life without it.

53. To whom is this passage probably being written?

a. Those who are in favor of cell phone use in schools
b. Those who are against cell phone use in schools
c. Those that are in favor of text messaging in school
d. Those that are against text messaging in school
e. The passage is not written to any of these audiences

54. What is the best title for this passage?

a. Texting Problems
b. Cell Phones Can Spell Trouble
c. Texting and Students
d. Teacher Beware
e. Technology Today

Refer to the following for questions 55 - 56:

Many female marathon runners today may not realize that the Boston Marathon was not always open to women participants. It was not until 1972 that women were welcome to register and officially participate in the race. Before that, some women would attempt to take part in the race in ways that would not divulge their gender. One method was registering with just their first initial and last name. In almost all instances, this type of deception was discovered and the runner was disqualified.

55. Based on what is discussed in the passage, which statement is most likely to be true?

a. Those that used deception to run in the Boston Marathon were arrested.
b. There are women alive today who ran as men in the Boston Marathon.
c. No women ran in the Boston Marathon prior to 1972.
d. The Boston Marathon is still biased toward men.
e. Women runners probably never wanted to race in the Boston Marathon.

56. According to the passage, what best describes the actions most women took so that they could run in the Boston Marathon prior to 1972?

a. Lie about their gender
b. Bribe race officials
c. Run with a male
d. Hide from officials
e. Threaten officials with lawsuits if they were not granted entry into the race

Writing

Refer to the following for questions 1 - 4:

In the following section, there are underlined parts to each sentence. One of the underlined parts is incorrectly written. Choose the letter that corresponds with the incorrect underlined part of the sentence. If the entire sentence is correct as written, choose E for No error.

1. We gawked at him as he drug the picnic table closer to the grill area.

a. gawked at
b. drug
c. closer to
d. grill area
e. No error

2. We must ensure that Mike proceeds Ann when the students line up for the graduation ceremony.

a. ensure that
b. proceeds
c. line up
d. graduation ceremony
e. No error

3. Marcy believed her parents had ought to have told her she was still grounded for the weekend.

a. believed
b. had ought
c. have told her
d. grounded
e. No error

4. Brianna says less children enrolled in our camp program this summer than last summer.

a. Brianna says
b. less children
c. enrolled
d. than
e. No error

Refer to the following for questions 5 - 23:

In the following section, there are underlined parts to each sentence. One of the underlined parts is incorrectly written. Choose the letter that corresponds with the incorrect underlined part of the sentence. If the entire sentence is correct, choose NO ERROR.

5. If you <u>put</u> your backpack by the door, you will <u>insure</u> you <u>won't forget</u> to <u>take it</u> home.

    a.   put
    b.   insure
    c.   won't forget
    d.   take it
    e.   No error

6. Let's write the <u>entire sign</u> in <u>capitol</u> letters so that it <u>can be seen</u> by people <u>who</u> are driving by.

    a.   entire sign
    b.   capitol
    c.   can be seen
    d.   who
    e.   No error

7. The <u>student's</u> <u>attitude in</u> math class probably ended up having a <u>negative</u> <u>affect</u> on his grade.

    a.   student's
    b.   attitude in
    c.   negative
    d.   affect
    e.   No error

8. All of the <u>students</u> <u>except</u> Marcus for the <u>free spirited</u> boy <u>that he is</u>.

    a.   students
    b.   except
    c.   free spirited
    d.   that he is
    e.   No error

9. <u>One flu patient</u> had an <u>averse</u> reaction to the drug and <u>had to</u> be <u>hospitalized</u> for a week.

    a.   One flu patient
    b.   averse
    c.   had to
    d.   hospitalized
    e.   No error

10. Grandfather said that when <u>he died</u> he wanted <u>his assets</u> <u>divided</u> <u>among</u> his two sons.

    a.   he died
    b.   his assets
    c.   divided
    d.   among
    e.   No error

11. "I hope Mrs. Johnson lets us swim in her pool." Pam said.

   a. "I
   b. lets
   c. swim
   d. pool." Pam
   e. No error

12. No one was able to provide a credible explanation for why the vase had simply fallen off the shelf.

   a. No one
   b. was able
   c. credible
   d. simply fallen
   e. No error

13. The book's table of contents didn't provide much information about the subjects covered in each chapter.

   a. book's
   b. table of contents
   c. much information
   d. each chapter
   e. No error

14. With Wilson injured and Anderson sick, it is highly unlikely that any school records will be broken in todays track meet.

   a. With Wilson injured and Anderson sick
   b. highly unlikely
   c. school records
   d. todays track meet
   e. No error

15. My Mother still likes to talk about the hard time she had with my twin brother and me when we were in junior high school.

   a. My Mother
   b. the hard time
   c. and me
   d. junior high school
   e. No error

16. This class of biology students is superior than the one she taught last semester.

   a. This class of
   b. biology students is
   c. superior than the one she
   d. taught last semester
   e. No error

17. Since the baby was born with a congenital heart defect, she immediately had to have surgery.

   a. Since
   b. was born
   c. congenital
   d. had to have
   e. No error

18. His uncle, who is a <u>doctor will</u> be joining <u>us</u> on the <u>camping trip</u>.

    a.   His uncle
    b.   doctor will
    c.   us
    d.   camping trip
    e.   No error

19. The people, <u>who sat in the last row</u>, paid <u>half price</u> for <u>their seats</u>.

    a.   The
    b.   who sat in the last row
    c.   half price
    d.   their seats
    e.   No error

20. The dog <u>ran away</u> <u>just as</u> he had to go to <u>work this</u> was no <u>laughing matter</u>.

    a.   ran away
    b.   just as
    c.   work this
    d.   laughing matter
    e.   No error

21. <u>I am</u> <u>going to go</u> to the museum this afternoon even if <u>their not</u> <u>interested in</u> accompanying me.

    a.   I am
    b.   going to go
    c.   their not
    d.   interested in
    e.   No error

22. <u>Underneath</u> his <u>gruff exterior</u> was a man <u>that was loving</u> and <u>sensitive and</u> who had just nursed three sick kittens back to health.

    a.   Underneath
    b.   gruff exterior
    c.   that was loving
    d.   sensitive and
    e.   No error

23. The <u>Frankel's</u> house <u>had been</u> on the market for at least seven months <u>so we were</u> surprised <u>when it was finally</u> sold.

    a.   Frankel's
    b.   had been
    c.   so we were
    d.   when it was finally
    e.   No error

Refer to the following for questions 24 - 40:

Select the best version of the underlined part of the sentence. If you think the original sentence is best, choose the first answer.

24. Jake **borrowed his parents** car without permission so they had no way to get to work.

   a. borrowed his parents car
   b. borrowed his parent's car
   c. borrowed the parents car
   d. borrowed his Parents car
   e. borrowed his parents' car

25. **Irregardless of the weather,** we will still hold the picnic at the park.

   a. Irregardless of the weather,
   b. Irregardless because of the weather,
   c. Irregardless of weather
   d. Regardless of the weather,
   e. Regarding the weather

26. Now that both of my brothers are married, I have **two sister's-in-law.**

   a. two sister's-in-law.
   b. two sisters'-in-law.
   c. two sisters-in-laws.
   d. two sister-in-laws.
   e. two sisters-in-law.

27. When questioned, most students **said the Math test** was too difficult.

   a. said the Math test
   b. say the Math test
   c. said the math test
   d. say the math test
   e. said that the Math test

28. **An only child Jane** enjoyed the company of her parents.

   a. An only child Jane
   b. An only child Jane,
   c. An "only" child, Jane
   d. An only child, Jane
   e. An "only" child Jane

29. Many people were not able to figure out **where the meeting was at.**

   a. where the meeting was at
   b. where the meeting was
   c. where, the meeting was at
   d. where at the meeting was
   e. at where was the meeting

227

30. Each student should bring their backpacks to the assembly.

   a. Each student should bring their backpacks
   b. Each student should bring backpacks
   c. Each student should bring they're backpacks
   d. Each student should bring his backpack
   e. Each student should bring his or her backpack

31. If you are not able to take part in class today, please set down at the side table.

   a. please set down at the side table.
   b. please set at the side table
   c. please sit at the side table
   d. please, set down at the side table
   e. please, sit at the side table.

32. Most of the tickets were sold the first day they were available.

   a. the first day they were available.
   b. the first day the tickets were available.
   c. the first day they are available.
   d. the first day the tickets are available.
   e. the first day they were "available."

33. A new state high jump record was set by Oscar Smith.

   a. A new state high jump record was set by Oscar Smith.
   b. A new state high jump record is set by Oscar Smith.
   c. A new state high jump record was being set by Oscar Smith.
   d. Oscar Smith set a new state high jump record.
   e. Oscar Smith sets a new state high jump record.

34. Whispering so low that no one could hear her.

   a. Whispering so low that no one could hear her.
   b. Whispering so low no one could hear her.
   c. Whispering low so no one could hear her.
   d. She is whispering so low no one can hear her.
   e. She is whispering so low that no one is hearing her.

35. Terry grabs the phone and talked to the police officer.

   a. Terry grabs the phone and talked to the police officer.
   b. Terry grabbed the phone and talks to the police officer.
   c. Terry grabs the phone and is talking to the police officer.
   d. Terry grabbed the phone and is talking to the police officer.
   e. Terry grabs the phone and talks to the police officer.

36. She didn't realize it would take so much time to clean the house she was late for the party.

   a. take so much time to clean the house she was late
   b. take so much time to clean the house, she was late
   c. take so much time to clean the house; she was late
   d. take so much time to clean the house - she was late
   e. take so much time to clean the house and therefore she was late

37. **"This box can't be used." "The gift is too big,"** Sharon said.

   a. "This box can't be used." "The gift is too big,"
   b. "This box can't be used. "The gift is too big,"
   c. "This box can't be used." The gift is too big,"
   d. "This box can't be used "The gift is too big,"
   e. "This box can't be used. The gift is too big,"

38. We were surprised that **most people's views involved** spending money from the treasury.

   a. most people's views involved
   b. most peoples views involved
   c. most peoples' views involved
   d. most peoples' view's involved
   e. most people's views' involved

39. No one in the room seemed **to notice Jack and I walk in late.**

   a. to notice Jack and I walk in late.
   b. to notice I and Jack I walk in late.
   c. to notice me and Jack walk in late.
   d. to notice Jack and me walk in late.
   e. to notice Jack and myself walk in late.

40. **Each of the diamonds are worth over** ten thousand dollars.

   a. Each of the diamonds are worth over
   b. Each of the diamonds is worth over
   c. Each of the diamonds are valued at over
   d. Each of the diamonds goes for over
   e. All of the diamonds is worth over.

Refer to the following for question 41:

PASSAGE A

Thank you for contacting me to express your concerns over the proposed elimination of the EPA's Clean Power Plan, which seeks to reduce carbon pollution by power plants and address the risks of climate change. I welcome feedback from my constituents and I appreciate your interest in this issue. I am pleased to tell you that I am a staunch advocate for addressing climate change and that I would oppose any measure that sought to eliminate the Environmental Protection Agency's Clean Power Plan.

President Barack Obama proposed the Clean Power Plan in June 2014 as a part of his Climate Change Action Plan. The Clean Power Plan sets standards for carbon pollution from power plants and could result in a 30 percent reduction in carbon pollution from the power sector by 2030. Climate change has the potential to cause a tremendous amount of potentially catastrophic consequences for people around the world. Scientists agree that human action, such as carbon pollution by power plants, is the cause for a majority of the current warming. While the situation is an increasing cause for concern, most scientists also agree that it is not too late to take action to stop this serious threat to our planet. Climate change is a cause for national concern, requiring national solutions, and as your Congressman, I will support legislation that seeks to stop the causes and to moderate the effects of climate change.

I am honored to be your representative in Congress and I hope that my office can be a useful resource for you now and in the future. For more information, please visit my office online at www.HankJohnson.house.gov and do not hesitate to contact me if you have any future questions or concerns.

Sincerely,

Henry C. "Hank" Johnson, Jr.
Member of Congress

PASSAGE B

Thank you for contacting me regarding the Environmental Protection Agency's (EPA) Clean Power regulations. I appreciate hearing from you and am grateful for the opportunity to respond.

The Clean Power regulations were introduced by the EPA on August 3, 2015. Under these regulations, existing power plants will be required to reduce their emissions 32 percent by 2030 and must submit a plan outlining their strategy for doing so by 2016. States also have the option to engage in a regional "cap and trade" system where emission credits can be traded in order to ease states' transition to new emission standards.

The authority to impose federal carbon mandates lies with Congress, not the EPA. These regulations will ultimately result in what could be called an "energy tax" that will be felt in the form of higher electricity bills for consumers. I share your concerns with overreaching rules and regulations promulgated by unelected officials at the EPA and have been actively fighting them in the Senate. Coal-fired power plants provide 36 percent of Georgia's electricity and support nearly 8,800 Georgia jobs. When these Clean Power regulations were originally proposed in 2014, I wrote a letter to the EPA expressing my concern over the detrimental impact the rule would have on electricity providers, consumers and the US economy as a whole.

On May 13, 2015, I cosponsored S.1324, the *Affordable Reliable Electricity Now Act of 2015*. This bill would allow states to opt out of the Clean Power regulations. The implementation of these regulations would also be halted until states that have filed lawsuits against the EPA have completed their proceedings, and the federal government would be prohibited from withholding highway funding from states that fail to submit an implementation strategy. I will keep your thoughts and concerns in mind if the *Affordable Reliable Electricity Now Act* is brought to the Senate floor for consideration.

Thank you again for contacting me. Please visit my webpage at http://isakson.senate.gov/ for more information on the issues important to you and to sign up for my e-newsletter.

Sincerely,

Johnny Isakson

United States Senator

GRAPHIC

41. In an essay approximately 400-600 words long, write a well-developed argument evaluating the pros and cons of the Clean Power Plan. This must include: (1) a claim that shows knowledge and comprehension of this subject; (2) valid and logical reasoning that builds upon the arguments in both passages; (3) support for your claim using enough pertinent evidence from all three sources above; and (4) an anticipation of, and response to, at least one counterclaim. Write in your own words (except for quotations) for an adult, educated audience while consistently using precise, clear language in an appropriate tone and style. Make sure your final draft follows all the writing conventions for standard American English.

42. Wiretapping and spying policies of the National Security Agency have been a topic of interest lately, with much discussion taking place over the need for security as it relates to the right to individual privacy. Please write a multiple-paragraph persuasive essay (approximately 350–500 words) discussing whether you support or oppose government collection of private data for the purpose of national security.

Mathematics

Refer to the following for question 1:

Kyle bats third in the batting order for the Badgers baseball team. The table below shows the number of hits that Kyle had in each of 7 consecutive games played during one week in July.

Day	Monday	Tuesday	Wednesday	Thursday	Friday	Saturday	Sunday
Hits	1	2	3	1	1	4	2

1. What is the mean of the numbers in the distribution shown in the table?

    a. 1

    b. 2

    c. 3

    d. 4

    e. 7

Refer to the following for question 2:

An MP3 player is set to play songs at random from the fifteen songs it contains in memory. Any song can be played at any time, even if it is repeated. There are 5 songs by Band A, 3 songs by Band B, 2 by Band C, and 5 by Band D.

2. What is the probability that the next two songs will both be by Band B?

    a. $\frac{1}{25}$

    b. $\frac{1}{9}$

    c. $\frac{1}{5}$

    d. $\frac{1}{3}$

    e. $\frac{1}{2}$

3. Marielle says the best descriptor of the data set {67, 2, 67, 73, 85, 60, 68} is the range. Choose the option that best describes Marielle's error.

    a.   Marielle is incorrect because the range should never be used to describe a data set.

    b.   Marielle is incorrect because this data set has an outlier.

    c.   Marielle is incorrect because the mean is always the best choice for describing a data set.

    d.   Marielle is incorrect because the median is best for a data set this small.

    e.   Marielle is incorrect because the range for this data set is too small.

4. Forty students in a class take a test that is graded on a scale of 1 to 10. The histogram in the figure shows the grade distribution, with the x-axis representing the grades and the y-axis representing the number of students who obtain each grade. If the mean, median, and mode values are represented by n, p, and q, respectively, which of the following is true?

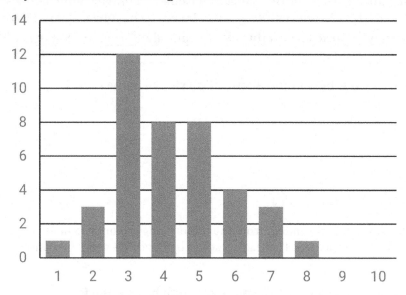

a. $n > p > q$
b. $n > q > p$
c. $q > p > n$
d. $p > q > n$
e. $q > n > p$

5. Which of the following choices could display data in a misleading way?

a. Starting the y-axis at zero, even when dealing with very large numbers
b. Listing categorical data in alphabetical order along the x-axis
c. Choosing very small intervals for the y-axis to exaggerate differences in data
d. Letting the number of data points determine the number of bins for a histogram
e. Including all data collected, even if it is not consistent with the outcome you were hoping for

6. Identify the median for the data set {53, 81, 85, 82, 91, 72}.

a. 81.5
b. 81
c. 77
d. 38
e. 83.5

7. Kylie describes the mode of the data set {67, 29, 57, 27, 38, 91} as zero. Which option best explains Kylie's interpretation of the data?

a. Kylie is correct because there is no value that occurs more than any other value so our mode is zero.
b. Kylie is incorrect because 27 and 29 can be averaged to find a mode of 28.
c. Kyle is correct because when we add all of our numbers and divide by 6 we get zero.
d. Kylie is incorrect because zero is not a value in the data set, therefore it cannot be the mode.
e. Kylie is incorrect because zero is never a valid mode for a data set.

8. Joe plans to flip two coins. Which of the following choices demonstrates using the counting principle to determine the probability of both coins landing on tails?

a. $\frac{1}{2}$

b. TT, TH, HT, HH

c. 2×2

d. $2 + 2$

e. $\frac{1}{2} \times \frac{1}{2}$

9. An ice-cream shop offers sundaes that include a choice of an ice cream flavor, a topping, and a sauce (either hot fudge or caramel). The different ice cream flavors are chocolate, vanilla, and strawberry. The choices of toppings are sprinkles and cherries. Which of the following tree diagrams correctly shows the total number of ice-cream sundaes that could be created using one flavor of ice cream, one topping, and either hot fudge or caramel?

a.

b.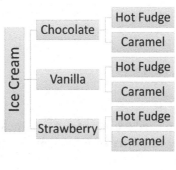

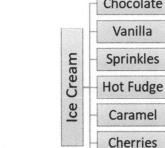

c.

d.

e.

10. What is the probability of spinning a D on the spinner below?

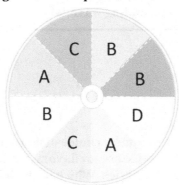

a. $\frac{1}{8}$

b. $\frac{1}{7}$

c. $\frac{3}{8}$

d. $\frac{5}{8}$

e. $\frac{6}{7}$

11. Edward draws a card from a standard deck of cards, does not replace it, and then draws another card. What is the probability that he draws a heart and then a spade?

a. $\frac{1}{16}$

b. $\frac{1}{2}$

c. $\frac{1}{17}$

d. $\frac{13}{204}$

e. $\frac{1}{3}$

12. Solve for y when $\frac{y}{2} - 8 = 0$.

a. $y = 4$

b. $y = 8$

c. $y = 2$

d. $y = 16$

e. $y = 6$

13. **What is the probability of spinning a 2 on the first try on the spinner below?**

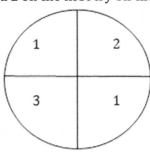

a. $\frac{1}{2}$

b. $\frac{1}{3}$

c. $\frac{1}{4}$

d. $\frac{2}{3}$

e. $\frac{2}{4}$

14. **Portia tosses a coin 1,000 times. Which of the following best represents the number of times she can expect to get tails?**

a. 350

b. 400

c. 450

d. 500

e. 1,000

15. **Given the double bar graph shown below, which of the following statements is true?**

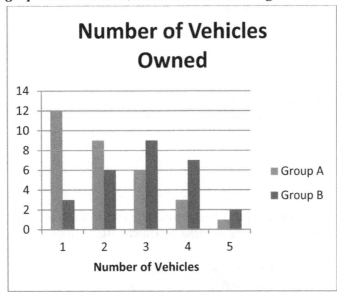

a. Group A is negatively skewed, while Group B is approximately normal.

b. Group A is positively skewed, while Group B is approximately normal.

c. Group A is positively skewed, while Group B is neutral.

d. Group A is approximately normal, while Group B is negatively skewed.

e. Group A is approximately normal, while Group B is positively skewed.

16. Aniyah has two pairs of jeans and three shirts. How many different outfits can she create, assuming each outfit consists of one pair of jeans and a shirt?

 a. 9 outfits
 b. 5 outfits
 c. 6 outfits
 d. 8 outfits
 e. 12 outfits

17. A six-sided die is rolled one time. What is the probability of the roll yielding an odd number?

 a. 10%
 b. 20%
 c. 25%
 d. 30%
 e. 50%

18. Of the twenty students in the classroom, half are boys and half are girls. If all students handed in their homework, what is the probability that the top homework sheet belongs to a girl?

 a. 20%
 b. 25%
 c. 30%
 d. 40%
 e. 50%

19. A bag contains 5 red marbles, 4 green marbles, and 3 yellow marbles. What is the probability that Fran pulls a red marble, keeps that marble in her possession, and then pulls a green marble?

 a. $\dfrac{5}{36}$
 b. $\dfrac{1}{6}$
 c. $\dfrac{7}{132}$
 d. $\dfrac{5}{33}$
 e. $\dfrac{4}{11}$

20. Simplify $8(x + 2) - 7 + 4(x - 7)$.

 a. $5x + 23$
 b. $5x - 23$
 c. $12x - 19$
 d. $12x + 19$
 e. $12x + 37$

21. Justin wants to re-carpet his rectangular bedroom. The bedroom has a length of 12 feet and a width of 10 feet. Which of the following measures should Justin calculate to determine the amount of carpet he will need?

 a. Justin should calculate the perimeter of his bedroom.
 b. Justin should calculate the area of the floor of his bedroom.
 c. Justin should calculate the volume of his bedroom.
 d. Justin should calculate the circumference of his bedroom.
 e. Justin should calculate the surface area of his bedroom.

22. There are 100 bacteria in a Petri dish. The number of bacteria doubles every day, so that on the first day, there are 100 bacteria; on the second, there are 200; on the third, there are 400; and so on. Write a formula for the number of bacteria on the nth day.

    a. $b(n) = 100 \times 2^{n-1}$
    b. $b(n) = 100n$
    c. $b(n) = 100n^2$
    d. $b(n) = 200(n - 1)$
    e. $b(n) = 200n^2$

23. A pump fills a cylindrical tank with water at a constant rate. The function $L(g) = 0.3g$ represents the water level of the tank (in feet) after g gallons are pumped into the tank. The function $w(t) = 1.2t$ represents the number of gallons that can be pumped into the tank in t minutes. Write a function $L(t)$ for the water level of the tank after t minutes.

    a. $L(t) = 0.25t$
    b. $L(t) = 0.36t$
    c. $L(t) = 0.9t$
    d. $L(t) = 3.6t$
    e. $L(t) = 4t$

24. Solve for x: $(2x - 6) + 4x = 24$

    a.   0
    b.   -3
    c.   5
    d.   -5
    e.   3

25. There is a big sale taking place at the clothing store on Main Street. Everything is marked down by 33% from the original price, p. Which of the following expressions describes the sale price, S, to be paid for any item?

    a. $S = p - 0.33$
    b. $S = p - 0.33p$
    c. $S = 0.33p$
    d. $S = 0.33(1 - p)$
    e. $S = p + 0.33p$

26. If Fahrenheit, (°F) and Celsius, (°C) are related by the formula $°F = \left(\frac{9}{5}\right)°C + 32$, what is the temperature in Fahrenheit of a location with an average temperature of 20 °C?

    a.   58°
    b.   63°
    c.   68°
    d.   73°
    e.   78°

27. The possible combinations of candy bars and packages of suckers that Amanda may purchase are represented by the graph shown below.

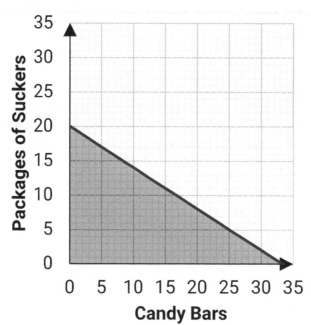

Which of the following inequalities represents the possible combinations of candy bars and packages of suckers that she may purchase?

a. $y \leq -\frac{1}{2}x + \frac{40}{3}$

b. $y \leq -\frac{2}{5}x + 20$

c. $y \leq -\frac{3}{5}x + 20$

d. $y \leq -\frac{5}{3}x + \frac{80}{3}$

e. $y \leq -\frac{2}{3}x + \frac{80}{3}$

28. If the two lines $2x + y = 0$ and $y = 3$ are plotted on a typical xy-coordinate grid, at which point will they intersect?

a. $\left(-\frac{3}{2}, 0\right)$

b. $\left(-\frac{3}{2}, 3\right)$

c. $\left(\frac{3}{2}, 3\right)$

d. $(4, 1)$

e. $(4.5, 1)$

Refer to the following for question 29:

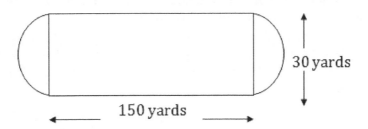

29. The diagram shows the outline of a racetrack, which consists of two long, straight sections, and two semi-circular turns. Given the dimensions shown, which of the following most closely measures the perimeter of the entire track?

    a.   180 yards
    b.   300 yards
    c.   360 yards
    d.   395 yards
    e.   425 yards

30. CF is a straight line. Angle BDF measures 45°. What is the measure of angle BDC?

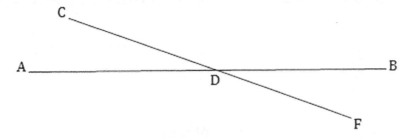

    a.   45°
    b.   135°
    c.   180°
    d.   225°
    e.   315°

31. Three rectangular gardens, each with an area of 48 square feet, are created on a tract of land. Garden A measures 6 feet by 8 feet; Garden B measures 12 feet by 4 feet; Garden C measures 16 feet by 3 feet. Which garden will require the least amount of fencing to surround it?

    a.   Garden A
    b.   Garden B
    c.   Garden C
    d.   All gardens will require the same amount of fencing
    e.   It cannot be determined from the information provided

32. Natasha designs a square pyramidal tent for her children. Each of the sides of the square base measures x ft, and the tent's height is h feet. If Natasha were to increase by 1 ft the length of each side of the base, how much more interior space would the tent have?

a. $\frac{h(x^2+2x+1)}{3}$ ft^3

b. $\frac{h(2x+1)}{3}$ ft^3

c. $\frac{x^2h+3}{3}$ ft^3

d. $\frac{x^2h}{3}$ ft^3

e. 1 ft^3

33. Which angle measure forms a complementary angle when combined with an angle measure of 48°?

a. 42°

b. 48°

c. 52°

d. 90°

e. 132°

34. Which of the following values is closest to the diameter of a circle with an area of 314 square inches?

a. 2π in

b. 10 in

c. 20 in

d. 31.4 in

e. 100 in

35. In the figure below, ΔJKL is dilated to the image $\Delta J'K'L'$.

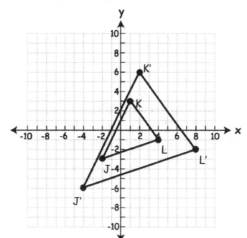

What is the scale factor of the dilation?

a. $\frac{1}{3}$

b. $\frac{1}{2}$

c. 2

d. 3

e. $\frac{1}{4}$

36. A new ramp is being installed at the entrance to a building.

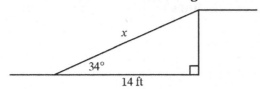

Based on the figure above, what is the length of the ramp, shown by x?

a. $14 \cos 34°$ ft
b. $\dfrac{14}{\cos 34°}$ ft
c. $\dfrac{14}{\tan 34°}$ ft
d. $\dfrac{14}{\sin 34°}$ ft
e. $14 \sin 34°$ ft

37. A hotel's Internet service costs guests $3.00 for the first hour of use and $0.15 for each five minutes over that. A woman uses the service for 3 hours and 10 minutes. What will her Internet charge be?

a. $3.90
b. $5.60
c. $6.90
d. $7.20
e. $9.30

38. Solve for x:

$$\frac{1}{6} \div \frac{3}{8} = x$$

a. $x = \dfrac{1}{16}$
b. $x = \dfrac{4}{9}$
c. $x = 2\dfrac{3}{8}$
d. $x = \dfrac{1}{2}$
e. $x = 2\dfrac{1}{3}$

39. What is the average of $\dfrac{7}{5}$ and 1.4?

a. 1.4
b. 2.8
c. 4.2
d. 5.6
e. 7.4

40. Which of the following would NOT satisfy $x \geq \dfrac{2}{5}$?

a. $x = \dfrac{5}{11}$
b. $x = \dfrac{3}{7}$
c. $x = \dfrac{1}{2}$
d. $x = \dfrac{1}{3}$
e. $x = \dfrac{7}{15}$

41. A recipe calls for 2 cups of water for every 6 cups of flour. Josie wants to make a smaller batch using only 2 cups of flour. How much water should she use?

a. $\frac{1}{2}$ cup

b. 2 cups

c. $\frac{2}{3}$ cup

d. $2\frac{2}{3}$ cups

e. 12 cups

42. Kendra uses the pie chart below to represent the allocation of her annual income. Her annual income is $40,000.

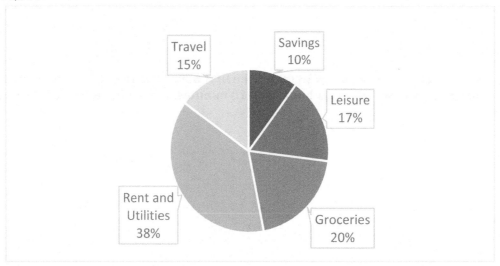

Which of the following statements is true?

a. The amount of money she spends on travel and savings is more than $11,000.

b. The amount of money she spends on rent and utilities is approximately $15,000.

c. The amount of money she spends on groceries and savings is more than $13,000.

d. The amount of money she spends on travel and leisure is more than $17,000.

e. The amount of money she spends on leisure is less than $5,000.

43. What is 40% of 360?

a. 90

b. 120

c. 144

d. 176

e. 270

44. What is the simplest form of $\frac{3}{8} \times \frac{3}{8}$?

a. $\frac{3}{4}$

b. $\frac{6}{8}$

c. $\frac{9}{64}$

d. 1

e. $1\frac{1}{8}$

45. Identical rugs are offered for sale at two local shops and one online retailer, designated Stores A, B, and C, respectively. The rug's regular sales price is $296 at Store A, $220 at Store B, and $198.00 at Store C. Stores A and B collect 8% in sales tax on any after-discount price, while Store C collects no tax but charges a $35 shipping fee. A buyer has a 30% off coupon for Store A and a $10 off coupon for Store B. Which of these lists the stores in order of lowest to highest final sales price after all discounts, taxes, and fees are applied?

    a.   Store A, Store B, Store C
    b.   Store B, Store A, Store C
    c.   Store B, Store C, Store A
    d.   Store C, Store A, Store B
    e.   Store C, Store B, Store A

46. Which of the following numbers is a prime number?

    a.   4
    b.   11
    c.   15
    d.   33
    e.   88

47. Which number is equivalent to 2^{-3}?

    a. $\frac{1}{2}$
    b. $\frac{1}{4}$
    c. $\frac{1}{8}$
    d. $\frac{1}{12}$
    e. $\frac{1}{16}$

48. Rachel spent $24.15 on vegetables. She bought 2 pounds of onions, 3 pounds of carrots, and $1\frac{1}{2}$ pounds of mushrooms. If the onions cost $3.69 per pound and the carrots cost $4.29 per pound, what is the price per pound of mushrooms?

    a. $2.25
    b. $2.60
    c. $2.75
    d. $2.80
    e. $3.10

49. A pair of $500 earrings is offered today at a 25% discount. If it is your birthday month, the store will take another 5% off of the discounted price. What does Mary pay for the earrings, since this is her birthday month?

    a. $250.50
    b. $300.00
    c. $356.25
    d. $405.75
    e. $400.00

50. Herbert plans to use the earnings from his lemonade stand, according to the table below, for the first month of operations. If he buys $70 worth of lemons, how much profit does he take home?

Cash Flow Item	Percentage of Total Earning Used on Item

Lemons	35%
Sugar	20%
Cups	25%
Stand improvements	5%
Profits	15%

a. $15
b. $20
c. $30
d. $35
e. $40

51. On Day 1, a driver averages 60 miles per hour for 15 hours of a 2,000-mile car trip. If he maintains this average speed and duration on Day 2, how far will he be from his destination at the end of the day?

a. 200 miles
b. 400 miles
c. 500 miles
d. 700 miles
e. 900 miles

52. Which of the following fractions is in lowest terms?

a. $\frac{6}{50}$
b. $\frac{12}{100}$
c. $\frac{3}{25}$
d. $\frac{12}{10}$
e. $\frac{12}{4}$

53. Lauren had $80 in her savings account. When she received her paycheck, she made a deposit, which brought the balance up to $120. By what percentage did the total amount in her account increase as a result of this deposit?

a. 35%
b. 40%
c. 50%
d. 80%
e. 120%

54. On a typical April day at Mayes Junior High, 8% of the 452 students who attend the school will be absent. About how many students will be absent on April 20?

a. 36
b. 38
c. 40
d. 42
e. 44

55. A long-distance runner does a first lap around a track in exactly 50 seconds. As she tires, each subsequent lap takes 20% longer than the previous one. How long does she take to run 3 laps?

    a. 72 seconds
    b. 150 seconds
    c. 160 seconds
    d. 180 seconds
    e. 182 seconds

56. Raul, Eli, Henry, and Lex all bought the same shirt from different stores for different prices. They spent $18.00, $18.50, $15.39 and $19.99 respectively. What is the average price the four men spent for the shirt?

    a. $15.97
    b. $16.97
    c. $17.97
    d. $18.97
    e. $19.97

Answer Key and Explanations

Reading

1. C: Although it never specifically addresses the babysitter, the directions are clearly instructions for how to take care of a little girl. A mother or father would not need this information written down in such detail, but a babysitter might. You can infer the answer in this case.

2. D: You cannot assume gender, and the note never indicates whether the writer is male or female. You can tell that the writer is the main caretaker of the child in question, so "parent" is the best choice in this case. A teacher or nurse might be able to write such a note, but parent is probably more likely, making it the best choice.

3. C: According to the author, the major clash between England and Scotland stemmed from religious differences. The countries clashed over Catholic and Protestant beliefs, causing tension among the citizens as well as members of the royal families.

4. B: According to the text, Queen Elizabeth I died in 1603. With no heir to her throne, the son of her cousin, James Stuart, was crowned king.

5. D: Paragraph 4 states that James and his wife lost many children during infancy. His son survived infancy, but the English feared that he would be raised Catholic and eventually become king, influencing Catholicism throughout England. To avoid this, they fabricated a story of his death and created a rumor that the king had replaced the young prince with an imposter, forcing James, his wife, and their young son to flee.

6. E: While England and the Scottish Lowlands were Protestant, the Highlands were accepting of Catholicism and even formed a group of Catholic followers known as "Jacobites."

7. E: When Queen Elizabeth I of England died, she had no heir. Therefore, her cousin's son, James, became King of England. He was named King James I of England, while already crowned King James VI of Scotland.

8. A: In paragraph 4, the author writes, "Mary gave birth to a son, but the story quickly circulated that the royal child had died, and the child named James's heir was a foundling smuggled in." We can use context clues to determine that the rumored child was illegitimate, and therefore most likely an orphan with no lawful rights to the throne.

9. C: An inference is a conclusion we make based on evidence and reasoning without the text explicitly giving us the information. The text states that King James II was being accused of having an illegitimate son as heir to the throne. The text also states that, rather than risk the safety of his family, James chose to flee with his wife and son, relinquishing his rightful seat as the King of England. From this, we can infer that King James II was committed to his family.

10. B: King James II was believed to be raising his son as a Catholic. The English were so fearful at the thought of a Catholic king that they created rumors of an illegitimate son, forcing James to flee England and abdicate his throne.

11. A: The term "Jacobites" refers to a group of Catholics inspired by the young King James II. The group was named to reflect the Latin version of James' name and gathered to practice Catholicism in the Highlands.

12. B: Although it is true that true that Mary Beatrice suffered the loss of many infants and Queen Elizabeth I was part of a troubled royal family, neither of these statements summarize the central idea of the passage. The author's main assertion is that the troubles between England and Scotland were largely due to a clash in religious beliefs.

248

13. D: The passage clearly states that the State Department's main responsibility is foreign policy (D). Disaster help (C) and treaty negotiation (E) are responsibilities that may fit within the category of foreign policy, but they are only parts of the department's main role. Economic aid (A) and food (B) are resources that the State Department may provide to help countries recover from disasters, but providing these resources is still not the department's main role.

14. A: A "celestial entity" is a body in space (A). The passage says that Earth is not the only celestial entity and then supports this by stating that "there are other large bodies in the solar system." Also, since Earth is a celestial entity, the definition of "celestial entity" must be something that describes Earth. Earth is not a star grouping (B), cosmic alien (C), solar flare (D), or a star unit (E), but it is a body in space.

15. C: The passage states that Newton considered the ideas of both Aristotle and Galileo when conducting his own work. This implies that he used those ideas when he came up with his three laws of motion (C). According to the passage, only parts of Galileo's work were proven false (A). Also, the passage does not discuss the current relevance of Galileo's work, but his influence on Newton and his laws suggests that his ideas are still relevant (D). There is also no information in the passage about a personal relationship between Aristotle and Galileo (B). The passage states that other celestial entities have gravitational pulls (E).

16. B: The passage states that blogs that are popular and have a consistently high number of readers can earn income for the blogger (B). This also means that not all blogs help the blogger make money (A). The passage also states that not every blogger creates a blog to make money (C), and advertisements are one of the ways bloggers can earn an income through a blog (D). However, according to the passage, companies tend to only advertise on blogs that have many frequent visitors, so bloggers may have a difficult time convincing companies to advertise on their blogs (E).

17. D: The passage mentions that introverts tend to be more comfortable by themselves rather than in social situations. A person who chooses a career as a stand-up comedian (A), an event organizer (B), a Master of Ceremonies (C), or a street musician (E) will most likely need to interact with others frequently to do his or her job well. A career as a painter is likely to require less social interaction than the other four options (D). According to the information in the passage, a profession as a painter is the most likely of these jobs to be chosen by an introvert.

18. E: Choice E is the only statement that is reasonably supported by the information in the passage, as introverts are more comfortable by themselves and are likely to enjoy solitary tasks. While introverts may tend to be more comfortable alone than in large groups, this does not provide enough evidence to suggest that introverts rarely have friends (A). On the other hand, the passage describes extroverts as having an easy time making friends and being among others, but does not necessarily mean that extroverts are bored without other people around (B). Extroverts' tendency, according to the passage, to act without an abundance of forethought also does not mean that they are necessarily insensitive (D). Additionally, the information in the passage explains the differences between introverts and extroverts, but these differences are not enough to support the statement that introverts and extroverts do not get along (C).

19. B: Lines 1–4 of the passage explain that *extrovert* and *introvert* are terms used to describe personality characteristics (B). These characteristics do not determine an individual's personal happiness (A) or reliably indicate a person's demographic (C), culture (D), or intelligence (E).

20. A: In the third paragraph of the passage, extroverts' actions are described as "apparent" (A). This means that their actions are often easy for others to perceive, suggesting that they are not secretive (C). While the passage says extroverts often act without forethought, this does not mean that their actions are completely subconscious (B). The passage also does not give any information about whether or not extroverts' actions are admired (D) or done out of kindness and care (E).

21. C: Although all five options are arguably benefits to eliminating mandatory attendance laws, the term "economical" tells us we're looking for a cost-effective advantage. According to the author, the cost of enforcing compulsory education is money ill-spent and could be better spent on students who *want* to be there.

22. E: According to the author, many problems that arise in schools are a direct result of students who are forced to be there. The author believes that attendance laws should be abolished in order to make education more valuable to students with a desire to learn.

23. B: The author believes that education is failing because teachers and schools spend far too much time disciplining behavior issues and mandating attendance. Teachers could better serve conscientious students if given the opportunity to fail or dismiss those who are disrupting the education of others.

24. D: An assumption is something we believe to be true because it is something we have been taught to believe and do not question. Here, the author is assuming that most parents want a high school education for their children. There is no evidence in the text supporting that claim, but the author believes it to be true based on his own experiences and beliefs.

25. E: Although all five options reflect the author's beliefs, only one of them describes the central idea, or main idea, of the writing. The author is trying to prove that abolishing mandatory attendance laws would create better school environments for the students with a genuine desire to learn. The other answer choices are used as supporting evidence to reinforce that claim.

26. C: A summary is a brief statement used to describe the main idea of writing, or a portion of that writing. The first paragraph of this article mentions all five choices, but the main idea is that abolishing mandatory attendance laws would improve the quality of education in schools. The other answer choices list ways in which the abolition of these laws could improve the climate of education or reasons why this abolition is necessary.

27. C: The author's main idea is that abolishing mandatory attendance laws would allow teachers the ability to dismiss disruptive students, preserving the sanctity of schools as a place for students to receive an esteemed education. Bullet three does not support that specific claim, but instead describes an issue with the grading of such students.

28. B: According to the text, mandatory attendance laws undermine the integrity of schools because teachers have no choice but to provide all students, regardless of behavior or attendance, the same educational opportunities. When there is no recourse for disrupting the learning environment, schools can be perceived as day cares or, as the author described, "indoor street corners."

29. D: An inference is defined as a conclusion reached on the basis of evidence and reasoning. Throughout the passage, the author has provided several reasons why students with behavior or attendance concerns should not be afforded the opportunity to disrupt the education of others. From these claims, we can infer that the author believes education is a privilege to those who want to put in the effort and not a birthright of every juvenile in a community.

30. C: Context clues are hints we can use within an author's writing to determine the meaning of an unknown word. The author writes, "Teachers could stop policing recalcitrant students and start educating." We can use context clues to determine that the term "recalcitrant" most similarly describes students who are disobedient, if they require the policing of teachers.

31. A: The main idea of this passage is to provide an overview of Chapter 11 (A). While both paragraphs give information that readers can use to infer why a company would file for Chapter 11 (B), this is not the purpose of the passage. The passage also includes a few details about legal rules associated with Chapter 11 (C), these are only details related to the main idea. The second paragraph describes actions a company may take after filing (D), but paragraph one does not discuss this, so this cannot be the main idea. The passage does not list any rights that creditors have under Chapter 11 (E), so this also cannot be the main idea.

32. A: The last sentence of the passage states that the changes are intended to restore the company to profitability and repay creditors. These are steps toward achieving solvency (A). While saving money (B), maintaining salaries (C), and keeping creditors at bay (D) may be part of the process of achieving solvency, and are likely goals of the company, they are only parts or steps within executives' overall goal. Creating a smaller company (E) is not mentioned in the passage.

33. E: The passage states that employee benefits can be affected during reorganization (E). Another likely part of reorganization is a change in management (D). The passage states that Chapter 11 is a legal filing (B) used to give a company protected time before it must pay its creditors, meaning that creditors do not receive payment during Chapter 11 proceedings (A). This also means that most of the company's debts should be repaid once these proceedings are complete (C).

34. E: The passage states that the Miranda decision did establish protections for suspects in police custody (E). The passage only mentions that people cannot be forced to testify if their testimony will be self-incriminating, but it does not say that people, in general, cannot be forced to testify (A). The passage specifically states that suspects in police custody have the right to remain silent (B). It also clearly says that the Miranda decision was part of a 1966 Supreme Court case (D) and, while the Miranda decision and the Fifth Amendment are related, they are two distinct things (C).

35. A: Each paragraph of this passage refers to aspects of self-incrimination and rights related to self-incrimination (A). The passage only discusses this aspect of the legal system, not the legal system as a whole (B). Similarly, the passage only discusses one right of suspects, not suspects' rights in general (E). The passage only briefly mentions how the Miranda decision came about (C). While the passage mentions that the Miranda decision was a result of a 1966 Supreme Court case, the passage does not describe the circumstances or other information about the case (D).

36. D: The introductory sentence should provide an overview that is supported by the details that follow. Answer A mentions maps and topographic details, but does not discuss topographic maps. Answers B and C both mention topographic maps, but they also include specific uses for topographic maps that are not discussed in the passage. Answer E introduces a method of creating topographic maps, which is not relevant to the details in the passage. Answer D specifically mentions topographic maps, is relevant to the details in the rest of the passage, and prepares the reader for the topic and information to follow.

37. D: Although this passage describes an opera, the feelings experienced by the characters would not be considered musical (D). The passage does mention that the American officer falls in love with Butterfly, so it is reasonable to describe the characters' feelings as romantic (A). *Poignant* (B), *crushing* (C), and *tragic* (E) all refer to feelings of intense emotional distress, which are expressed through both Butterfly and the officer's reactions at the end of the passage. These terms clearly describe the characters' feelings, making *musical* the correct answer.

38. B: The passage uses schools segregated by neighborhood (B) as an example of de facto segregation. Large schools (A) are not necessarily an example of de facto segregation, as the size of the student body alone does not reveal the presence or lack of segregation in the school. Diverse (C), integrated (D), and heterogeneous (E) schools would all have students from a variety of backgrounds or demographics, so none of these would be an example of de facto segregation.

39. A: The end of the passage says "de facto segregation can still be found in our country," meaning that de facto segregation still exists today (A). The passage lists some negative consequences of de facto segregation, showing that it was, and still is, a serious problem (B). According to the passage, during the 1960s, students who lived in low-income neighborhoods suffered the consequences of de facto segregation (C). The passage also states that de facto segregation is based on socioeconomic factors, meaning that de facto segregation is not always characterized by race (D), and it does not create equality (E).

40. C: Corrosion due to heat (C) is not mentioned in the passage. According to the passage, contact with water (D) and contact with oxygen (E) are causes for iron corrosion, exposure to elements (A) causes copper corrosion, and silver corrosion occurs over time (B).

41. E: The passage notes that "competition between markets keeps prices at a particular level" (E). The passage also states that sellers may adjust prices depending on whether or not consumers purchase goods, and sellers may be corporations (C) or individuals (D), but sellers do not determine prices (A). Market economies also entail very little government involvement, so the government does not determine prices in such an economy (B).

42. B: The passage states that the problem in a story, or the story problem (B), can be called conflict. While the conflict is a type of situation, not every situation in a story (A) is a conflict. Conflicts may also be part of a character's growth process (D) or something the character experiences (E), but these do not have to occur through conflicts. Most conflicts have resolutions (C), but conflicts are not resolutions, themselves.

43. E: The passage describes several elements of a good story, including characters with whom readers can connect (E). The passage states that good stories establish conflict early in the story, not in the middle (B), and that the resolution should be unpredictable (D) to help readers become more invested in the story and the characters' actions. According to the passage, stories where the main character explicitly states what he or she has learned (A) are not as successful as stories that require readers to decide what the lesson is for themselves. The passage also does not discuss whether it is better for stories to have one or multiple conflicts (C).

44. B: The passage mentions that handwriting notes can, on occasion, be more reliable than using a recording device during an interview (B). The passage also mentions that it can be difficult to take notes quickly and legibly. In other words, note taking can be slow (A), and handwritten notes may be difficult to read after the interview (E). The first paragraph states that relying on handwritten notes during an interview can distract journalists and cause them to look away from the person they are interviewing (C) and miss small details like body language (D).

45. A: In the passage, the first paragraph gives two examples of body language when it describes an interview subject closing his eyes and trembling sightly. This implies that body language is nonverbal, physical cues. A shocked look (B), wringing hands (C), blinking (D), and a glance (E) are all examples of body language, since they are nonverbal, physical actions. Answering a question quietly is not an example of body language because it is a verbal response (A).

46. A: Although the other options are all good practices to ensure that a recorder will work when it is needed, handwriting notes while recording an interview is the best way for journalists to make sure that they have reliable notes from an interview (A). Bringing extra batteries (B) and tapes (C), increasing the volume (D), and ensuring the recorder is on (E) are all wise things to do, but they still may not prevent all malfunctions that may occur when using a recorder.

47. C: "Tape Recording an Interview" (C) is relevant to each section of the passage. The passage includes details related to writing notes (A) and body language (D), but since neither of these are the main idea, titles focused on these topics are not the best choices. Tape recording an interview is only one part of interviewing, so the title "Conducting an Interview" (B) is too broad for this passage. The passage also only talks about problems that occur when taking notes, not problems with interviews in general, so "Problems with Interviews" (E) is also not the best title.

48. B, C: The passage mentions advantages and disadvantages to both processes. Note-taking is described as being difficult to do efficiently and legibly, and it carries with it the necessity for frequently looking away from the interview subject. Choices A and E, on the other hand, are reasons that note-taking may be superior to audio recording. Technology can fail unexpectedly, causing information to be lost. Choice D alludes to a potential drawback of both methods, namely that non-verbal cues may be missed.

49. D: The passage clearly states that "Florence is not the capital of Italy" (D). The passage also explains that Florence is at the center of Italy (C). According to the passage, tourists still visit to see the city's architecture, and artists still visit Florence for inspiration. These facts support the statements that Florence is still relevant (E) and an artistic center (B). The first paragraph of the passage discusses the city's impact and artistic significance during the Italian Renaissance, showing that Florence has a rich cultural history (A).

50. E: *Burgeoned* means "multiplied," or "prospered." In the context of the passage, *exploded* can mean the same thing (E). The other words have meanings that imply different actions. *Dwindled* (A), *stagnated* (B), and *deteriorated* (D) imply that something is decreasing rather than prospering. These do not match the events the passage describes. *Originated* (C) means "started" and does not make sense in the context of the passage.

51. C: Answer C would be the most appropriate as the second sentence in the passage. Answers B, D, and E are all sentences that discuss whether or not students appreciate scaffolding techniques. These would not fit well in the passage because the passage focuses on teachers and scaffolding, not how students feel about scaffolding. Answer A gives a potential definition for scaffolding. However, this sentence does not fit the rest of the information in the passage or the purpose of the passage. Answer C is relevant to all of the information in the passage and flows well with the other sentences.

52. E: Answer E is relevant to the passage and expands upon the information in the last sentence. Answer A provides information that is already implied in the last sentence, so it would not add helpful information to the passage. Answer B is contrary to the second sentence in the passage, which says that conflict mediation is sometimes unnecessary. The information in answer C does not build upon the ideas in the passage and shifts the topic. Answer D repeats information that is already stated in the passage and does not expand upon the last idea in the passage.

53. E: The passage provides facts about cell phone text messages and does not appear to address any particular audience. Choices A, B, C, and D all define an audience based on their opinions concerning using cell phones or texting during school. Cell phone use in schools is only discussed in the second paragraph, so the target audience for the passage is not likely to be any of these.

54. C: Each paragraph in the passage discusses teenagers and texting. Answer C is a title that is relevant to information throughout the passage and summarizes the topic. Answers A and B suggest that the passage is about problems with texting or cell phones. While the passage discusses problems related to texting and cell phones, the last section is not about problems with texting, so these titles are not the best choices. Answer D suggests that the passage is about problems that may arise for teachers. While the passage discusses problems related to using cell phones in school, this is not the main point of the passage. Answer E suggests that the passage is about modern technology. While the passage does discuss modern technology, it specifically focuses on teenagers and their use of modern technology. Answer E is too broad of a title for this passage.

55. B: Some women who ran as men in the Boston Marathon prior to 1972 could still be alive today (B). The passage does not suggest that the women who ran as men were arrested (A) or that the individuals who currently manage the Boston Marathon have a male bias (D). The passage clearly mentions that women ran in the Boston Marathon as men (C). The choice of female runners to run as men implies that they did want to race (E).

56. A: The passage says that women attempted to conceal their gender (A). While it is possible that some women attempted to bribe (B), hid from (D), or threatened to sue race officials (E), none of these actions are mentioned in the passage. Running with a male in the race (C) is also not mentioned in the passage.

Writing

1. B: The past tense of *drag* is *dragged*, not *drug*.

2. B: *Precedes* means "to come before" and is the appropriate choice in this sentence. *Proceeds* means "to carry on."

3. B: *Had ought* is considered to be bad grammar. *Ought* should be used alone in this sentence.

4. B: *Less* is a comparative adjective used with things that cannot be counted or are talked about as a single unit, as in *less afraid* or *less gasoline*. *Fewer* is used when talking about people or about objects and things that are considered in units, as in *fewer students* or *fewer apples*.

5. B: The correct word is *ensure*—to make certain by stressing an action taken beforehand.

6. B: *Capitol* refers to the capitol building. The correct word here is *capital*, which means an uppercase letter.

7. D: "Affect" means *to influence* whereas "effect" means *end result*.

8. B: *Except* means "instead of." Here, the word should be *accept*.

9. B: To be averse to something is to be reluctant to take part in it or to loath it:

She was averse to going to the beach since she was afraid of the big waves.

The word here should be "adverse," which means to have a bad reaction or the opposite reaction that was expected.

10. D: With two people, *between* is used. When speaking of more than two people, *among* is used.

11. D: The sentence is not complete until *said.* Instead of a period after *pool*, a comma should be used.

12. E: The sentence is correct as it is written.

13. E: The sentence is correct as it is written.

14. D: *Today's* tells when which track meet we are referring to. The noun is in the possessive form and needs to have an apostrophe –*s*.

15. A: "Mother" is not capitalized here since it is not being used as a proper noun: I hope my mother won't talk about it. I hope Mother won't talk about it.

16. C: "Superior to" or "smarter than" should be used here. "Superior" is not ordinarily used with "than."

17. E: The sentence is correct as it is written.

18. B: The phrase "who is a doctor" must be included in commas. It is a nonrestrictive (unneeded) clause and it can be removed from the sentence without losing the main idea of the sentence: His uncle will be joining us on the camping trip.

19. B: There should be no commas around this restrictive phrase. The phrase is dependent on the rest of the sentence to create the sentence's meaning.

20. C: This is a run-on sentence. A period should be placed between "work," and "this."

21. C: "They're" should be used here: They are

22. C: Since a person is the subject of the sentence, "who" and not "that" should be used here.

23. A: Since the Frankels are a family, the correct usage would be plural possessive. Thus, the apostrophe should be outside the s.

24. E: Since "they" indicates more than one parent, the plural possessive form of parent should be used here.

25. D: *Irregardless* is not considered to be a conventional English word. *Regardless* is the correct word to use in this sentence.

26. E: *Sisters-in-law* is the plural of *sister-in-law.*

27. C: Only those subjects that are proper nouns (e.g., English, Spanish) are capitalized.

28. D: A comma is used to separate the phrase at the beginning of the sentence from the rest of the sentence to prevent the sentence from being misread.

29. B: The sentence ends in a preposition, which is an example of incorrect grammar.

30. E: The subject refers to the individual (each) student. Students only have one backpack. Response D may be correct if the students are from a group of all males, but the sentence does not indicate this to be so.

31. C: The word "set" is not a synonym for "sit." "Sit" must be used here.

32. A: The sentence is correct as it is written.

33. D: The sentence should begin with Oscar Smith as the subject, putting it in active form.

34. D: This sentence is a fragment – it is not a complete sentence. It needs a subject, which "she" provides.

35. E: The sentence begins in the present tense: *grabs.* The sentence needs to continue in the present tense throughout.

36. C: This is a run-on sentence and the semi-colon is needed to break it into two simple sentences. A period would have also worked to separate the two main ideas here.

37. E: Quotation marks are not closed between sentences. They open at the beginning of the dialogue and close when the person or character is finished speaking.

38. A: The sentence is correct as it is written.

39. D: The nominative case, *Jack and me,* should be used here since they are objects of notice. To test this, take out "Jack and" and read the sentence: to notice *me* walk in late.

40. B: The sentence refers to the singular: *each* diamond. Each is worth over ten thousand dollars.

41. Essay question graders commonly look for the following elements in a strong response: strong content knowledge, clear organization, and effective arguments or examples. Language and usage are not usually strictly graded, but can make a big impact on the clarity of your ideas.

Please use the provided rubric to make sure your response meets these common criteria. Try to have a friend or family member grade your response for you or take a break after writing your response and return to grade it with fresh eyes.

CONSTRUCTED RESPONSE RUBRIC

Domain	Description
Content Knowledge	<ul><li>The response directly addresses every part of the prompt.</li><li>The response demonstrates independent knowledge of the topic.</li><li>The response discusses the topic at an appropriate depth.</li></ul>
Organization	<ul><li>The response introduces the topic, usually with a thesis statement or by restating the prompt.</li><li>The response directly addresses the prompt by providing a clear and concise answer or solution.</li><li>The answer or solution is supported by logical arguments or evidence.</li><li>The response restates the main idea in the conclusion.</li></ul>
Arguments and Examples	<ul><li>The response provides a reasonable answer to the prompt.</li><li>The answer is supported by strong reasoning or evidence.</li><li>The response develops ideas logically and connects ideas to one another.</li><li>The reasoning and evidence provided act to support a unified main idea.</li></ul>
Language and Usage	<ul><li>The response demonstrates effective use of grammar and uses varied sentence structure throughout the response.</li><li>The response demonstrates correct use of spelling, punctuation, and capitalization.</li><li>The response demonstrates strong and varied use of vocabulary relevant to the topic and appropriate for the intended audience.</li></ul>

42. Essay question graders commonly look for the following elements in a strong response: strong content knowledge, clear organization, and effective arguments or examples. Language and usage are not usually strictly graded, but can make a big impact on the clarity of your ideas.

Please use the provided rubric to make sure your response meets these common criteria. Try to have a friend or family member grade your response for you or take a break after writing your response and return to grade it with fresh eyes.

CONSTRUCTED RESPONSE RUBRIC

Domain	Description
Content Knowledge	• The response directly addresses every part of the prompt. • The response demonstrates independent knowledge of the topic. • The response discusses the topic at an appropriate depth.
Organization	• The response introduces the topic, usually with a thesis statement or by restating the prompt. • The response directly addresses the prompt by providing a clear and concise answer or solution. • The answer or solution is supported by logical arguments or evidence. • The response restates the main idea in the conclusion.
Arguments and Examples	• The response provides a reasonable answer to the prompt. • The answer is supported by strong reasoning or evidence. • The response develops ideas logically and connects ideas to one another. • The reasoning and evidence provided act to support a unified main idea.
Language and Usage	• The response demonstrates effective use of grammar and uses varied sentence structure throughout the response. • The response demonstrates correct use of spelling, punctuation, and capitalization. • The response demonstrates strong and varied use of vocabulary relevant to the topic and appropriate for the intended audience.

Mathematics

1. B: The mean, or average, is the sum of the numbers in a data set divided by the total number of items in the set. This data set has 7 items (one for each day of the week). The total number of hits that Kyle had during the week is the sum of the numbers in the right-hand column. The sum is 14, so the mean is 2 because $14 \div 7 = 2$.

2. A: Since 3 of the 15 songs are by Band B, the probability that any one song will be by that band is $\frac{3}{15} = \frac{1}{5}$. The probability that two successive events will occur is the product of the probabilities for any one event or, in this case, $\frac{1}{5} \times \frac{1}{5} = \frac{1}{25}$.

3. B: The data set {67, 2, 67, 73, 85, 60, 68} contains seven numbers, six of which are within 15 units of each other. The seventh piece of data, 2, is an outlier, meaning it is much greater or smaller than the rest of the data. Using the range of this data set, 83 (because $85 - 2 = 83$), would give the impression that the entire data set greatly varies, which is not the case. For this type of data set, the median would be a better representation of the set because the outlier does not have as great an effect.

4. A: The mean, or average, of the distribution can be computed by multiplying each grade by the number of students obtaining it, summing all products, and then dividing by the total number of students. Here, $n = 4.2$. The median is the value for which an equal number of students have received higher or lower grades. Here, $p = 4$. The mode is the most frequently obtained grade, and here $q = 3$. Thus, $n > p > q$.

5. C: When displaying data collected in a survey, we must always choose intervals appropriate for the data collected. This includes starting our y-axis at zero, and choosing intervals that are appropriate for the data being collected. For example, imagine we are comparing the purchase prices of homes in an area. If the homes sold for $280,000, $282,000, and $284,000, most people would consider the homes to have sold for very similar prices, given that $2,000 increments are only marginally different when describing the cost of a house. If these prices were graphed with y-axis intervals of $10.00, the bar representing the $284,000 house would be much higher than the bar representing the house that sold for $282,000, even though the difference in price is only $2,000. That graph would mislead people into thinking the houses sold for prices that were considerably different from each other, which was not the case.

6. A: The median is the middle number of a data set when the set is listed from least to greatest. To find the median, we must first rewrite our set from least to greatest as: 53, 72, 81, 82, 85, 91. Because there are six data values, we have two numbers, 81 and 82, that can be described as the "middle numbers." To find the median of the set, we must find the mean of the two middle numbers. The mean of 81 and 82 is 81.5, so the median of our entire data set is also 81.5.

7. D: In the data set {67, 29, 57, 27, 38, 91} there is no value that occurs more than any other value. However, we cannot describe the mode as "zero" because that would imply that the value "0" is part of the data set and appears more than any other value. When we have a data set without any repeating numbers, we must describe that set as having "no mode," rather than "zero."

8. B: The counting principle is the strategy in which we list out all of the possible combinations that *could* occur in order to determine the probability of a specific event occurring. Here, Joe is flipping two coins and trying to find the probability of both coins landing on tails. When we write out all of the possible flip combinations we get: TT, TH, HT, HH. Using this strategy, we would then circle the outcomes that meet our designated outcome (both coins landing on tails) and determine that the probability is 1 out of 4, or $\frac{1}{4}$. Although $\frac{1}{2} \times \frac{1}{2}$ would lead us to this answer, it is not an example of the counting principle being applied.

9. A: A tree diagram shows the different combinations possible by listing each option as a sort of hierarchy. To start, we list all possibilities for the first category. Here, our first category is ice cream flavor, so we need three branches to represent the three different flavors. Next, we must decide between three different toppings. Because each topping can be paired with any flavor, we need two branches coming from each flavor, to show all the flavor/topping combinations. Finally, we must decide on hot fudge or caramel. Again, each choice can be added to any of our already existing combinations, so we'll need two more branches coming from each topping choice. When finished, we can follow the branches from top to bottom to see every possible combination of ice cream sundae that can be created. So, the correct option shows every possible branch.

10. A: Experimental probability is a ratio of how many times the spinner will land on the specific letter to the total number of places the spinner can land. In this case, there are eight possible places where the spinner may land. The D is present only in one space, so the probability of landing there is 1 to 8 or $\frac{1}{8}$.

11. D: Since he does not replace the first card, the events are dependent. The sample space will decrease by 1 for the second draw because there will be one fewer card to choose from. Thus, the probability may be written as $P(A \text{ and } B) = \frac{13}{52} \times \frac{13}{51}$, or $P(A \text{ and } B) = \frac{169}{2,652} = \frac{13}{204}$.

12. D: To solve for y, we must first complete the inverse of any addition or subtraction. Here, we need to add 8 to both sides of the equation. This simplifies our equation to $\frac{y}{2} = 8$. Next, we need to complete the inverse of division, which is multiplication. When we multiply both sides of the equation by 2, we find that $y = 16$. To check our answer, we can insert 16 into our original equation. Because $\frac{16}{2} - 8 = 0$, we know we have the correct value for y.

13. C: There are four, equally possible places the spinner may land. The digit 2 is only present in one space, so the probability of landing there is 1 out of 4 or $\frac{1}{4}$.

14. D: The theoretical probability of getting tails is $\frac{1}{2}$. Thus, she can expect to get a total of $\frac{1}{2} \times 1{,}000$ tails, or 500 tails.

15. B: Data is said to be positively skewed when there are a higher number of lower values, indicating data that is skewed right. Data is said to be negatively skewed when there are a higher number of higher values, indicating that the data is skewed left. An approximately normal distribution shows an increase in frequency, followed by a decrease in frequency, of approximately the same rate, following a general bell curve. Therefore, Group A is positively skewed, and Group B is approximately normal.

16. C: To find the number of options Aniyah can create, we can start by making an ordered list of the different options. To start, we can assign each piece of clothing an abbreviation, such as J1 for the first pair of jeans or S1 for shirt number 1. When we list all of the different options in an organized way, we find the following combinations: J1/S1, J1/S2, J1/S3, J2/S1, J2/S2, J2/S3. We can count the numbers of combinations created to conclude that Aniyah is able to create six different outfits from two pairs of jeans and three shirts. Another way to solve this problem is to simply multiply the number of options within each category. There are two options for jeans and three options for shirts. The product of 3 and 2 is 6, again confirming that Aniyah has six possible outfit combinations.

17. E: A die has a total of six sides, with a different number on each side. Three of these numbers are odd, and three are even. When rolling a die, the probability of rolling an odd number is 3 out of 6 or $\frac{3}{6}$. Reducing the fraction, yields a $\frac{1}{2}$ or 50% chance an odd number will be rolled.

18. E: Out of the twenty students in the classroom, half are girls. That means there is a 1 in 2, or 50%, chance that the homework handed in will belong to a girl.

19. D: To find the probability of Fran pulling two different marbles from the bag, we must find the probability of each event occurring individually, then multiply those probabilities together. To start, we can determine that Fran's chance of pulling a red marble is $\frac{5}{12}$ because there are 5 red marbles out of a total 12 marbles. Next, we must determine that Fran has a $\frac{4}{11}$ chance of pulling a green marble because there are 4 green marbles out of a new total 11 marbles. Notice, our total must now be reduced to 11 because Fran has one marble already in her possession. When we multiply our two events, $\frac{5}{12} \times \frac{4}{11}$, we get $\frac{20}{132}$, or $\frac{5}{33}$. The chance of Fran pulling a red marble followed by a green marble is $\frac{5}{33}$.

20. C: To solve, first multiply through the parentheses and then combine like terms:

$$8(x + 2) - 7 + 4(x - 7) = 8x + 16 - 7 + 4x - 28$$
$$= 12x - 19$$

21. B: Area is the measure we use to calculate the number of square units that will fit into a plane surface. To re-carpet his bedroom, Justin must calculate the total number of square feet that must be covered in order to fill the floor space. To find area, Justin should multiply the length of his bedroom, 12 feet, by the width, 10 feet. Because $12 \times 10 = 120$, Justin will need 120 square feet of carpet for his bedroom.

22. A: The number of bacteria forms a geometric sequence: 100, 200, 400, 800, 1,600, etc. Notice that, if you ignore the two zeroes, these numbers are all powers of 2 (i.e. 2^0, 2^1, 2^2, 2^3, 2^4, etc.). In other words, they are all 100 multiplied by a power of 2, so the sequence can be written as an exponential function of the form $y = 100 \times 2^n$. However, since this sequence begins with an exponent of 0 on the first day, rather than 1, and an exponent of 1 on the second day rather than 2, you need to subtract 1 from n to get the correct power. Thus, the function $b(n) = 100 \times 2^{n-1}$ represents the number of bacteria on the nth day.

23. B: The first function $L(g)$ gives the water level after g gallons are pumped into the tank. The second function $w(t)$ gives the number of gallons pumped into the tank after t minutes, which the first function calls g. Consequently, we can have L act on w: the composition of the functions $L(w(t))$ is the water level of the tank after t minutes. Calculate $L(w(t))$.

$$L(w(t)) = 0.3 \times w(t)$$
$$L(t) = 0.3 \times 1.2t$$
$$L(t) = 0.36t$$

Thus, the function $L(t) = 0.36t$ represents the water level of the tank after t minutes.

24. C: To solve, isolate x by rearranging the equation:

$$2x - 6 + 4x = 24$$
$$6x - 6 = 24$$
$$6x = 30$$
$$x = 5$$

25. B: To calculate S, first calculate the discount, and then subtract it from the original price, p. In this case, the discount is 33% of p, or $0.33p$. Thus, $S = p - 0.33p$.

26. C: To find the temperature in degrees Fahrenheit, plug 20 into the formula for degrees Celsius and solve.

$$°F = \left(\frac{9}{5}\right)(20) + 32 = 36 + 32 = 68$$

Therefore, the temperature in degrees Fahrenheit is 68°.

27. C: The y-intercept of the inequality is 20. The slope can be determined by calculating the ratio of the change in y-values per change in corresponding x-values. Choose any two points to calculate the slope. For example, the points $(0,20)$ and $(25,5)$ can be used.

$$m = \frac{y_2 - y_1}{x_2 - x_1} = \frac{5 - 20}{25 - 0} = \frac{-15}{25} = -\frac{3}{5}$$

Therefore, the slope is –0.6. Write the inequality in slope-intercept form. Use the less than or equal to sign ($\leq$) because the line is solid and the graph is shaded below the line.

$$y \leq -\frac{3}{5}x + 20$$

28. B: Since the second line, $y = 3$, is horizontal, the intersection must occur at a point where $y = 3$. Substitute $y = 3$ into the equation and solve for x.

$$2x + (3) = 0$$
$$2x = -3$$
$$x = -\frac{3}{2}$$

Therefore, the point where these two lines will intersect is at $\left(-\frac{3}{2}, 3\right)$.

29. D: First, add the two straight, 150-yard portions. Also, note that the distance around the two semi-circular turns combine to form the circumference of a circle. The radius, r, of that circle is $\frac{1}{2}$ the dimension that is shown as the width of the track, or 15 yards. Now, take the formula for the circumference of a circle, $C = 2\pi r$, and add it to the length of the two straight portions of the track.

$$\text{Length} = (2\pi \times 15) + (2 \times 150) \approx 394.25$$

Therefore, the closest approximation of the perimeter is 395 yards.

30. B: Since CF is a straight line, its measure is 180°. Since $\angle BDF = 45°$, then:

$$\angle CDB = 180° - 45° = 135°$$

31. A: To solve, find the perimeter (sum of all sides) of each garden.

Garden A: 6 ft by 8 ft rectangle, 6 ft + 8 ft + 6 ft + 8 ft = 28 ft

Garden B: 12 ft by 4 ft rectangle, 12 ft + 4 ft + 12 ft + 4 ft = 32 ft

Garden C: 16 ft by 3 ft rectangle, 16 ft + 3 ft + 16 ft + 3 ft = 38 ft

The smallest perimeter, Garden A, will require the least amount of fencing.

32. B: The volume of a square pyramid can be calculated using the formula $V = \frac{Bh}{3}$, where B is the area of the base and h is the height of the pyramid. Therefore, the volume of Natasha's tent is $\frac{x^2 h}{3}$. If she were to increase by 1 ft the length of each side of the square base, the tent's volume can be calculated by substituting $x + 1$ for x in the original tent volume formula.

$$\frac{(x+1)^2 h}{3} = \frac{(x^2 + 2x + 1)(h)}{3} = \frac{x^2 h + 2xh + h}{3} = \frac{x^2 h}{3} + \frac{2xh + h}{3}$$

Notice this is the volume of Natasha's tent, $\frac{x^2 h}{3}$, increased by $\frac{2xh+h}{3}$, or $\frac{h(2x+1)}{3}$. This is how much more interior space the tent would have.

33. A: Complementary angles are two angles that equal 90° when added together:

$$90° - 48° = 42°$$

34. C: The area of a circle is given by $A = \pi \times r^2$, where r is the radius of the circle. Since π is approximately 3.14, we can solve for $r = \sqrt{\frac{A}{\pi}} = \sqrt{\frac{314 \text{ in}^2}{3.14}} = \sqrt{100 \text{ in}^2} = 10$ in. Now, the diameter is twice the radius, or 2×10 in $= 20$ in. Therefore, the diameter is 20 inches.

35. C: To determine the scale factor of the dilation, compare the coordinates of $\Delta J'K'L'$ to the coordinates of ΔJKL. J is at $(-2, -3)$ and J' is at $(-4, -6)$, which means that the coordinates of J were multiplied by a scale factor of 2 to get the coordinates of J'. K is at $(1,3)$ and K' is at $(2,6)$. L is at $(4, -1)$ and L' is at $(8, -2)$. The coordinates of K and L were also multiplied by a scale factor of 2 to get to the coordinates of K' and L'. Therefore, the scale factor of the dilation is 2.

36. B: Based on the location of the 34°, the 14 ft section is the adjacent leg and the ramp length is the hypotenuse of the right triangle. Therefore, in order to solve for x, it needs to be set up as $\cos 34° = \frac{\text{adjacent}}{\text{hypotenuse}}$ or $\cos 34° = \frac{14}{x}$. The value of x is found by rearranging the equation to be $x = \frac{14}{\cos 34°}$.

37. C: To solve, first figure out how much she owes over the $3.00 base fee. For each five minutes, she pays an extra 15 cents. For each hour after the first one, she will pay:

$$12 \times 0.15 = \$1.80$$

She has used the service for an extra 2 hours and 10 minutes. Two hours of additional time is:

$$\$1.80 \times 2 = \$3.60$$

Ten minutes of additional time is:

$$\$0.15 \times 2 = \$0.30$$

Adding these two values gives an additional cost of $3.90. Add this to the base fee of $3 for the first hour to get a total bill of $6.90.

38. B: To divide fractions, multiply the dividend (the first fraction) by the reciprocal (turn it upside down) of the divisor (the second fraction):

$$\frac{1}{6} \div \frac{3}{8} = \frac{1}{6} \times \frac{8}{3}$$
$$= \frac{8}{18}$$
$$= \frac{4}{9}$$

39. A: The value of the fraction, $\frac{7}{5}$, can be evaluated by dividing 7 by 5, which yields 1.4. The average of 1.4 and 1.4 is $\frac{1.4 + 1.4}{2} = 1.4$.

40. D: To compare fractions with unlike denominators, we can rewrite each fraction with equivalent denominators. To do so, we must first identify the least common denominator, or LCD. The LCD is the least common multiple of the denominators. Here, the LCDs between $\frac{2}{5}$ and the answer choices are 55, 35, 15, and 10. Next, we must rewrite each fraction for comparison, while maintaining equivalence. Let's start with $\frac{5}{11}$. Our new denominator, 55, is five times greater than our original denominator, 11. To maintain equivalence, we must make our new numerator five times greater than our original numerator. To do so, we multiply our original numerator, 5, by 5, which equals 25. That makes our new fraction $\frac{5}{55}$. We do the same for $\frac{2}{5} = \frac{22}{55}$, and once our denominators are equivalent, we can simply compare our numerators to determine the greater value. Because 25 is greater than 22, we know that $\frac{25}{55}$ is greater than $\frac{22}{55}$, or $\frac{5}{11} > \frac{2}{5}$. We follow the same logic to evaluate each answer choice to find that $\frac{1}{3} < \frac{2}{5}$.

41. C: To start, we can write our ratio in fractional form as $\frac{2 \text{ cups of water}}{6 \text{ cups of flour}}$. We know Josie wants to lessen the flour to only 2 cups, making our proportion $\frac{2 \text{ cups of water}}{6 \text{ cups of flour}} = \frac{x \text{ cups of water}}{2 \text{ cups of flour}}$. To find the value of x, we can cross multiply the two diagonal values we know, 2 and 2, and divide their product by the remaining value, 6. $2 \times 2 = 4$, and $4 \div 6 = \frac{4}{6}$, which simplifies to $\frac{2}{3}$. This means Josie should use $\frac{2}{3}$ of a cup of water for every 2 cups of flour.

42. B: The amount of money she spends on travel and savings is $(0.15 + 0.10) \times \$40{,}000 = 0.25 \times \$40{,}000 = \$10{,}000$, so choice A is false. The amount of money she spends on rent and utilities is equal to $0.38 \times \$40{,}000 = \$15{,}200$, which is approximately $15,000, so choice B is true. The amount of money she spends on groceries and savings is $(0.20 + 0.10) \times \$40{,}000 = 0.30 \times \$40{,}000 = \$12{,}000$, so choice C is false.

The amount of money she spends on leisure is $0.17 \times \$40,000 = \$6,800$, so choices D and E are false. Therefore, choice B is the correct answer.

43. C: Because 40% is the same as 0.40, multiply 360 by 0.40 to get 144.

44. C: Multiply the numerators by one another to get the new numerator ($3 \times 3 = 9$), and the denominators by one another to get the new denominator ($8 \times 8 = 64$). The result ($\frac{9}{16}$) is in simplest form.

45. A: Calculate the final sales price of the rug at each store.

$$1.08(0.7 \times \$296) = \$223.78 \text{ at Store A}$$
$$1.08(\$220 - \$10) = \$226.80 \text{ at Store B}$$
$$\$198 + \$35 = \$233 \text{ at Store C}$$

Therefore, the stores in order of lowest to highest prices are Store A, Store B, Store C.

46. B: A prime number is a natural, positive, non-zero number that can only be factored by itself and 1. This is the case for 11. 4 is not a prime number because 2 is a factor of 4: $2 \times 2 = 4$. 15 is not a prime number because 3 and 5 are factors of 15: $3 \times 5 = 15$. 33 is not a prime number because 3 and 11 are factors of 33: $3 \times 11 = 33$. 88 is not a prime number because 2, 4, 8, 11, 22, and 44 are factors of 88: $2 \times 44 = 88$, $4 \times 22 = 88$, and $8 \times 11 = 88$.

47. C: According to the exponent rule $a^{-n} = \frac{1}{a^n}$, the expression 2^{-3} is equivalent to $\frac{1}{2^3}$. Since $2^3 = 2 \times 2 \times 2 = 8$, this expression is equivalent to $\frac{1}{8}$.

48. B: To answer this question, we first determine the total cost of the onions and carrots, since these prices are given. This will equal $2 \times \$3.69 + 3 \times \$4.29 = \$20.25$. Next, this sum is subtracted from the total cost of the vegetables to determine the cost of the mushrooms: $\$24.15 - \$20.25 = \$3.90$. Finally, the cost of the mushrooms is divided by the quantity in lbs to determine the cost per lb:

$$\text{Cost per lb} = \frac{\$3.90}{1.5} = \$2.60$$

Therefore, the mushrooms cost $2.60 per pound.

49. C: This question requires two steps. The first step is to determine the discounted earring price by multiplying $500 by 0.75 (75%, the amount that isn't taken off from the discount, as a decimal).

$$\$500 \times 0.75 = \$375$$

The second step is to use the birthday discount. With the birthday discount, she will still pay 95% (100%–5%) of the discounted price, so multiply $375 by 0.95.

$$\$375 \times 0.95 = \$356.25$$

Since this is Mary's birthday month, she pays $356.25 for the pair of earrings.

50. C: If $70, the amount used to buy more lemons, represents 35% of Herbert's earnings, then 1% corresponds to $\frac{\$70}{35} = \$2$. To determine how much profit he takes home, multiply the dollar amount that represents 1%, which is $2, by 15 to get $2 \times 15 = \$30$. Therefore, Herbert takes home $30 in profit.

51. A: Multiply 60 mph by 15 hours to find out how far he drove on Day 1:

$$60 \text{ mph} \times 15 \text{ hr} = 900 \text{ mi}$$

If he does the same on Day 2, he will have driven a total of 1,800 miles. He will have 200 miles left to go on a 2,000-mile trip.

52. C: Analyze each option to see if it can be further reduced. $\frac{6}{50}$ can be reduced to $\frac{3}{25}$ by dividing the numerator and denominator by 2, so it is not in lowest terms. $\frac{12}{100}$ can be reduced to $\frac{3}{25}$ by dividing the numerator and denominator by 4, so it is not in lowest terms. $\frac{12}{10}$ can be reduced to $\frac{6}{5}$ or $1\frac{1}{5}$ by dividing the numerator and denominator by 2, so it is not in lowest terms. $\frac{12}{4}$ can be rewritten as 3, so it is not in lowest terms. $\frac{3}{25}$ is the only fraction that cannot be simplified or rewritten as a mixed number, so it is the correct answer.

53. C: To solve, use the percentage increase formula.

$$\text{Percentage Increase} = \frac{\text{new} - \text{initial}}{\text{initial}} \times 100$$

In this case, the initial value is \$80, and the new value is \$120.

$$\text{Percentage Increase} = \frac{120 - 80}{80} \times 100 = \frac{40}{80} \times 100 = 50\%$$

Therefore, the total amount in her account increased by 50%.

54. A: To determine how many students will be absent, multiply the percentage of students who will be absent by the total number of students.

$$8\% \times 452 = 0.08 \times 452 = 36.16$$

Therefore, about 36 students will be absent on April 20.

55. E: If the first lap takes 50 seconds, the second one takes 20% more, or $T_2 = 1.2 \times T_1 = 1.2 \times 50 = 60$ seconds, where T_1 and T_2 are the times required for the first and second laps, respectively. Similarly, $T_3 = 1.2 \times T_2 = 1.2 \times 60 = 72$ seconds, the time required for the third lap. To find the total time, add the times for the three laps together: $50 + 60 + 72 = 182$ seconds.

56. C: The average is found by adding the four prices and then dividing by 4.

$$\frac{18.00 + 18.50 + 19.99 + 15.39}{4} = \frac{71.88}{4} = 17.97$$

So, the average price is \$17.97.

Praxis Practice Test #2

Reading

Refer to the following for questions 1 - 5:

Elementary grade students should be able to describe today's weather, as well as the climate of the area in which they live. Depending on their developmental level, students should be able to provide information about whether they live in a dry and hot climate, a tropical climate, or a climate with warm summers and cold winters, often referred to as a continental climate. Students should recognize there are a large number of factors that can affect climate such as: the land and water features of a region, ocean currents, the latitude of an area, and different landforms that may be present.

Students should be aware of how these aspects affect the climate. Elevation is an interesting subject for students to consider. Students should discuss how those areas with a high elevation and close proximity to the equator will experience climatic conditions that are different from those areas with a low elevation that are also located near the equator. Ocean currents can have an effect on a region's climate, and mountain ranges can buffer winds, often causing an area to be warmer than the same area without such wind shields. Teachers should strive to help students develop a clear understanding about how climate and weather are related but have different meanings.

1. According to the passage above, what is a true statement about students in elementary schools?
a. All students should be able to talk about the climate of their area and other areas.
b. All students should be able to describe current weather conditions.
c. All students should be able to tell how mountains affect climate.
d. All students should be able to explain how landforms affect climate.
e. All statements are true.

2. Which word best describes seasonal climate, like that of the northeast United States?
a. Tropical
b. Dry
c. Hot
d. Mild
e. Continental

3. According to the passage, what can mountains do to an area's climate?
a. Block the wind and make it mild
b. Block the wind and make it warmer
c. Increase the wind and make it milder
d. Increase the wind and make it warmer
e. Nothing

4. Of the choices listed, which one does NOT have an effect on an area's climate?
a. Weather balloons
b. Ocean currents
c. An area's elevation
d. Mountain ranges
e. Proximity to the equator

5. Which word best describes the relationship between the words weather and climate?

    a. They are synonyms
    b. They are antonyms
    c. They are homonyms
    d. They are homophones
    e. They are related words

Refer to the following for questions 6 - 8:

Vocational counseling at the high school level can be invaluable to students, especially those students who may not know the profession they would eventually like to pursue. Good vocational counseling can be very helpful to steer students to the major or career field that works best with their strengths and interests. Not all high schools have vocational counselors on staff, so in many places a school's guidance counselor will be responsible for this job too.

A skilled vocational counselor will first assist students in assessing those areas where they hold their highest interest and abilities. A number of evaluation instruments can be used to evaluate a student's talents, abilities, and personality traits, and often fields a student may not have considered previously will be discovered during this assessment.

6. Which of the following would be a good title for the passage?

    a. An Overview of Vocational Counseling
    b. Why Students Need Vocational Counseling
    c. The Duties of the Vocational Counselor
    d. The Counselor in the School
    e. The Value of the Vocational Counselor

7. According to the passage, the students who benefit most from vocational counseling tend to be:

    a. Those who use evaluation instruments.
    b. Those who are honest about their interests.
    c. Those who already know their eventual career choice.
    d. Those who have a vocational counselor in their school.
    e. Those who do not have a chosen profession.

8. The main purpose of the passage is to:

    a. Argue for vocational counseling as a career choice.
    b. Give positive and negative ideas about vocational counseling.
    c. Talk about evaluation instruments.
    d. Tell what vocational counseling can do for students.
    e. Provide reasons to have vocational counselors on-site.

Refer to the following for questions 9 - 10:

Delaying their initial entry to school can cause some children to actually fall behind their peers in learning. Some studies have shown differing early childhood academic achievement results when comparing children from low-income families with those living in middle-income homes. Children from low-income homes tend to begin school with weaker skills than their peers from more advantaged backgrounds. Holding young children back a year before they begin their academic career is sometimes thought to help them mature before beginning school. This practice may actually backfire for some of those children from low-income households. During the additional year at home, these children are thought to miss opportunities to cultivate the basic skills that they could develop while taking part in a learning environment – skills suggested to be absent in some low-income families.

9. According to the passage, which of the following is true?
a. Children from low-income homes are always weaker in basic skills than children from higher-income homes.
b. Holding children back a year from starting school is always a mistake.
c. Children from high-income homes often begin school with stronger basic skills than children from lower-income homes.
d. All kids benefit most from starting school on time.
e. Learning at school is preferable to learning at home.

10. What is the main purpose of this passage?
a. To persuade parents to have their kids begin school on time.
b. To explain the problems teachers have with some students.
c. To tell that not all students are starting school with the same basic skills.
d. To explain the disparity in basic skills when kids initially enter school.
e. To highlight the significant differences among students coming from high- and low-income households.

Refer to the following for question 11:

Title IX, part of the Higher Education Act, was signed into law by Richard Nixon in 1972. Title IX prohibited colleges and universities accepting Federal funds to discriminate against students based on gender. The law affected athletics by greatly enhancing and increasing the opportunities for women in college sports.

11. Which of the following would be a supporting detail which could add depth to the passage above?
a. The year after the legislation passed, women's participation in sports increased 45% from the year before.
b. Richard Nixon was eventually impeached for his role in the Watergate scandal.
c. The Summer and Winter Olympics were held later that year.
d. Many male sports heroes became famous during that time in history.
e. Some sports were not interesting to women.

Refer to the following for question 12:

It is important for students at all grade levels to be read aloud to daily at school. Teachers should read aloud for 20 minutes to a half hour and should choose books that encourage students' appreciation of literature, increase their vocabulary, and promote reading as an enjoyable activity. As the teacher reads aloud, he or she should encourage discussion of vocabulary words, story conflict, opinions of certain characters in the story, and predictions about what may happen next in the book.

12. According to the passage, all of the following statements are true EXCEPT:
a. Older students can still benefit from being read aloud to.
b. Student opinions are not as important as discussions about vocabulary words.
c. Predicting what will happen in a story is an important skill for all students.
d. Read-aloud books should contain challenging words.
e. Teachers should ask questions as they read.

Refer to the following for questions 13 - 14:

There are several important rules regarding Five Oaks guests' vehicles. Please ensure you understand and abide by these regulations and indicate such by initializing 5 and returning a copy of this sheet to the front office.

Parking tickets will be issued for those vehicles left in the main lot overnight. If you plan to spend the night at Five Oaks, please 10 ensure you have registered your vehicle, secured and displayed a window label, and are parked in the side lot. We cannot be responsible for tickets issued by the city Police Department.

15 If you are returning to Five Oaks after 11:00 p.m., please use the four-digit pass code to enter the side parking lot. This code changes every 48 hours and should be kept confidential.

20 Thank you for your attention to these rules which are in effect for your safety and the safety of others at Five Oaks.

13. According to the passage, which of the following is an example of going against regulations?
   a. Displaying a window label
   b. Parking in the side lot
   c. Using the pass code
   d. Registering a vehicle
   e. Overnight parking in the main lot

14. According to the passage, which of the following is NOT true?
   a. Five Oaks is a highly secure facility.
   b. The pass code is predictable.
   c. Police patrol the parking lot.
   d. The side lot is locked at night.
   e. In the past, some guests had cars towed.

Refer to the following for question 15:

The cloze exercise is an important component of students' reading comprehension process. When students read unfamiliar words, they often substitute what they believe to be a synonym to fill in that space in the sentence. The cloze activity asks the student to do essentially the same thing. As they complete a cloze exercise, students call on their prior knowledge and also use context clues within the sentence to fill in a blank as their comprehension of text is assessed.

15. Which of the following was not a reason for a cloze exercise?
   a. Assess spelling
   b. Assess text comprehension
   c. Assess vocabulary
   d. Assess use of context clues
   e. Assess synonym use

Refer to the following for question 16:

The Dawes Act was passed in 1887 and was designed with the goal of turning Native Americans into landowners and farmers. The federal law provided families with one of two options: 160 acres of reservation farm land or double that amount for cattle grazing. The land ownership was believed by the government to be a huge incentive for the Native Americans to take steps toward citizenship and become individuals rather than being dependent on their tribes. As the Native Americans accepted land, their hunting rights on reservation land were restricted. Since hunting and reservation life was an important component of Indian culture, these people were not altogether happy about the turn of events.

16. Which of the following facts is not a reason the government offered land to the Native Americans?
a. To help them become landowners
b. To help them become individuals
c. To help them maintain their rich culture
d. To help them become farmers
e. To help begin the citizenship process

Refer to the following for questions 17 - 18:

One component of good story writing is showing and not telling. Showing can be achieved through descriptions of settings and events, and through characters' appearances, words, and actions to show what is happening in the story rather than directly telling information as though the story is being narrated by the writer:

It was a cold and rainy morning. The first track meet of the season was scheduled for that day.

Instead of telling the reader information this way, it's often better to show the information. For example, the characters can show information through their words and actions:

Marissa shivered as she stood next to Jessica on the sidewalk. "Why didn't I bring my coat?" Marissa whined. "It's going to feel like this on the bus, too! And why does it have to rain the morning of our first track meet?"

"I know. I hope it isn't cancelled. I really wanted to see how my meet times were looking. I want to move up to a varsity slot so bad." Jessica huddled close to Marissa and craned her neck to look down the street. She glanced at her watch and frowned.

By having the two characters show the information, the reader has jumped right into the story and learned about the characters in the first few sentences.

17. Which of the following is NOT shown through the characters' words and actions?
a. The bus has not yet arrived to pick up the track team.
b. It is cold outside.
c. Marissa is on the varsity team, while Jessica is not.
d. Marissa and Jessica are friends.
e. Jessica cares about her performance.

18. What is a true statement about showing and not telling a story?
a. It is one component of good story writing.
b. It gives the writer's voice to the story.
c. It means providing factual information.
d. It always involves narrating a story.
e. It keeps the readers from knowing the characters.

Refer to the following for questions 19 - 22:

It is important for teachers to model and teach good science lab safety at every opportunity. Students need to be reminded that serious accidents and injuries can occur if they are not attentive to dangers present in the lab. Review practices students will use to take great care in the lab.

Understanding the experiment is an important component of lab safety. Encourage the students to reread the experiment steps a few times and to follow all directions precisely. There should be an adequate supply of safety goggles and students should use them when they are working with any chemicals, glassware, or hot materials. Good practice often dictates having students wear goggles and a lab apron at most times they are working in the science lab.

Students should wear plastic gloves when they are working with chemicals and should be aware of methods of disposing of used gloves. Oven mitts are essential equipment when students are working with heat or flames. Remind students that glass can get hot enough to cause serious burns. Glassware is present throughout a science lab and students should be careful to report broken or chipped glass and to refrain from touching any broken glass. Students should also exercise extreme care when working with knives, scissors, and other sharp and potentially dangerous equipment in the laboratory.

Students with long hair should make sure it is tied back and loose-fitting clothing (e.g., jackets, scarves) should be removed or secured when students are working with fire. Help students appreciate the ease and speed with which flammable materials can become extremely dangerous.

Show students how chemicals and non-reusable lab materials should be correctly disposed of and review the importance of following these guidelines. Provide adequate time at the end of a lab session for students to wash their hands carefully and thoroughly, whether they were wearing gloves or not. Students will be using these basic lab rules throughout their years in a lab – making sure they are using good practices now can ensure their appreciation for the lab and its materials for years to come.

19. Where would this passage most likely appear?
   a. In a student's high school handbook
   b. On a lab equipment label
   c. In the page immediately before each science experiment
   d. In a teacher's science text
   e. In a student's science text

20. Which sentence would be the best addition to paragraph 3?
   a. Glass does not change appearance when it is hot.
   b. Some students may misread instructions for an experiment.
   c. Students should complete lab reports after each experiment.
   d. Teachers should be trained in CPR.
   e. Students can get hurt in a lab.

21. What is the main idea of this passage?
   a. Accidents can happen in the lab.
   b. Good lab practices are important for students to learn.
   c. Teachers are responsible for teaching about lab equipment.
   d. Labs should have safety equipment.
   e. Students can learn quite a bit in the lab.

22. According to the passage, what is a true statement about the lab?

   a. If students are wearing gloves, they may not need to wash their hands.
   b. Broken glass can only be handled by those wearing oven mitts.
   c. Loose-fitting clothing may be unsafe to wear in a lab.
   d. Plastic gloves can protect users against heat.
   e. Teachers usually do not wear lab aprons.

Refer to the following for questions 23 - 24:

     Judith Sargent Murray's writings over two hundred years ago provided significant insight into perceptions about the intellectual differences between men and women. During Sargent's lifetime—the 1750s to 1820—men were often thought of as naturally intellectually superior to women. In her writing, Sargent argued that men were not mentally advantaged, they had been educated and that was the reason for their perceived intellectual superiority. Women of those colonial times were largely unschooled.

     Sargent contended that women were intellectual equals to men but that they needed the opportunity to be educated. Since they were the primary teachers for their children, Sargent asserted that when women were educated, the entire culture benefited.

23. Based on the facts in the passage, what prediction could you make about children of educated colonial women?

   a. They were smarter than children of uneducated colonial women.
   b. They were just as smart as children of uneducated colonial women.
   c. Their intelligence depended on their father's education level.
   d. Generalizations about children cannot be made.
   e. They were intellectually equal to their mother.

24. As used in the passage (beginning of paragraph 2), what does the word *contended* most nearly mean?

   a. Terminated
   b. Denied
   c. Concurred
   d. Valued
   e. Argued

Refer to the following for question 25:

     Desalination is a process used to convert sea water to drinkable water. It is used in those areas where there is a shortage of water for drinking, cooking, washing, and bathing. Although desalination works well and is not difficult to do, it is a very expensive process.

     To remove the salt from seawater, the water is first heated until it evaporates. The vapor formed during the evaporation process is put into contact with very cold pipes, causing it to turn back into water. The resulting water is free from salt and is drinkable.

25. Which of the following sentences would be a relevant detail to add to the first paragraph above?

   a. In those areas where it is used, desalination is a necessity.
   b. People have probably never heard of desalination.
   c. Most people would be shocked at its cost.
   d. Water is important to daily life.
   e. People should instead be conserving water.

Refer to the following for question 26:

When students take part in inquiry-based learning, most models prescribe first defining the problem. Students brainstorm inquiry questions to help them learn more about how to resolve the problem. Questions can take a variety of formats and will have varying degrees of usefulness.

Closed-ended questions, those that can be answered with a *yes*, *no*, or other one-word response, tend to provide the least amount of usable data. Open-ended questions, those that can have more than a few correct answers, yield the best information as students work to resolve their identified problem. Students will have to refer to an assortment of resources as they research possible answers to their question.

26. According to the passage, what is the best explanation for not asking close-ended questions?
   a. The teacher has to ask too many of them.
   b. They take too long to create.
   c. They only provide one-word responses.
   d. They do not define the problem.
   e. They are usually misunderstood by students.

Refer to the following for questions 27 - 28:

Print newspapers today are in survival mode. The past decade has been an unsettled one for national and local papers as online technology has provided enhanced opportunities for readers to get news. Add our country's current poor economy to the equation and publishers of most large national newspapers don't need to read quarterly figures. They know their circulation continues to fall.

Some newspapers have experimented with charging a fee for access to their online news. Successful subscription-based online newspapers have content that is both unique and valuable. Since many reputable websites offer their news at no charge and it is updated constantly, it is difficult for most newspapers to charge a fee and compete online. Print newspapers must figure out ways to keep their readers loyal, produce revenue, and stay viable in today's changing world. Most newspaper executives know that the window of time to adapt to the market narrows each week.

27. Based on the information given, what is the main reason for the decline of print newspapers?
   a. Rising costs
   b. Poor quality
   c. Changing interests
   d. The internet
   e. Fall in circulation

28. What does the last sentence of the passage most nearly imply?
   a. All newspapers will fail soon.
   b. Newspapers must act quickly to save the medium.
   c. The economy is not improving.
   d. Newspapers must set up websites.
   e. There are only a few newspapers left.

Refer to the following for question 29:

During both fission and fusion—two types of nuclear reactions—small quantities of matter are changed into large amounts of energy. Fission involves breaking down. One large nucleus is split into smaller pieces. Nuclear fission is commonly used as a form of energy.

With fusion two light nuclei fuse, or combine, to form one larger nucleus. Unlike fission, fusion has not been used as a reliable and useable alternate form of energy despite it being a powerful nuclear reaction that causes change.

29. What is true about both fission and fusion?
a. Both involve breaking down.
b. Both involve combining nuclei.
c. Both are commonly used as an energy source.
d. Both are unreliable.
e. Both are nuclear reactions.

Refer to the following for question 30:

China's Yangtze River (also known as the Chang) is the longest river in Asia. The Yangtze flows from Tibet, a mountainous region in southwest China, mainly eastward through the center of China, past the city of Shanghai, and finally emptying into the Pacific Ocean. Since the river is so long—about 4,000 miles—the Yangtze is an important transportation and trade route in China.

30. According to the passage, which statement is not true?
a. All other rivers in Asia must be less than 4,000 miles in length.
b. Tibet is west of Shanghai.
c. The Chang River is the longest river in China.
d. All shipping originates in Tibet.
e. All four statements are false.

Refer to the following for questions 31 - 32:

School vouchers were initially introduced as a solution for those students who were dissatisfied with their zoned public school. Vouchers provided those students with what can best be described as a grant to attend a more highly regarded private school in their area. Some schools in our country are under-performing. Educational assessments do not meet set minimum standards, so school vouchers were seen as one solution for dissatisfied students.

Vouchers do not always resolve the problem. Sometimes students may want to attend a private school but won't have transportation there. Other students may be content in their present underperforming school but are unsure what to do when their classmates leave. Jobs and funding may be lost if enough students leave a school, often eroding the school's performance further.

Since they do not take government funding, many private schools do not have to attain the same standards as public schools. Some private schools may not accept students who are not of a certain academic level and academically challenged students may not be helped at all by vouchers. Private schools often do not have trained teachers and programs in place to work with those students who need remediation or particular types of individualized instruction.

31. According to the passage, what does NOT typically happen when many students leave a particular underperforming school?

    a. New students are admitted at the same rate.
    b. The school population decreases.
    c. Schools lose government funding.
    d. The school becomes weaker.
    e. The staff loses jobs.

32. Which student may be most helped by the voucher system?

    a. An academically challenged student
    b. A student happy in his present school
    c. A student with friends at his school
    d. A student who is dissatisfied with his school
    e. A student with a private school near his present school

Refer to the following for questions 33 - 34:

As a plunger is depressed, air inside the wide rubber cup is pushed out. This depression action forms a strong, airtight seal around the top of a clogged pipe and the plunger cup is held fast by the air pressure of the user. Continued plunging—pressing down on the plunger—causes an increase in pressure inside the clogged pipe and will usually force out whatever may be causing the clog.

33. What word best describes the organization of this passage?

    a. Inferring
    b. Hypothesizing
    c. Explaining
    d. Observing
    e. Modeling

34. As used in the passage, what does the word "depressed" most nearly mean?

    a. Very unhappy
    b. Decreased appreciably
    c. Exhaled hard
    d. Ignored completely
    e. Pushed down

Refer to the following for question 35:

>   Blogs can be created and written on any subject and even about nothing. Bloggers, as those who write blogs are usually referred, may write a daily dose of wisdom about baseball, childrearing, looking for a job, looking for a boyfriend, or just about what they do every day.

>   Many bloggers hope to interest as many readers as they are able to. Serious bloggers, those who update their online journal with regularity, usually hope to gain and hold onto a regular audience.

35. According to the passage, which of the following statements is true?
a. Some bloggers do not update their blog regularly.
b. All bloggers want many readers.
c. Serious bloggers write on serious subjects.
d. Bloggers need a defined subject to write on.
e. Bloggers are people who read blogs.

Refer to the following for questions 36 - 39:

Conflict mediation in many schools requires staff to use specific problem-solving strategies. These tactics are employed with the students involved in the conflict and a teacher or student acting as mediator. A student is a peer mediator and has been trained in conflict resolution. The student mediator uses specific prompts to encourage the involved students to brainstorm ways to resolve the problem. The students are guided to work toward a resolution they both are comfortable with. This meeting of the minds does not always successfully resolve the conflict but is usually considered a positive step to attempt to have students work out problems in a mature and socially acceptable way.

36. According to the passage, who must act as a mediator?
a. An administrator
b. Teacher or student
c. Teacher
d. Student
e. Someone directly involved

37. What is true about conflict mediation?
a. It always creates a successful resolution.
b. It rarely works as it is supposed to.
c. It involves separating problem students.
d. It solves problems among peer mediators.
e. It involves specific strategies.

38. As used in the passage, what does the word "prompt" most nearly mean?
a. Suggestion
b. Punctual
c. Brainstorm
d. Time saver
e. Rapid

39. What is true of the resolution within a conflict resolution session?

    a.   One mediator creates the resolution.

    b.   It is one that will work quickly.

    c.   It is usually one that will separate the students.

    d.   It is one that both parties will agree with.

    e.   It is one that is guaranteed to be successful.

Refer to the following for questions 40 - 45:

    Introductions between two professional people who do not know each other involve introducing the lowest-ranked person (often the youngest) to the higher-ranking person. A new teacher aide at a school would be introduced to the principal:

Ellen, this is Jane Wilson. Jane is working in Pete Richards' classroom and comes to us from Reed Elementary.

    Then introduce the two people in reverse:

Jane, Ellen Kennedy is our school's principal. She has been with East Side High for the past seven years. Ellen's office is right over there.

    Sometimes a person's name is tricky. The correct pronunciation or the name to be used should be clarified as part of the introduction:

Karen, I'd like you to meet Angelique DeMarco. Angie will be working as a student teacher for the next three months in Chris Maxwell's first grade classroom.

George, this is Illiyo Lee. Illiyo goes by the name Ellie. She is visiting our school this week from Tokyo.

    In reverse:

Ellie, George Smith is our district's curriculum director. George's office is here in our school and I'm sure he will be happy to answer any questions you may have this week.

    Making introductions deliberately and correctly puts everyone at ease. Sometimes the person making the introduction may feel uncomfortable in the role, but those being introduced will be grateful for the time taken to put them at ease.

40. A bank president is being introduced to a new hire. Who is introduced to whom?

    a.   The bank president is introduced to the new hire.

    b.   The new hire is introduced to the bank president.

    c.   The older of the two is introduced to the younger of the two.

    d.   The younger of the two is introduced to the older of the two.

    e.   It does not matter.

41. According to the passage, what usually occurs after one person is introduced to another?

    a.   They are introduced in reverse.

    b.   They are asked their names.

    c.   They are invited to shake hands.

    d.   They go back to what they were doing.

    e.   They pronounce their names.

42. According to the passage, what should be done if a person has a difficult name to pronounce?

a. Skip that part of her name
b. Make a joke about it
c. Clarify the correct way to say it
d. Ask the person to say it
e. Use an initial

43. When are formal introductions most often used?

a. In all settings
b. In a casual setting
c. In a professional setting
d. In a school setting
e. In an uncomfortable setting

44. What is the usual goal for introducing two people?

a. Make those involved more comfortable
b. Review business protocol
c. Take time in a meeting
d. Ensure the highest-ranking person knows everyone
e. Ensure the lowest-ranking person knows everyone

45. A city government official and an administrative assistant will be introduced. Who does the introducing?

a. The city government official
b. The administrative assistant
c. A third person
d. Both the city government official and the administrative assistant
e. It does not matter

Refer to the following for questions 46 - 48:

About 17 million children and adults in the United States suffer from asthma, a condition that makes it hard to breathe. Today it is a problem that is treatable with modern medicine. In days gone by, there were many different superstitions about how to cure asthma. Some people thought that eating crickets with a little wine would help. Eating raw cat's meat might be the cure. Another idea was to try gathering some spiders' webs, rolling them into a ball, and then swallowing them. People also thought that if you ate a diet of only boiled carrots for two weeks, your asthma might go away. This carrot diet may have done some good for asthma patients, since the vitamin A in carrots is good for the lungs.

46. Which of the following would be a good title for the passage?

a. Asthma in the United States
b. Methods of Treating Asthma
c. Old Wives' Tales
d. Superstitions about Asthma
e. Carrot Diets

47. The fact that 17 million children and adults in the United States suffer from asthma is probably the opening sentence of the passage because:

a. It explains why people in times gone by might have found a need to try homemade cures.
b. It creates a contrast between today and the past.
c. It lets the reader know that many people have asthma.
d. It is a warning that anyone could get asthma.
e. Asthma makes it hard to breathe.

48. The main purpose of the passage is to:

a. Describe herbal remedies
b. Explain some of the measures for treating asthma from long ago
c. Define superstitions
d. Extol the virtues of modern medicine
e. Explain why asthma came about

Refer to the following for questions 49 - 50:

In the 1970s, Buffalo Point became part of a public park. Since that time, the area has been flooded many times in such a way that the landscape was changed. There is a boat landing on the Buffalo River which periodically changes due to high water moving gravel either on or off of the land, and as people go there for recreational purposes they may see changes annually. The boat landing is next to Painted Bluff, so called because it is splashed with shades of brown and gray. The top half of Painted Bluff is St. Peter Sandstone, while the bottom is dolomite. Painted Bluff towers up to 320 feet over the river, but the majority of the bluff cannot be seen due to plant life that grows over approximately the 70-foot mark.

49. According to the passage, which of the following is true?

a. You cannot know what Buffalo Point will look like from year to year.
b. You cannot know what Painted Bluff will look like from year to year.
c. High water takes gravel away from the boat landing every year.
d. Painted Bluff is formed entirely from dolomite.
e. Painted Bluff goes up around 70 feet over the Buffalo River.

50. What is the main purpose of this passage?

a. To describe Painted Bluff
b. To explain why the boat landing is unsafe
c. To describe Buffalo Point
d. To point out that Buffalo Point is a public recreational area
e. To discuss public parks from the 1970s

Refer to the following for questions 51 - 52:

During the last 100 years of medical science, the drugs that have been developed have altered the way people live all over the world. Over-the-counter and prescription drugs are now the key for dealing with diseases, bodily harm, and medical issues. Drugs like these are used to add longevity and quality to people's lives. But not all drugs are healthy for every person. A drug does not necessarily have to be illegal to be abused or misused. Some ways that drugs are misused include taking more or less of the drug than is needed, using a drug that is meant for another person, taking a drug for longer than needed, taking two or more drugs at a time, or using a drug for a reason that has nothing to do with being healthy. Thousands of people die from drug misuse or abuse every year in the United States.

51. According to the passage, which of the following is an example of misusing a drug?
   a. taking more of a prescription drug than the doctor ordered
   b. taking an antibiotic to kill harmful bacteria
   c. experiencing a side effect from an over-the-counter drug
   d. throwing away a medication that has passed the expiration date
   e. not using a childproof lid

52. According to the passage, which of the following is not true?
   a. over-the-counter drugs are used for medical issues
   b. every year, thousands of people in the United States die due to using drugs the wrong way
   c. medical science has come a long way in the last century
   d. all drugs add longevity to a person's life
   e. legal drugs are sometimes abused

Refer to the following for questions 53 - 54:

In 1954, the US Supreme Court overturned the doctrine of "separate but equal" in the landmark case of *Brown v. Board of Education*. From that point on, segregation in schools was illegal. But the Civil Rights movement began long before that. The NAACP worked for decades in opposition to segregated schools and in favor of equality before *Brown v. Board of Education* occurred. Booker T. Washington was a strong African American (who had a white father) that had been born into slavery and grew up to become a dominant leader. He definitely wanted a better future for black people, but he thought blacks should work together and be non-confrontational. He did a lot to progress working relationships between black and white people. Washington actually kept the NAACP from being developed in southern states, because he was staunchly in favor of people doing for themselves and not depending on others. After his death the organization popped up all over the south. When the *Brown v. Board of Education* decision happened, many white people were totally surprised. Not so in the African American community.

53. According to the passage, what happened in 1954?
   a. "Separate but equal" was established
   b. The Supreme Court determined that "separate but equal" was legal
   c. "Separate but equal" was overturned
   d. Booker T. Washington was born
   e. The Civil Rights movement was made illegal

54. How did many white people feel when the *Brown v. Board of Education* decision was reached?
 a. In favor
 b. In opposition
 c. Nonconfrontational
 d. Dominant
 e. Surprised

Refer to the following for questions 55 - 56:

In April 1917, the United States declared war on Germany. A considerable number of people were not certain that it was needed, and some were against it. The war was generally opposed by progressives and socialists, as well as a number of ordinary civilians. Many who were against going to war were just regular people that didn't want to be drafted or who were against the war due to religious reasons.

The Council of National Defense worked at putting out propaganda. A Committee on Public Information dispensed publications, arranged for speakers, and managed the corps of Four Minute Men. The latter went around giving short speeches in theaters, schools, and churches. The purpose of the speeches was to portray the war in a positive light and promote war activities, such as war savings stamp campaigns, liberty loan campaigns, and Red Cross efforts.

All over the United States there was national hysteria about the war. People became overzealous with anti-German and anti-immigrant thoughts and actions. Here are some examples of the mob-mentality obsession:

- Most schools no longer allowed German for foreign-language instruction.
- "Liberty cabbage" was suggested to replace the word "sauerkraut."
- German measles was occasionally called "liberty measles."
- At the symphony, music composed by Germans was commonly not allowed.
- A lot of German-Americans could not keep or find jobs and were shunned by community members.
- South Dakota banned German as a language to be used on the phone.

The efforts at patriotism even went so far as to cause violence and "patriotic murder." People who were opposed to the war or government were also targets, even if they were not German. People were afraid of insurrection and full of illogical hatred. The Espionage Act, Trading with the Enemy Act, and Sedition Act are examples of how far people were willing to go in trying to be patriotic.

The climate of the times had been created by the war and the propaganda being spread so thoroughly throughout the country. It was very hard for a true conscientious objector to find a way through the mire of mob mentality. The country was in a patriotic frenzy, and innocent people lost their rights to freedom and free speech because of it.

55. Which of the following is NOT an example of mob mentality as listed in the passage?
 a. Renaming the German measles
 b. Allowing German music at the symphony
 c. German-Americans being unable to find jobs
 d. Not allowing the German language on the phone
 e. Patriotic murder

56. Which of the following lists people who were opposed to war?

a. Progressives, socialists, and certain groups of religious people
b. Progressives, socialists, and the military
c. The Council of National Defense, South Dakota, and mobs
d. Mobs and schools
e. All people who were drafted

Writing

Refer to the following for questions 1 - 40:

Select the best version of the underlined part of the sentence. If you think the original sentence is best, choose the first answer.

1. <u>She sang beautiful</u> despite her sadness.

a. She sang beautiful
b. She sings beautiful
c. She sings beautifully
d. She sang beautifully
e. She sung beautiful

2. <u>One of our bicycles are</u> missing.

a. One of our bicycles are
b. One of our bicycles is
c. One of our bicycles, are
d. One, of our bicycles, are
e. One, of our bicycles, is

3. <u>"Are you Don Adams," he asked?</u>

a. "Are you Don Adams," he asked?
b. "Are you Don Adams?" He asked.
c. "Are you Don Adams?," he asked.
d. "Are you Don Adams," He asked?
e. "Are you Don Adams?" he asked.

4. We have enough students for another <u>Science, English, and Health class.</u>

a. Science, English, and Health class.
b. Science, English, and health class.
c. science, English, and Health class.
d. science, english, and health class.
e. science, English, and health class.

5. <u>We had spaghetti and meatballs, garlic bread, and salad.</u>

a. We had spaghetti and meatballs, garlic bread, and salad.
b. We had spaghetti, and meatballs, garlic bread, and salad.
c. We had, spaghetti and meatballs, garlic bread and salad.
d. We had, spaghetti, and meatballs, garlic bread, and salad.
e. We had spaghetti and meatballs; garlic bread, and salad.

6. When he accepted the award, Mr. Stewart said "that he had never been so wonderfully honored in his life."

a. said "that he had never been so wonderfully honored in my life."
b. said that "he had never been so wonderfully honored in his life."
c. said that "he had never been so wonderfully honored in my life."
d. said that he had "never been so wonderfully honored in my life."
e. said that he had never been so wonderfully honored in his life.

7. George sounded excited as he tells his mother about the trip to the factory.

a. George sounded excited as he tells his mother
b. George sounded excited and he tells his mother
c. George sounds excited as he told his mother
d. George sounds excited and he told his mother
e. George sounded excited as he told his mother

8. Feeling weak after running in the long race.

a. Feeling weak after running in the long race.
b. Feeling weak since she had been running in the long race.
c. Feeling weak on account of running in the long race.
d. She was feeling weak on account of running in the long race.
e. She was feeling weak after running in the long race.

9. The leaves were raked all day by Sergio and Gina.

a. The leaves were raked all day by Sergio and Gina.
b. The leaves were being raked all day by Sergio and Gina.
c. Sergio and Gina raked leaves all day.
d. Sergio and Gina had raked leaves all day.
e. Leaves were raked all day by Sergio and Gina.

10. Her hand-sewn dress was beautiful she was proud to wear it to the dinner party.

a. Her hand-sewn dress was beautiful she was proud to wear it to the dinner party.
b. Her hand-sewn dress was beautiful, she was proud to wear it to the dinner party.
c. Her hand-sewn dress was beautiful; she was proud to wear it to the dinner party.
d. Her hand-sewn dress was beautiful so that therefore she was proud to wear it to the dinner party.
e. Her hand-sewn dress was beautiful but she was proud to wear it to the dinner party.

11. "I hope we find Boots." "He'll be a hungry and tired cat if he spends the night out here,"

a. "I hope we find Boots." "He'll be a hungry and tired cat if he spends the night out here,"
b. "I hope we find Boots." He'll be a hungry and tired cat if he spends the night out here,"
c. "I hope we find Boots. "He'll be a hungry and tired cat if he spends the night out here,"
d. "I hope we find Boots. He'll be a hungry and tired cat if he spends the night out here,"
e. "I hope we find Boots" "He'll be a hungry and tired cat if he spends the night out here,"

12. Two of our dogs like to bark at the vacuum cleaner.

a. Two of our dogs like to bark
b. Two of our dog's like to bark
c. Two of our dogs' like to bark
d. Two of our dogs like to "bark"
e. Two of our dog's like to "bark"

13. Driving <u>past the park, the new swimming pool was seen</u>.

    a. past the park, the new swimming pool was seen.
    b. past the park, he is seeing the new swimming pool.
    c. past the park, the new swimming pool was shown.
    d. past the park, he saw the new swimming pool.
    e. past the park, the new swimming pool was seen by him.

14. All of the revisions need to be <u>approved by Ellen Jackson and I</u>.

    a. approved by Ellen Jackson and I.
    b. approved by Ellen Jackson and myself.
    c. approved by myself and Ellen Jackson.
    d. approved by Ellen Jackson and me.
    e. approved by I and Ellen Jackson.

15. <u>It was he who wrote the email.</u>

    a. It was he who wrote the email.
    b. It was him who wrote the email.
    c. It was himself who wrote the email.
    d. It was him who had written the email.
    e. It was he who had written the email.

16. The <u>scout leader, who had been standing in the road, were</u> hurt in the collision.

    a. scout leader. who had been standing in the road, were
    b. scout leader who had been standing in the road were
    c. scout leader, who had been standing in the road was
    d. scout leader, who had been standing in the road, was
    e. scout leader who had been standing in the road was being

17. <u>Using foreign coins is not permitted in our store.</u>

    a. Using foreign coins is not permitted in our store.
    b. Using foreign coins are not permitted in our store.
    c. To be using foreign coins is not permitted in our store.
    d. To be using foreign coins are not permitted in our store.
    e. Using foreign coins, they are not permitted in our store.

18. <u>The turtle trapped himself inside our screened-in porch.</u>

    a. The turtle trapped himself inside our screened-in porch.
    b. The turtle had trapped himself inside our screened-in porch.
    c. The turtle trapped him- or herself inside our screened-in porch.
    d. The turtle trapped itself inside our screened-in porch.
    e. The turtle had been trapping itself inside our screened-in porch.

19. <u>"Does your salad taste okay," she asked?</u>

    a. "Does your salad taste okay," she asked?
    b. "Does your salad taste okay," She asked?
    c. "Does your salad taste okay?" she asked.
    d. "Does your salad taste okay?," she asked.
    e. "Does your salad taste okay." She asked.

20. Most students missed <u>Spanish, Math, and Science today.</u>

    a. Spanish, Math, and Science today.
    b. Spanish, math, and Science today.
    c. Spanish, Math, and science today.
    d. Spanish, math, and science today.
    e. spanish, math, and science today.

21. She passed <u>the salt and pepper, the butter, and the ketchup to</u> the other table.

    a. the salt and pepper, the butter, and the ketchup to
    b. the salt, and pepper, the butter, and the ketchup to
    c. the salt and pepper, the butter and the ketchup to
    d. the salt, and pepper, the butter, and the ketchup, to
    e. the salt and pepper, the butter, and the ketchup, to

22. Minerals are nutritionally significant elements <u>that assist to make your body</u> work properly.

    a. that assist to make your body
    b. that help your body
    c. that making your body
    d. that work to make your body
    e. that hinder your body to

23. Of the two, <u>the oldest brother</u> had a much more difficult time in school.

    a. the oldest brother
    b. the older brother
    c. the earliest brother
    d. the best brother
    e. the better brother

24. The duck waddled toward the pond, her five ducklings following just behind her.

    a. her five ducklings following just behind her
    b. and then there were five ducklings following in back of her
    c. therefore the ducklings were following behind
    d. and so her five ducklings were following just behind her
    e. her five ducklings

25. <u>Fair teachers understand that he or she</u> cannot treat any student with favoritism.

    a. Fair teachers understand that he or she
    b. Fair teachers understand that he
    c. Fair teachers understand that she
    d. Fair teachers understand that they
    e. Fair teachers understand that their

26. We will begin with painting <u>first, and then secondly</u> we will start the decoupage process.

    a. first, and then secondly
    b. firstly, and then secondly
    c. first, and then second
    d. first, then second
    e. first, second

27. The hidden passageway in the bowels of the castle <u>remained a well kept secret</u>.

a. remained a well kept secret
b. remained a well-kept secret
c. remained a wellkept secret
d. was always going to be a secret
e. would always be a secret

28. Another view of the test results had been planned to be provided by a different doctor.

a. Another view of the test results had been planned to be provided by a different doctor.
b. She will need to get new test results from a different doctor.
c. A different doctor has planned to provide another view of the test results.
d. Several new views of the results are provided and planned with a different doctor.
e. A couple of views of the test results are planned to be provided by a different doctor.

29. <u>I dare not whisper</u> the deadly secret to a single soul.

a. I dare not whisper
b. I should not whisper
c. I cannot tell anyone
d. I swore not to tell
e. I whispered

30. The scientist said we did need not trouble our minds with trivial details.

a. The scientist said we did need not trouble
b. The scientist said we did not trouble
c. The scientist said do not worry
d. The scientist did not need to do
e. The scientist said we need not trouble

31. Every teacher ought set a good example for his or her students.

a. Every teacher ought set a good example
b. Every teacher ought to set a good example
c. Teachers are required to set a good example
d. It is important for teachers to set good examples
e. One teachers should set a good example

32. The Math Committee worked to make sure students <u>had options to participate in</u> contests, book work, computer games or memory practice games.

a. had options to participate in
b. met the requirements for
c. were allowed to do
d. could choose one of the following:
e. opted to do one of the following:

33. Forgetting to feed the dog was a honest mistake.

a. Forgetting to feed the dog was a honest mistake.
b. She honestly forgot to feed the dog.
c. The dog went hungry.
d. Forgetting to feed the dog was an honest mistake.
e. Forgetting to feed her dog was an honest mistake.

34. On his first day at the news station, the new anchorman had to determine <u>where his desk was at</u>.

    a.   where his desk was at

    b.   the location of the desk

    c.   which desk would belong to him

    d.   what to put on his new desk

    e.   where his desk was

35. The gentleness of the summer sky while the buttercups shined like the stars.

    a.   The gentleness of the summer sky while the buttercups shined like the stars.

    b.   The buttercups shone like stars against the gentle summer sky.

    c.   The gentle summer sky even as the buttercups shined as though they were stars.

    d.   The summer sky gentleness while the buttercups shined like the stars.

    e.   The gentleness of the summer sky at the same time that the buttercups shined like the stars.

36. He got up bright and early and he spent a whole hour taking a shower.

    a.   He got up bright and early and he spent

    b.   He got up as early as he could and he took

    c.   He arose before the dawn; and he spent

    d.   He got up bright, and early, and he spent

    e.   He got up bright and early, and he spent

37. The principal added an additional break time into the teachers' busy schedules.

    a.   The principal added an additional break time

    b.   The principal decided that he needed to add another break time

    c.   The principal added another break time

    d.   The principal added a third break time

    e.   The principal gave the teachers another break time

38. The cow cumbersome crossed the wide, grassy field.

    a.   The cow cumbersome crossed the wide, grassy field.

    b.   The cow cumbersome crossed the wide grassy field.

    c.   The cow cumbersomely crossed the wide, grassy field.

    d.   The cow did his best to cross the wide, grassy field.

    e.   The cow went across the field.

39. The girl was so popular in her own school <u>that the other students treated her like a God</u>.

    a.   that the other students treated her like a God.

    b.   that the other students treated her like a god.

    c.   and so all the other students wanted her to be a god.

    d.   that she thought she was a god.

    e.   that she felt like a god.

40. Cecile White is from Sylacauga, Alabama, the teacher of the year.

    a.   Cecile White is from Sylacauga, Alabama, the teacher of the year.

    b.   Cecile White is the teacher of the year and was from Sylacauga, Alabama.

    c.   Cecile White, who is from Sylacauga, Alabama, is the teacher of the year.

    d.   Cecile White was the teacher of the year in Sylacauga, Alabama.

    e.   Although Cecile White is from Sylacauga, Alabama, she is the teacher of the year.

Refer to the following for question 41:

PASSAGE A

Thank you for contacting me to express your concerns over the proposed elimination of the EPA's Clean Power Plan, which seeks to reduce carbon pollution by power plants and address the risks of climate change. I welcome feedback from my constituents and I appreciate your interest in this issue. I am pleased to tell you that I am a staunch advocate for addressing climate change and that I would oppose any measure that sought to eliminate the Environmental Protection Agency's Clean Power Plan.

President Barack Obama proposed the Clean Power Plan in June 2014 as a part of his Climate Change Action Plan. The Clean Power Plan sets standards for carbon pollution from power plants and could result in a 30 percent reduction in carbon pollution from the power sector by 2030. Climate change has the potential to cause a tremendous amount of potentially catastrophic consequences for people around the world. Scientists agree that human action, such as carbon pollution by power plants, is the cause for a majority of the current warming. While the situation is an increasing cause for concern, most scientists also agree that it is not too late to take action to stop this serious threat to our planet. Climate change is a cause for national concern, requiring national solutions, and as your Congressman, I will support legislation that seeks to stop the causes and to moderate the effects of climate change.

I am honored to be your representative in Congress and I hope that my office can be a useful resource for you now and in the future. For more information, please visit my office online at www.HankJohnson.house.gov and do not hesitate to contact me if you have any future questions or concerns.

Sincerely,

Henry C. "Hank" Johnson, Jr.
Member of Congress

PASSAGE B

Thank you for contacting me regarding the Environmental Protection Agency's (EPA) Clean Power regulations. I appreciate hearing from you and am grateful for the opportunity to respond.

The Clean Power regulations were introduced by the EPA on August 3, 2015. Under these regulations, existing power plants will be required to reduce their emissions 32 percent by 2030 and must submit a plan outlining their strategy for doing so by 2016. States also have the option to engage in a regional "cap and trade" system where emission credits can be traded in order to ease states' transition to new emission standards.

The authority to impose federal carbon mandates lies with Congress, not the EPA. These regulations will ultimately result in what could be called an "energy tax" that will be felt in the form of higher electricity bills for consumers. I share your concerns with overreaching rules and regulations promulgated by unelected officials at the EPA and have been actively fighting them in the Senate. Coal-fired power plants provide 36 percent of Georgia's electricity and support nearly 8,800 Georgia jobs. When these Clean Power regulations were originally proposed in 2014, I wrote a letter to the EPA expressing my concern over the detrimental impact the rule would have on electricity providers, consumers and the US economy as a whole.

On May 13, 2015, I cosponsored S.1324, the *Affordable Reliable Electricity Now Act of 2015*. This bill would allow states to opt out of the Clean Power regulations. The implementation of these regulations would also be halted until states that have filed lawsuits against the EPA have completed their proceedings, and the federal government would be prohibited from withholding highway funding from states that fail to submit an implementation strategy. I will keep your thoughts and concerns in mind if the *Affordable Reliable Electricity Now Act* is brought to the Senate floor for consideration.

Thank you again for contacting me. Please visit my webpage at http://isakson.senate.gov/ for more information on the issues important to you and to sign up for my e-newsletter.

Sincerely,

Johnny Isakson

United States Senator

GRAPHIC

41. In an essay of approximately 100-200 words, identify which passage argues more effectively. Identify which specific claims each writer makes. Identify what evidence each provides to support his claims, and evaluate whether that evidence is sufficient, relevant, and valid. Support this evaluation using examples from each of the passages. Write your essay for an adult, educated audience in your own words (except for quotations). Your final draft should adhere to standard American English writing conventions.

42. There is at present a heated debate over the role of the United States in foreign affairs. Some experts argue that the cost and unintended consequences of American intervention are so great that the United States should simply mind its own business. Others assert that America's economic and political power necessitate foreign intervention, both to protect American interests and human rights. Another group derides these opposing views as condescending to the people of other countries, and suggests that the United States consult with foreign countries before becoming involved in their affairs.

In an organized, coherent, and supported essay explain what you think the United States should do and why it should do so. Address the pros and cons.

Mathematics

1. Giselle is selling notebooks at the school store. She earns $45.00 for selling 30 notebooks. How much is Giselle charging for each notebook?

    a. $135.00
    b. $3.00
    c. $1.25
    d. $3.50
    e. $1.50

Refer to the following for question 2:

Kyle bats third in the batting order for the Badgers baseball team. The table below shows the number of hits that Kyle had in each of 7 consecutive games played during one week in July.

Day	Monday	Tuesday	Wednesday	Thursday	Friday	Saturday	Sunday
Hits	1	2	3	1	1	4	2

2. What is the mode of the numbers in the distribution shown in the table?

    a. 1
    b. 2
    c. 3
    d. 4
    e. 7

3. Find the mean of the data set $\{76, 193, 83, 43, 105\}$.

    a. 80
    b. 83
    c. 100
    d. 150
    e. 500

4. A regular deck of cards has 52 cards, four of which are aces. What is the chance of drawing three aces in a row?

    a. $\frac{1}{52}$
    b. $\frac{1}{156}$
    c. $\frac{1}{2,000}$
    d. $\frac{1}{5,525}$
    e. $\frac{1}{132,600}$

5. A combination lock uses a three-digit code. Each digit can be any one of the ten available integers 0–9. How many different combinations are possible?

    a. 1,000
    b. 100
    c. 81
    d. 30
    e. 9

6. Consider the data set {196, 832, 736, 271, and 573}. Which of the following best describes the range of the data set?

    a. 377
    b. 636
    c. 1,028
    d. 5
    e. 573

7. Find the mode(s) of the data set {84, 29, 84, 93, 93, 84, 39, 84, 29, 93, 93, 29}.

    a. 84
    b. 93
    c. 29
    d. 84 and 93
    e. 29, 84, and 93

8. Find and interpret the range for the data set {78, 29, 57, 10, 3, 84}.

    a. The range of the data set is 6, which means that the values differ by a maximum of 6.
    b. The range of the data set is 43.5, which means the average value in the set is 43.5.
    c. The range of the data set is 81, which means the values of the set differ by no more than 81 units.
    d. The range of the data set is 13.5, which means that the standard deviation is less than 13.5.
    e. The range of the data set is 43, which means the middle number is 43.

9. Given the table below, which of the following best represents the probability that a student is enrolled at TAMU or prefers lattes?

	Latte	Cappuccino	Frappuccino	Total
TAMU	350	225	175	750
NMSU	325	300	275	900
Total	675	525	450	1,650

    a. 55%
    b. 60%
    c. 65%
    d. 70%
    e. 75%

10. In a game of chance, 3 dice are thrown at the same time. What is the probability that all three will land on a 6?

    a. $\frac{1}{6}$
    b. $\frac{1}{18}$
    c. $\frac{1}{30}$
    d. $\frac{1}{36}$
    e. $\frac{1}{216}$

11. Solve for x:

$$(2x - 3) + 2x = 9$$

   a. 1
   b. −2
   c. 3
   d. −3
   e. 2

12. What is the value of x in the following equation?

$$15 - x = 78$$

   a. 5.2
   b. 63
   c. −63
   d. 93
   e. −93

13. Which of the following could be a graph of the function $y = \frac{1}{x}$?

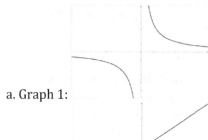

   a. Graph 1:

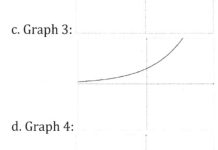

   b. Graph 2:

   c. Graph 3:

   d. Graph 4:

   e. Graph 5:

14. What is the value of y in the following equation?

$$4y + 16 = 60$$

a. 4
b. 11
c. 12
d. 15
e. 19

15. Given the equation $\frac{3}{y-5} = \frac{15}{y+4}$, what is the value of y?

a. $\frac{4}{45}$
b. $\frac{4}{29}$
c. $\frac{29}{4}$
d. 45
e. 54

16. Rafael has a business selling computers. He buys computers from the manufacturer for $450 each and sells them for $800. Each month, he must also pay fixed costs of $3,000 for rent and utilities at his store. If he sells n computers in a month, which of the following equations can be used to calculate his profit?

a. $P = n(\$800 - \$450)$
b. $P = n(\$800 - \$450 - \$3,000)$
c. $P = \$3,000 \times n(\$800 - \$450)$
d. $P = n(\$800 - \$450) - \$3,000$
e. $P = n(\$800 - \$450) + \$3,000$

17. Which of the following expressions is equivalent to $3\left(\frac{6x-3}{3}\right) - 3(9x + 9)$?

a. $-3(7x + 10)$
b. $-3x + 6$
c. $(x + 3)(x - 3)$
d. $3x^2 - 9$
e. $15x - 9$

18. If $A = \begin{bmatrix} 1 & -3 \\ -4 & 2 \end{bmatrix}$ and $B = \begin{bmatrix} 1 & -3 \\ -4 & -2 \end{bmatrix}$, then what is $A - B$?

a. $\begin{bmatrix} 2 & -6 \\ -8 & 0 \end{bmatrix}$
b. $\begin{bmatrix} 0 & 0 \\ 0 & 0 \end{bmatrix}$
c. $\begin{bmatrix} 0 & 0 \\ 0 & 4 \end{bmatrix}$
d. $\begin{bmatrix} 0 & 3 \\ 4 & 2 \end{bmatrix}$
e. $\begin{bmatrix} 0 & -6 \\ -8 & 4 \end{bmatrix}$

19. What is the approximate area of the shaded region between the circle and the square in the figure shown below? Use 3.14 for π.

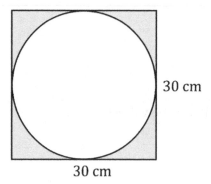

30 cm

30 cm

    a.   177 cm^2
    b.   181 cm^2
    c.   187 cm^2
    d.   190 cm^2
    e.   193 cm^2

20. A triangle has angles measuring 40°, 100°, and 40°. Which of the following choices accurately describes the triangle?

    a.   It is an acute equilateral triangle.
    b.   It is an acute isosceles triangle.
    c.   It is an obtuse isosceles triangle.
    d.   It is an acute scalene triangle.
    e.   It is an obtuse scalene triangle.

21. A rainbow pattern is designed from semi-circles as shown below.

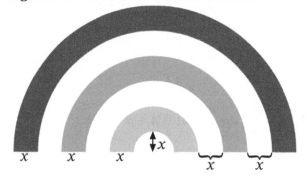

x x x x x x

Which of the following gives the area A of the shaded region as a function of x?

    a. $A = \frac{21x^2\pi}{2}$
    b. $A = 21x^2\pi$
    c. $A = 42x^2\pi$
    d. $A = 82x^2\pi$
    e. $A = \frac{21x^2\pi}{4}$

22. The letter H exhibits symmetry with respect to a horizontal axis, as shown in the figure, as everything below the dashed line is a mirror image of everything above it. Which of the following letters does NOT exhibit horizontal symmetry?

a. C
b. D
c. E
d. I
e. Z

23. The volume of a rectangular box is found by multiplying its length, width, and height. If the dimensions of a box are $\sqrt{3}$, $2\sqrt{5}$, and 4, what is its volume?

a. $2\sqrt{60}$
b. $2\sqrt{15}$
c. $4\sqrt{15}$
d. $8\sqrt{15}$
e. $24\sqrt{5}$

24. Which pair of angles is equal to 180°?

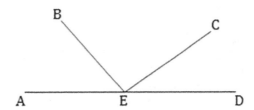

a. ∠AEB and ∠BEC
b. ∠CED and ∠BEC
c. ∠AEB and ∠CED
d. ∠AEC and ∠BED
e. ∠AEB and ∠BED

25. Express the area of the given right triangle as a function of x.

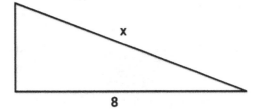

a. $A(x) = 4x$
b. $A(x) = \dfrac{x\sqrt{64-x^2}}{2}$
c. $A(x) = 4\sqrt{x^2 - 64}$
d. $A(x) = 64 - \sqrt{x^2}$

295

e. $A(x) = 32 - \sqrt{\frac{1}{2}x^2}$

26. Triangle ABC below is an equilateral triangle, not drawn to scale. Which statement is true about side BC?

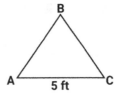

a.   It measures less than 5 ft.
b.   It measures greater than 5 ft.
c.   It measures 2.5 ft.
d.   It measures 5 ft.
e.   It measures 10 ft.

27. Which of the following is true about the relationship between the two triangles shown below?

 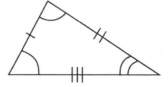

a.   The triangles are similar.
b.   The triangles are congruent.
c.   The triangles are equilateral.
d.   The triangles are both congruent and equilateral.
e.   The triangles are both similar and congruent.

Refer to the following for question 28:

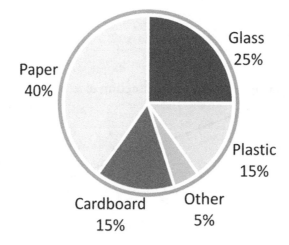

28. If there is a total of 50,000 tons of materials recycled every month, approximately how much paper is recycled every month?

    a. 15,000 tons
    b. 20,000 tons
    c. 40,000 tons
    d. 50,000 tons
    e. 60,000 tons

29. Express 18% as a decimal.

    a. 0.018
    b. 0.18
    c. 1.8
    d. 0.0018
    e. 0.108

30. A television that regularly costs $400 is offered today at a price reflecting 20% off. When a customer shows a Super Saver card, another 5% is deducted at the register. What does a customer with a Super Saver card pay for the television today?

    a. $380
    b. $375
    c. $300
    d. $304
    e. $270

31. Krystal purchased a pair of sunglasses for $19.99 and a scarf for $27.50. She paid with a $50.00 bill. How much change did she receive?

    a. $47.49
    b. $17.49
    c. $3.61
    d. $2.99
    e. $2.51

32. Simplify the expression $(10 + 4 \times 3) \div 2$.

    a. 22
    b. 21
    c. 6
    d. 20
    e. 11

33. Which of the following expressions is equivalent to the expression $(17 + 18) + 2$ according to the associative property?

    a. $35 + 2$
    b. $(18 + 17) + 2$
    c. $17 + 2(9 + 1)$
    d. $17 + (18 + 2)$
    e. $17 + 20$

34. Everyone in a class has blue, green, or brown eyes. 40% of the students have brown eyes and 90% of the other students have blue eyes. What can we infer from this information?

   a. We can infer that there is a majority of students with brown eyes.
   b. We can infer that there is a majority of students with blue eyes.
   c. We can infer that there is a majority of students with green eyes.
   d. We can infer that there is an equal number of students with each eye color.
   e. We cannot infer anything from this information.

35. Mary's basketball team is losing tonight's game 42–15. Mary scores a three-point shot. How many more three-point shots will someone on her team have to score in order to tie the game?

   a. 5
   b. 6
   c. 7
   d. 8
   e. 9

36. Which of the following is the largest number?

   a. 0.003
   b. 0.02
   c. 0.1
   d. 0.20
   e. 0.300

37. Simplify: $|7 - 5| - |5 - 7|$

   a. −4
   b. −2
   c. 0
   d. 2
   e. 4

38. Put the following numbers in order from the least to greatest $2^3, 4^2, 6^0, 9, 10^1$.

   a. $2^3, 4^2, 6^0, 9, 10^1$
   b. $6^0, 9, 10^1, 2^3, 4^2$
   c. $10^1, 2^3, 6^0, 9, 4^2$
   d. $6^0, 2^3, 9, 10^1, 4^2$
   e. $2^3, 9, 10^1, 4^2, 6^0$

39. Which of the following expressions is equivalent to $x^3 x^5$?

   a. $2x^8$
   b. x^{15}
   c. x^2
   d. x^8
   e. $2x^{15}$

40. A crane raises one end of a 3,300-pound steel beam. The other end rests upon the ground. If the crane supports 30% of the beam's weight, how many pounds does it support?

   a. 330 lb
   b. 700 lb
   c. 990 lb
   d. 1,100 lb
   e. 2,310 lb

41. Write $\frac{42}{7}$ as a percentage.

   a. 6%
   b. 600%
   c. 60%
   d. 0.6%
   e. 0.06%

42. Solve for x: $\left(\frac{2}{5}\right) \div \left(\frac{2}{3}\right) = x$

   a. $x = \frac{1}{4}$
   b. $x = \frac{4}{15}$
   c. $x = 1\frac{2}{3}$
   d. $x = \frac{3}{5}$
   e. $x = 3\frac{1}{2}$

43. Mrs. Patterson's classroom has sixteen empty chairs. All of the chairs are occupied when every student is present. If $\frac{2}{5}$ of the students are absent, how many students make up her entire class?

   a. 16 students
   b. 24 students
   c. 32 students
   d. 36 students
   e. 40 students

44. 30% of a woman's paycheck goes to health insurance, 15% goes to savings, and 32% goes to taxes. After these deductions, what percentage of the check is remaining?

   a. 19%
   b. 23%
   c. 38%
   d. 77%
   e. It cannot be determined from the information given.

45. Brenda buys a pair of shoes for $62.00. The next day she sees that the shoes are on sale for 25% off. How much money would Brenda have saved if she had waited a day?

   a. $9.92
   b. $15.50
   c. $25.00
   d. $46.50
   e. $52.08

46. John buys 100 shares of stock at $100 per share. The price goes up by 10%, and he sells 50 shares. Then, prices drop by 10%, and he sells his remaining 50 shares. How much did he get for the last 50 shares?

   a. $4,900
   b. $4,950
   c. $5,000
   d. $5,050
   e. $5,500

47. The weight in pounds of five students is 112, 112, 116, 133, and 145. What is the median weight of the group?

    a. 112 lbs
    b. 116 lbs
    c. 118.5 lbs
    d. 123.5 lbs
    e. 140 lbs

48. A cereal manufacturer claims to include 16 ounces in each container, with a standard deviation of 0.2 ounces. A random sample of 30 containers shows a mean of 16.1 ounces. Which of the following statements is true?

    a. The manufacturer's claim is likely true, as evidenced by a p-value less than 0.05.
    b. The manufacturer's claim is likely true, as evidenced by a p-value greater than 0.05.
    c. The manufacturer's claim is likely false, as evidenced by a p-value less than 0.05.
    d. The manufacturer's claim is likely false, as evidenced by a p-value greater than 0.05.
    e. Not enough information is provided to make a conclusion.

49. Three teachers from a county are chosen at random to attend a conference for high school science educators. What is the approximate probability that two women from the same department will be chosen?

	Biology	Chemistry	Physics
Women	26	31	20
Men	16	11	25

    a. 8.6%
    b. 9.6%
    c. 10.7%
    d. 11.9%
    e. 13.8%

50. Which of the following statements is NOT true?

    a. In a negatively skewed distribution, the tail is on the left.
    b. In a positively skewed distribution, the median is greater than the mode.
    c. In a normal distribution, the curve is symmetrical.
    d. In a normal distribution, the mean is at the peak.
    e. In a positively skewed distribution, the median is closer to the third quartile than the first.

51. Which of the following best represents the standard deviation of the data below?

8, 10, 11, 13, 13, 16, 17, 20

    a. 2.9
    b. 3.4
    c. 3.6
    d. 4.0
    e. 4.6

52. A small company is divided into three departments, as shown. Two individuals are chosen at random to attend a conference. What is the approximate probability that two women from the same department will be chosen?

	Department 1	Department 2	Department 3
Women	12	28	16
Men	18	14	15

- a. 8.6%
- b. 9.5%
- c. 10.7%
- d. 11.2%
- e. 13.8%

53. A random sample of 241 children ages 5 to 10 were asked these three questions:

 Do you like baseball?
 Do you like basketball?
 Do you like football?

The results of the survey are shown below. If these data are representative of the population of students at the school, which of these is least probable?

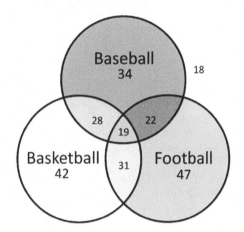

- a. A child chosen at random likes football.
- b. If a child chosen at random likes baseball, he also likes at least one other sport.
- c. If a child chosen at random likes baseball and basketball, he also likes football.
- d. A child chosen at random likes basketball and baseball.
- e. A student chosen at random does not like baseball, basketball, or football.

54. Which of the following correlation coefficients represents the weakest correlation?

- a. 0.3
- b. −0.1
- c. 0.4
- d. −0.9
- e. 0.6

55. A student scores 71 on a final exam. Another student scores 86 on the exam. The class average is 81, with a standard deviation of 10 points. What percentage of the class scored within the range of these two students' scores?

    a. 53.28%

    b. 58.94%

    c. 68.35%

    d. 64.11%

    e. 71.28%

56. How many different seven-digit telephone numbers can be created in which no digit repeats and in which zero cannot be the first digit?

    a. 5,040

    b. 35,280

    c. 362,880

    d. 544,320

    e. 3,265,920

Answer Key and Explanations

Reading

1. B: The passage mentions that elementary school students should be able to talk about today's weather and their area's climate (B). A student's ability to discuss other climates (A) and how landforms affect climate (D) depends on his or her developmental level, according to the passage. Only the current weather and the climate the student lives in are listed in the passage as things all students should be able to describe.

2. E: The passage defines continental climate as a climate with seasons. The passage suggests that tropical (A), dry (B) and hot (C), and mild (D) climates do not have seasons like continental climates do.

3. B: The passage clearly states that a mountain can buffer winds and cause an area to be warmer. Answer A correctly states that mountains block wind, but incorrectly states that this makes nearby areas have a mild climate. Answers C and D both incorrectly state that mountains allow more wind in an area. Answer E is incorrect because the passage does explicitly list some effects mountains can have on a climate.

4. A: The passage mentions the effects that ocean currents (B), elevation (C), mountains (D), and proximity to the equator (E) can have on an area's climate. Weather balloons (A) are simply used to study weather, and they are not mentioned in the passage.

5. E: The passage states that weather and climate have different meanings. They have related meanings, but they are neither synonyms (A) nor antonyms (B). They also do not have similar spellings or pronunciations, so they are not homonyms (C) or homophones (D). However, they are often used within the same basic subject area, so they are related words (E).

6. A: Answer A, "An Overview of Vocational Counseling," most accurately describes the content of the passage, so it is the correct choice. This passage describes the role of the vocational counselor (C) and how vocational counseling benefits students (B). Since the passage covers several aspects of vocational counseling, answers B, C, and E would not be good titles because they are not broad enough to accurately describe the passage. The passage also specifically discusses vocational counseling, so a title that focuses on school counselors in general would also not be appropriate (D).

7. E: The passage describes vocational counseling as a useful tool for students who are not sure what career they want to pursue, or do not have a chosen profession (E). Students who receive vocational counseling will likely have a vocational counselor at their school (D) and may use evaluation instruments (A). These students should also be honest about their interests to receive the best results (B). However, these factors do not determine whether or not a student needs or would benefit from vocational counseling. Students who already know what career they wish to pursue will not benefit from vocational counseling as much, as the purpose of this counseling is to help them make this decision (C).

8. D: This passage gives the reader basic information about vocational counseling and how it helps students (D). Answers A, B, and E suggest that the purpose of the passage is to persuade readers to form an opinion or take action regarding vocational counseling. This is not the purpose of the passage, as it is expository. The purpose of the passage is also not to talk about evaluation instruments (C), as they are a detail mentioned only in the second paragraph.

9. C: The passage states that "children from low-income homes tend to begin school with weaker skills than their peers from more advantaged backgrounds," which has the same meaning as answer C. Answers A, B, and D include absolute statements that claim something is true for all students. The passage discusses generalizations, not circumstances that always apply to all students, so these answers are incorrect. The passage does not clearly discuss learning at home, so answer E is also incorrect.

10. D: The main purpose of the passage is to inform readers of factors that can cause a disparity in basic skills in students when they begin attending school (D). While this passage discusses the benefits of allowing children to start school on time, it is not a persuasive passage (A). While the passage mentions how the income level of students' parents or guardians (E) can contribute to the visible disparity in students' basic skills (C), these are details discussed in the passage, so neither is the main purpose of the passage. Teachers and their potential problems with students (B) are not mentioned in the passage.

11. A: Answer A describes the impact of Title IX on women's participation in sports. This sentence is relevant to the passage and expands upon the information in the last sentence. Answer B mentions Richard Nixon, who was mentioned in the passage, but this detail is not relevant to the rest of the passage. Answers C and D include information related to sports, but are also not relevant to the passage. Answer E discusses some women's lack of interest in sports. While this is relevant to the main idea of the passage, it does not support or build upon the information in the passage.

12. B: The passage states that the teacher should encourage discussions about vocabulary words and students' opinions, meaning that they are of equal importance (B). Students' predictions about a story's plot (C) and their acquisition of new vocabulary words (D) are both also listed as important topics teachers should lead students to discuss. According to the passage, teachers can ask questions to encourage these discussions as they read (E). The passage states that reading aloud to students is beneficial for students at any grade level, which includes older students (A).

13. E: In lines 7–8, the passage notes that parking tickets will be issued for vehicles left in the main lot overnight. Overnight guests are instructed to register their vehicles (D), display a window label (A), and park in the side lot (B), so these actions do not violate regulations. The pass code is for guests who need to access Five Oaks after 11:00 p.m., so it is neither an instruction or against regulations (C).

14. B: The passage says that the pass code changes every 48 hours, implying that it is unpredictable and secure (B). The need for a pass code to enter the side lot after 11:00 p.m. implies that the side lot is locked at night (D). The instructions to park in the side lot to avoid receiving a ticket from the city police shows that police are patrolling the facility's parking lot (C). The passage does not mention cars being towed in the past (E), but it does not give evidence that this has not happened.

15. A: Spelling skills (A) are not clearly mentioned in the passage or measurable through the cloze exercise, so answer A is the best choice. The cloze exercise is described as a reading comprehension tool, meaning that it can help evaluate students' text comprehension (B). The passage states that students must use context clues (D) and prior knowledge, which includes vocabulary (C), to fill in blanks during the cloze exercise, so it can also evaluate these skills. The passage also compares the cloze exercise to activities that require students to use synonyms to understand unknown words, which suggests that the cloze exercise also reflects a student's ability to use synonyms (E).

16. C: The passage clearly states that the goal of the Dawes Act was to turn Native Americans into landowners (A) and farmers (D) and that the government hoped this would encourage Native Americans to pursue citizenship (E) and adopt more individualistic lifestyles (B). However, the law deprived many Native Americans of important aspects of their culture, showing that maintaining Native American culture (C) was not a reason the government offered land to Native Americans.

17. C: Jessica says that she wants to be on the varsity team, which shows that she is not on the team. However, the characters do not say or do anything to show whether Marissa is on the varsity team or not (C). Marissa's words show that the characters will be riding a bus, and Jessica's actions show that they are still waiting for the bus to arrive (A). Marissa's words and actions show that it is very cold outside (B). Marissa and Jessica's actions show that they are friends (D), since they talk to each other and stand close together in the cold. Jessica's words about her meet times and her desire to be on the varsity team show that she cares about her performance (E).

18. A: The introductory sentence of this passage clearly states that showing instead of telling is a component of good story writing (A). Voice in writing (B) is more often achieved through word choice and is not mentioned in the passage. The purpose of showing instead of telling is not to give facts (C) or narrate a story (D). It is instead often used to make descriptions more engaging for the reader. Showing can also help readers know the characters better, as evidenced by the passage (E).

19. D: The passage describes what teachers should do while working with students, therefore, teachers are the audience for this passage (D). Students should be aware of lab safety practices, but this passage is not intended for students, so it would not appear in a student's handbook (A) or science text (E). This passage also applies to a variety of lab situations and materials, so it would not appear on the label for any given lab equipment (B). Also, since this passage covers a variety of information, it would not need to be printed before the instructions for each science experiment (C).

20. A: The third paragraph describes gloves and glassware, so a response about hot glassware (A) would provide an additional detail that is relevant to the information in the paragraph. A sentence about students misreading instructions for an experiment (B) may be relevant to the passage, but it is not directly relevant to this paragraph. Similarly, a sentence stating that students can get hurt in a lab (E) is relevant to the whole passage, but it is also implied throughout the passage and does not strengthen paragraph 3. Whether or not students complete lab reports after experiments (C) is not relevant to this passage (C). While CPR training for teachers (D) can promote students' safety, it is not mentioned in the passage or specifically related to lab safety or proper use of gloves and glass.

21. B: Accidents in the lab (A), instruction over the use of lab equipment (B), and safety equipment (C) are all discussed in the passage. However, these are all details that are included under the main topic of good lab practices that students should learn (B). This is the main idea and applies to each paragraph in the passage, while the other options are only relevant to parts of the passage. While labs are designed for students to learn (E), the passage is about students learning safely rather than students learning a great deal of information.

22. C: According to lines 36–38 in the passage, loose-fitting clothing is unsafe to wear when students are working with fire. This means that, in general, loose-fitting clothing may be unsafe to wear in the lab (C). Lines 46–49 state that students should always wash their hands after completing an experiment, even if they were wearing gloves (A). The passage also states in lines 28–30 that students should report broken glass and avoid touching it at all (B). Oven mitts are listed as the proper safety equipment when working with heat (D) in lines 23–25. The passage does mention that students should wear aprons most of the times they're in the lab, but does not offer any information on whether or not teachers wear aprons in the lab (E).

23. A: According to the passage, one reason Sargent believed women should be educated was because they were the primary teachers for their children. This suggests that an educated mother would educate her child, meaning that children of educated colonial women would most likely be smarter than children of uneducated women (A). This also means that children of educated women would not be intellectually equal to children of uneducated women (B). The passage does provide enough information to make a generalization about the children's education and intelligence (D), but does not give information to support a generalization comparing a child's education or intelligence to their mother's (E). It also does not mention the influence of the father's education on the child's intelligence (C).

24. E: In the context of the passage, the idea Sargent "contended" seems to be one she suggested, believed, and defended. Based on this context, *argued* (E) is the closest in meaning to *contended*. Neither *terminated* (A), which means ended, or *denied* (B), which means rejected, fit in this sentence because both of these words would suggest that Sargent disagreed or disliked the idea. While using *concurred* (C) would mean that Sargent agreed with the claim, Sargent was making her own claim, meaning that she had no need to agree with another person or idea. *Valued* (D) is also a close fit, as it means appreciated or respected, but it does not reflect that Sargent had to support and defend her claim.

25. A: The necessity of the desalination process (A) is an important detail that is relevant to the information in the first paragraph. The cost of desalination (C) and the importance of usable water (D) are briefly mentioned in the first paragraph, but these sentences do not provide any new information, so they would not expand upon the information in the first paragraph. People's knowledge of desalination (B) and the conservation of water (E) are not relevant to the information given in the first paragraph.

26. C. As stated in the passage, closed-ended questions only provide a small amount of usable information (C), so they are not a useful tool in the context of inquiry-based learning. The passage does not discuss questions made by the teacher (A), the amount of time it takes to make questions (B), or how often students understand close-ended questions (E). The problem is also defined before inquiry questions are created, so neither close-ended or open-ended questions should define the problem (D).

27. D: The internet's role in the decline of print newspapers is emphasized throughout the passage (D). Readers' changing interests (C) and decreases in circulation (E) are both mentioned in the passage, but these are described as less impactful factors than the internet. The passage does not discuss the cost of making newspapers (A) or the quality of newspapers (B).

28. B: The last sentence suggests that newspaper executives see a need to make decisions and changes and have a limited amount of time to do so. "Newspapers must act quickly to save the medium" (B) is a reasonable conclusion based on this idea. While the last sentence implies that newspaper executives must act quickly, it does not predict the fate of all newspapers, or suggest that newspapers will fail soon (A). The last sentence does not mention the economy (C), newspaper websites (D), or a scarcity of newspapers (E).

29. E: The passage clearly describes both fission and fusion as nuclear reactions (E). The process of fission involves breaking down matter (A), while fusion involves combining nuclei (B). The passage also states that fission has been used as a form of energy (C), but fusion has not, and is also not as reliable as fission (D).

30. D: The passage suggests that a great deal of shipping originates in Tibet, but it does not support the statement that all shipping originates there (D). According to the passage, the Yangtze River is almost 4,000 miles long, and is the longest river in Asia. This means that the rest of Asia's rivers must be shorter than 4,000 miles (A), and the Yangtze River must be the longest river in China (C). The passage also says that the river begins in Tibet, in Southwest China, and flows eastward past Shanghai, meaning that Tibet must be west of Shanghai (B).

31. A: The passage states that jobs and funding are at risk of decreasing when many students leave the school at once, so it is not reasonable to assume that new students are admitted at the same rate that former students left (A). Since the school population decreases (B) and government funding (C) and jobs (E) are likely to decrease, schools that experience a large group of students leaving typically become weaker overall (D).

32. D: According to the passage, the voucher system was designed for students who were not satisfied with their school (D). Students who are happy with their school (B) are not likely to take advantage of the voucher system. The passage states that some private schools may not admit academically challenged students (A), so these students may not always benefit from school vouchers. Whether or not a student has friends at school (C) does not determine whether the student is satisfied with the school, and this is not discussed in the passage. The proximity of a private school to a student's school does not necessarily impact a student's satisfaction with their school (E).

33. C: The passage describes what happens when a plunger is used to clear a clogged pipe and why this process works. This is best described as an explanation (C). While the passage does describe a chain of events, it also explains why these events happen, meaning that the passage, as a whole, is not an observation (D). The passage is also simply explaining how plungers work, it is not providing an example or modeling the use of a plunger (E). Inferring (A) means asking a question, and hypothesizing (B) means to propose an unproven idea. The passage does neither of these things.

34. E: "Depressed" is used in the passage to describe how a plunger is pushed down (E) to make it work. "Very unhappy" (A) is not an action, and it is also not logical for the plunger to be decreased (B), so these answers can be eliminated. The passage also says that when the plunger is depressed, air moves. If the user exhaled on the plunger (C) or ignored it (D), this would not cause the air inside the cup to move.

35. A: The passage mentions that serious bloggers update their blog regularly, implying that bloggers who are not serious about blogging may not do this (A). The passage states that bloggers are people who write blogs (E), and although many bloggers want as many readers as possible, not all bloggers have this goal (B). All bloggers, including serious bloggers, may write about any topic (C), or even a variety of topics (D).

36. B: In line 5, the passage clearly states that a teacher or student may act as mediator (B), so mediators are not limited to being only teachers (C) or only students (D). It is unlikely that someone directly involved in the conflict would be a mediator, and this idea is not supported by the passage (E). The passage also does not mention administrators (A).

37. E: Lines 1–3 of the passage state that specific strategies are used in conflict mediation (E). The process of conflict mediation described in the passage includes bringing involved students together (C) so the teacher or peer mediator can lead them through a mature and respectful discussion (D). While lines 13 and 14 explain that conflict mediation does not always lead to a successful resolution (A), lines 14–17 suggest that conflict mediation often succeeds in achieving other positive results (B).

38. A: The passage states that the mediator uses specific prompts to help students brainstorm solutions. This means the mediator is making suggestions (A) to guide the students' discussion and decision. In this sentence, the word *prompt* must be a noun, so *punctual* (B) and *rapid* (E) are not possible definitions, since they are adjectives. *Brainstorm* (C) is already used in the same sentence as a verb, so it also cannot be the meaning of *prompt*. There is also no evidence in the passage to support the idea that the mediator would want to speed up the discussion or resolution, so *time-saver* (D) is not a logical meaning of *prompt* in this sentence.

39. D: Lines 10–12 explain that the resolution should be one that both of the students involved are comfortable with, which implies that both students agree with the resolution (D). While the mediator helps the students reach a resolution, the passage says the mediator's role is to guide the students involved to create a resolution (A). To do this, the mediator talks to the students together, rather than separately (C). The passage does not mention how long the session lasts, so it is unclear whether or not a session works quickly (B). Lines 12–14 also state that the session does not always successfully result in a resolution (E).

40. B: The passages states that the lower-ranking person is introduced to the higher-ranking person (B). In this case, the bank president is the higher-ranking person, so the bank president would not be introduced to the new hire (A). Although the lower-ranking person is often younger, this is not always the case, so the order of introductions does not depend on age (C)(D).

41. A: The passage says that after the lower ranking person has been introduced to the higher-ranking person, the two people are introduced in reverse (A). The person introducing the individuals will have already learned the two people's names (B) and how they are pronounced (E). The passage does not mention shaking hands (C) or what occurs after the introduction (D).

42. C: The passage states that the correct pronunciation of an unfamiliar name should be clarified during the introduction (C). None of the other options, skipping the difficult part of a person's name (A), joking about a person's name (B), asking a person to pronounce their own name (D), and shortening a person's name to an initial (E), are mentioned in the passage.

43. C: The passage mentions that these types of introductions occur between two professional people (C). School settings may be included in professional settings, as those who work at a school are professionals (D). These introductions are likely too formal for most casual settings (B), and are certainly not best for all settings

(A). One purpose of these introductions is to put individuals at ease, but the passage does not support the idea that these introductions are specifically for uncomfortable conversations (E).

44. A: In the last paragraph, the passage says that introductions help put everyone at ease, or make everyone more comfortable (A). The passage does not discuss reviewing business protocol (B) or taking up time in meetings (C), and these are not logical answers based on the given information. The passage also only discusses introductions between two people; it does not state that it is important for the highest-ranking (D) or lowest-ranking (E) person to have met everyone.

45. C: The passage describes an introduction process where one person introduces two other people to each other. The ranks of the people being introduced does not matter; a third person (C) will be introducing them. This means that in this situation, neither the city government official (A) or the administrative assistant (B) will introduce themselves.

46. D: Since the passage describes superstitions from days gone by about treating asthma, answer choice D is the correct one. The other choices are either too broad and general (choices A, B, and C) or too specific (choice E).

47. A: The reader can infer from the opening sentence that if so many people have asthma today, many would probably have had asthma long ago as well. Even though the environment today is different than it was long ago, people would still have suffered from the condition. The sentence explains why people long ago may have needed to try homemade methods of treating the condition. (Although choice C is also accurate, it does not explain why the sentence would be placed at the beginning of the passage.)

48. B: The purpose of the passage is to describe different measures that people took for asthma long ago, before the advent of modern medicine. Answer choice A, herbal remedies, is incorrect because the majority of the "medicine" described in the passage is not herbal. The passage does not, as in answer choice C, define superstitions. Nor does it praise modern medicine, as answer choice D suggests.

49. A: The passage states that the boat landing at Buffalo Point changes annually because the river water moves gravel in and out of the area. Painted Bluff (B) is not described as changing annually. Answer choice C is partially correct, but the passage says that the gravel comes both on and off the land there, not just off. Answer choice D is also partially right, but the top half of Painted Bluff is not dolomite. Answer choice E is incorrect.

50. C: The entire passage is a description of Buffalo Point. Answer choice A, Painted Bluff, is included in the description as part of the explanation of what Buffalo Point is like. Answer choice B is incorrect. Answer choice D is true, but it is not the main purpose of the passage.

51. A: Of all the choices listed, only answer choice A is an example of misusing a drug. It is listed as one of the ways that drugs are misused in the middle of the passage. Taking more or less of a prescription drug than the amount that the doctor ordered can be harmful to one's health. The other answer choices are not examples of misuse, nor do they appear in the passage. Make sure all of your answer choices are based on the passage given rather than information you may know or assume from other sources.

52. D: The passage does not say that ALL drugs add longevity. It says that drugs that are healthy and used properly add longevity. The word *all* makes the statement untrue.

53. C: All of the other statements use words that are in the passage, but they are written in such a way that they are all false. Only answer choice C has a true statement according to the passage.

54. E: You will find the answer in the second to last sentence of the passage. All of the other word choices are used in the passage, but *surprised* is the only one that describes how many white people felt.

55. B: The passage does mention choice B, German music at the symphony, but it states the opposite: German music was not allowed. Answer choice E, patriotic murder, is not in the bulleted list in the passage, but it follows the list and is still in the passage as an example of mob-mentality patriotism.

56. A: While mob mentality is certainly a factor in the passage, *mobs* in general is not a noun that describes a group of people opposed to war. Some people who were drafted were against the war, but not all. The military was not listed as a group who was opposed to war; rather, civilians were more likely to be opposed.

Writing

1. D: *Beautifully*, the adverb form of *beauty* must be used here since it is describing a verb (sang).

2. B: *Is*, the singular form of *to be* must be used here since the sentence refers to just one of the bicycles.

3. E: The first part of the sentence is the question: Are you Don Adams? This part of the sentence is enclosed by quotation marks since it is being said by "him."

4. E: Only subjects that are proper nouns are capitalized, here – just English.

5. A: The sentence is correct as it is written. Spaghetti and meatballs go together as a unit and should not be separated by a comma.

6. E: Quotation marks should enclose only those words that a speaker says. Here, the speaker is not directly quoted.

7. E: Since the sentence begins in the past tense, the rest of the sentence must be in the past tense as well.

8. E: As presented, the original words do not form a fragment, not a complete sentence with a subject and a verb. The correct response is a sentence and demonstrates better usage than the answer choice before it.

9. C: This sentence is in passive voice. The subject of the sentence should be performing the action rather than having the action done to him/her/it.

10. C: The original sentence is a run-on sentence-two sentences joined together with no punctuation to separate them. A semi-colon must be added after *beautiful*.

11. D: Quotation marks are closed when a speaker has finished what he or she is saying not between sentences of dialogue.

12. A: The sentence is correct as it is written.

13. D: The original sentence is in passive voice and does not provide a subject. Answer choice D provides the best sentence structure.

14. D: The objective case, *Ellen Jackson and me*, is used here. To test whether I or *me* is the correct form to use, remove Ellen Jackson: "All of the revisions need to be approved by *me*."

15. A: The sentence is correct as it is written.

16. D: The subject of the sentence is one person. The singular verb was must be used in order for the subject to agree with the verb.

17. A: The sentence is correct as it is written.

18. D: The gender of most animals in the wild is not known, so "it" is used.

19. C: The question is this part of the sentence: "Does your salad taste okay?" The question mark is placed at the end after *okay*. A comma is not added after a question mark that is part of dialogue.

20. D: When written in a sentence, only school subjects that are proper nouns are capitalized.

21. A: The items are part of a list, with *salt and pepper* considered to be one unit and the other two items as separate units.

22. B: Answer choice B is precise and clear. Answer choice A keeps the meaning, but is awkward and wordy. Answer choice C uses the wrong verb tense. Answer choice D would put the word *work* into the sentence twice. It is not completely incorrect, but it is not the best choice. Answer choice E changes the original meaning of the sentence.

23. B: When comparing two people or things, the correct comparative word would be *older* rather than *oldest*. If there were more than two, you would use the comparative word *oldest*. The other choices change the intended original meaning of the sentence. The same is true for the comparative words *better* and *best* or *less* and *least*.

24. A: The sentence is precise and clear in its original form. This type of sentence is an absolute construction, including a noun and a modifier. Absolute constructions squeeze two sentences into one. In this case the modifier is a participle phrase.

25. D: The plural subject *teachers* agrees with the pronoun *they*. Pronouns have to agree with gender, number and person. If the subject had been singular, such as *teacher*, then the pronoun would have needed to also be singular. In that case the correct sentence might have been: A fair teacher understands that he or she cannot treat any student with favoritism.

26. C: When putting things or people in order, the words must agree in the series. You can use *first, second, third,* and so forth, or you may use *firstly, secondly, thirdly,* and so forth. In this sentence, answer choice C is the best choice because the two words *first* and *second* agree in the series, and in this case it sounds better. *Firstly* and *secondly* sound awkward. Also, it is correct to use *and then* in the sentence rather than answer choice D which uses only the word *then*.

27. B: *Well* and *kept* put together forms a compound adjective. In this case the compound adjective was written with an adverb and a past participle. When the two together come before and modify a noun, such as *secret*, they must be hyphenated as such: *well-kept secret*.

28. C: The style in the original sentence is awkward because it has a double passive voice. Change the first passive verbs into an active verb and the sentence will simply sound better. Even though answer choice B sounds good and is grammatically correct, you cannot choose it because of the pronoun *she*. The original sentence does not specify gender.

29. A: The sentence is clear and precise in its original form.

30. E: The word *need* is being used as an auxillary verb in this sentence. It does not go together with *did* or any form of *do* unless it is being used as a main verb. The following is an example of *need* being used as a main verb together with *do*: *We do need to trouble our minds.*

31. B: The word *ought* is an auxiliary verb that should go together with the word *to* in formal writing. It is sometimes used in speech without the word *to* (especially in particular regions), but is not considered correct in written English. There are some cases where *ought* can be correctly used without *to* in questions, such as: *Ought the teacher set a good example?*

32. A: The sentence is clear and precise in its original form.

33. D: The only problem with the sentence is the use of the adjective *a* rather than *an*. You cannot assume gender (such as *she* or *her*).

34. E: The use of the word *at* at the end of the sentence is unnecessary. It is a dangling preposition. Remove the word *at* to make it clear and precise.

35. B: The original sentence has dependent clauses with words that LOOK like verbs but do not ACT like verbs. The entire sentence is a fragment. Answer choice B is the only one that adds a subject and verb to change the fragment into a complete sentence.

36. E: The original is a run-on sentence. There should be a comma to separate the two thoughts. The use of a semicolon only works if you remove the word *and*, as follows: He got up bright and early; he spent a whole hour taking a shower.

37. C: The two words *added* and *additional* are redundant. Grammatically, it is not wrong, but the two words are similar enough that they seem like the same word. It is awkward. Taking out the *additional* makes the sentence more precise without changing any of the meaning.

38. C: The word *cumbersome* is an adjective, but the placement in the sentence calls for an adverb. Add *ly* to the word to make modify the verb. If it had been used as an adjective, it would have come before the noun as follows: *the cumbersome cow.*

39. B: The word *god* should not be capitalized because it is not being used as a name. When the word is non-specific and not used as a name, it should be written with the lowercase *g*.

40. C: There are two facts in the sentence that need to be connected without ending up with a run-on sentence. The original is already a run-on sentence. Answer choice C is the only choice that is not confusing or awkward. It states the two facts and connects them in such a way that the sentence makes sense. Answer choice D actually changes the meaning of the sentence since it states that she is the teacher of the year IN Sylacauga, Alabama. The original sentence never says that. It only says that she is FROM Sylacauga. We have no idea where she lives now. Answer choice E uses the word *although*, which implies that she got the award in spite of being from that city.

41. Essay question graders commonly look for the following elements in a strong response: strong content knowledge, clear organization, and effective arguments or examples. Language and usage are not usually strictly graded, but can make a big impact on the clarity of your ideas.

Please use the provided rubric to make sure your response meets these common criteria. Try to have a friend or family member grade your response for you or take a break after writing your response and return to grade it with fresh eyes.

CONSTRUCTED RESPONSE RUBRIC

Domain	Description
Content Knowledge	• The response directly addresses every part of the prompt. • The response demonstrates independent knowledge of the topic. • The response discusses the topic at an appropriate depth.
Organization	• The response introduces the topic, usually with a thesis statement or by restating the prompt. • The response directly addresses the prompt by providing a clear and concise answer or solution. • The answer or solution is supported by logical arguments or evidence. • The response restates the main idea in the conclusion.
Arguments and Examples	• The response provides a reasonable answer to the prompt. • The answer is supported by strong reasoning or evidence. • The response develops ideas logically and connects ideas to one another. • The reasoning and evidence provided act to support a unified main idea.
Language and Usage	• The response demonstrates effective use of grammar and uses varied sentence structure throughout the response. • The response demonstrates correct use of spelling, punctuation, and capitalization. • The response demonstrates strong and varied use of vocabulary relevant to the topic and appropriate for the intended audience.

42. Essay question graders commonly look for the following elements in a strong response: strong content knowledge, clear organization, and effective arguments or examples. Language and usage are not usually strictly graded, but can make a big impact on the clarity of your ideas.

Please use the provided rubric to make sure your response meets these common criteria. Try to have a friend or family member grade your response for you or take a break after writing your response and return to grade it with fresh eyes.

CONSTRUCTED RESPONSE RUBRIC

Domain	Description
Content Knowledge	• The response directly addresses every part of the prompt. • The response demonstrates independent knowledge of the topic. • The response discusses the topic at an appropriate depth.
Organization	• The response introduces the topic, usually with a thesis statement or by restating the prompt. • The response directly addresses the prompt by providing a clear and concise answer or solution. • The answer or solution is supported by logical arguments or evidence. • The response restates the main idea in the conclusion.
Arguments and Examples	• The response provides a reasonable answer to the prompt. • The answer is supported by strong reasoning or evidence. • The response develops ideas logically and connects ideas to one another. • The reasoning and evidence provided act to support a unified main idea.
Language and Usage	• The response demonstrates effective use of grammar and uses varied sentence structure throughout the response. • The response demonstrates correct use of spelling, punctuation, and capitalization. • The response demonstrates strong and varied use of vocabulary relevant to the topic and appropriate for the intended audience.

Mathematics

1. E: Each notebook costs $1.50. To find the cost of each notebook, we must divide the total amount of money earned, $45.00, by the number of notebooks sold, 30. When we divide 45 by 30, we know that 30 can "fit" into 45 one time, with a remainder of 15. We can turn our remainder into a fraction by making our remainder the numerator and our divisor the denominator, creating the fraction $\frac{15}{30}$, or $\frac{1}{2}$. When working with money, 1 whole and $\frac{1}{2}$ represents one and a half dollars, or $1.50. Giselle charged $1.50 for each notebook.

2. A: The mode is the number that appears most often in a set of data. If no item appears most often, then the data set has no mode. In this case, Kyle had 1 hit for a total of 3 times. There were 2 times that he had 2 hits. Also, on 1 day, he had 3 hits. Then, on another day, he had 4 hits. 1 hit happened the most times, so the mode of the data set is 1.

3. C: The mean of a data set is considered a measure of center. To calculate the mean (sometimes known as the "average"), we must first find the sum of all numbers included in the data set. Here, the sum of 76, 193, 83, 43, and 105 is 500. Next, we need to divide the sum of our data set by the number of values included in the set. This data set contains 5 values, so we'll divide our sum, 500, by 5. The quotient of 500 and 5 is 100, making our mean 100.

4. D: The probability of getting three aces in a row is the product of the probabilities for each draw. For the first ace that is $\frac{4}{52}$, since there are 4 aces in a deck of 52 cards. For the second, it is $\frac{3}{51}$, since 3 aces and 51 cards remain. And for the third, it is $\frac{2}{50}$. So, the overall probability is $P = \frac{4}{52} \times \frac{3}{51} \times \frac{2}{50} \times \frac{24}{132,600} \times \frac{1}{5,525}$.

5. A: In this probability problem, there are three independent events (each digit of the code), each with ten possible outcomes (the numerals 0–9). Since the events are independent, the total number of possible outcomes equals the product of the possible outcomes for each of the three events.

$$P = P_1 \times P_2 \times P_3 = 10 \times 10 \times 10 = 1,000$$

This result makes sense when we consider trying every possible code in sequence, beginning with the combinations 0-0-0, 0-0-1, 0-0-2, etc. In ascending order, the last three-digit combination would be 9-9-9. Although it may seem that there would be 999 possible combinations, there are in fact 1,000 when we include the initial combination, 0-0-0.

6. B: To calculate the range of any data set, we must find the difference between the largest value (known as the maximum) and the smallest value (known as the minimum). In this data set, our maximum is 832, while our minimum is 196. The difference of 832 and 196 is 636, so the range of the data set is also 636.

7. D: The mode of any data set is the value(s) that appears most often. Here, we have two values, 84 and 93, that both occur four times. No other value occurs more than four times so we can say that we have two modes: 84 and 93.

8. C: We calculate the range of any data set by subtracting the smallest value from the largest value, or the maximum – the minimum. Here, our maximum is 84, while our minimum is 3. Because $84 - 3 = 81$, our range is 81. The range tells us how "spread out" our data is. Having a range of 81 means that our data is spread out by no more than 81 units.

9. C: To find the probability that a student is enrolled at TAMU or that a student prefers lattes, the addition rule needs to be used. The addition rule adds the probabilities of two independent events and subtracts the probability that both events are true to avoid double counting. The probability may be written as $P(A \text{ or } B) = \frac{750}{1,650} + \frac{675}{1,650} - \frac{350}{1,650}$, which simplifies to $P(A \text{ or } B) = \frac{1,075}{1,650} \approx 65\%$. Therefore, the probability is approximately 65%.

10. E: For each die there is a $\frac{1}{6}$ chance that a 6 will be on top because a die has 6 sides. The probability that a 6 will show for each die is not affected by the results from another roll of the die. In other words, these probabilities are independent. So, the overall probability of throwing 3 sixes is the product of the individual probabilities: $P = \frac{1}{6} \times \frac{1}{6} \times \frac{1}{6} = \frac{1}{6^3} = \frac{1}{216}$. Therefore, the probability that all three dice will land on a 6 is $\frac{1}{216}$.

11. C: To solve, rearrange the equation and simplify by combining like terms:

$$(2x - 3) + 2x = 9$$
$$2x - 3 + 2x = 9$$
$$4x - 3 = 9$$
$$4x = 12$$
$$x = 3$$

12. C: The equation can be rearranged and simplified as follows:

$$15 - x = 78$$
$$15 - 78 = x$$
$$-63 = x$$

13. A: This is a typical plot of an inverse variation where the product of the dependent and independent variables, x and y, is always equal to the same value. In this case, the product is always equal to 1. So, the plot is in the first and third quadrants of the coordinate plane. As x increases and goes to infinity, y decreases and goes to zero while keeping the constant product. In contrast, graph 2 is a linear plot for an equation of the form

$y = x$. Graph 3 is a quadratic plot for the equation $y = x^2$. Graph 4 is an exponential plot for the equation $y = 2^x$. And, Graph 5 is another linear plot corresponding to $y = \frac{x}{4} + 1$.

14. B: To solve, isolate y on one side of the equation:

$$4y = 60 - 16$$
$$4y = 44$$
$$y = 11$$

15. C: Solve this equation by first using cross multiplication.

$$3(y + 4) = 15(y - 5)$$

From here, distribute on both sides.

$$3y + 12 = 15y - 75$$

Subtract $3y$ from both sides.

$$12 = 12y - 75$$

Add 75 to both sides of the equation.

$$87 = 12y$$

Finally, divide both sides by 12 and simplify the fraction.

$$\frac{87}{12} = \frac{29}{4} = y$$

16. D: Rafael's profit on each computer is given by the difference between the price he pays and the price he charges his customer, or $\$800 - \$450$. If he sells n computers in a month, his total profit will be n times this difference, or $n(\$800 - \$450)$. However, it is necessary to subtract his fixed costs of $\$3,000$ from this to compute his final profit per month. This gives the complete equation:

$$P = n(\$800 - \$450) - \$3,000$$

17. A: To simplify the expression, start by distributing the 3s.

$$3\left(\frac{6x - 3}{3}\right) - 3(9x + 9)$$

$$6x - 3 - 27x - 27$$

Then, combine like terms.

$$(6x - 27x) + (-3 - 27)$$

$$-21x - 30$$

Since this isn't one of the answer choices, manipulate it to match one of the choices given. Factor out a –3 from each term.

$$-3(7x + 10)$$

18. C: When subtracting A from B, the difference matrix can be written as $\begin{bmatrix} 1-1 & -3-(-3) \\ -4-(-4) & 2-(-2) \end{bmatrix}$, which reduces to $\begin{bmatrix} 0 & 0 \\ 0 & 4 \end{bmatrix}$.

19. E: The area of the square is $A = s^2 = (30 \text{ cm})^2 = 900 \text{ cm}^2$. The area of the circle is $A = \pi r^2 = (3.14)(15 \text{ cm})^2 \approx 707 \text{ cm}^2$. The area of the shaded region is equal to the difference between the area of the square and the area of the circle, or $900 \text{ cm}^2 - 707 \text{ cm}^2$, which equals 193 cm^2.

20. C: Any triangle with an angle measuring over 90° is considered an obtuse triangle. Because this triangle has an angle measuring 100°, we must classify it as obtuse. Since we have two 40-degree angles, we know that the sides opposite those angles must be the same length. A triangle with two equivalent sides is described as an isosceles triangle. This triangle must be described as an obtuse isosceles triangle.

21. A The area of a circle is πr^2, so the area of a semicircle is $\dfrac{\pi r^2}{2}$. Illustrated below is a method which can be used to find the area of the shaded region.

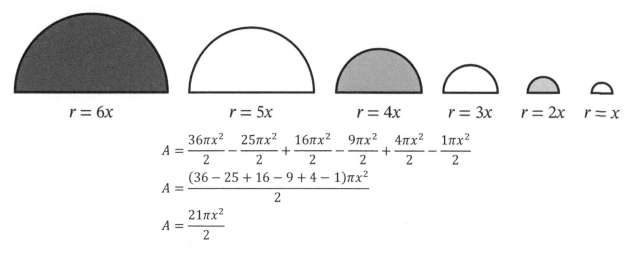

$r = 6x$ $\qquad r = 5x$ $\qquad r = 4x$ $\qquad r = 3x$ $\quad r = 2x$ $\quad r = x$

$$A = \frac{36\pi x^2}{2} - \frac{25\pi x^2}{2} + \frac{16\pi x^2}{2} - \frac{9\pi x^2}{2} + \frac{4\pi x^2}{2} - \frac{1\pi x^2}{2}$$

$$A = \frac{(36 - 25 + 16 - 9 + 4 - 1)\pi x^2}{2}$$

$$A = \frac{21\pi x^2}{2}$$

22. E: All of the other capital letters shown are symmetrical with respect to a horizontal axis drawn through the middle, as in the H shown in the figure. Only Z is not symmetrical in this respect.

23. D: The volume of the box is the product of $\sqrt{3}$, $2\sqrt{5}$, and 4. To multiply two or more square root radicals, multiply the coefficients and then multiply the radicands.

$$\sqrt{3} \times 2\sqrt{5} \times 4 = 8\sqrt{3}\sqrt{5} = 8\sqrt{15}$$

Then, simplify the radicand if possible by factoring out any squares. Since 15 cannot be factored into any square factors, it cannot be simplified further.

24. E: Choose two angles that take up the entire line, since a straight line has a measure of 180°.

25. C: The area of a triangle is $A = \frac{1}{2}bh$, where b and h are the lengths of the triangle's base and height, respectively. The base of the given triangle is 8, but the height is not given. Since the triangle is a right triangle and the hypotenuse is given, the triangle's height can be found using the Pythagorean theorem.

$$8^2 + h^2 = x^2$$
$$h^2 = x^2 - 64$$
$$h = \sqrt{x^2 - 64}$$

To find the area of the triangle in terms of x, substitute $\sqrt{x^2 - 64}$ for the height and 8 for the base of the triangle into the area formula, $A = \frac{1}{2}bh$.

$$A(x) = \frac{1}{2}(8)(\sqrt{x^2 - 64})$$
$$A(x) = 4\sqrt{x^2 - 64}$$

26. D: An equilateral triangle means that all sides are the same length.

27. E: Since the two triangles have all three corresponding pairs of sides and corresponding pairs of angles marked congruent, then the two triangles are congruent. Similar triangles are the same shape but not necessarily the same size; they have congruent angles. All congruent triangles are similar triangles, so the correct choice is that the triangles are both similar and congruent. An equilateral triangle has three congruent sides and angles measuring 60° each, so these triangles are not equilateral.

28. B: The chart indicates that 40% of the total recycled material is paper. Since 50,000 tons of materials are recycled every month, the total amount of paper will be 40% of 50,000 tons, or $\frac{40}{100} \times 50,000 = 20,000$. Therefore, there are approximately 20,000 tons of paper recycled every month.

29. B: To convert a percent into a decimal, change the percent sign to a decimal point and move the it two places to the left (or divide by 100).

30. D: To solve, first subtract the 20% discount ($\$400 \times 0.20 = \$80$) from the original price:

$$\$400 - \$80 = \$320$$

Then take the 5% discount ($\$320 \times 0.05 = \$16$) from the total:

$$\$320 - \$16 = \$304$$

31. E: First, we must determine the total amount of money Krystal spent. To do so, we must add the cost of the sunglasses, $\$19.99$, and the scarf, $\$27.50$. To add decimals, we stack the numbers so that the decimal points are directly on top of one another. Then, we add using the traditional algorithm, bringing the decimal point straight down into our sum. This gives us a total cost of $\$47.49$. To determine Krystal's change, we must subtract our total, $\$47.49$, from $\$50.00$. Again, we must be sure to stack our decimal points directly on top of one another. Then we subtract as normal, bringing our decimal point straight down into our answer. We need to be careful that we borrow when necessary. The difference of $\$50.00$ and $\$47.49$ is $\$2.51$. Krystal will receive change in the amount of $\$2.51$.

32. E: When there are two operations within our parentheses, we must follow the order of operations *within* the parentheses as well. Because multiplication comes before addition, we must start by finding the product of 4 and 3, which is 12. Next, we add 10 and 12 to get 22. Finally, we can divide 22 by 2 to arrive at our final answer, 11.

33. D: The associative property states that moving the parentheses when adding or multiplying a string of numbers will not affect the sum or product. The associative property is often used to group compatible numbers in an effort to assist with mental math. By rewriting the problem as $17 + (18 + 2)$, we have grouped our compatible numbers, 18 and 2. These are considered compatible numbers because they have a sum of 20, which is an easy number to calculate mentally. Once we have the sum of 20 we can include our final addend, 17, to arrive at our total of 37.

34. B: Regardless of the exact number of students, we can determine the relative percentages of each eye color. We are given that 40% of the total have brown eyes, which means that 100% − 40% or 60% of the students have either blue or green eyes. Since 90% of those have blue eyes, we know that 10% of those 60% have green eyes, or 6% of the students have green eyes. Now, 90% of 60% can be found by converting both percentages to decimals and multiplying them. $(0.9) \times (0.6) = 0.54$, which is equivalent to 54%. So, in total, 40% have brown eyes, 54% have blue eyes, and 6% have green eyes. Therefore, we can definitively say that blue eyed students are the majority.

35. D: To solve, first add Mary's shot to the score: 42–18. Subtract the figures to see how many points still need to be scored: $42 - 18 = 24$. Divide by three, since three points are attained with each shot: $24 \div 3 = 8$.

36. E: A is a number in the thousandths; B is a number in the hundredths. C, D, and E are in tenths. Three-tenths (0.300) is the largest of these choices.

37. C: The vertical operators indicate absolute values, which are always positive. Start by simplifying the expressions inside the absolute value bars.

$$|7 - 5| - |5 - 7|$$

$$|2| - |-2|$$

Then, evaluate the absolute values and subtract. Since absolute value is always positive, both $|2|$ and $|-2|$ are equal to 2.

$$2 - 2 = 0$$

38. D: When a number is raised to a power, you multiply the number by itself by the number of times of the power. For example, $2^3 = 2 \times 2 \times 2 = 8$. A number raised to the power of 0 is always equal to 1. So, 6^0 is the smallest number shown. Similarly, for the other numbers:

$$9 = 9; 10^1 = 10; 4^2 = 4 \times 4 = 16$$

Since $1 < 8 < 9 < 10 < 16$, we can write the order as $6^0, 2^3, 9, 10^1, 4^2$.

39. D: In order to multiply two powers that have the same base, add their exponents because of the exponent rule $a^m \times a^n = a^{m+n}$. Therefore, $x^3 x^5 = x^{3+5} = x^8$.

40. B: It is helpful to recall that percentages can be converted to decimals. 30% of 3,300 is $0.3 \times 3,300 = 990$. Therefore, the crane supports 990 pounds.

41. B: To solve, divide the numerator by the denominator and multiply by 100:

$$\frac{42}{7} \times 100 = 6 \times 100 = 600\%$$

42. D: To divide fractions, multiply the divisor (the second fraction) by its reciprocal (turn it upside down). Then, reduce or simplify the fraction:

$$\frac{2}{5} \times \frac{3}{2} = \frac{6}{10} = \frac{3}{5}$$

43. E: There are 16 empty chairs. This gives $\frac{2}{5}$ of the total enrollment. So, the full class must be:

$$\text{Class} = \frac{5}{2} \times 16 = 40 \text{ students}$$

Another option is to use proportions.

$$\frac{2}{5} = \frac{16}{x}$$

First, cross multiply to get: $2x = 80$. Then, divide each side by 2 to solve for x. So, $x = 40$, which means there are 40 students in the entire class.

44. B: To solve, first find what percent of the paycheck is taken out: $30\% + 15\% + 32\% = 77\%$. Subtract this number from 100% to find out the amount of her paycheck that is remaining: 23%.

45. B: To determine how much Brenda would have saved, first find out the sale price of the shoes and then subtract this price from the amount Brenda paid. The sale price of the shoes is:

$$\$62 \times 0.75 = \$46.50$$

Then, subtract this amount from the amount Brenda paid:

$$\$62 - \$46.50 = \$15.50$$

Brenda would have saved $15.50 if she had waited a day.

46. B: The stock first increased by 10%, or $10 (10% of $100), to $110 per share. Then, the price decreased by $11 (10% of $110), so that the sell price was $110 − $11 = $99 per share, and the sell price for 50 shares was $99 \times \$50 = \$4,950$.

47. B: The median is the value in a group of numbers that separates the upper-half from the lower-half, so that there are an equal number of values above and below it. Order the numbers from least to greatest.

$$112, 112, 116, 133, 145$$

In this distribution, there are two values greater than 116, and two values below it, so 116 is the median.

48. C: A z-test may be used, since the population standard deviation is known. A z-score may be calculated using the formula $z = \frac{\bar{X} - \mu}{\frac{\sigma}{\sqrt{n}}}$. Substituting the sample mean, population mean, population standard deviation, and sample size into the formula gives $z = \frac{16.1 - 16}{\frac{0.2}{\sqrt{30}}}$, which simplifies to $z \approx 2.74$. The p-value is approximately 0.006, which is less than 0.05. Thus, there does appear to be a significant difference between what the manufacturer claims and the actual number of ounces found in each container. The claim is likely not true, due to a p-value less than 0.05.

49. D: There are three ways in which two women from the same department can be selected: two women can be selected from Biology, two women can be selected from Chemistry, or two women can be selected from Physics. Since the events of choosing one woman and then another are both independent events, multiply the two probabilities together to get the probability of choosing two women from the same department.

Biology	**Chemistry**	**Physics**
$\frac{26}{129} \times \frac{25}{128} = \frac{650}{16,512}$	$\frac{31}{129} \times \frac{30}{128} = \frac{930}{16,512}$	$\frac{20}{129} \times \frac{19}{128} = \frac{380}{16,512}$

Since any of these is a distinct possible outcome, the probability that two men will be selected from the same department is the sum of these outcomes.

$$\frac{650}{16,512} + \frac{930}{16,512} + \frac{380}{16,512} = \frac{1,960}{16,512} \approx 0.119 = 11.9\%$$

50. E: In a positively skewed distribution, the median is closer to the first quartile than the third.

51. D: The standard deviation is equal to the square root of the ratio of the sum of the squares of the deviation of each score from the mean to the square root of the difference of n and 1. The mean of the data set is 13.5. The deviations are −5.5, −3.5, −2.5, −0.5, −0.5, 2.5, 3.5, and 6.5. The sum of the squares of the deviations may be written as:

$$30.25 + 12.25 + 6.25 + 0.25 + 0.25 + 6.25 + 12.25 + 42.25 = 110$$

Division of this sum by $n - 1 = 7$ gives 15.71. The square root of this quotient is approximately 4.0.

52. C: There are three ways in which two women from the same department can be selected. Two women can be selected from the first department, or two women can be selected from the second department, or two women can be selected from the third department.

Department 1	Department 2	Department 3
$\frac{12}{103} \times \frac{11}{102} = \frac{132}{10,506}$	$\frac{28}{103} \times \frac{27}{102} = \frac{756}{10,506}$	$\frac{16}{103} \times \frac{15}{102} = \frac{240}{10,506}$

Since any of these is a distinct possible outcome, the probability that two men will be selected from the same department is the sum of these outcomes:

$$\frac{132}{10,506} + \frac{756}{10,506} + \frac{240}{10,506} = \frac{1,128}{10,506} \approx 0.107, \text{ or } 10.7\%$$

53. E: Determine the probability of each option (if s = likes baseball, b = likes basketball, and f = likes football).

For choice A, this is the total number of students in the football circle of the Venn diagram divided by the total number of students surveyed:

$$P(f) = \frac{47 + 22 + 19 + 31}{241} = \frac{119}{241} \approx 49.4\%$$

For choice B, this is the total number of students in the baseball circle and also in at least one other circle divided by the total number in the baseball circle:

$$P(s \cup f | b) = \frac{28 + 19 + 22}{28 + 19 + 22 + 34} = \frac{69}{103} \approx 67.0\%$$

For choice C, this is the number of students in the intersection of all three circles divided by the total number in the overlap of the baseball and basketball circles:

$$P(s | b \cap f) = \frac{19}{19 + 28} = \frac{19}{47} \approx 40.4\%$$

For choice D, this is the number of students in the intersection of the basketball circle and the baseball circle.

$$P(s \cap b) = \frac{28 + 19}{241} = \frac{47}{241} \approx 19.5\%$$

For choice E, this is the number of students outside of all the circles divided by the total number of students surveyed:

$$P([c \cup b \cup f]') = \frac{18}{241} \approx 7.5\%$$

Since Choice E has the lowest probability, it is the correct answer.

54. B: Weak correlation coefficients are those with absolute values close to 0. Since –0.1 has an absolute value of 0.1 and 0.1 is closer to 0 than any of the absolute values of the other correlation coefficients in the answer choices, it is the weakest.

55. A: Two z-scores should be calculated, one for each student's score. The first z-score may be written as $z = \frac{71-81}{10}$, which simplifies to $z = -1$. The second z-score may be written as $z = \frac{86-81}{10}$, which simplifies to $z = 0.5$. The percentage of students scoring between these two scores is equal to the sum of the two mean-to-z areas. A z-score with an absolute value of 1 shows a mean-to-z area of 0.3413. A z-score of 0.5 shows a mean-to-z area of 0.1915. The sum of these two areas is 0.5328, or 53.28%.

56. D: There are nine ways to assign the first digit since it can be any of the numbers 1–9. There are nine ways to assign the second digit since it can be any digit 0–9 EXCEPT for the digit assigned in place 1. There are eight ways to assign the third number since there are ten digits, two of which have already been assigned. There are seven ways to assign the fourth number, six ways to assign the fifth, five ways to assign the sixth, and four ways to assign the seventh. So, the number of combinations is $9 \times 9 \times 8 \times 7 \times 6 \times 5 \times 4 = 544{,}320$.

Another way to approach the problem is to notice that the arrangement of nine digits in the last six places is a sequence without repetition, or a permutation. (Note: this may be called a partial permutation since all of the elements of the set need not be used.) The number of possible sequences of a fixed length r of elements taken from a given set of size n is permutation $_nP_r = \frac{n!}{(n-r)!}$. So, the number of ways to arrange the last six digits is $_9P_6 = \frac{9!}{(9-6)!} = \frac{9!}{3!} = 60{,}480$. Multiply this number by nine since there are nine possibilities for the first digit of the phone number. $_9P_6 \times 9 = 544{,}320$.

Practice Tests #3, #4, and #5

To take these additional Praxis practice tests, visit our bonus page:
mometrix.com/bonus948/praxcore

How to Overcome Test Anxiety

Just the thought of taking a test is enough to make most people a little nervous. A test is an important event that can have a long-term impact on your future, so it's important to take it seriously and it's natural to feel anxious about performing well. But just because anxiety is normal, that doesn't mean that it's helpful in test taking, or that you should simply accept it as part of your life. Anxiety can have a variety of effects. These effects can be mild, like making you feel slightly nervous, or severe, like blocking your ability to focus or remember even a simple detail.

If you experience test anxiety—whether severe or mild—it's important to know how to beat it. To discover this, first you need to understand what causes test anxiety.

Causes of Test Anxiety

While we often think of anxiety as an uncontrollable emotional state, it can actually be caused by simple, practical things. One of the most common causes of test anxiety is that a person does not feel adequately prepared for their test. This feeling can be the result of many different issues such as poor study habits or lack of organization, but the most common culprit is time management. Starting to study too late, failing to organize your study time to cover all of the material, or being distracted while you study will mean that you're not well prepared for the test. This may lead to cramming the night before, which will cause you to be physically and mentally exhausted for the test. Poor time management also contributes to feelings of stress, fear, and hopelessness as you realize you are not well prepared but don't know what to do about it.

Other times, test anxiety is not related to your preparation for the test but comes from unresolved fear. This may be a past failure on a test, or poor performance on tests in general. It may come from comparing yourself to others who seem to be performing better or from the stress of living up to expectations. Anxiety may be driven by fears of the future—how failure on this test would affect your educational and career goals. These fears are often completely irrational, but they can still negatively impact your test performance.

Elements of Test Anxiety

As mentioned earlier, test anxiety is considered to be an emotional state, but it has physical and mental components as well. Sometimes you may not even realize that you are suffering from test anxiety until you notice the physical symptoms. These can include trembling hands, rapid heartbeat, sweating, nausea, and tense muscles. Extreme anxiety may lead to fainting or vomiting. Obviously, any of these symptoms can have a negative impact on testing. It is important to recognize them as soon as they begin to occur so that you can address the problem before it damages your performance.

The mental components of test anxiety include trouble focusing and inability to remember learned information. During a test, your mind is on high alert, which can help you recall information and stay focused for an extended period of time. However, anxiety interferes with your mind's natural processes, causing you to blank out, even on the questions you know well. The strain of testing during anxiety makes it difficult to stay focused, especially on a test that may take several hours. Extreme anxiety can take a huge mental toll, making it difficult not only to recall test information but even to understand the test questions or pull your thoughts together.

Effects of Test Anxiety

Test anxiety is like a disease—if left untreated, it will get progressively worse. Anxiety leads to poor performance, and this reinforces the feelings of fear and failure, which in turn lead to poor performances on subsequent tests. It can grow from a mild nervousness to a crippling condition. If allowed to progress, test anxiety can have a big impact on your schooling, and consequently on your future.

Test anxiety can spread to other parts of your life. Anxiety on tests can become anxiety in any stressful situation, and blanking on a test can turn into panicking in a job situation. But fortunately, you don't have to let anxiety rule your testing and determine your grades. There are a number of relatively simple steps you can take to move past anxiety and function normally on a test and in the rest of life.

Physical Steps for Beating Test Anxiety

While test anxiety is a serious problem, the good news is that it can be overcome. It doesn't have to control your ability to think and remember information. While it may take time, you can begin taking steps today to beat anxiety.

Just as your first hint that you may be struggling with anxiety comes from the physical symptoms, the first step to treating it is also physical. Rest is crucial for having a clear, strong mind. If you are tired, it is much easier to give in to anxiety. But if you establish good sleep habits, your body and mind will be ready to perform optimally, without the strain of exhaustion. Additionally, sleeping well helps you to retain information better, so you're more likely to recall the answers when you see the test questions.

Getting good sleep means more than going to bed on time. It's important to allow your brain time to relax. Take study breaks from time to time so it doesn't get overworked, and don't study right before bed. Take time to rest your mind before trying to rest your body, or you may find it difficult to fall asleep.

Along with sleep, other aspects of physical health are important in preparing for a test. Good nutrition is vital for good brain function. Sugary foods and drinks may give a burst of energy but this burst is followed by a crash, both physically and emotionally. Instead, fuel your body with protein and vitamin-rich foods.

Also, drink plenty of water. Dehydration can lead to headaches and exhaustion, especially if your brain is already under stress from the rigors of the test. Particularly if your test is a long one, drink water during the breaks. And if possible, take an energy-boosting snack to eat between sections.

Along with sleep and diet, a third important part of physical health is exercise. Maintaining a steady workout schedule is helpful, but even taking 5-minute study breaks to walk can help get your blood pumping faster and clear your head. Exercise also releases endorphins, which contribute to a positive feeling and can help combat test anxiety.

When you nurture your physical health, you are also contributing to your mental health. If your body is healthy, your mind is much more likely to be healthy as well. So take time to rest, nourish your body with healthy food and water, and get moving as much as possible. Taking these physical steps will make you stronger and more able to take the mental steps necessary to overcome test anxiety.

Mental Steps for Beating Test Anxiety

Working on the mental side of test anxiety can be more challenging, but as with the physical side, there are clear steps you can take to overcome it. As mentioned earlier, test anxiety often stems from lack of preparation, so the obvious solution is to prepare for the test. Effective studying may be the most important weapon you have for beating test anxiety, but you can and should employ several other mental tools to combat fear.

First, boost your confidence by reminding yourself of past success—tests or projects that you aced. If you're putting as much effort into preparing for this test as you did for those, there's no reason you should expect to fail here. Work hard to prepare; then trust your preparation.

Second, surround yourself with encouraging people. It can be helpful to find a study group, but be sure that the people you're around will encourage a positive attitude. If you spend time with others who are anxious or cynical, this will only contribute to your own anxiety. Look for others who are motivated to study hard from a desire to succeed, not from a fear of failure.

Third, reward yourself. A test is physically and mentally tiring, even without anxiety, and it can be helpful to have something to look forward to. Plan an activity following the test, regardless of the outcome, such as going to a movie or getting ice cream.

When you are taking the test, if you find yourself beginning to feel anxious, remind yourself that you know the material. Visualize successfully completing the test. Then take a few deep, relaxing breaths and return to it. Work through the questions carefully but with confidence, knowing that you are capable of succeeding.

Developing a healthy mental approach to test taking will also aid in other areas of life. Test anxiety affects more than just the actual test—it can be damaging to your mental health and even contribute to depression. It's important to beat test anxiety before it becomes a problem for more than testing.

Study Strategy

Being prepared for the test is necessary to combat anxiety, but what does being prepared look like? You may study for hours on end and still not feel prepared. What you need is a strategy for test prep. The next few pages outline our recommended steps to help you plan out and conquer the challenge of preparation.

STEP 1: SCOPE OUT THE TEST

Learn everything you can about the format (multiple choice, essay, etc.) and what will be on the test. Gather any study materials, course outlines, or sample exams that may be available. Not only will this help you to prepare, but knowing what to expect can help to alleviate test anxiety.

STEP 2: MAP OUT THE MATERIAL

Look through the textbook or study guide and make note of how many chapters or sections it has. Then divide these over the time you have. For example, if a book has 15 chapters and you have five days to study, you need to cover three chapters each day. Even better, if you have the time, leave an extra day at the end for overall review after you have gone through the material in depth.

If time is limited, you may need to prioritize the material. Look through it and make note of which sections you think you already have a good grasp on, and which need review. While you are studying, skim quickly through the familiar sections and take more time on the challenging parts. Write out your plan so you don't get lost as you go. Having a written plan also helps you feel more in control of the study, so anxiety is less likely to arise from feeling overwhelmed at the amount to cover.

STEP 3: GATHER YOUR TOOLS

Decide what study method works best for you. Do you prefer to highlight in the book as you study and then go back over the highlighted portions? Or do you type out notes of the important information? Or is it helpful to make flashcards that you can carry with you? Assemble the pens, index cards, highlighters, post-it notes, and any other materials you may need so you won't be distracted by getting up to find things while you study.

If you're having a hard time retaining the information or organizing your notes, experiment with different methods. For example, try color-coding by subject with colored pens, highlighters, or post-it notes. If you learn better by hearing, try recording yourself reading your notes so you can listen while in the car, working out, or simply sitting at your desk. Ask a friend to quiz you from your flashcards, or try teaching someone the material to solidify it in your mind.

STEP 4: CREATE YOUR ENVIRONMENT

It's important to avoid distractions while you study. This includes both the obvious distractions like visitors and the subtle distractions like an uncomfortable chair (or a too-comfortable couch that makes you want to fall asleep). Set up the best study environment possible: good lighting and a comfortable work area. If background music helps you focus, you may want to turn it on, but otherwise keep the room quiet. If you are using a computer to take notes, be sure you don't have any other windows open, especially applications like social media, games, or anything else that could distract you. Silence your phone and turn off notifications. Be sure to keep water close by so you stay hydrated while you study (but avoid unhealthy drinks and snacks).

Also, take into account the best time of day to study. Are you freshest first thing in the morning? Try to set aside some time then to work through the material. Is your mind clearer in the afternoon or evening? Schedule your study session then. Another method is to study at the same time of day that you will take the test, so that your brain gets used to working on the material at that time and will be ready to focus at test time.

STEP 5: STUDY!

Once you have done all the study preparation, it's time to settle into the actual studying. Sit down, take a few moments to settle your mind so you can focus, and begin to follow your study plan. Don't give in to distractions or let yourself procrastinate. This is your time to prepare so you'll be ready to fearlessly approach the test. Make the most of the time and stay focused.

Of course, you don't want to burn out. If you study too long you may find that you're not retaining the information very well. Take regular study breaks. For example, taking five minutes out of every hour to walk briskly, breathing deeply and swinging your arms, can help your mind stay fresh.

As you get to the end of each chapter or section, it's a good idea to do a quick review. Remind yourself of what you learned and work on any difficult parts. When you feel that you've mastered the material, move on to the next part. At the end of your study session, briefly skim through your notes again.

But while review is helpful, cramming last minute is NOT. If at all possible, work ahead so that you won't need to fit all your study into the last day. Cramming overloads your brain with more information than it can process and retain, and your tired mind may struggle to recall even previously learned information when it is overwhelmed with last-minute study. Also, the urgent nature of cramming and the stress placed on your brain contribute to anxiety. You'll be more likely to go to the test feeling unprepared and having trouble thinking clearly.

So don't cram, and don't stay up late before the test, even just to review your notes at a leisurely pace. Your brain needs rest more than it needs to go over the information again. In fact, plan to finish your studies by noon or early afternoon the day before the test. Give your brain the rest of the day to relax or focus on other things, and get a good night's sleep. Then you will be fresh for the test and better able to recall what you've studied.

STEP 6: TAKE A PRACTICE TEST

Many courses offer sample tests, either online or in the study materials. This is an excellent resource to check whether you have mastered the material, as well as to prepare for the test format and environment.

Check the test format ahead of time: the number of questions, the type (multiple choice, free response, etc.), and the time limit. Then create a plan for working through them. For example, if you have 30 minutes to take a 60-question test, your limit is 30 seconds per question. Spend less time on the questions you know well so that you can take more time on the difficult ones.

If you have time to take several practice tests, take the first one open book, with no time limit. Work through the questions at your own pace and make sure you fully understand them. Gradually work up to taking a test under test conditions: sit at a desk with all study materials put away and set a timer. Pace yourself to make sure you finish the test with time to spare and go back to check your answers if you have time.

After each test, check your answers. On the questions you missed, be sure you understand why you missed them. Did you misread the question (tests can use tricky wording)? Did you forget the information? Or was it something you hadn't learned? Go back and study any shaky areas that the practice tests reveal.

Taking these tests not only helps with your grade, but also aids in combating test anxiety. If you're already used to the test conditions, you're less likely to worry about it, and working through tests until you're scoring well gives you a confidence boost. Go through the practice tests until you feel comfortable, and then you can go into the test knowing that you're ready for it.

Test Tips

On test day, you should be confident, knowing that you've prepared well and are ready to answer the questions. But aside from preparation, there are several test day strategies you can employ to maximize your performance.

First, as stated before, get a good night's sleep the night before the test (and for several nights before that, if possible). Go into the test with a fresh, alert mind rather than staying up late to study.

Try not to change too much about your normal routine on the day of the test. It's important to eat a nutritious breakfast, but if you normally don't eat breakfast at all, consider eating just a protein bar. If you're a coffee drinker, go ahead and have your normal coffee. Just make sure you time it so that the caffeine doesn't wear off right in the middle of your test. Avoid sugary beverages, and drink enough water to stay hydrated but not so much that you need a restroom break 10 minutes into the test. If your test isn't first thing in the morning, consider going for a walk or doing a light workout before the test to get your blood flowing.

Allow yourself enough time to get ready, and leave for the test with plenty of time to spare so you won't have the anxiety of scrambling to arrive in time. Another reason to be early is to select a good seat. It's helpful to sit away from doors and windows, which can be distracting. Find a good seat, get out your supplies, and settle your mind before the test begins.

When the test begins, start by going over the instructions carefully, even if you already know what to expect. Make sure you avoid any careless mistakes by following the directions.

Then begin working through the questions, pacing yourself as you've practiced. If you're not sure on an answer, don't spend too much time on it, and don't let it shake your confidence. Either skip it and come back later, or eliminate as many wrong answers as possible and guess among the remaining ones. Don't dwell on these questions as you continue—put them out of your mind and focus on what lies ahead.

Be sure to read all of the answer choices, even if you're sure the first one is the right answer. Sometimes you'll find a better one if you keep reading. But don't second-guess yourself if you do immediately know the answer. Your gut instinct is usually right. Don't let test anxiety rob you of the information you know.

If you have time at the end of the test (and if the test format allows), go back and review your answers. Be cautious about changing any, since your first instinct tends to be correct, but make sure you didn't misread any of the questions or accidentally mark the wrong answer choice. Look over any you skipped and make an educated guess.

At the end, leave the test feeling confident. You've done your best, so don't waste time worrying about your performance or wishing you could change anything. Instead, celebrate the successful completion of this test. And finally, use this test to learn how to deal with anxiety even better next time.

> **Review Video: <u>Test Anxiety</u>**
> Visit mometrix.com/academy and enter code: 100340

Important Qualification

Not all anxiety is created equal. If your test anxiety is causing major issues in your life beyond the classroom or testing center, or if you are experiencing troubling physical symptoms related to your anxiety, it may be a sign of a serious physiological or psychological condition. If this sounds like your situation, we strongly encourage you to seek professional help.